FEMINIST PERSPECTIVES ON EQUITY AND TRUSTS

Cavendish
Publishing
Limited

London • Sydney

Titles in the *Feminist Perspectives in Law* series

FEMINIST PERSPECTIVES ON EQUITY AND TRUSTS

Edited by
Susan Scott-Hunt
Principal Lecturer in Law
Middlesex University
and
Hilary Lim
Principal Lecturer in Law
University of East London

Cavendish
Publishing
Limited

London • Sydney

First published in Great Britain 2001 by Cavendish Publishing Limited,
The Glass House, Wharton Street, London WC1X 9PX, United Kingdom
Telephone: + 44 (0)20 7278 8000   Facsimile: + 44 (0)20 7278 8080
Email: info@cavendishpublishing.com
Website: www.cavendishpublishing.com

© Cavendish Publishing   2001

British Library Cataloguing in Publication Data

Scott-Hunt, Susan
Feminist perspectives on equity and trusts
1 Equity – England 2 Equity – Wales 3 Trust and trustees –
England 4 Trust and trustees – Wales
I Title II Lim, Hilary
346.4'2'004

ISBN 1 85941 606 3

Printed and bound in Great Britain

For Barkis, Emily and Chneah

Whilst we can claim that this series is unique, this particular volume, on equity and trusts, has a particular claim to uniqueness. Not only is it, to our knowledge, the first volume of essays written by feminists in this area of law, it is also the first volume of essays in the critical tradition ever to be published on equity and trusts. The few previous volumes of essays published, in this country in particular, have concentrated on doctrinal issues with, at best, a policy gloss or social context to that work, rather than drawing more broadly from the wide range of historical and philosophical material which is available to develop a critical approach to the subject area. Although the development of such an approach can be glimpsed in journal articles and occasionally in the plethora of student texts available, there has, to date, been no attempt made to draw this material together.

Many factors have probably played in to this lack of development – not least of which is the rather shaky status given to the subject in law schools in this country. Although 'the subject' remains a compulsory element in exemption courses, in practice, it has often been dealt with as a series of topics in which trusts has been given a particular status, although frequently taught as part of a property based course, and equitable remedies has found a place either at the end of a trusts course or at the end of common law courses. The subject, at the level of teaching, seems to have imploded. Many equity and trusts textbooks on close inspection, are really trusts books with a brief resume of equity as history and a small number of chapters on equitable remedies. None of this helps develop an overall 'feel' for the area. Further, both in teaching and in research, some of the most exciting material (in developmental terms) has been ceded to other courses: banking, intellectual property, entertainment law, etc, all draw material from equitable origins but can situate and explore that material so much more successfully than in the paucity of time usually given to the teaching of equity *per se*. And it seems that a generation of scholars who might well have put their intellectual effort into equity and trusts have been understandably seduced by the intellectual attractions of restitution law.

Perhaps there is an even deeper reason for this lack of intellectual engagement with the subject area *per se*, perhaps it goes back to the common lawyers unease with the role of equity. Not only does there remain a tension as to whether to regard the area as 'truly assimilated' into law, but the old characterisations of equity as somehow less stable, more discretionary and, therefore, more open to abuse, seem to still play through as a kind of fear fantasy of what law might be if it were not properly regulated by clear doctrinal detail and sound judicial reasoning. Would it be too much to suggest that this image of equity continues to function as a kind of feminine 'other'? A place onto which we can project our fears of law, as well as recognising that we are desirous of change and flexibility and need some place in which we can express underlying ethical ideas and principles but need to be able to contain them. The female figurations of equity, mercy and justice are required, but so is the firm placing of them on the margins and the firm assurance that any seepage from them will be controlled and contained. One way of doing this has been to emphasise equity as a black letter subject and to focus on trusts as a functional outcome.

But it would be wrong to simply suggest that equity is the feminine against the maleness of law: just as it would be wrong to suggest that equity is 'women's law' or has been of particular and peculiar benefit to women. The essays in this volume make it clear that feminist work has gone beyond such simplistic accounts. Nevertheless, there is something particularly intriguing in bringing out the first critical volume in the area as feminist scholarship. There is a real sense in which a feminist engagement with equity and trusts does derive from, and speak to, this sense of otherness in equity. In recovering the area and developing critical scholarship, it seems particularly apposite that it should be feminists who have produced this volume of work and we hope that it will provide an impetus for further critical scholarship.

Indeed, there are signs that such scholarship in equity and trusts is now very necessary. As we become more conversant with developments in other common law jurisdictions, commonwealth ones in particular, we become more aware of the need for fuller consideration of the potential between different equitable remedies (including trusts) and the principles upon which they are based. Within our own jurisdiction, the increasingly constitutionalist approach to all law, both within the statutory bodies and the courts, requires that we think much more carefully about principles rather than simply remain focused on doctrine. There is much to be done and we welcome this volume as a contribution to the development of new and innovative scholarship in this area. To those who still think and teach (or are taught) equity and trusts as a rather boring but necessary black letter subject, this volume should come as welcome relief. To those critical scholars who, to date, have seen little to examine in the area, this volume should provide data to suggest otherwise. To those scholars within the area who, to date, have hinted at possibilities in texts and begun to explore issues in journal articles, this volume should be read as a chance for more sustained and focused scholarship which might bring us together as a network of scholars in this area of law.

We know that it was a very hard task for the editors of this volume to bring this collection together and to get it out in the time scale they were given. We are very grateful to them for all that work, it has been a huge challenge and they were very brave in undertaking it. We have no doubt that it will prove to have been very worthwhile and we are very proud to have this volume in our series. Our thanks, as ever, to all the editorial group at Cavendish, who worked at great speed on this volume at a time when they were under enormous pressure. Our thanks also for the support of our readers of this series – here is a volume from which we are sure you will gain a great deal, now is the time to let go of all those old prejudices held about equity and trusts. It is not boring!!!!!

Anne Bottomley and Sally Sheldon

CONTRIBUTORS

Rosemary Auchmuty started her academic life in Australia as an historian. After moving to London, she studied law as a mature student at the Polytechnic of Central London, now the University of Westminster, where she teaches Land Law and Trusts on the LLB and Women's Legal History and Jurisprudence on the LLM Women and Law. Her research is on women's history and jurisprudence and she has recently published *A World of Women: Growing Up in the Girl's School Story* (1999). She also contributed 'Lesbian law, lesbian legal theory' to Griffin, G and Andermahr, S, *Straight Studies Modified: Lesbian Interventions in the Academy* (1996).

Anne Bottomley lectures at the University of Kent in the areas of trusts and property. She has published a number of articles developing feminist pespectives on substantive law, as well as on feminism and legal theory. Anne is a member of the editorial group of Feminist Legal Studies and she is co-editor, with Sally Sheldon, of the *Feminist Perspectives on Law* series for Cavendish. Her recent work includes 'Women and trust(s): portraying the family in the gallery of law', in Bright, S and Dewar, J (eds), *Land Law: Themes and Perspectives* (1998).

Maggie Conway worked for a number of years in a variety of commercial environments, including banking, insurance and computing. She is now a Senior Lecturer in Law at the University of North London, where she specialises in property and trusts. Maggie is currently working for her PhD on land law and the 19th century novel.

Alison Dunn primarily researches in the area of equity, focusing in particular on the redress of unconscionability and on charitable trusts. In addition to looking at trustees' powers of investment, she is currently engaged in empirical research on the legal and practical effect of restrictions against political activities and campaigning placed on charities. She has recently edited a collection entitled *The Voluntary Sector, the State and the Law* (2000). In 1999, she published 'Charity law as a political option for the poor' in the Northern Ireland Legal Quarterly and 'Equity is dead: long live equity!' in the Modern Law Review.

Kate Green has spent much of her academic life at the University of East London researching and writing in the fields of property and feminist legal theory. She has now left academic life in order to pursue her life as a dancer and dance teacher. She recently published 'What is this thing about female circumcision?' (1998, with Hilary Lim) in Social and Legal Studies. She also contributed 'Citizens and squatters: under the surfaces of land law' to Bright, S and Dewar, J (eds), *Land Law: Themes and Persepctives* (1999).

Catherine Hobby has lectured at the University of East London since 1993. Her teaching interests are in the areas of labour law and industrial relations. She recently contributed to 'Personal rights' in *Atkin's Encyclopaedia of Court Forms in Civil Proceedings* (1998) on discrimination, official secrecy, confidentiality, privacy, public order and harassment. She is currently writing a volume on whistleblowing for the Institute of Employment Rights.

Hilary Lim teaches equity and child law at the University of East London. Her recent publications include a contribution on children's rights to *Feminist Perspectives on Child Law* (2000, with Jeremy Roche) and 'Caesareans and cyborgs' for Feminist Legal Studies (1999).

Susan Scott-Hunt joined Middlesex University after a career in practice in criminal law and civil law both in the US and Britain. Her teaching interests have included equity and trusts, contract law and legal systems. One of her current areas of focus is internet-based learning. Her research interests are in financial fraud and she recently published 'Fraud, market manipulation and insider dealing in US and UK bond markets' in *Bond Markets: Law and Regulation* (1999, with Helen Parry). Previously, she contributed 'Commercial law and insider trading' to *Amicus Curiae* (1998).

Jane Scoular is a Lecturer in Law at the University of Strathclyde. She recently held a position as Visiting Scholar at the Centre for Law and Society at New York University, where she worked in the area of mediation. Her publications include 'Feminist jurisprudence', in Jackson, S and Jones, J, *Contemporary Feminist Theories* (1998). She is currently editing a book on family law entitled *Family Dynamics* (forthcoming, 2001).

Claire de Than has held lecturing posts as the University of East London, Queen Mary and Westfield and SOAS, before moving to the University of Westminster, where she has taught since 1995 in the areas of equity, criminal law and human rights. Her research interests include civil liberties, human rights, criminal fraud and comparative law. She recently published *Essential Human Rights Cases* (1999, with S Nash, M Furse and M Amos). Previously, with Edwin Shorts, she wrote *Civil Liberties: Legal Principles of Individual Freedom* (1998). She has published two related articles in the December 2000 and February 2001 issues of the Journal of Criminal Law.

Malcolm Voyce is a Senior Lecturer in Law at Macquarie University. He teaches trusts, succession, social security and taxation. He has recently completed a major project on rural inheritance and divorce in Australia.

Simone Wong lectures at the University of Kent. Her particular research interests include equitable doctrines in the family home. Simone's latest publications include 'When trust(s) is not enough: an argument for the use of unjust enrichment for home-sharers' (1999) for Feminist Legal Studies and 'Constructive trusts over the family home: lessons to be learned from other commonwealth jurisdictions' (1998) for Legal Studies.

ACKNOWLEDGMENTS

We would like to thank all the contributors to this volume and Susanna Owen for her insightful comments. Our thanks also go to Jo Reddy and Cara Annett at Cavendish Publishing for their support. We owe a special debt of gratitude to Anne Bottomley for all her encouragement and interest in the project. Finally, we have to express our great appreciation to Pat Berwick and Sharon Senner for their hard work and unfailing kindness.

CONTENTS

Contents

TABLE OF CASES

TABLE OF STATUTES

TABLE OF ABBREVIATIONS

AC	Appeal Cases
All ER	All England Law Reports
All ER (D)	All England Reporter
ALJR	Australian Law Journal Reports
ALR	Australian Law Reports
Amb	Ambler
App Cas	Appeal Cases
Atk	Atkyns
BLR	Bengal Law Reports
Bro CC	Brown's Reports of Cases in Chancery
Can BR	Canadian Bar Review
CFLQ	Child and Family Law Quarterly
Ch	Chancery Division
Ch App	Chancery Appeal
Ch D	Chancery Division
CLR	Common Law Reports
CLR	Commonwealth Law Reports
Co Rep	Coke's King's Bench Reports
Conv	Conveyancer and Property Lawyer
Crim LR	Criminal Law Review
Cro Eliz	Croke's Kind's Bench Reports
De G & Sim	Gex and Simons
DLR	Dominion Law Reports
EAT	Employment Appeal Tribunal
ECR	European Court Reports
Edin LR	Edinburgh Law Review
EHRR	European Human Rights Reports
Eq Ca Ab	Abridgement of Cases in Equity
ER	English Reports
Fam	Family Division
Fam LR	Family Law Reports (Australia)

FLR	Family Law Reports
FLS	Feminist Legal Studies
Harv LR	Harvard Law Review
ICR	Industrial Court Reports
ILJ	Industrial Law Journal
IRLR	Industrial Relations Law Reports
IRS	Industrial Relations Services
Jac & W	Jacob's and Walker's Chancery Reports
JLS	Journal of Law and Society
JLSS	Journal of the Law Society in Scotland
JR	Judicial Review
J & R	Johnson and Herring
JSWFL	Journal of Social Welfare and Family Law
KB	King's Bench Law Reports
K & J	Kay and Johnson's Vice Chancellor's Reports
LS	Legal Studies
LTR	Law Times Reports
LQR	Law Quarterly Review
MLR	Modern Law Review
My & Cr	Myline & Craig
NLJ	New Law Journal
NSWLR	New South Wales Law Reports
NSWR	New South Wales Reports
NZLR	New Zealand Law Reports
OJLS	Oxford Journal of Legal Studies
Os H LJ	Osgoode Hall Law Journal
OR	Ontario Reports

Prec Ch	Precedents in Chancery
PL	Public Law
QB	Queen's Bench Law Reports
R	Rettie
Rep Ch	Reports in Chancery
RPC	Reports of Patents, Design and Trade Marks Cases
SALR	South Australia Law Reports
SC	Scottish Cases
SCLR	Scottish Civil Case Reports
Sim	Simons
SJ	Solicitor's Journal
SLG	Scots Law Gazette
Sm & G	Smale & Gifford's
SLT	Scottish Law Times
SR (NSW)	New South Wales State Reports
State Tr	Howell's State Trials
TLR	Times Law Reports
Vern	Vernon's Chancery Reports
VLR	Victorian Law Reports
Ves	Vesey
WLR	Weekly Law Reports
WN	Weekly Notes

INTRODUCTION

Susan Scott-Hunt and Hilary Lim

Much contemporary writing on equity is marked by its optimism for the future, applauding the flexibility of its doctrines and remedies, projecting it into the 21st century as a vibrant, modern servant of commerce. Although history has always had a peculiar saliency both in equity and in the teaching of equity, history is almost 'shrugged off' in this 'future of equity' approach.[1] In the rush towards the new millennium, the widespread potential for equity or, more specifically, the trust, on an international plane is highlighted and even those who express doubts about these expansionist plans record admiration for the trust as a 'valuable means of safeguarding assets'.[2] Many textbooks now have healthy sections on trusts 'in the modern world' and there is a growing emphasis upon catching up with events outside the classroom in the City. 'Traditional' interventions by equity in the 'family home' are safely tucked away in a separate doctrinal compartment.[3] The road ahead is open and clearly marked. A safe journey requires only a few interesting technical adjustments and modifications to the vehicle.

This largely cheerful and untroubled account is not one which commentators from feminist perspectives readily share. While any feminist engagement with law is conscious of its siren call, feminists have an even more tentative and doubtful approach to equity and equitable doctrine. Women writing about equity find themselves trapped by history and an old and powerful mythology that is difficult to think and write beyond. Chancery holds its particular temptations. The story of equity's role in relation to women in law runs something like this. Equity 'mitigates the harshness of the common law', smoothing rough formalistic edges with her gentle touch, whispering entreaties in a melodious voice. In this, equity is woman's special friend and protector, interceding when woman's place, the home, is threatened by the treachery, greed or egoistic foolishness of woman's male companion. It is a story located firmly in equity's supposed old heartland – the family. Presented as history, the layers of its endless repetition lie heavy. It is an alluring myth and, as Scoular suggests in this volume, it is hard to resist the warmth of this supposed friendly association of woman with equity.

Different stories have been produced and the chapters in this book join a growing effort to construct alternative accounts of equity. Here, the contributors explore the complex truth, the faithfulness and falsity of equity's friendship, valuing the tokens of that friendship neither as pure precious metal nor mere paste and paint. Many of the chapters are, in part, revisionist,

---

1   The 'saliency of history' in equity and the 'future of equity approach' are discussed in O'Donnell and Johnstone, 1997, pp 25–30, 64.
2   Willoughby, 1999, p 112. Scoular, Chapter 6, in this volume, points out that there is extensive resistance to an expansion of equity, in the English legal sense, into the Scots legal system.
3   Dewar, 1998 and Bottomley, Chapter 12, in this volume.

what Bottomley calls 'ground clearing' exercises. They rake over familiar and unfamiliar territory, revealing 'the perfidy of law in all its many manifestations'. Thus, Conway and Auchmuty's chapters explore both equity's historical protection of some married women from the disabilities of coverture and the restraint against anticipation, and the destruction of women's common law rights in order to protect male succession. Scott-Hunt's chapter continues this footwork, tracing the role of secrecy in equity with particular attention to the secret trust and *donatio mortis causa*. Lim touches upon a another kind of 'ground clearing' in her discussion of the legal encounter between the Islamic *waqf* and the trust, which challenges received histories of law and women.

The result of this type of 'ground clearing', however, is neither a simple debunking of equity's supposed sisterly affection, nor equity's demonisation, but a recognition of the places and ways where equity has helped and hindered particular women at particular times. On the one hand, some 'ground clearing' efforts unearth the balance sheet, the price that women have paid for equity's protection; the reinforcing of stereotypical images of women as dependent and vulnerable. In this, they build upon a seam of earlier feminist writing on the constitution of women as subjects in equity, but choose to do this on less obvious or familiar discursive territory. De Than's chapter on women and equity's *in personam* remedies suggests that, for example, the non-gender neutrality of rules on the execution of search orders perpetuates a differential treatment dependent upon an image of dependency.

Hobby's chapter, on women as whistleblowers, takes up this theme. She argues that courts treat male and female employees who expose mismanagement and illegality differently, disadvantaging women, because the legal system is unwilling to accept an image of women compelled by personal conscience and motivated by moral principle. For instance, she contrasts the adjectives applied to male whistleblowers ('distinguished,' 'principled') with those applied to women ('silly', 'misguided'). Scott-Hunt examines the personal fraud theory supporting secret trusts and looks at the language used by courts to describe the 'equitable obligations that bind a man's conscience'.

On the other hand, some contributions are concerned not so much with ground clearing as 'digging', showing ways in which apparently gender-neutral rules subtly act to the disadvantage of women. Thus, Voyce examines, in the context of pastoral accounting within Australia, how the de-centred State rules through a diversity of structures, including the capital and income rules in trust law, to regulate individual lives to the disadvantage of women life tenants and heirs. Several contributors, including Voyce, have noticed the historical absence, and the growing modern population, of women's voices as actors in the law; as litigators and trustees. While Stretton, Cioni and Spring's historical work has shown a more active view of ordinary women in contact with law than the orthodox sources, such as reported case law, would suggest, women's general invisibility is still a conundrum for feminist legal scholarship (de Than, Dunn, Scott-Hunt).

Many of the contributions to this collection, therefore, break out of the boundaries of equity's feminist 'ghettos', the 'common intention constructive trust' and 'undue influence' to explore, as well, the subtle particularities of equity's expression and censorship of women's voices. They search for equity's impact upon women within the interstices of the law; the ordinary realms in which trusts are employed and administered and the multitude of contexts in which equity claims as its own, a category of relationship, a duty, a way of acting or a value. Dunn's paper is concerned with the representation of women on boards of trustees, examining the manner in which women trustees exercise and monitor their powers of investment. She questions whether the reasons for the 19th century 'prudent man of business' test endure and are justified today. Scott-Hunt discusses the seemingly anachronistic secret trust and *donatio mortis causa*. Her 'modest' conclusion that these devices permit, upon occasion, a pragmatic response to women's interests is just one illustration of a strategic approach adopted by several contributors.

Various chapters introduce ideas about feminism's strategic engagement with law in the area of equity and trusts as a whole multi-surfaced fabric. These voices do not necessarily call for a collapse into an overarching doctrine of unconscionability, or for a move 'back to principles', but something both simpler and more complex, ambiguous and contradictory. Bottomley argues for the advantage of the 'common intention constructive trust' over the remedial constructive trust, lessening the dependency of women litigants on male courts' discretion. Green and Lim suggest that the protection of a 'special equity' for women, in the context of emotionally transmitted debt, may be the best thing on offer at the present time. Scott-Hunt argues that women's interests may be protected in some instances by equity's long standing doctrinal inconsistencies, which allow it to operate flexibly. Wong, de Than and Hobby ask whether statutory approaches offer the best strategy for women, even though they may produce inconsistency and/or doctrinal confusion.

Several chapters directly or indirectly engage in what Bottomley's chapter identifies as a second kind of 'ground clearing': rising clear of the ground to assess the complete landscape of legal principles and to identify the forces and constructs which serve to constrain women's progress and obscure women's footprints in law. Important amongst these obstructions is the binary bond of the private/public dichotomy. Under the commonplace statements about equity's development into the new territories of the commercial world lie assumptions which are of concern for feminists. Concepts like 'the family home', 'the market' and 'the city' come already loaded. To suggest that equity and the trusts are shifting from the realm of the family into the field of business is to conjure up the 'natural division' between the private and the public, the world of women from the world of men. Some contributors discuss this directly (Green and Lim, Scoular, Conway). All are concerned with the blurring of these boundaries and pursuing the separation. Despite the urge towards different sites for discussion, the starting point in a number of chapters is still the family home, although not necessarily to move somewhere else, be it the market or the city (Auchmuty, Scoular, Green and Lim). Wong's essay charts the familiar territory of co-habitees from a different vantage point; the experience of another Commonwealth jurisdiction with statutory intervention. Whether women are advantaged by statutory approaches which limit the court's exercise of discretion, is a pressing question in light of the Law Commission's forthcoming consultation on potential family home legislation. Hobby raises a similar question about the effect of legislation, albeit in a somewhat different context.

Another theme interwoven throughout the collection is the presence or absence of evidence of women's different styles, values or 'ethics'. Auchmuty argues that 'few non-legal sources' have been as 'influential on legal theory' as the work of psychologist Carol Gilligan. Contributors to this collection are no exception in falling under this influence. Auchmuty's chapter deals with feminist scholarship on law and literature. Critiquing Posner's rejection of notions of gender in law, she argues that Gilligan's 'ethic of care' operates in relation to law as moral decision making based on a highly principled different set of rules. While equity has the potential to express the 'ethic of care' in producing judgments sympathetic to some women, (although it is a fiction that equity speaks for women), male judges' deafness to the true tenor of women's different 'voice' renders them unable to feel empathy for women. Hobby suggests that whistleblowers, both men and women, may exhibit a moral voice combining the ethic of care and the ethic of rights – an ethic of rebellion. Belinda Fehlberg's research into women's moral decision making in the context of sexually transmitted debt is also a recurring point of reference for a number of contributors (Scoular, Auchmuty, Green and Lim). Dunn's chapter juxtaposes evidence of women's different management style to equity's formulation of the 'reasonably prudent man of business' in relation to a trustee's duty to invest the trust fund.

One final thread running through most of the chapters is a concern with our role as teachers of equity and trusts: what are we doing as feminists teaching equity and why are we teaching equity? A number of contributors express their problems with some existing course texts quite explicitly, including the urge to find new, challenging, cross-cultural materials with the potential to disrupt the established patterns of the curriculum (de Than, Lim, Bottomley). For this reason alone, the kind of feminist 'ground clearing' undertaken here remains necessary, and will do so for the foreseeable future. Implicit in most of the essays is a further concern with what students imbibe about equity and how to ensure a critical focus. What we hope this collection will do is provide a beginning, the possibility of different and new conversations in our lecture halls and seminar rooms. By way of illustration, at the workshop where the papers here were presented, the abiding presence of Lord Denning in student consciousness, particularly on equity courses, was raised. We remembered one student in our classes many years ago who, in the context of a discussion about the images of women in equitable discourse, said directly and succinctly that: 'Denning was good to women, provided they were elderly and white.' It is a timely reminder that it is through dialogue that we can begin to subvert both ourselves as teachers and the texts of law. Our students may resist equity's temptations and mythology, while appreciating its pragmatic possibilities, more readily than, perhaps, their teachers do.

CHAPTER 1

THE FICTION OF EQUITY

Rosemary Auchmuty

Richard Posner's *Law and Literature,* first published in 1988, is an important contribution to a burgeoning field of scholarship. Better known for his advocacy of an economic approach to law, Posner argues that 'legal education is incomplete without the ethical insights afforded by an immersion in literature',[1] thus calling into question the much-vaunted autonomy of the law and the objectivity of legal judgments. If feminists, for the most part, have been critical of the Law and Economics movement,[2] they have shown, for the most part, much sympathy for the Law and Literature movement.[3] In particular, they have welcomed its attempt to seek out alternative analyses of law and justice to those found in strictly legal sources and the expression of alternative viewpoints, the voices of those silenced or unrepresented in the legal process. They have supported the move to include the study of legal ideas in literature in the education of lawyers and judges to help them to understand alternative or minority points of view, and to provide women and minority law students with the expression of views they can recognise and identify with, since the need to learn to 'think like a lawyer' is often experienced by these students as a profoundly alienating experience.[4]

By the time Posner came to revise and update his *Law and Literature* in 1998, there was a substantial body of feminist scholarship in the field. Obviously feeling that this needed to be addressed, Posner curiously inserted his critique of the feminist contribution to Law and Literature in the middle of an explication of the significance of equity. Here he takes to task those literary scholars who conceptualise law as excessively rigid and formalistic, in part because they do not understand the role of equity. In *The Merchant of Venice,* for example, Terry Eagleton sees Shylock as representing law and Portia, 'not-law', but, for Posner, Portia 'personifies the spirit of equity'.[5] Posner offers a 'Table of Legal Antimonies' to explain how common law systems have never 'embraced the legalist position in undiluted form', the formalistic descriptors in the left hand column (law, rule, objectivity, judge finds law and so on) balanced by the flexible terms on the right (equity, discretion, subjectivity,

---

1   Posner, 1998, publisher's 'blurb'.
2   Eg, Frug, 1992, pp 111–24.
3   Eg, West, 1993; Heinzelman and Wiseman, 1994; Murphy, 1996; and St Joan and McElhiney, 1997.
4   Eg, Worden, 1985; and DuBois *et al*, p 11.
5   Posner, 1998, p 109.

judge makes law). This leads him to ask: 'Has law gender? Some feminists believe that the legalistic approach to law reflects a distinctively male way of thinking. It is remarkable how often, in literature, the view of law expressed by the terms on the right hand side of my table is personified by a woman and the opposing view by a man.'[6] This abrupt change of direction seems to be due to the fact that both groups categorise law as rigid, since plainly feminist legal scholars are not unaware of equity. Posner proceeds to examine the feminist proposition by analysing the ideas in Susan Glaspell's short story 'A jury of her peers' (1917)[7] and Carol Gilligan's *In a Different Voice* (1982), concluding that 'the "ethic of care" of which Gilligan speaks is no more a female preserve in law than it is in literature'.[8] 'The suggestion is excessively dichotomous both in its strict gendering of the polar conceptions of law and in its assumption that law does or can embrace one of the poles to the exclusion of the other.'[9]

Although Posner's reasoning is not entirely clear, what I take him to be saying is that the ethic of care, as a basis for moral reasoning, is not confined to women; that it is already embodied in American law through the equitable jurisdiction and at the hands of particular judges ('For every Langdell there has been a Cardozo, for every Frankfurter a Murphy, for every Rehnquist a Brennan, for every Scalia a Blackmun, and for every Easterbrook a Reinhardt');[10] and that there is no distinctively female approach to legal questions. In literature, too, Posner asserts, 'the principal exemplars ... of the alleged feminine outlook on law are the creation of men' (Shakespeare, for example).[11] It follows that there is no need to seek out women's voices either in law or in literature, because what women have to say is already encompassed by the law and literature produced by men.

Posner has described himself as a 'conservative feminist'[12] but, although some scholars have acknowledged with gratitude his contribution to feminist perspectives on law (mainly through provoking them into argument),[13] his is not a name usually associated with feminist legal thought. Indeed, there are many points a feminist might quarrel with in Posner's succinct dismissal of

---

6 Posner, 1998, p 121.

7 Posner points out that the story 'A jury of her peers' is loosely based on a real case, *State v Hossack* 89 NW 1077 (Iowa 1902), and is discussed by Angel, M, 'Criminal law and women: giving the abused woman who kills a jury of her peers who appreciates trifles' (1996) 33 American Criminal Law Review 230, and Mustazza, L, 'Gender and justice in Susan Glaspell's "A jury of her peers"' (1988) 2 Law and Semiotics 271. See, also, Camilleri, 1990.

8 *Ibid*, Posner, p 124.

9 *Ibid*, p 123.

10 *Ibid*, p 125.

11 *Ibid*, p 123.

12 Posner, 1989.

13 Eg, Nussbaum, 1995.

the notion of gender in law (five pages in a book of more than 400) but, for the purposes of this chapter, I would like to focus on his identification of Gilligan's 'ethic of care' with (among other devices) equity, and its corollary, that equity expresses 'women's voice', at least when employed by certain 'caring' judges. My view is that women's voices, that is, their ways of conceptualising moral dilemmas, have rarely found expression in law or equity, and that they are more likely to present themselves outside the legal discourse – in literature written by women, for example.

This chapter will explore the relationship between Gilligan's ethic of care, women's voices, and equity, according to the following plan. First, I will outline Gilligan's arguments in *In A Different Voice* and the ways in which her insights have been critiqued or accepted within feminist legal scholarship. It is my view that Posner has seriously misunderstood Gilligan's thesis, mainly through his reduction of her thesis to a simplistic notion that men reason one way and women another. This misses Gilligan's more important methodological point, that mainstream scholarship privileges a particular model of moral development and diminishes, excludes, or disqualifies the approaches to moral dilemmas often articulated by women and girls.

Then, where Posner denies the possibility of women's different voice, I will show that, in respect of moral dilemmas which end up in court, we can and do see distinctly 'different' ways of analysing legal problems, that these often fit Gilligan's 'ethic of care', that they are often articulated by women, and that these 'different' ways of seeing legal issues are not, in fact, always satisfied by equity. I point out the value of looking to sources outside law – literary sources like fiction and autobiography – to find an expression of women's voices on the subject of legal issues.

Posner dismisses the need to read literature actually produced by women to find 'women's voice'; indeed, he insists on only reading the *best* literature – which, for him, means the 'classics', works which have passed the 'test of time'.[14] This leaves out contemporary literature, and literature which has only recently resurfaced after decades of neglect – which means most published writing by women: 'Feminist literary critics are trying to boost the reputation of a number of women writers, some hitherto unknown, but it is too early to say whether their efforts will succeed. That is always the case with literature and the arts; it takes many years to separate the wheat from the chaff.'[15] I would argue, on the contrary, that it is often in popular fiction and the work of less 'important' figures that we are likely to find the different voices Gilligan describes.

The next section of this paper analyses in more depth Posner's claim that the ethic of care has been embodied in the operation of equity across the

---

14   Posner, 1998, p 5.
15   *Ibid*, p 12.

centuries. I argue that, although equity has that potential, it has rarely been allowed to do so, or not for long. I move then to Posner's argument that the ethic of care has been employed in the judgments of particular 'caring' judges. As an English equivalent of Cardozo or Brennan, I have selected Lord Denning, the great exponent of equity; but I conclude that, although Denning was often sympathetic to women, his legal analysis did not exemplify Gilligan's ethic of care, being based upon a set of principles about deservingness which had more in common with an ethic of rights.

In conclusion, I argue, of course, for the inclusion of women's voices within law, but with no clear strategy beyond the feminist knowledge that all systems offer spaces for resistance, and that two good starting points might well be the flexibility of equity and the educative models provided by literary sources which give voice to women's ideas about law.

THE ETHIC OF CARE AND FEMINIST LEGAL RESEARCH

There can be few non-legal sources as influential on legal theory as psychologist Carol Gilligan's *In a Different Voice* (1982). Gilligan observed through a series of empirical studies that men make moral judgments according to an ethic of rights (or justice, or equality) and women according to an ethic of care, or desire to avoid pain. Men, Gilligan suggests, measure situations against abstract rules designed for the general good. If individuals occasionally suffer through being judged by those rules, they are perceived as unfortunate casualties of a fundamentally good system, but the rules are still applied, since they apply to everyone equally. Women, however, focus on relationships and outcomes – on *what works* for the individual in that context. Faced with a moral problem, they try to find a way out of the difficulty which gives the best result and causes the least possible pain to all participants:

> Care becomes the self-chosen principle of a judgment that remains psychological in its concern with relationships and response but becomes universal in its condemnation of exploitation and hurt. Thus a progressively more adequate understanding of the psychology of human relationships – an increasing differentiation of self and other and a growing comprehension of the dynamics of social interaction – informs the development of an ethic of care.[16]

Mainstream accounts of psychological development, however, categorise this 'female' method of moral reasoning as less advanced than the abstract reference to principle preferred by most men. Gilligan argues that, on the contrary, women's moral reasoning is as highly developed as men's and she points out that, because men tend to see their own behaviour as the norm,

16 Gilligan, 1993, p 7.

4

they fail to appreciate that the 'female' method is not inferior to the 'male', but simply different.

Gilligan was not the first, or the only, feminist to notice that women perceive and construe moral issues differently from men. But her work, more than that of many others (for example, Nel Noddings, whose *Caring: A Feminist Approach to Ethics and Moral Education*, makes a similar argument and has also been influential), transferred very readily to law, especially the paradigm case she borrowed from Kohlberg of the boy Jake and the girl Amy's responses to the dilemma of Heinz (should he steal the drug for his dying wife?), which involved a whole range of issues of law and justice.

Since Gilligan, feminist legal scholars can hardly work in the area of difference without at least a reference to her work. 'I thought to make scholarly history by being the first feminist writer in a decade to produce a whole article without citing Carol Gilligan's book', quipped Linda Hirschman in 1992, before finding herself obliged to cite it.[17] Some, like Carrie Menkel-Meadow, embraced its insights with relief and optimism: for her, the analysis helped to explain why women like herself who worked in law were forced to learn to be 'bilingual', to think like a lawyer as well as like a woman.[18] Menkel-Meadow was one of the first feminists to see the work's relevance to legal reasoning:

> In conventional terms Jake would make a good lawyer because he spots the legal issues of excuse and justification, balances the rights, and reaches a decision, while considering implicitly, if not explicitly, the precedential effect of his decision. But ... Amy's approach is also plausible and legitimate, both as a style of moral reasoning and as a style of lawyering. Amy seeks to keep the people engaged; she holds the needs of the parties and their relationships constant, and hopes to satisfy them all (as in a negotiation), rather than selecting winner (as in a lawsuit) ... She looks beyond the 'immediate lawsuit' to see how the 'judgment' will affect the parties.[19]

Martha Minow also finds much to admire in Gilligan's work. She takes the view that Gilligan's 'different voice' does not mean women's voice but, rather, a voice which is different from the mainstream accounts – a reading which, Gilligan has always insisted, is the correct one.[20] Minow argues that legal problems involving difference, not simply of gender, but also of race, age, disability and so on, can best be tackled by reference to a range of alternative ways of reasoning.[21]

---

17 Hirschman, 1992, p 315.
18 DuBois *et al*, 1984, p 49.
19 Menkel-Meadow, 1985, p 198.
20 DuBois *et al*, 1984, p 38.
21 Minow, 1990.

Other feminists, however, have been disturbed by the apparent essentialism of Gilligan's argument. They point to the 'caring' men and 'uncaring' women who clearly disprove any generalisation about gender differences, and to the danger of playing into the hands of conservatives who would use this research to give scientific validity to their wish to return women to a domestic and 'caring' role in the home.[22] Catharine MacKinnon views the ethic of care as a product of gender oppression; in a genuinely egalitarian non-patriarchal society, she observes, women might have a totally different approach to moral and legal issues.[23] Joan Williams also rejects the idea that women tend to reason according to an ethic of care: 'to the extent this is true, it is merely a restatement of male and female gender roles under the current gender system'.[24] The validity of Gilligan's research methodology has been attacked, other studies being cited which show fewer differences between men and women in their approach to moral reasoning.[25] Some black scholars and most postmodernists have rejected the theory as 'homogenising' and based on the experience of a particular group of white middle class women.[26]

To all her critics, Gilligan has responded by trying to re-focus attention on what, for her, is the central issue: not whether (all) men and women adopt different forms of moral reasoning, but the fact that mainstream psychology (and law) privileges one form of moral reasoning and marginalises or excludes others.[27] To those who criticise her methodology, she explains that conventional methodologies are not designed to deal with women's accounts – that was the point of her work – so she had adopted a different technique: 'In listening to women, I sought to separate their descriptions of their experience from standard forms of psychological interpretation and to rely on a close textual analysis of language and logic to define the terms of women's thinking.'[28] To those who denied that gender differences are as profound as Gilligan found, and commented that women can score just as high on 'justice' readings as men, she has replied by saying that the association of the ethic of care with women 'is an empirical observation, and it is primarily through women's voices that I trace its development. But this association is not absolute, and the contrasts between male and female voices are presented here to highlight a distinction between two modes of thought and to focus a problem of interpretation rather than to represent a generalization about

---

22 See Kerber *et al*, 1986, p 304; and Rhode, 1990, in Bartlett and Kennedy, 1991, p 336.

23 MacKinnon, 1989, p 51; and DuBois *et al*, 1985, p 74.

24 Williams, 1989, in Bartlett and Kennedy, 1991, p 112.

25 Kerber *et al*, 1985, pp 310–21.

26 *Ibid*, p 321.

27 *Ibid*, p 326.

28 *Ibid*, p 328.

either sex'.[29] And, naturally, women, especially educated women, understand how to reason according to an ethic of rights – we could hardly succeed in law school if we could not – but this, she asserts, 'has no bearing on the question of whether they would spontaneously choose to frame moral problems in this way'.[30]

For postmodern feminists, Gilligan's work is problematic, because it appears to replace the single universalist theory of mainstream psychology with a different single universalist theory: that of women's different voice.[31] In fact, as Gilligan explained in conversation with critics, including MacKinnon, her research did not take a unified view of 'women'. She did include black women in her studies, but omitted to mention it; finding that these women represented a high level of 'integration of justice and care', she found an explanation in the fact that they had been interviewed by a white male – 'there is the whole dominance issue right there'.[32] Clearly, more complexity is present in Gilligan's work than the over-simplified critiques would indicate, but Gilligan herself admits that more attention to differences between and among women was needed.

Linda Nicholson, from a postmodernist position, has argued for the usefulness of feminist theorising which 'situates the categories within historical frameworks', proposing a non-essentialist reading of Gilligan which takes into account the criticisms of MacKinnon and Joan Williams.[33] Mary Joe Frug showed that *In a Different Voice* can be interpreted both conservatively and progressively, since the text is sufficiently ambiguous to be able to ignore the apparent essentialism of the categories. She herself was optimistic about its usefulness 'as a methodology for challenging gender'.[34]

This seems to me the best approach for legal feminists, but it is one which Posner's superficial account entirely misses. He cites none of these contributions to the debate. In the last few years, there has been renewed interest in applying Gilligan's ideas of a 'different voice' (or, more usually, these days, 'voices') to feminist scholarship in law, in particular critiques of rights and discussions of citizenship, often in an international or European context. Selma Sevenhuijsen, for example, speaks of citizens 'judging with care' on the basis of Gilligan's model of 'female' moral reasoning, though she rejects its gendered nature.[35] Nancy Hirschmann has written in defence of rights, once viewed with suspicion and distrust by many legal feminists

---

29 Gilligan, 1993, p 2.
30 Kerber *et al*, 1985, p 328.
31 Fraser and Nicholson, 1990, p 32.
32 DuBois *et al*, 1985, p 77.
33 Nicholson, 1990, p 9.
34 Frug, 1992, pp 30–49.
35 Sevenhuijsen, 1998, pp 15, 53, 64.

including herself, suggesting that feminists may selectively reclaim rights provided attention is given to 'particularity and specificity of need'[36] – an ethic of rights tempered by an ethic of care. This recent feminist work takes Gilligan's proposal, that both voices need to be heard in moral reasoning, a step further, by arguing for the destruction of the binary system itself. Women's characteristics, they point out, will always be undervalued in such a system under patriarchy. A more promising vision, Ruth Lister suggests, 'is that of a "woman-friendly" citizenship that combines elements of the gender-neutral and gender-differentiated approaches, while at the same time remaining sensitive to the differences that exist between women'. 'This is best advanced,' she argues, 'through the subversion, transcendence, or critical synthesis of the original dichotomies.'[37]

THE ETHIC OF CARE AND EQUITY

Even given the *caveat* about Gilligan's essentialist categories, it is striking how often her observations about the way women approach moral dilemmas are borne out by legal research, including research in the field of equity. In an article of 1993, Anne Bottomley explored competing 'languages of claim' in property law.[38] Or take Belinda Fehlberg's *Sexually Transmitted Debt*.[39] This is an examination of sureties who agreed to charge their assets with their spouse's or partner's business liabilities, and ended up with horrific debts. Fehlberg interviewed 22 sureties, including two men, as well as a number of debtors, lenders, and lawyers. In a careful analysis of the sureties' motives for agreeing to a charge on their assets, including the family home, Fehlberg uncovered a complex interplay of factors which demonstrated that women tend to make moral decisions on the basis of a different set of considerations from those employed by the laws governing such situations and the courts which enforce them. The women Fehlberg interviewed uniformly lacked financial power within their relationships: they might control the family finances on a day to day basis, they might even have substantial earnings of their own, but the major financial decisions were always made by the men, and 'very few women considered they had the *right* to control' the couple's assets.[40] Not surprisingly, then, they tended to go along with their partner's business decisions, so could not, in all fairness, be considered to be equal bargaining parties. 'When you love someone, you just do what they ask you to

---

36 Hirschmann, 1999, pp 30–50.
37 Lister, 1997, p 9.
38 Bottomley, 1993.
39 Fehlberg, 1997.
40 *Ibid*, p 119.

do', Ms Fenwick (a teacher) confessed.[41] This tendency was reinforced, in some cases, by physical or emotional pressure on the part of the men, so that women who might have had reservations about signing as sureties were really coerced into agreeing. 'I was just forced. There's no other word really to describe it. Not physically forced, but forced ...'[42] The difficulty for the court, here, lay in whether it could recognise this kind of emotional blackmail as a legal wrong. In other cases, however, the determining factors in the women's decisions were ones which played no part at all in the courts' reasoning: the desire to sustain family relationships, the avoidance of conflict (including violence or the threat of it) and the need to demonstrate loyalty and trust.[43] 'Loyalty is the main thing, isn't it?' asked Ms Fenwick. 'It would be totally disloyal not to [sign].'[44]

This comment demonstrates the inadequacy of the test devised by the House of Lords in *Barclays Bank v O'Brien* (1994)[45] to determine whether a surety has been the object of undue influence, misrepresentation or duress. Creditors can avoid being fixed with constructive notice of such a legal wrong if they take 'reasonable steps' to insist that the surety is advised to receive independent legal advice about the consequences of signing. But Fehlberg's interviewees made it clear that neither knowledge of the risks, which most of them understood, nor independent legal advice, would have facilitated, or even made possible, a refusal to act as security to their spouse or partner. As Mrs Inness put it, 'If I'd had independent advice, I'd still have had no choice ...'[46] Mrs Elliot added tellingly: 'You have a choice whether you're going to stay married or not, and that's really what you're down to, isn't it?'[47] Fehlberg concludes: 'Gilligan's research does lend support to the proposition that a woman requested by her husband to execute a security would be likely to view her decision less in terms of law, economic considerations or property, than in terms of the negative impact that her refusal to act as surety would have on their relationship.'[48] These surety cases are precisely the kinds of situation in which equity may intervene to assist those who have been the victims of recognisable legal injustice. But the sureties Fehlberg studied had not been helped by equity, since the courts had not recognised any injustice in their particular cases.[49] The women, however, felt strongly that they had been

---

41 Fehlberg, 1997, p 148.
42 *Ibid*, p 182.
43 *Ibid*, pp 174, 187.
44 *Ibid*, p 182.
45 [1994] 1 AC 180.
46 Fehlberg, 1997, pp 41, 173.
47 *Ibid*, p 182.
48 *Ibid*, p 86.
49 The male sureties also lost out, but had not suffered the same structural disadvantages as the women: they had not, eg, been threatened by their partners, nor did they feel they agreed to sign in order to preserve the relationship.

victims of injustice. 'I just feel it's terribly unfair,' Mrs Hayes concluded. 'I ended up with the debts, and everyone else is living happily ever after.'[50]

EQUITY AND WOMEN'S VOICE/S

The work of Fehlberg and others lends credence to an argument that the concerns and viewpoints of women who came into contact with late 20th century English and American legal ideas and processes were not, Posner to the contrary, well accommodated by those ideas and processes. Equity may, in contrast to law, take the circumstances of the litigants into account, and it purports to look to the intent rather than the form. But, as Fehlberg's research showed, the circumstances and the intent are interpreted according to particular modes of reasoning which do not always, or even usually, bear much resemblance to the way women view the problem.

Though Posner clearly identifies equity as one of the vehicles for the expression of the (so called 'female' but, for him, ungendered) 'ethic of care', he does not really develop his discussion of equity in any depth. He does, however, focus on the idea of 'the alleged female outlook on law'[51] as contextual, concrete rather than abstract, flexible, and discretionary – attributes we tend to associate with equity. This is where I think that Posner's glib assumption that equity and the ethic of care are one and the same thing leads him into error. Since equity is seen as dichotomous with law, his view of a justice system based solely on an ethic of care is one where law is altogether absent: a system without rules, outside the rule of law. This is evident from his warning that: '... if society goes too far in making the administration of law flexible, particularistic, "caring", the consequence will be anarchy, tyranny, or both, which is why "people's justice" is rightly deprecated.'[52] But what Gilligan describes is, of course, not moral decision making without rules but moral decision making based on a different set of rules. Her theory that these are distinctively 'female' does rather seem to be borne out by Posner's inability to grasp what she is getting at.

One important reason why equity rarely embodies women's points of view is precisely because there is often no place for them within law and the legal process to be heard or because, if heard, they are not understood. The sorry saga of disputes over the family home in English trust law is a classic instance of judges operating entirely within the equitable domain, but failing to hear the woman's point of view or to comprehend her approach to justice. This is abundantly clear from the first case on the issue, *Re Rogers* (1948),[53]

---

50 Fehlberg, 1997, p 229.
51 Posner, 1998, p 123.
52 *Ibid*, p 125.
53 *In Re Rogers' Question* [1948] 1 All ER 328.

which set the tone for the ensuing 50 years-plus of debate. Mr and Mrs Rogers bought a house soon after they married in 1939. It was actually Mrs Rogers who found the house and opened negotiations with the seller. It was she, too, who paid the £100 deposit when contracts were exchanged. But it was Mr Rogers who arranged the mortgage to cover the remaining £900 of the asking price of £1,000. The contract, conveyance, mortgage and indemnity insurance required by the building society were all put in the husband's name, and he undertook to pay – and, in the event, did pay – the monthly mortgage instalments. In 1947, the marriage broke down. Dividing up the assets, the couple reached deadlock over the house. Mr Rogers claimed that it was his. Mrs Rogers claimed that, on the contrary, it was *hers*. Neither would budge from that position, so the dispute went to court.

Of course, in law, Mr Rogers was right: the house was in his name. But the fact that Mrs Rogers had paid the initial deposit of £100 entitled her to an interest under the doctrine of the resulting trust, and the High Court judge duly awarded her a one-10th share. Using resulting trusts in this kind of situation was quite novel at the time, and Roxburgh J truly thought that equity had come to Mrs Rogers' defence against the harshness of the strict application of law. Mrs Rogers did not think so at all, and Mr Rogers begrudged her even the 10%. Both appealed.

In the Court of Appeal, Mr Rogers contended that the deposit paid by his wife had been a loan to him at the time of the purchase and that, therefore, his sole obligation to his wife was to repay the £100. He said the house was, and had always been intended to be, his alone. Mrs Rogers, however, said exactly the same thing. She declared that the fact that her husband had paid all the mortgage instalments had absolutely no bearing on the question of ownership of the property; all it meant was that he was taking responsibility for the 'household expenses' which, as a husband and major breadwinner, 'it would be his proper function to discharge'.[54] Evidence was brought to show that she had fought strenuously to have the contract placed in her name but had been unsuccessful. Though not spelt out in the case report, it was clear that the building society would not deal with a married woman.

The brief case report reveals that Mrs Rogers' (male) counsel tried to distance himself from her grand claim. He merely asked for a larger share, where she claimed the whole house – a view the court plainly found incomprehensible. 'In the circumstances, it seems to me wholly unreasonable to suppose that the wife thought she could both have her cake and eat it [that is, be supported by her husband and get the house]', expostulated Evershed LJ.[55] Yet that is exactly what she did think.

---

54 *In Re Rogers' Question* [1948] 1 All ER 328, p 329.

55 *Ibid*, p 330.

We know nothing about Mrs Rogers beyond the few facts given in the case report. We know nothing of her background, whether she had children or not, whether she had a paid job or not. And we do not know why she thought the house was hers. But we can guess. Her point of view is perfectly logical if you locate it, not in the discourses of law and equity, but in the domestic ideology of her day. Women's place was in the home: this maxim, born of the social upheaval which followed the Industrial Revolution, led to the Victorian notion of 'separate spheres' which still held sway through the first half of the 20th century. In the 1920s and 1930s, married women were expected to be full time housewives and mothers[56] and were discouraged – often banned – from working in paid employment.[57] If women's place was in the home, which men were bound to provide for their families, then it followed logically that the home was women's place; Mrs Rogers differed from her silent sisters only in articulating this as a literal truth rather than a figure of speech.

Here we have, then, a clash of viewpoints – of analysis – of reasoning. Mrs Rogers' view makes sense, but it is not the sense of law or equity. Equity recognised her 'contribution' to the home in the form of the £100 deposit. But Mrs Rogers would not have seen this as her sole or, indeed, her most important contribution to the home. Her contribution would have lain in the housework, the childcare, in *homemaking*.

This is all conjecture, of course, but it can be supported by a mass of evidence from extra-judicial sources. The popular literature of the period (women's magazines and advertisements, for example) fairly rammed home the message about women's place and women's role.[58] Moreover, women's own writings (in novels and autobiographical work) tell a very different tale of 'ownership' from that of law or equity.

Here, for example, is an extract from the wartime Mass Observation diary of a working class housewife called Nella Last:

> If I could, I'd gather my dear, wide-windowed house and take it far away, and hide it safely in some quiet spot ... [I know] it's only a semi-jerry-built modern house, with little of value in it. I keep telling myself that, but then the soft sheen of my 'autumn-tiled' fireplace or my gay bright curtains or the polished, panelled hall takes my eye, and ... my hand goes out to stroke a cushion or curtain, or to move my brass tray to catch the sun.[59]

For Mrs Last, the house is plainly *her* house, lovingly furnished and tended, not beautiful, not valuable, but *hers*.

---

56 'In the interwar years only one desirable image was held up to women by all the mainstream media agencies – that of the housewife and mother. This single role model was presented to women to follow and all other alternative roles were presented as wholly undesirable.' Beddoe, 1989, pp 3, 8.

57 *Short v Poole Corp* [1925] All ER 74.

58 Eg, Opie, 1997, 1998; Ballaster *et al*, 1991.

59 Broad and Fleming, 1981, p 117.

And the same is true for Laura in Mollie Panter-Downes's novel of 1947, *One Fine Day*, who muses, after the departure of her solicitor husband for work in the morning: '[T]he debris of breakfast things looked cold, awful, as though they were the mummified remains of some meal eaten a thousand years ago. But she sat down among them and poured out a last cup of tea. Ah, how good! Now, said the house to Laura, we are alone together. Now I am yours again.'[60] *Now I am yours again.* Laura's husband is here depicted as an intruder in the domestic sphere. Only when the man has gone can the truth be told: it is not his house, but hers.

'LOOKING AFTER' WOMEN

In so far as the ethic of care can be taken to mean taking care of the interests of those ill-protected by law, as Posner appears to think, there is a long history of equity's purporting to protect the interests of women. Accounts of the development of property law have represented the courts of equity as particularly sympathetic to women's sufferings under the common law. Scholars have argued that women's legal position improved across the 16th, 17th and 18th centuries, largely because of the increasingly sophisticated use of trusts in marriage settlements.[61] Until recently, the strict settlement has been explained as a property device which owed its origins in part to the desire of loving fathers to provide for their daughters and younger sons instead of simply following the rules of primogeniture.[62] The restraint on anticipation, invented by Lord Thurlow in 1791 to prevent a married woman from alienating her separate property, was justified throughout the century and a half of its existence as a safeguard for women's rights. The object of the restraint was to make it impossible for a husband to force his wife to transfer her property to him or to offer it as security for his debts – to 'kick or kiss' her out of her entitlement.[63] The woman thus shielded was (in Dicey's words), 'absolutely guarded against the possible exactions or persuasions of her husband, and received a kind of protection which the law of England does not provide for any other person except a married woman'.[64] More recently, Lord Denning made chivalrous use of equitable principles to try to produce justice for women in the context of disputes over the family home.

It has been difficult, even for women, to resist this version of history which places equity at the centre of women's improving legal situation. The

---

60 Panter-Downes, 1985, p 17.
61 Eg, Cioni, 1985.
62 Eg, Stone, 1997.
63 Kenny, 1879, p 104.
64 Dicey, 1962, p 379.

American historian Mary Beard, for example, writing in 1949, took William Blackstone severely to task for producing an oft-quoted account of women's legal position which only considered the common law, and totally ignored their rights in equity.[65] But considering the extraordinary influence of Blackstone's pronouncements – in Victorian England, they had the force of law and were accepted uncritically, not only by the courts, but by many feminist campaigners on legal matters (Ray Strachey's 1928 study of first wave feminism, *The Cause*, suffers from this fault) – it was perhaps not surprising that Beard saw equity as offering women greater scope and protection than law. Though non-legally trained feminists must have had difficulty grasping the intricate distinctions between the two jurisdictions, it is noteworthy that Barbara Leigh Smith Bodichon, a leading light in the married women's property campaigns, was not so deceived, either by Blackstone or by the claims of equity. In her *Brief Summary ... of the Most Important Laws Concerning Women*, she did not portray equity as representing women's rights, nor did she call for the extension of the equitable rules to all women. She merely observed that equity bestowed certain limited rights on certain well to do women (such as herself) which the common law did not – and then called for a different kind of rights for women, the rights enjoyed by men.[66]

More recent research by legal feminists has all but dismantled equity's claim to offer women special protection. Tim Stretton's exhaustive study of *Women Waging Law* in the (equitable) Court of Requests in Tudor times has demonstrated that 'it is misleading to represent equity as women's legal saviour'.[67] Eileen Spring has challenged the traditional view of strict settlements as providing for women who would have lost out under common law rules. She has shown that, on the contrary, the common law rules were perceived as allowing property to fall into women's hands much too frequently, and the strict settlement was developed to restrict or actually deny their access to it.[68] Stretton comments that this finding 'serves as an important reminder that the flexibility offered by rival jurisdictions to the common law could be used to thwart women's entitlements as well as to protect or extend them'.[69]

Part of the explanation for equity's refusal to protect women's rights in any consistent fashion lies in the courts' inability or refusal to hear what women were saying. In earlier centuries, this was not so much because women did not appear in court in person – in fact they did, as Stretton found, in greater numbers than one would have supposed[70] – as because their

---

65 Beard, 1946, p 85.
66 Bodichon, 1854.
67 Stretton, 1998, p 28.
68 Spring, 1993.
69 Stretton, 1998, p 32.
70 *Ibid*, p 40.

stories, and also their personalities, had to be moulded to fit into preconceived stereotypes of deservingness. It was perilous enough to go to law, in an age which depicted the ideal woman as modest and confined to the private sphere, and many women then, as now, feared the legal process, because of the opportunities it presented for character assassination by opponents and counsel. In court, therefore, they would try to present themselves (or to be presented) as independent, shrewd and self-sufficient, or weak, ignorant and helpless, as their claim and strategy demanded – and, in either case, as virtuous.

Stretton comments on the deliberate silencing of women's voices: '[T]here was a right way and a wrong way to go to law. The right way was for a women to say little, leaving her counsel to argue all aspects of her case on her behalf, in other words to entrust her affairs to a man ... The wrong way was for a woman to break silence and speak vigorously, confidently, and like a man whenever the opportunity presented itself.'[71] It hardly needs saying that the strident, confident woman still wins few friends in court, while stereotypes continue to dominate the legal discourse in matters concerning women, even at the hands of female counsel. As Helena Kennedy explains in *Eve Was Framed*, to depart from these norms might risk losing the court's sympathy for one's client.[72]

As for the restraint on anticipation, described by England's first woman barrister as a device 'to protect married women against their own folly or their husband's greed',[73] it can equally plausibly be seen as protection for the assets of the woman's family of origin against an interloping husband, and it operated as a severe check on married women's ability to make use of their capital or anticipate their income. This meant that the 19th century wife, unlike her 18th century predecessor, could not conduct her own business or even provide for her family in the event of her husband's inability to do so. In *Re Wood* (1885),[74] for example, a solicitor's clerk in his 50s lost his job through illness and was unable to find another. His wife applied to release some of the funds in her marriage settlement to pay for the children's education. The Court of Appeal refused: '[T]hey did not consider it would be for the benefit of the family that the small property should be eaten up. On the contrary, it might be for their benefit that the husband, who had hitherto been unable to get work and on whom there was not the slightest imputation, should not have the stimulus to induce him to procure work in any way removed.'[75] Yet the debates over the restraint on anticipation, which was not abolished until well into the 20th century,[76] raises many of the same issues as Belinda

---

71 Stretton, 1998, p 54.
72 Kennedy, 1992, p 33.
73 Normanton, 1932, p 120.
74 (1885) 1 TLR 192.
75 *Ibid*, p 193.

Fehlberg's work on women sureties. The reality of patriarchal power within 19th century marriage meant that many husbands did put pressure on their wives to give up their separate property or use it to secure their husbands' business debts. Indeed, the restraint had been created in direct response to the sad case of Mrs Vernon who, not realising the consequences of her action, conveyed her separate estate as security for her husband's debts; thus, 'while the wax was yet warm upon the deed', as the report most graphically puts it, 'the creditors got a claim on it'.[77] A century later, successive Vice Chancellors were still commenting on the stream of applications coming to court where 'it has been evident that the object of removing the restraint was in reality to benefit the husband'.[78] Who knows if the Victorian court's refusal to help the husband made things easier for the anxious wife than the unprotected status of her late 20th century counterpart?

There is evidence that some judges listened carefully to women who asked to have their restraints lifted. Fry J advised that the women be separately examined.[79] Chitty J was 'very strict in finding out that it is according to their own free will',[80] while Kekewich J stated: 'Regarding the restraint on anticipation as intended for the protection of the wife, I view these applications with extreme jealousy; and when they are occasioned, as is often the case, by the husband's extravagance, I never grant them unless satisfied that the wife's happiness will be seriously endangered by refusal or will really be advanced by such order as is asked.'[81] Mrs Cathcart, in lengthy litigation against her solicitor, Mr Hood Barrs, conducted her own case: this elicited exasperated commentary from the judges in the seven reported cases. Lord Esher MR did 'not wonder that there has been considerable doubt as to the effect of what took place in the earlier applications in the case of *Hood Barrs v Cathcart*, owing to the fact that the defendant insisted on arguing her own case'.[82] But, as in modern case law, there can be no certainty that the judges actually heard the women's own version of the transaction. So much depends on the questions asked, the assumptions made, and the straitjacket of 'thinking like a lawyer' – that is, sticking to the 'legal' issues, and not straying from the 'point' – which often filters out the very concerns which weigh most with women.

---

76 The creation of new restraints was abolished by the Law Reform (Married Women and Tortfeasors) Act 1935. All existing restraints were abolished by the Married Women (Restraint Upon Anticipation) Act 1949, a private Bill adopted by the Government at the behest of Countess Mountbatten of Burma.

77 *Pybus v Smith* [1791] 3 Bro CC 341.

78 *Tamplin v Miller* [1882] WN 44.

79 *Hodges v Hodges* (1882) 20 Ch D 749, p 753.

80 *In Re Currey, Gibson and Way (No 2)* [1887] 56 LTR 80.

81 *Paget v Paget* [1898] 1 Ch 47, p 55.

82 *Hood Barrs v Cathcart* [1894] 2 QB 559, p 561.

What does emerge clearly, however, is that women under settlements were obliged to rely on the skill and honesty of male trustees and solicitors (some of whom lacked both),[83] instead of being able to control their own finances and develop the competence that comes with experience. Tim Stretton makes this point about women in the 16th and 17th centuries: 'Parents made arrangements with parents and future sons-in-law or with trustees, and while daughters were consulted, their involvement was often circumscribed.'[84] It was always men who prepared and signed the documents, and women tended to accept any financial arrangements their husbands proposed. In *Mara v Browne* (1895), for example, North J observed of the wife:

> ... though she showed no signs of being a clever woman of business, she seemed fairly intelligent. Her evidence was to the effect that she lived with her husband at Torquay, and had entire confidence in, and left all business matters to, him; that she never remembered any occasion on which she was personally consulted at all as to investments; that her husband used to tell her what was going on about the trust ... and if he thought all was right she did too ...[85]

The parallel with Fehlberg's surety cases 100 years later is glaringly obvious.

The lessons to be learnt from this account of some of equity's claims to protect women are that, across the centuries, women have indeed required protection from the abuse of patriarchal power and that equity has from time to time operated to 'mitigate the harshness of the common law' (as the textbooks put it), as it impacts on women ... and at other times not. What is most striking is that equitable interventions which have the potential to assist women are, nevertheless, susceptible of co-option and use by men against women. Perhaps this should not surprise us, since men had complete control of the development of law and the legal process until after the First World War, and still dominate it at the highest levels, and – perhaps more importantly – because men have also dominated the dissemination of knowledge. Men's control of publishing, the media and advertising, and of the educational curriculum at every level, has meant that most women still grow up with no more financial or legal understanding than their 19th century counterparts; more to the point, they still lack power in financial and legal transactions, even where they have the expertise. The source of women's powerlessness may be material, but it may also, as Fehlberg showed, be the result of decision making according to a set of priorities different from those of patriarchal institutions like law and the finance industry. The result is that

---

83 Eg, Kay LJ told Mr Hood Barrs, solicitor, who appeared for himself, that one point he advanced was 'a perfectly impossible argument to any one who studies the Act of Parliament, and to any one who has the slightest pretensions to be a lawyer'. *In Re Lumley ex p Hood Barrs* [1896] 2 Ch 690, p 692.

84 Stretton, 1998, p 120.

85 *Mara v Browne* [1895] 2 Ch 69, p 89.

women still need protection against the exercise by their husbands and the big credit institutions of their strict legal rights.

The fact that women prioritise loyalty and trust and looking after the family over safeguarding their own legal position and standing up for their own rights and wishes means that their version of events will continue to conflict with the way the law sees it – and this will almost always act to women's detriment. Equity has come to the aid of women many a time, but it has never spoken *for* women, nor represented women's viewpoint. It is but another of patriarchy's discourses and, despite its heroic reputation, it does not embody Gilligan's ethic of care, and it still lets women down.

THE 'FLEXIBILITY' OF EQUITY

In textbook accounts, equity is depicted as the opposite or the complement of common law: flexible where law is strict, discretionary where law is obligatory, humane in its concern for 'justice' rather than 'rights'. This is certainly Posner's view in *Law and Literature* and central to his claim that equity both embodies the ethic of care and speaks for women. Yet I would argue that the vaunted flexibility of equity is an illusion. Until the advent of Lord Denning, there had been no new equitable developments for a century. 'Harman J said in 1950 that "Equity is presumed not to be past the age of child-bearing". But in 1952, it had no child living which was not at least 100 years old.'[86] In 1952, Denning, then a Lord Justice of Appeal, gave a lecture at University College, London on 'The Need for a New Equity'. He pointed out that rules established for good and valid reasons may cease to make sense when social conditions change. They should, therefore, be replaced with different rules which take account of these new conditions. It is clear from the text of his speech that Denning did not expect the new equity to come from either the judges (who 'are forbidden to legislate') or the House of Lords ('for they are bound by their own mistakes'); he looked, instead, to 'the new spirit which is alive in our universities'.[87] In the event, it was Lord Denning who became the embodiment of that new spirit, who, disregarding his own precept about judges' inability to make law, seized the nettle and began to use equity with a flexibility which bordered on recklessness.

Fifty years on, while many of Denning's challenges to law have been incorporated in modified form into statute, his flexible application of equity has been replaced with a much more cautious approach. Today, when a landmark equitable decision is made, which really seems to unsettle the legal status quo, you can be sure that the broad application of the new principle will

---

86   Denning, 1981, pp 176–77.
87   *Ibid*, p 177.

be speedily cut down to size in the cases which follow. The landmark judgment may be confined to its facts. A stricter test may be substituted for the original broad brush formulation. The House of Lords, in particular, makes a habit of reducing the application of equitable principles to a narrow set of circumstances which makes a mockery of equity's pretensions to be flexible or even very different from law. *Williams and Glyn's Bank v Boland*,[88] for example, sent shock waves through the mortgage industry: for the first time, lenders would have to take account of the little woman at home! But, when the Court of Appeal extended the protection offered to Mrs Boland to Mr and Mrs Flegg,[89] the House of Lords seized on a technical rule to remove it, despite their similar situation and the fact that the Fleggs were unquestionably deserving.

Property law in the second half of the 20th century has seen the role of equity repeatedly expanding and contracting, one moment (in Denning's words) 'fluid and adaptable', the next 'rigid and technical'.[90] In this struggle, the protagonists have often been the Court of Appeal and the House of Lords, representing (certainly in Denning's view) the forces of progress and of reaction. But, even where the former's equitable interventions were victories on behalf of the women concerned, the latter's (usually successful) efforts to restrain or even snuff them out put paid to any long standing challenge to patriarchy.

The family home has been the principal site of this struggle of wills across more than half a century. The combination of factors which led to the dispute in *Re Rogers* gave Lord Denning scope to develop a new role for equity: the great increase in home ownership, the increase in divorce, the rise in cohabitation outside marriage, and the inability of much-praised property law reforms of 1925 to deal with co-ownership problems never contemplated by its patriarchal creators.

The Court of Appeal used trust law to find a 'just' solution for Mrs Rogers, but Denning was not interested in a simple trust formulation which, though 'equitable', was almost as mechanical and rigid in its application as law. He took a much more radical approach in the two new principles he evolved, with some support (and much opposition) from his brother judges through the 1950s and 1960s. These principles were the deserted wife's equity, intended to prevent a deserting husband from selling the family home over his ex-wife's head, and 'family assets', the doctrine that married couples automatically (in the absence of other arrangements) co-own the matrimonial home. 'It seems to me,' declared Denning LJ in *Rimmer v Rimmer*, his first such case, 'that when the parties, by their joint efforts, save money to buy a house,

---

88 *Williams & Glyn's Bank Ltd v Boland* [1981] AC 487.
89 *City of London Building Society v Flegg* [1988] AC 54.
90 Denning, 1981, p 176.

which is intended as a continuing provision for them both, then the proper presumption is that the beneficial interest belongs to them jointly.'[91]

Both these principles derived from Denning's view that husbands should be breadwinners and wives should be homemakers, with logic and chivalry dictating that a woman who fulfilled her proper role in marriage should not be disadvantaged thereby in the event of a marital breakdown for which she was not to blame.

It is plain that Denning's views on gender were conservative but, on the other hand, the series of cases in which he developed the deserted wife's equity and the family assets doctrine were welcomed by women at the time, since they took account of women's actual material and ideological situation. In that limited sense, then, he spoke for women. But many senior judges did not like Denning's decisions, because they made a mockery of land law rules. How could the deserted wife's equity be held to bind third parties when it was not (could not be) registered? And 'family assets' sounded dangerously like 'community of property', a foreign notion which was not a part of English law, and should only be introduced, if it be their will, by Parliament.

The end result was that the House of Lords struck down both the deserted wife's equity[92] and family assets.[93] Public outcry did, indeed, lead to parliamentary intervention, but the spouse's right of occupation was a poor substitute for the deserted wife's equity, since it required a spouse to register her right in order for it to bind third parties. Not only were few women aware that they should do this, but fewer still would contemplate, even with the requisite knowledge, adopting what could only be seen as a hostile and untrusting course of action in the context of a 'happy' marriage. In place of family assets, Parliament offered ss 4 and 37 of the Matrimonial Proceedings and Property Act 1970, which took divorcing couples out of the land law regime altogether.[94]

For all other co-ownership situations, Lord Diplock's constructive trust formulation in *Gissing*[95] established the guiding principle from which the courts have not deviated (let alone progressed) in the ensuing 30 years. This is in spite of the fact that the judges in *Gissing* raised a number of problems with the narrowness of the test which have still not been accommodated. Lord Reid, for example, was worried about the fact that financial contributions to

---

91 [1953] 1 QB 63, p 73.

92 *National Provincial Bank Ltd v Ainsworth* [1965] AC 1175.

93 *Gissing v Gissing* [1971] AC 886.

94 Section 4 gave the court power to transfer property on divorce, taking account of the contributions of each party to the welfare of the family, including housework and childcare. Section 37 provided that contributions by spouses without a legal interest in the home to improvements in the property would give them a share or, if they already had a share under an implied trust, an increased share.

95 *Gissing v Gissing* [1971] AC 886.

the household which were not directly referable to the purchase of the home would not be taken into account in assessing interests in the home: 'I can see no good reason for this distinction and I think that in many cases it would be unworkable ... Is she to be deprived of a share if she says "I can pay in enough to pay for the household bills," but given a share if she says "I can pay in £10 a week regularly"[?]'[96] Phillimore LJ, in the Court of Appeal, was concerned about not including women's non-financial contributions: 'If she had not gone on earning and in addition done all the housework and cooking, he would hardly have been able to meet his financial obligations and also save £3,500 in 10 years.'[97]

The courts' refusal to move on the family home front demonstrates that there is a limit to how much equity can be permitted to disturb the legal status quo – particularly where big financial interests are concerned – and the social status quo – particularly where men's interests are concerned. Belinda Fehlberg has noted how the Court of Appeal decision in *Barclays Bank v O'Brien* recognised that some wives might still need equity's special protection because of their continuing social inequality. However, the House of Lords replaced this approach with a test which appeared to strike a balance between the interests of the sureties and those of the creditors. The result has been a series of 'creditor-sympathetic' judgments and a paucity of decisions favourable to women.[98] We are forced to the conclusion that equitable interventions in court, even where they appear to strike a blow for women in the original case, are always going to be whipped into line, the principle watered down, its application restricted, the test re-stated in ever-narrower terms, the discretion all but removed. The House of Lords' judgment in *Lloyd's Bank v Rosset*[99] is perhaps the clearest modern example of this tendency and how it works to the manifest disadvantage of women. In searching for evidence of an implied intention that a non-legal partner might have a share in the family home, Lord Bridge decided that it was unlikely that anything less than a financial contribution to the purchase price would do. Most claimants are women, yet women are much less likely to make financial contributions to the home than men. This is partly because women have less access to money than men. They tend to occupy lower paid jobs, and to be paid less in the same jobs, and since they are expected to be responsible for childcare and housework, they are often forced to give up remunerative positions for work which fits in with these duties or no paid work at all. But it is also because heterosexual couples' financial arrangements tend to fall in gendered ways: women use their money for household goods and expenses,

---

96 *Gissing v Gissing* [1971] AC 886, p 896.
97 *Gissing v Gissing* [1969] 2 Ch 87, p 101.
98 Fehlberg, 1997, pp 37–42.
99 [1991] 1 AC 107, p 132.

the children, and extras like holidays (as Mrs Burns did in *Burns v Burns*),[100] while men use theirs for the mortgage and home improvements (as Mr Burns did). Judges know this. They have known it for decades. Yet, despite the public outcry which greeted the decision in *Burns v Burns* in 1984, the House of Lords was quite content to perpetuate the injustice of equity's treatment of women into the 1990s.[101]

In this respect, then, the claim that equity is flexible and context-based is as false as the claim that it speaks for women and defends their interests. Equity, like law, operates to maintain patriarchal power and, by denying women access to assets they have worked for, contributes substantially to their disempowerment.

THE 'CARING' JUDGE

At first sight, Lord Denning might be seen as the English equivalent of American judges Cardozo and Brennan, suggested by Posner as representing an equitable and caring approach to law as opposed to a 'masculine' concern with the strict application of rules. Certainly, Denning was the antithesis of the unthinking obeyer of rules. Rules which irked him were grandly swept away, to be replaced by the clever elaboration of equitable principles focused squarely, it would seem, on a consideration of context, relationships, and consequences. Yet underlying his apparent concern with particulars lay a world view which was clearly premised on rights and entitlements.

In 1953, he wrote that 'the law recognises the natural state of affairs whereby the man's proper function is to work to provide for his wife and family; and the woman's proper place is to look after the home and bring up the children'.[102] He never deviated from this philosophy. For this reason, while he would do his utmost to assist deserted wives, he would never reward a deserting wife. He disliked too much independence in a woman. Giving the Eleanor Rathbone Memorial Lecture in Liverpool in 1960, he tactlessly observed that there had been one historical period in which women had achieved a high degree of equality: 'It was in the Roman Empire, and it should serve as a warning of the dangers to which equality may give rise ... This freedom proved to be disastrous to the Roman society.'[103]

---

100 *Burns v Burns* [1984] Ch 317.

101 For a much more sophisticated account of what happened to narratives of women in property disputes after Denning, see Bottomley, 1993.

102 Denning, 1953, p 98.

103 Denning, 1960, pp 3–4.

This prejudice, amounting almost to a maxim of equity, coloured Denning's attitude to women in court. Nowhere is it clearer than in those property disputes where he decided against the woman. *Bedson v Bedson*[104] involved a couple who jointly owned (as joint tenants in equity) a house in which the husband also carried out his draper's business. The wife, who had left home with the children, wanted the house sold so that she could realise her half-share. In the county court, however, the judge awarded her only £272 worth, on the grounds that the house had only been put in joint names to avoid death duties if anything happened to the husband, the contract had been in the husband's sole name, and he had paid the entire purchase price of £4,000. Mrs Bedson appealed to the Court of Appeal, which accepted that she was a joint tenant and entitled to half the value of the house, but denied her application for sale. Lord Denning's judgment is worthy of close study to uncover his reasons and the language used to justify this decision.

Denning's approach was always to begin by introducing his characters in their setting. Mr Bedson, we are told, was 'a regular soldier serving in the Life Guards ... [who] attained the distinguished and responsible rank of Corporal of Horse'.[105] In 1960, he retired with a grant of £2,000 and savings of £3,000, obtained through doing extra work designing badges and heraldry, all of which he put towards the purchase of the family home and stock for his shop on the ground floor. From the start, therefore, we have a picture of Mr Bedson as industrious and praiseworthy. The business was carried out by the couple in partnership, 'the wife helping in the shop, and the husband doing all the management'.[106] The wife was paid £3 a week.

Next comes a telling paragraph. Recounted in classic Denning style, point by point in a series of principal clauses, it loses none of its dramatic impact by the deadpan presentation:

> In 1963, the wife's mother inflicted herself on them. She was a disturbing influence. The wife gave up helping in the shop. On Sept 9, 1963, the wife deserted the husband, taking the three children with her. She went to live in a house in the neighbourhood and herself went out to work at a factory earning £9 a week. On Nov 18, 1963, she complained to the magistrates that the husband had deserted her and had wilfully neglected to provide her with reasonable maintenance. On Jan 14, 1964, the magistrates dismissed both her complaints. They awarded the wife no maintenance, but they ordered the husband to pay £2 10s a week for each child, making £7 10s a week in all. He has regularly paid this sum, though it has been a great strain on his resources. He has lived himself most frugally to make ends meet. The £7 10s was so difficult that the magistrates reduced it to £6 a week; and this he has just managed to afford.[107]

---

104 [1965] 3 All ER 307.
105 *Ibid*, p 309.
106 *Ibid*, p 310.
107 *Ibid*, p 310.

I have quoted this section at length because it is so revealing of Denning's abilities to tailor his decision to his sympathies while appearing simply to set out the facts objectively. Not that there is any pretence of objectivity in the treatment of the mother-in-law, of course, but mothers-in-law have always been fair game in fact and fiction, and Denning was playing to an audience. Moreover, by placing the blame on her mother, Denning manages to seem unjudgmental about the wife. Meanwhile, the husband continues to be presented in a favourable light. He has obediently paid out maintenance for the children, despite the hardship this causes him. Life is clearly a struggle for Mr Bedson.

But there must be another side to this story: the wife's side. These facts could be interpreted quite differently. Note, for instance, that Mrs Bedson was forced to go to court to get maintenance for the children. This suggests that it was not being paid up to that point. We are told that the husband has been back to court to get the amount reduced. But we are not told how his family is faring on that reduced sum. We learn that Mrs Bedson is able to get £9 a week in a factory job. This indicates that her labour in her husband's business was paid at an undervalue. Elsewhere in the judgment, we are told that she has given up any claim to a share in the business. A different reading of these facts might well conclude that Mrs Bedson has been economically exploited. With three children, reduced maintenance and a full time job, life is almost certainly a struggle for Mrs Bedson too – but we are not told this.

Bedson is an instance where Lord Denning (along with the other two judges in the Court of Appeal) used equity to deny a woman the normal statutory remedy in these sorts of trust for sale disputes. 'If the wife deserted her husband and leaves the matrimonial home, the court will not order a sale at her request where it would be inequitable to do so', Denning declared.[108] As with all equitable decisions, this purports to be based on the particular facts, the context, the personalities and the probable consequences of the decision. The court's refusal to order a sale allowed the husband to continue to work on the premises. But there is no evidence that the court took into account the consequences for Mrs Bedson of her inability to realise the capital in her jointly owned home. This case shows, then, that not only can equity be used against women's interests, but that context-based, apparently caring judgments like this do not necessarily employ Gilligan's ethic of care. Denning's overriding concern was his rule that *equity will not assist a deserting wife*. In this sense, he was as concerned with rules and rights as any judge.

---

108 *Bedson v Bedson* [1965] 3 All ER 307, p 312.

LISTENING TO WOMEN

In 1985, in one of the first attempts to apply Gilligan's findings to law, Carrie Menkel-Meadow foresaw the transformative power of women's voices in the legal profession. In describing the conflicting forces within law, she started out, like Posner, by identifying equity with 'woman's voice' and the ethic of care: '... there is a tendency for one set of characteristics in a system to mitigate the excesses of another. In this sense, the legal system can be seen to encompass both the male and female voices already. Thus, the harshness of the law produced the flexibility of equity, and conversely, the abuse of flexibility gave rise to rules of law to limit discretion.'[109] But, Menkel-Meadow noted, in all systems there is a tendency for the 'male' form to prevail. 'Thus, equity begins to develop its own harsh rules of law and universalistic regulations applied to discretionary decisions, undermining the flexibility that discretion is supposed to protect. Because men have, in fact, dominated by controlling the legal system, the women's voice in law may be present, but in a male form.'[110] Unlike Posner, then, Menkel-Meadow came to doubt equity's power to speak adequately for women. So do I. The promise of equity has been dangled before us to deceive women into thinking that our interests are served by the law, our voices heard, and that we have nothing to complain about. But, as Menkel-Meadow indicates, the flexibility of equity is all too often curbed by the rules protecting the power of men. (In the conclusion to his discussion of Susan Glaspell's story, Posner observes: 'Read literally, "A Jury of her Peers" endorses a "battered wife" defense to murder so encompassing as to place most husbands outside the protection of the law.'[111] This seems to me to make a similar point.)

It is a fiction that equity speaks for women, or even looks after our interests; indeed, we are more likely to find the expression of women's ideas about law in real fiction, or in autobiography, or in personal interviews with women. Our laws and legal processes make little room for women's versions of events. We may debate whether this exclusion is deliberate – I think it is! – in any case, it is now so entrenched it would take a huge effort of will to change it. What, then, should women do? We could all be educated to think like lawyers, and thus avoid the problems that follow from acting according to an ethic of care. We could swamp the legal institutions and, masters of the ethic of rights, change all the rules so that they benefit women rather than men. Or we could argue for the incorporation of the ethic of care into legal reasoning. To help us achieve this, we could do far worse than to look to literature to see how equity's flexible jurisdiction could be broadened to encompass all those different voices.

---

109 Menkel-Meadow, 1985, p 302.
110 *Ibid*.
111 Posner, 1998, pp 125–26.

CHAPTER 2

EQUITY'S DARLING?

Maggie Conway

INTRODUCTION

It is a truth universally acknowledged that equity has been the special friend of womankind, even that equity is a Sister.[1] However, what is universally acknowledged is not necessarily true. While it is undeniably the case that equity has, from time to time, assumed the white knight role and ridden to the rescue of some damsel caught in the toils of the common law, it is much less certain that equity could ever rightfully claim to be a girl's best friend.

This chapter will consider the role of equity historically, in the context of inheritance, marriage and widowhood, divorce and separation. The purpose is not to recast equity as the enemy of women, nor to propose that the common law should now occupy the female-friendly throne vacated by equity, but to argue that the situation is more complex. Equity has assisted some women, some of the time, but not all women and not consistently. It must be stated that not all women were able to benefit from equity's intervention. Women from rich families were able to have their property protected by trust on marriage. Although the Court of Requests, part of the Exchequer, provided a form of inexpensive equitable jurisdiction, most women from poor families, if they encountered law at all, would be subject to the common law. This chapter will concentrate on the role played by equity in dealing with the property of women from relatively wealthy families.

Equity's credentials as the protector of women, historically, stem from the particular legal disabilities attaching to the married woman in English jurisprudence. Blackstone was able to put a positive 'spin' on this. 'Even the disabilities which the wife lies under, are for the most part intended for her protection and benefit. So great a favourite is the female sex of the laws of England.'[2] These disabilities are well known. During coverture, the woman's identity was merged with that of her husband – the fiction of marital unity. A

---

1   See, eg, Stretton, 1998, especially Chapters 3 and 4; and, in modern times, Scott LJ in the Court of Appeal decision in *Barclays Bank plc v O'Brien*: '... special equitable rules continued to apply to married women' (1993) QB 109, CA, p 138, leading to the conclusion that wives are 'a specially protected class'.

2   *Blackstone's Commentaries on the Laws of England*, 1765, London, Vol 1, p 433, quoted in Stretton, 1998, p 24.

married woman could not own property in her own right, she could neither sue nor be sued, had no rights over her own children, was not entitled to her own earnings, and did not even have to wait for her wedding day to find herself coming under the dominion of her husband-to-be, with the doctrine of restraint on anticipation. Single women were, of course, disenfranchised, but did have legal capacity, which their married sisters lacked. 'It was not the fact of being female, but the status of wife that entailed severe legal disabilities.'[3]

The origins of the fiction of marital unity are debatable:

> ... its religious origins lay in the one flesh doctrine of Christianity, its empirical roots in the customs of medieval Normandy. Its introduction into English law after the Norman Conquest signalled a decline in the status of English wives which reached a nadir in the early capitalism of the 16th and 17th centuries. But what is most striking about the long course of the concept of marital unity is its ability to serve the needs of those shifting social structures: the kin-oriented family of the late Middle Ages, the patriarchal nuclear family of early capitalism, and even the more companionate nuclear family of the late 18th century.[4]

Christianity played a part in advocating the notion of the desirability of submissive and obedient wives, but was not the origin of the idea. 'There is no doubt that Greeks and Romans, both men and women, had always accepted wifely subordination as an integral part of a well ordered family.'[5] 'The church fathers certainly thought that male domination was an important constituent of the Christian family. But, although they often cited the Bible for the submissive role of the wife, they never claimed that it would have been a particularly Christian idea. On the contrary, they believed that it was a commonly accepted part of the natural order.'[6] The idea of the 'natural order' was also invoked to support the idea that men and women, or at least husbands and wives, occupied separate spheres, public and private respectively.

The disabilities within marriage were not addressed directly by equity, but women from wealthy families could have their property protected by trustees and specified to be for their sole and separate use, so that a husband would not have access to the property, nor be able to use it to settle his debts. When the marriage was in difficulty, and the parties had separated or divorced, further problems arose. Not the least of these was the confusion of jurisdictions dealing with particular matters. No civil divorce was available before 1857,[7] but in the preceding centuries, different procedures and arrangements were possible to enable the parties to live apart. 'From the

---

3   Holcombe, 1983, p 4.
4   Quoted in Doggett, 1993, p 70.
5   Arjava, 1996, p 131.
6   *Ibid*, p 132.
7   Matrimonial Causes Act 1857.

Middle Ages to 1857, there was no formal change at all in the official doctrine and practice of the canon law.'[8] The common law and equity had both complementary and conflicting roles in the process. The theoretical difficulties of the exact nature of marriage were not satisfactorily resolved – status or contract.

Marriage, at least amongst the landed classes, was often an exercise in dynastic engineering. The use of entails, settlements and the observance of primogeniture were inconsistent with the public policy of free alienability of land. However, the landed classes and the conveyancers combined were able to overcome these difficulties to their own satisfaction. The net effect of such practices was to limit severely the possibility of wives owning and dealing with property in their own right or daughters inheriting and thereby interfering with the male line of succession. Equity in these developments, as far as women were concerned, was by no means an invariably benign influence.

Throughout the 19th century, most of the legal disabilities for wives were eventually dealt with by legislation. The various Married Women's Property Acts, from the 1870s,[9] enabled married women to own property and keep their own earnings. Civil divorce, in 1857, changed the marital landscape and the Settled Land Act 1882, by giving the powers of management to the tenant for life, took much of the sting out of the strict settlement. Such changes, of course, were not taking place in a political and social vacuum, but a lengthy consideration of the wider political, social, economic and religious forces, which wrought such changes in the 19th century, is beyond the scope of the present discussion.

Equity's traditional role of alleviating the harshness of the common law was perhaps more evident historically in protecting the rights of wives than of women generally. This practice continued into modern times: for example, Lord Denning's famous campaign to create the 'deserted wives' equity'.[10] It could be argued, however, that equity in some instances was used to defeat and destroy women's common law rights in order to protect succession in the male line.

It will be argued in this chapter that equity, far from being the inevitable defender of women's rights, has occasionally provided the mechanism by which women's rights have been postponed or even eliminated. The common law, on the other hand, has not historically been the inevitable enemy of

---

8   Stone, L, 1990, p 307.

9   Married Women's Property Act 1870; Married Women's Property Act 1882.

10   Ultimately, Lord Denning's campaign had a victory of a kind in Parliament. Wives were able to register a Class F Land Charge under the Land Charges Act 1972, s 2(7), which would protect their occupation during the marriage. Unmarried women did not even have this level of protection.

women. Nor should the role of legal practitioners, in and out of parliament, be ignored in this history.

'IS THERE YET ANY PORTION OR INHERITANCE FOR US IN OUR FATHER'S HOUSE?'

(Leah and Rachel, *Genesis*)

As Eileen Spring argues,[11] the common law was not hostile to women in terms of inheritance. Where a daughter was the heiress at law, that is, a family with no sons but a daughter, she had a common law right to inherit. 'The most important rules governing succession to lands were those of the common law. Of these the principal was primogeniture. Males excluded females of equal degree. Among males of equal degree only the eldest inherited, but females inherited together as co-heiresses.'[12] Operation of law, then, would transfer property to women, although only in default of a male heir. Where there was no power to alter the common law rule, daughters could inherit. It is the processes by which the common law rules were avoided that Eileen Spring investigates:

> From beginning to end, then, landowners' legal history is much to be seen as the effect to overcome the common law rights of daughters. It was heiresses whose rights threatened to divide estates. It was heiresses whose rights threatened to leave titles bare of land. It was heiresses who would alter the name tags associated with estates ... From the entail, to the use, to the strict settlement, what landowners were above all seeking was a means of dealing with the problem that female inheritance posed.[13]

It is Equity's role in these processes which will be addressed. Eileen Spring[14] identified the heiress at law as the target of these various devices – what she calls 'ordinary daughters', that is, daughters who were not the heiress at law, ranked with younger sons in that the estate might have to provide for them, but who would inherit neither title nor land. Clearly, if landowners considered it necessary and desirable to maintain patrilineal succession, then it was incumbent upon them and their conveyancers to devise means of avoiding the common law rules. The entail was one such device. 'In operation, an entail in tail male, whomever it was initially made on, proceeded by favouring collateral males over direct females, and this is undoubtedly the main point to be emphasised about collaterals.'[15] Estates of restricted inheritance were made

---

11 Spring, 1993.
12 Houlbrooke, 1984, p 229.
13 Spring, 1993, p 35.
14 *Ibid*, p 35.
15 *Ibid*, p 71.

possible by the statute *De Donis Conditionalibus* in 1285. 'The statute was widely construed, to enable donors to restrict categories of heirs in a way not possible at common law, thus a gift could be made to A and the heirs male of his body, whereas a gift to A and his heirs male, without words of procreation, passed a fee simple – which could descend to females – at common law.'[16]

However, since entails could be barred by various means, such as warranty or common recovery, and would eventually become subject to the rule against perpetuities,[17] it was clear that entails alone were not sufficient to guarantee succession in the male line. Nor would the prudent landowner rely on the common law rule of primogeniture. Sons might die, leaving a daughter or daughters to inherit. It has been noted by more than one commentator that, despite the lavish praise bestowed in the defence of the principle of primogeniture, most landowners took care to manage their affairs more actively. Since the Wills Act 1850, land could be devised by will and primogeniture applied automatically only to the intestate.

The strict settlement came to be the preferred method of arranging the transmission of property from one generation to the next. The modern form of settlement first emerged in the 17th century, as an elegant and typically English device to avoid the most stringent of the penalties for choosing the wrong side in the civil war. Land of traitors was forfeit, but if the traitor held only a life interest, then only the life interest could be forfeit. When land was settled, the form of the trust employed also operated very effectively to make inheritance in the female line a rare and precious thing. An example of equity not mitigating the harshness of the common law, but depriving women of their common law rights to inherit.

'In the simplest case, when it took place at the marriage of the eldest son, the settlement … limited the interest of the father to that of a life tenant, and made the eldest son a life tenant after the death of the father, the estate was to descend to his eldest son in tail.'[18] The purpose of this rather odd sounding arrangement was to keep the estate intact, by arranging for unitary, rather than partible inheritance, and to fragment the title, to reduce the possibility of any life tenant or tenant in tail endangering the estate by debt or sale. It was also, of course, an effective device to privilege sons over daughters.

Except for intestacy, primogeniture was not a legal requirement, and yet many landowners continued to observe the practice as though it were an obligation, not a choice. 'It was natural for an established landowner to feel that he was the temporary custodian of the family estate for his descendants.'[19] The settlement leaned in favour of primogeniture. 'The

---

16 Baker, 1971, p 149.
17 *Duke of Norfolk's Case* [1683] 3 Cas in Ch 1 Poll 223.
18 Habakkuk, 1994, p 2.
19 *Ibid*, p 5.

passionate emotional attachment to the principle of primogeniture was, after all, frequently demonstrated in the debates on the modest proposal to make the law on intestacy relating to real estate the same as that which already provided for equal division in the case of personal property.'[20] This equality was not, in fact, achieved until the Administration of Estates Act 1925.

The settlement could not work effectively until a way was found to preserve contingent remainders because of the concept that no living person could have an heir, and the doctrine of merger as held in *Shelley's Case*.[21] This was achieved by interposing a trust to avoid the abeyance of seisin, thus overcoming the 'common law's reluctance to accept contingent remainders'.[22]

Just as primogeniture was not obligatory, neither was the strict settlement ever given any official sanction. It was essentially a private matter between the landowner and his conveyancer. The landowner willed the end and the conveyancer provided the means. The third element required to make the settlements effective was that should they come to court, they would be enforced. Once contingent remainders were accepted and the rule against perpetuities was avoided, settlements were enforced. Once again, equity, by way of the trust, was used to defeat the common law rights of daughters to inherit. 'The strict settlement was biased towards primogeniture; there was never any doubt that the elder son and his issue inherited before his younger brother, and that the sons took precedence over daughters.'[23] There was evidently a voluntary element to these arrangements. 'The settlement of landed estates would not have lasted so long had it not commanded the acquiescence of the younger siblings ...'[24]

Conveyancers would draw up the settlements in the knowledge of the problems which might be encountered, where settlements conflicted with common law principles. Free alienability of land was clearly not an attainable goal where land was settled in one family for generations. There was also a potential problem with the rule against perpetuities, and the common law had, for centuries, leaned against perpetuities. The settlements were enforceable as trusts, and since land in settlement was commonly resettled from time to time, the perpetuity problem was avoided. 'The rule against perpetuities which developed in the 17th century sought to balance the interests of competing generations by limiting the power to establish dynastic trusts.'[25] '[D]uring the 18th and 19th centuries, any substantial landowner, and any conveyancer instructed by him, was subject to very strong pressure,

20 Thompson, 1963, p 69.

21 *Shelley's Case* [1581] 1 Co Rep 88b.

22 Simpson, 1986, p 99.

23 Habakkuk, 1994, p 30.

24 *Ibid*, p 64.

25 Finch, J, 1996, pp 29–30.

in terms of conformity with the practice adopted by members of the land-owning class and with precedents pervading both the training and the day to day activities of conveyancers, to adopt some variant of the strict settlement as a means of controlling the distribution of the landed estate.'[26] It seemed that some common law principles could be ignored with careful conveyances and appropriate practices, and some could not. 'The English wealthy man then followed the rule of primogeniture because he approved of it. But the law against perpetuities was not to his taste. He therefore eluded it by the means of strict family settlements.'[27]

Nevertheless, the tide of law reform was gathering pace in the 19th century and, eventually, even the strict settlement had to yield. The Settled Land Act 1882, by giving powers of management to the tenant for life, effectively ended the power of the father to rule from beyond the grave. The entail, the compromise between the living and the dead, managed to hang on a bit longer, and was not finally ended until 1996.[28] The same Act, although it preserved existing settlements, prevented the creation of new strict settlements.[29]

The role of the conveyancer in the process should not be underestimated. 'Within the legal profession, peculiar pride has also been taken in the way that conveyancing has become so technically difficult as to be unintelligible and mysterious, not only to ordinary laymen and clients, but also to ordinary lawyers, judges and legislators.'[30] 'The conveyancers worked as agents of members of the propertied classes who sought to maximise their control over their property ...'[31]

In terms of inheritance, then, it could be argued that the common law was a better friend to women than equity, and that equity by way of an alliance between dynastically minded landowners and artful conveyancers was deployed to deprive women of their rights which the common law would have provided. 'It was on the large rights that the common law gave to females that landowners had their eyes fixed, and against which their conveyancing stratagems were fundamentally designed.'[32]

---

26 Chesterman, 1984, p 130.

27 Johnson, 1909, p 13.

28 Trusts of Land and Appointment of Trustees Act 1996, s 5(1), Sched 1, where a person purports by an instrument coming into operation after the commencement of this Act to grant to another person an entailed interest in real or personal property, the instrument: (a) is not effective to grant an entailed interest; but (b) operates instead as a declaration that the property is held in trust absolutely for the person to whom an entailed interest in the property was purportedly granted.

29 *Ibid*, s 2(1). No settlement created after the commencement of this Act is a settlement for the purposes of the Settled Land Act 1925; and no settlement shall be deemed to be made under that Act after that commencement.

30 Staves, 1990, pp 57–58.

31 *Ibid*, p 40.

32 Spring, 1993, p 88.

'HIS DESIGNS WERE STRICTLY HONOURABLE, AS THE PHRASE IS: TO ROB A LADY OF HER FORTUNE BY WAY OF MARRIAGE'

(Henry Fielding, *The History of Tom Jones*)

The legal disabilities of the married woman before 1882[33] have been well rehearsed, in particular, that the common law did not recognise the existence of the wife during the marriage. There can be no doubt that the circumstances surrounding marriage and the transmission of property in England, historically, were patriarchal.

> Patriarchy, I take it, is a form of social organisation in which fathers appear as political and legal actors, acting publicly for themselves and as representatives of the women and children subordinated to them and dependent on them in families. In the property regimes of patriarchy, descent and inheritance are reckoned in the male line; women function as procreators and as transmitters of inheritance from male to male.[34]

'The provision of money and the getting of heirs was still the main function of women.'[35] Where the well endowed bride to be acquired her wealth is an interesting question, in the light of the foregoing discussion on inheritance. One route, of course, was the operation of law, whereby heiresses at law were allowed to inherit. Another is provision made in family settlements, where the land and title, if any, passed to the oldest son, and the estate provided portions for daughters and younger sons. 'From the second half of the 17th century, the evolution of the strict settlement meant it had become customary to make provision for younger sons and daughters.'[36] Eileen Spring argues[37] that writers of legal history have often represented portions for daughters as both generous and growing in size without taking into account the fact that portions were often paid to the heiress at law, who would, but for the machinations of landowners and their conveyancers, have inherited.

The main engines of perpetuating the system were the idea of primogeniture, entails and the strict settlement. 'Within the family itself, the strict settlement also represented an important patriarchal weapon against any other form of delinquency by heirs and heiresses.'[38] Within this very limited space, the common law made some provision for married women, and, more

---

33 Married Women's Property Act 1882.

34 Staves, 1990, p 4.

35 Lumis and Marsh, 1990, p 62.

36 Chesterman, 1984, p 131.

37 Cannadine, 1994, p 45.

38 Spring, 1993. See particularly pp 22–27 for a discussion of the argument that legal writers have failed to give proper importance to the exclusion of female heiresses and the significance of the marriage portion.

particularly, for widows. Common law dower provided that a widow should have one-third of the income of any real property of which her husband had been seised during his life. This provision had the potential to act as a fetter on the free alienability of land, and was eventually replaced by the jointure.

In those circumstances, it could be argued that equity assisted in the process of depriving widows of their dower, by recognising contingent remainders in settlements and treating them as vested interests, which both got round the perpetuity problem, and also made sure that there was no estate to which dower could attach. Dower could not attach to property held in trust. Susan Staves argues powerfully that the transition from dower to jointure was detrimental to widows.[39] It also represents another shift from status to contract. Dower rights were status-based, whereas the jointure was essentially contractual in nature.

The move from dower to jointure has been the subject of much academic debate. It clearly represents a move from status to contract, and it is equally clear that there was a trade off between portions and jointures. Not all commentators have interpreted the data as Spring has done, or accepted her argument that heiresses have been effectively cheated, and that equity has been instrumental in a kind of fraud. 'The female disinheritance thesis is framed by the glow of common law rights. But no adequate theory or explanation for why the common law rules ... took the form that they did is developed. It is as if it suffices that these rules were there. And that there was a later self-evident male conspiracy against dower.'[40]

What is less contentious is the contractual nature of the relationship between portion and jointure. 'Women who contributed portions to their marriage expected in return to be maintained should they be widowed. By the 16th century fewer and fewer wives put their faith in the common law right of dower enshrined in Magna Carta ...'[41] The ratio was an indication of the relative bargaining powers of the families, and there is some evidence to support the view that the size of portions increased over time in relation to the value of the jointure which it could secure. 'It has been pointed out that the average ratio of dowry (given by the father) to jointure (settled on the girl by the bridegroom's family) rose from four or three to one in the middle of the 16th century to between eight and 10 to one by the end of the 17th.'[42]

'In marriages between equals in aristocratic circles, portions of £10,000 to £50,000 were perhaps normal, and the bride would expect a jointure of 10% at least on her fortune ... In fact, the tariff laid down at the time of the marriage, both in respect of jointure and of portions for younger children whose

39   Staves, 1990, particularly Chapter 2, pp 27–55.
40   Murphy, 1996, p 625.
41   Stretton, 1998, p 27.
42   Fraser, 1989, pp 302–03.

numbers were unpredictable, was a minimum which was quite often augmented by will as circumstances and affection allowed.'[43] 'It was thus a complicated matter to arrive at the going rates of the marriage market and negotiations of some delicacy might be called for, with the family solicitor in reserve to say what was normal in any given case.'[44]

Paraphernalia, the personal clothing and ornaments which the bride brought to the marriage, was an exception to the general common law rule that all the wife's personal property at the time of the marriage belonged absolutely to the husband. Since the wife was the 'shadow' of her husband, she had no capacity to contract on her own behalf, but was entitled to pledge her husband's credit for necessaries. This corresponded to the common law duty of the husband to maintain his wife. The law of agency was used to explain the wife's ability to pledge, and it is interesting to observe that this agency argument has, until relatively recently, still been employed in the husband–wife nexus.[45] This despite the fact that separate property was established in 1882, and even the Inland Revenue accepted wives as individual tax payers only a century or so later, when separate taxation for husbands and wives was made possible.

A legal commentator, in 1800, when considering the law on marriage observed: '[I]t must have been a shock to a woman who was ignorant of her true position to learn when she married that ... she was not trusted by the law with a shillingsworth of property, and that any contract she made had as much efficacy as her husband's would have if he were an imbecile or in a state of hopeless intoxication.'[46] Married women, then, if they were to have anything to call their own, would have to rely on equity. The position at common law was unequivocal. 'So jealous was the law of any interference with the marital rights of the husband that, after one of the "favourite of the law" had agreed to marry him, she could not deprive him of any of her property without his consent.'[47] There was no corresponding obligation on a prospective husband to retain in his own control any property of which he may have been seised when proposing marriage. 'Despite the complexity of the legal rules relating to married women's rights in different categories of property, one fact stood out clearly and consistently – during marriage women had no property at their disposal; instead their husbands assumed ownership or at least control of their property.'[48]

---

43 Thompson, 1963, p 101.

44 *Ibid*, p 104.

45 See, eg, *Barclays Bank v O'Brien* [1994] 1 AC 180, where the agency argument was not accepted.

46 Lush, 1901, pp 349–50.

47 *Ibid*, p 358.

48 Holcombe, 1983, p 25.

'Marriage is the only actual bondage known to our law. There remain no legal slaves, except the mistress of every house.'[49] Equity could offer some relief by safeguarding some property to the wife's sole use. However, even this required that the trustees, as the legal owners, had the control and management of the property, and not the wife. Nevertheless, this was of some benefit and, given the difficulty of obtaining a divorce, ecclesiastical or civil, this could be of crucial importance.

Such settlements were not uncommon amongst the landed classes: all part of the extended and complex negotiations attendant upon a dynastic marriage. Pin money, income secured to the wife from her husband's estate during his lifetime, might also be agreed. The purpose of pin money is somewhat uncertain. It was clearly not intended to be used for the provision of necessaries, since the husband was under a common law obligation to provide those. Even this small measure of potential separate property for married women was of concern, and not permitted to flourish unchecked. '[T]he development of the legal doctrines concerning pin money between the Restoration and the early 19th century shows that the law having created a potentially threatening source of women's power in the married women's separate estate, soon appreciated that threat and responded by creating idiosyncratic rules for pin money and other forms of married women's separate property ...'[50]

These 'idiosyncratic rules' were developed as a result of 'cultural and political choices, not an inevitable development decreed by abstract legal logic'.[51] A recurring theme in any study of women's rights is the idea that the law is not impartial or disinterested, handing down Olympian decisions which have been dictated by sheer, ineluctable logic, but is a system operated by individuals and groups with power and privilege to protect. 'Feminist theory seeks to reveal the ways in which law reflects, reproduces, expresses, constructs and reinforces power relations along sexually patterned lines. In doing so, it questions law's claim to autonomy and represents it as a practice which is continuous with deeper social, political and economic forces which constantly seep through its supposed boundaries.'[52]

It was not only the rich and landed families who provided separate property for their daughters. 'Richard Potter [father of Beatrice Webb] gave most of his daughters an annuity of £250 with a promise of £5,000 to be paid within six months of his death. This money was provided for the daughter's own use, and hence could not be taken by her husband.'[53]

---

49 Mill, JS, 'The subjection of women', quoted in *The Vintage Book of Historical Feminism*, 1976, p 176.
50 Staves, 1990, p 161.
51 *Ibid*, p 161.
52 Lacey, 1988, p 7.
53 Caine, 1988, p 67.

It was clear that wives were very much at the mercy of their husbands. Of course, a study of cold legal documents by no means tells the whole story. 'A knowledge of the social and economic framework of marriage tells us little about the personal experiences of individuals.'[54] While this is undeniably true, there are countless histories of women trapped in miserable marriages with husbands who were lazy, cruel, unfaithful or worse, with no recourse at common law and not much assistance from equity. 'The personal influence of a woman with her husband and his kindness and good sense, prevent many a woman from having the least suspicion of the barbarous nature of those laws which would interpose but slight obstacles to her husband's treating her with the most unrelenting tyranny, did their mutual good understanding fail ...'[55]

It was clear that, by the 19th century, calls for reform were growing, and not only amongst the married women themselves. 'For law reformers in the 19th century the common law relating to a wife's property was the most basic disability suffered by married women ...'[56] One 19th century married woman who was a very active campaigner for law reform was Caroline Norton, whose own troubled marriage was the driving force behind her activities. She was instrumental in bringing about many changes in the law through her influential Whig connections, and was also fortunate in having some property secured to her own use, since her husband, George Norton, himself a lawyer, had no compunction about using the common law to his own advantage. This was the man who did not flinch at suing the Prime Minister of the day, Lord Melbourne, for criminal conversation. The case was lost, but Caroline Norton's reputation was ruined.

Left with few friends, no possibility of an ecclesiastical divorce, no access to her children and no right to maintenance, Caroline Norton had cause to be grateful that equity at least provided her with some income which she could call her own. '[H]er life interest in her father's estate had not been secured to her in law, and therefore was payable to Norton. But Mrs Sheridan had had money in her own right. Consequently, the £480 a year she bequeathed to Caroline was secured to her under the laws of Equity, so that Norton could not touch the money.'[57]

Caroline Norton, in fact, could take advantage of the property secured to her by equity, but her experience may not have been typical, even where such provision had been made. '[A]ccording to liberal political theory a wife who had separate property legally secured to her ought to have gained power. It frequently happened that despite separate property being secured to them, women were unwilling or unable even to hang on to it ... by husbands who

---

54 Caine, 1988, pp 86–87.
55 Reid, 1988, p 5.
56 Heward, 1998, p 163.
57 Chedzoy, 1992, p 231.

had physical or emotional power that rendered their wives' legal power nugatory.'[58]

Property law was notoriously slow to change. 'Between the Restoration and the Reform Act of 1832 ... the one notable change, the evolution of the strict settlement took place towards the middle of the 18th century.'[59] It would not have been possible to effect a system of separate property for wives without a comprehensive and radical overhaul of property law generally. That was not seriously contemplated until the 19th century was well advanced, and the role of the legal profession in stoutly resisting change has been well documented.[60]

The acknowledged shift from status to contract for marriage, based at least notionally on consent should, perhaps, have made a great difference, but the rather odd nature of the marriage contract has often been commented on. 'Marriage is called a contract but, feminists have argued, [it is] an institution in which one party, the husband, has exercised the power of a slave-owner over his wife ...'[61] Pateman has argued: '... far from being opposed to patriarchy, contract is the means through which modern patriarchy is constituted.'[62]

Peter Goodrich argues that the true nature of contracts has been ignored by failing to acknowledge the emotive and relational dimensions, while concentrating on the pretence of objectivity and 'arm's-length' negotiations. This failure of perception has been compounded in relation to the marriage contract.[63] It would be scarcely surprising then, if some married women were to be heard to say: 'Reader, I wish I had never married him.'

'... A WILD LATITUDINARIAN AND MISCHIEVOUS PRINCIPLE'

(Sir Charles Wetherell AG on the Divorce Bill)

The most striking feature of married life in 18th century England was the theoretical, legal and practical subordination of wives to their husbands ... even worse than the condition of the unhappily married, however, was the lot of those women who were separated or divorced. They automatically lost all contact whatsoever with their children, unless their husbands were willing to allow it, and they were also financially reduced to very small allowances, even if they were innocent parties.[64]

---

58 Staves, 1990, pp 134–35.
59 Manchester, 1980, p 302.
60 See Offer, 1981.
61 Pateman, 1988, p 154.
62 *Ibid*, p 2.
63 Goodrich, 1996, pp 19–22.
64 Stone, 1995, p 48.

Once married, though, it was no small matter to separate or divorce. During the interregnum, when the ecclesiastical courts were in abeyance, a practice of informal private separation agreements began to develop. The form of these agreements was essentially contractual in that, often, the husband would agree to pay an allowance and, in return, would be indemnified from responsibility for the wife's future debts. 'There was great initial reluctance by common lawyers to accept such a transfer of financial freedom and responsibility to a wife, since it ran counter to the ancient legal concept that a married woman had no legal personality and lacked powers to borrow, sue, or transact any legal business.'[65] And, furthermore: 'All these clauses made concessions to wives which were in partial or total contradiction with the common law, equity law in Chancery and canon law in the ecclesiastical courts.'[66]

The conflicting principles led to attempts by the common law courts to refuse to enforce the financial aspects of the agreements, on the basis that marriage was indissoluble, whereas equity would enforce the financial agreements but refused to enforce the separation. By the beginning of the 19th century, a *modus operandi* had emerged, whereby the separation agreements would be enforced provided they were made via trustees. 'It therefore seems likely that an important cause of the spread of these agreements in the last half of the 18th century was the willingness of the court of Chancery to enforce the financial terms swiftly and cheaply, so long as trustees were involved.'[67]

Although still married, both parties derived some benefit from these arrangements. Wives received some financial control, while husbands were able to make an announcement that they were no longer liable for their wives' debts. The husband had the additional bonus that, should his wife enter into an adulterous relationship, he would be entitled to seek an ecclesiastical divorce and pay no alimony. Separated husbands, on the other hand, had more leeway. For a husband to be divorced in the ecclesiastical courts, there had to be both adultery on his part, and also cruelty. Given that, until the landmark case of *Jackson*,[68] husbands had the common law right to chastise their wives, cruelty was notoriously difficult to establish.

'While the husband could keep a mistress with impunity, the slightest sexual step on the part of the separated wife would allow him to stop payment of the maintenance allowance, and the wife would thereafter be socially humiliated and financially ruined.'[69] There were an increasing number of separations and parliamentary divorces, reflecting the fact that the

---

65 Stone, 1990, p 150.

66 *Ibid*, p 153.

67 *Ibid*, p 161.

68 *R v Jackson* (1891) 1 QB 671.

69 *Ibid*, Stone, p 169.

19th century was a period of change and the widespread recognition that the legal system stood in need of reform. A number of different forces were providing the impetus for reform of the divorce law.

The royal parliamentary divorce between George IV and Caroline of Brunswick in 1820 lent some veneer of respectability to the process, while the increase in cases of bigamy and even wife sale indicated that there was demand for a way of ending marriages among the less wealthy as well as the wealthy. The system of obtaining a parliamentary divorce was particularly complex and attracted much criticism, adding to the weight of the reformers' argument. A royal commission was set up in 1850 to consider the matter, leading to a number of Bills which failed and, ultimately, the 1857 Act. The movement for women's suffrage and the sometimes complementary and sometimes conflicting movement for married women's property rights added another voice to the chorus. 'It is hardly surprising that another lobby for divorce reform, apart from the lawyers, was composed of upper middle-class women. But these women were more concerned with the protection of their property as wives than with equal access to divorce, which was to most of them a secondary consideration.'[70]

Caroline Norton, who was not generally in favour of women's rights, was inspired by her own circumstances, and had both the motive and the opportunity to play an instrumental role in the reform process. She was well connected in Whig political circles, and through her own writing was able to publicise the defects of the law, particularly in relation to the custody of infant children and the fact that married women had no control over their own earnings. The Law Amendment Society, which comprised many influential Whig lawyers, was also pushing for change.

One source of difficulty was the different jurisdictions and different forms of separation available. Ecclesiastical courts could grant divorce *a mensa et thoro* (from bed and board), which meant that the parties were still married, but not obliged to live together. The first parliamentary divorce was obtained by Lord Roos in 1670, and the second by Lord Macclesfield in 1698. However, parliamentary divorces were both procedurally complex and prohibitively expensive. A husband would first seek a divorce *a mensa et thoro* and then charge some other man with criminal conversation (adultery). If that charge carried, then a parliamentary divorce could be sought by private act of parliament. In the 18th century, 134 such divorces were granted and, in the 19th century (before 1857), only 90.[71]

William Maule J, in typically robust manner, expressed the absurdity of the process while giving judgment on Thomas Hall, who was convicted of

---

70 Stone, 1990, p 362.
71 Holcombe, 1983, Chapter 5.

bigamy. In advising him that he should have divested himself of one wife before taking another, the judge said:

> You have acted wrongly. You ought to have brought an action for criminal conversation; that action would have been tried before one of Her Majesty's judges at the assizes; you would probably have recovered damages; and then you should have instituted a suit in the Ecclesiastical Court for a divorce *a mensa et thoro*. Having got that divorce, you should have petitioned the House of Lords for a divorce *a vinculo*, and then you should have appeared by counsel at the bar of their Lordships' house. Then, if the Bill passed, it would have gone down to the House of Commons; the same evidence would possibly be repeated there; and if the royal assent had been given after that you might have married again. The whole proceedings would not have cost you more than £1,000.[72]

Of the parliamentary divorces granted, only four were obtained by women.[73] Women had an extra burden of proof to discharge. Mere adultery was not enough; cruelty or desertion was also required. In 1801, Jane Campbell sought a divorce when her husband was having an affair with her sister. Her brother-in-law obtained a divorce on the grounds of his wife's adultery, but Jane was refused. Eventually, she succeeded by introducing the taboo of incest. In 1829, Louise Turton succeeded on the same grounds, while in 1840, Mrs Battersby was granted a divorce on the basis that her husband had infected her with venereal disease, committed bigamy and deserted her. The fourth case was technically an annulment in 1850 by Georgina Hall, on the basis of bigamy. The rationale for this distinction appeared to be that if a wife committed adultery, then a spurious heir might be introduced into the family. Husbands who committed adultery were not, on the whole, likely to bring any 'spurious' offspring home, and so adultery was a lesser offence when committed by a husband. Lord Brougham, who was in favour of reform, cited the Scottish example, where divorce had been available for 300 years, and did not appear to have had a particularly deleterious effect on the national character.[74]

The call for reform was not unopposed. However, there comes a tide in the affairs of women, and finally, in 1857, civil divorce was introduced.[75] Men and women did not have equal access to divorce until 1932, and women who did not divorce, but remained married, did not have full rights to separate property at common law until the Married Women's Property Act 1882. The Married Women's Property Act 1870 permitted wives to keep their own earnings and property acquired after the marriage.

It could be argued that equity played at best a marginal role in these momentous developments for women. Some women, if they came from wealthy families, and if a settlement had been arranged for them whereby

---

72 Quoted in Hartsman, 1985, p 74.
73 *Ibid.*
74 See Leneman, 1998.
75 Matrimonial Causes Act 1857.

property was secured in trust for their sole use, might have some protection from the common law rules which applied to married women. Where parties had privately agreed to separate, equity would enforce the financial aspect of the agreement, where the common law would not recognise them. In terms of rights, the married woman in England suffered the most severe legal disabilities – she effectively ceased to exist as far as the common law was concerned, and equity availed her little. Such protection as equity did provide was not by way of a bonus, making women a 'specially protected class', but, instead, the barest recognition that married women existed at all, if only through the medium of a trust.

CONCLUSION

A discussion of the historical legal aspects of marriage, widowhood, divorce and inheritance from a feminist perspective relies primarily on legal developments. However, it should always be borne in mind that 'the law' is not an autonomous monolithic structure; it does not function in a hermetically sealed world, above and unaffected by social, political, economic, cultural and religious developments.

The strict settlement did not arise accidentally or inevitably. It was the result of landowners with dynastic ambitions, aided and abetted by the conveyancers' art, to design a vehicle which would safeguard inheritance in the male line, keep the estate intact for future generations and provide financial provision for other family members. The net result was to prefer males, even collateral males, to heiresses.

Equity's role in the development is complex. The strict settlement relied on the trust. It was also the method by which merger and unity of the title in the tenant in tail were avoided, by interposing contingent remainders held on trust, which both the common law and equity treated as vested interests. This was also the method by which the common law dower was rendered less effective, eventually being replaced by jointure provisions.[76] In those circumstances, far from being woman's protector, equity appeared to be used to defeat existing common law rights.

'How can it be, then, that this court [equity], self-consciously protective of women and children, and apparently progressive in their interests, appears to strip widows of their dower?'[77] Staves, who posed this question, answers it thus from a feminist viewpoint: '... basically nothing changed – not because English society as it changed continued to find appropriate forms of married women's property, but rather because the deeper structures of male

---

76 This process culminated in the Dower Act 1833.
77 Staves, 1990, p 31.

domination and female subordination persisted from the Anglo Saxons right through to the Family Provision Act of 1975 and beyond.'[78]

At the same time, the move from status to contract was facilitated by the assistance equity afforded to the process of removing status-based rights and replacing them with rights of a contractual nature. 'Between 1500 and 1760 ... communal protection by custom gave way to free competition in which women might need to go to law to enforce a contract.'[79] Marriage itself began to assume contractual status. Whether this development benefited women is doubtful, given the subordinate position women traditionally occupied in society, whether as women generally, or as wives in particular. The validity of contracts is predicated on the assumption that the contracting parties are bargaining on equal terms, and that the terms have been mutually agreed. The marriage contract does not fit that model and Carole Pateman argues that patriarchy was not defeated by the victory of contract over status, but merely consolidated in a modern form.[80]

Stretton argues that the common law is frequently represented as antagonistic to women's rights.[81] However, as he points out, when women were acting as ordinary litigants and not in some woman-specific role, the common law courts presented no extra obstacles.[82] Equity, on the other hand, with its traditional approach of substance over form, was undoubtedly beneficial to women, as women, in that the procedures were more forgiving. Women, because of their exclusion from access to legal documents and proofs, would not readily be able to prosecute actions in common law courts, even where they had the capacity.[83] The flexibility of equity was also evident in permitting widows to pursue actions which originated before or during coverture, often after many years. Widowhood was the first opportunity these women had to bring their cases, since they lacked legal personality during the marriage.[84] The Masters in the Court of Requests would even permit women to sue their husbands in exceptional circumstances, but this anomaly served only to highlight the precarious position of the married woman in the eyes of the law, only slightly modified by equity.[85]

Ultimately, the removal of the legal disabilities attaching to wives was brought about not by equity, but as part of the 19th century reform movements which saw the widening of the franchise, and other momentous

---

78 Staves, 1990, p 35.
79 Laurence, 1994, p 235.
80 Pateman, 1988, p 187.
81 Stretton, 1998, p 31.
82 *Ibid*, p 33.
83 *Ibid*, p 28.
84 *Ibid*, p 29.
85 *Ibid*, p 150.

social changes. Not that women were enfranchised at that time, but, nevertheless, change was afoot, and Parliament, in the end, recognised the separate existence of wives and granted them separate property rights. Wives had custody rights over their infant children, could keep their own wages and obtain civil divorces. Full legal equality with men in the eyes of the law was not to come until very much later, if it has come at all, but, again, without the agency of equity playing a particularly prominent role.

Equity, then, has been a friend to some women in some circumstances, particularly to married women before legislation made them discernible to the stern eye of the common law. In particular, women from wealthy families were able to avail themselves, through their fathers, their brothers, their husbands or their trustees, of equity's assistance. Single women and widows could, and did, use the common law courts freely and successfully for all kinds of legal matters. It was the married woman who truly needed a friend and it is arguable that offering some slight mitigation to a human being in a condition of theoretical, if by no means always actual, enslavement was a rather poor sort of friendship.

CHAPTER 3

THE *WAQF* IN TRUST

Hilary Lim

[The use] had apparent predecessors in other systems of law. Links have been suggested, for instance, with the Roman law concept of *fideicommissum*, with a Germanic form of executor called the *'salman'*; with the executor of a 'testament' of personal chattels recognised in the common law and ecclesiastical courts; and *even with* an Islamic legal concept called *'waqf'* (allegedly brought back to England by the crusaders ...).[1]

INTRODUCTION

The *waqf* is a legal mechanism, recognised and developed in Islam for more than 1,000 years. It permits 'an owner to settle' her 'property to the use of beneficiaries in perpetuity' and becomes *'waqf* upon a declaration by its owner (the *waqif*) permanently reserving its income for a specific purpose.'[2] Ultimately, all *awqaf*[3] (plural) must be dedicated to charity, but this purpose need not be immediate. There are two forms of *waqf*: first, the family endowment, where the property, that is, its usufruct or income, is held for the family of the *waqif*,[4] until the extinction of her descendants, whereupon it is diverted to a charitable purpose, which is a *waqf ahli* or *waqf dhurri*; or, secondly, the charitable endowment, which involves the permanent dedication of the property to a charitable purposes, known as *waqf khairi*.[5]

At first sight, the discussion about *awqaf* may seem somewhat out of place in a volume on equity. Given that I would not pretend any expertise in the field of Islamic law, the focus is, perhaps, all the more surprising. The initial impetus to begin what amounts to no more than preliminary research in this area was threefold. First, there are fleeting, casual references to *awqaf* in

---

1   Moffat, 1999, p 26, emphasis added.

2   Cattan, 1955, p 203.

3   I use the plural *awqaf*, although many writers in English use the even more anglicised *wakfs* or *waqfs*, for reasons which will become apparent in the course of the argument presented here.

4   Or other specific individuals.

5   Ali, 1885, p 179. He refers to these as 'quasi-public *wakf'*. See, also, Tucker, 1985, p 220, fn 131 (citing Baer, 1969) who suggests also that, due to the wide variety of ways in which revenue has been divided up, it is difficult to make 'any pristine distinction' between family and charitable *awqaf*, although she states that it has been important at certain times to make the legal distinction.

relation to the history of the trust in established textbooks, most notably in successive editions of Moffat's *Trusts Law Text and Materials*. Secondly, I had a chance encounter with a series of lectures by Syed Ameer Ali, which were published in 1885 as *The Law Relating to Gifts, Trusts and Testamentary Dispositions among the Mohammedans (According to the Hanafi, Maliki, Shafei and Shia Schools)*. Thirdly, my location, as a white woman in a new London University with a diverse student body, means that I am necessarily involved in the search for interdisciplinary and critical teaching materials to challenge the monoculturalism of the legal curriculum.[6]

This latter point is not a matter of celebrating difference but, as articulated effectively by O'Donnell and Johnstone, an attempt to develop new approaches to legal knowledge concerned with how culture is 'represented through law' and 'how such representations ... might be linked to wider histories of colonialism and racism'.[7] It can be argued that these curriculum issues are most important in areas, including equity, which O'Donnell and Johnstone regard as 'opaque', because these are the sites upon which to 'confront the accumulated, taken-for-granted and common sense assumptions which the law uses to understand the complex social world'.[8] The seemingly tentative links between *awqaf* and trusts are both interesting and challenging from such a perspective. They led me to an Islamic theory of trusts which deserves wider appreciation and a less transient appearance in the history of equity served up to undergraduate students.

In equity, 'history seems to acquire a special saliency',[9] in part because the principles and maxims to be discussed were created in what was, until 1875, a separate jurisdiction from the common law. This legal pluralism needs some explanation, as does the fact that the doctrines and remedies of this jurisdiction still tend to be taught at the beginning of the 21st century as a separate course. The histories which find their way into the average student textbook adopt a functionalist approach, together with what Anderson has called a 'doctrinal genealogy'.[10] Students, for instance, will be taught that equity, and its major conceptual creation the trust, are the product of pleas made to the King, via the Lord Chancellor, in the Middle Ages, which solidified into a body of rules implemented by the Court of Chancery. Equity, it will be said, filled the gaps where the rigid rules of the common law either failed to offer the complainant any remedy or caused injustice to a specific individual; a supplemental system 'to correct men's consciences for frauds,

---

6   O'Donnell and Johnstone, 1997, pp 20–21, make the point that there we are not often able to do this by looking at the whole curriculum and we should be careful not to overload students with additional reading.

7   *Ibid*, p 14.

8   *Ibid*, p 3.

9   *Ibid*, p 26.

10 Anderson, 1984, p 77.

breaches of trust, wrongs and oppression of what nature so ever they be, and to soften and mollify the extremity of the law'.[11]

Along the way, it is likely that the average student will gain the impression that equity was peculiarly the protector of women and children. In particular, it is widely recorded that the use provided a means to avoid the gross injustice of the common law and enabled landowners to make provision for their families, especially their daughters and younger sons and to avoid feudal taxation. In other words, the use provided a means to avoid the rigidity of the common law which did not permit the alienation of land through testamentary provision and favoured the eldest son. Furthermore, the gender cleavage of equity is emphasised through the idea that it mitigated the effects for a married woman of coverture, protecting her equitable right to property settled upon her for her use under the management of a trustee.

There is a developing 'revisionist' history, however, as is well documented elsewhere in this collection.[12] It suggests that equity and the trust did not provide simple protection from the rigours of the common law, but served as key mechanisms in women's subordination. Erickson has argued, for instance, that 'the twin pillars of common law control over women's economic fortunes – primogeniture in inheritance and coverture in marriage – were draconian in theory, but had less impact in practice'.[13] Spring has raised doubts as to whether equity should be regarded as being so obviously 'with the angels'. It should be remembered that both equity and common law started from the position that women, particularly married women, required protection, although the legal response was different in each system.

Spring has produced a detailed account of the manner in which equity came to be viewed as the branch of law associated with women, arguing for a more balanced view. The broad claim is that: '[I]f equity riddled common law doctrines ... it riddled those that were favorable to women quite as much as those that were unfavorable to them. Equity protected trusts, whatever their purpose, and not all trusts were in favor of women.'[14] Moreover, Spring argues that there is a coincidence between the establishment of the legal mechanism of the marriage settlement and the loss to women of inheritance rights. The advent of the trust, together with the testamentary power provided by the Statute of Wills in 1544, shows 'a great downward slide' for the

---

11 *Earl of Oxford's Case* (1615) 1 Rep Ch 1, p 6. The ubiquity of this history cannot be overemphasised. It may be detailed and critical as in Moffat, 1999, who devotes most of two chapters and some 50 pages to his basic description of the salient history, or it may be brief, as in Pearce and Stevens, 1998, where the 'historical introduction' occupies about 15 pages.

12 See, in particular, Conway, Chapter 2, in this volume.

13 Erickson, 1995, p 224.

14 Spring, 1993, p 121.

heiress.[15] She is not arguing that the generosity of the common law to females should be over-emphasised, but at the same time wishes to disrupt the established myths or preconceptions about equity.[16] What Spring suggests is the search for a history of the interrelationship between common law and equity, which can better understand what 'equitable developments meant in different periods and for different classes'.[17] Tim Stretton's exploration of women's experience of litigation in the Court of Requests, the 'poor man's Chancery',[18] in Elizabethan England makes another entry in this feminist history. He uncovers evidence of 'women waging law' which, in his own words, 'challenges long standing impressions of closeted female domesticity'.[19]

Given the above context, there is a hint in Syed Ameer Ali's lectures of a further reason why it may be relevant at this time to touch upon historical accounts of *waqf* endowment. He made the point, presumably for the benefit of contemporary 19th century European lawyers engaged in the legal occupation of Islamic law[20] that '[a]ny person who is trustworthy and otherwise qualified to discharge the duties of the office may be appointed *Mutawalli* (trustee) ... [and] in this respect men and women are alike'.[21] A number of commentators have recorded that, in contrast, it was not until the end of the 19th century that married women in England were released from a system by which they lost control of their property to their husbands upon marriage and could directly participate in trusts.

The picture of Muslim women deeply involved in the management of their own wealth, including the active creation and administration of *awqaf*, should not be a surprise. As Marsot has commented, women of all classes

---

15 Through statistical analysis she has also shown that, in 13th century England, about 33% of women were directly the heirs of their fathers, but between the 16th and 18th centuries, only 8% of estates went to women: see Spring, 1990, p 274.

16 Spring, 1993, pp 112–22, contends in the course of her argument that a number of women historians have perpetuated the myth through their 'tributes' to equity's role in enhancing the position of (married) women. In addition, she discusses the part that both JS Mill and FW Maitland played in establishing this particular analysis of equity's contribution to the history of women.

17 *Ibid*, p 122.

18 Stretton, 1998, p 7.

19 *Ibid*, p 8. Stretton suggests, p 32, that many of Spring's arguments 'have yet to be conclusively established empirically' but that 'the logic of her approach is compelling' and '[f]or aristocratic women at least, the common law could sometimes be the lesser of two evils'.

20 See Strawson, 1996; Lim, 1996a; and discussion below, pp 57–59.

21 Ali, 1895, p 246. The only exception being where the *mutawalli* has to perform religious duties in connection with the *waqf*, in which case, a woman cannot take on the office. One of the first cases he makes reference to is *Delroos Banoo Begum v Nawak Ashghur Ally* 15 BLR 167, which involved a woman who executed a *waqf-namah*, similar to a trust document, dedicating all her properties to pious purposes, although it was decided on the facts that no *waqf* had been constituted, in part because she continued to act as the owner of the property, rather than the *mutawalli*.

have owned property and endowed charities throughout Islamic history, while at times taking an active part in trade and commerce.[22] However, despite attempts to dislodge it over the last 20 years, the Orientalist vision of women occupying 'a despised and servile position in the social and economic order of Islamic civilization'[23] is still pervasive. Abundant new accounts, Orientalist, feminist and otherwise, in particular those concerned with the examination of court archives in the Ottoman period, combined with a perceived affiliation between *awqaf* and trusts, make it a pertinent moment to give attention to the historical importance of *waqf* property in Muslim women's lives. Moreover, while property rights have been seen as 'a key indicator not only of economic change, but also of women's status in the family and society, little attention ... has been paid to Muslim societies in comparative historical studies of women's property rights'.[24]

I am not endeavouring here, however, to make a comparison between these histories, but to suggest the placing of these new accounts of *waqf* endowment alongside the emerging feminist debate around equity and the trust. This distinction is important since I am trying to avoid what Gunning has termed the 'arrogant perception' which can be 'traced to Western civilisation',[25] amounting at times to little more than ideological tourism,[26] and from which feminism is not immune. She explains that:

> A key aspect of arrogant perception is the distance between 'me' and 'the other'. The 'I' as arrogant perceiver is a subject to myself with my own perceptions, motivations and interests. The 'other' in arrogant perception terms, is unlike me. The 'other' has no independent perceptions and interest but only those that I impose. Any evidence that the 'other' is organized around her own interests is evidence of defectiveness in the 'other'.[27]

Gunning devised a methodology 'for understanding culturally challenging practices',[28] including genital surgeries. The method, which Bulbeck argues 'walks the tightrope between interconnectedness and independence, between women's shared perspectives and their differences',[29] I suggest is a mechanism that can inform cross-cultural understanding well beyond the area of Gunning's immediate concern. Simultaneous recognition of interconnectedness and independence may appear to contain an inherent

---

22 Marsot, 1996.

23 Jennings, 1975, p 114.

24 Shatzmiller, 1995, pp 220–21. Meriwether and Tucker, 1999, pp 1–2, have recently argued that 'efforts to learn about women's lives in the past have been slower to develop than have studies of women in the contemporary Middle East, although they have gained considerable momentum in the past 10 years'.

25 Gunning, 1991–92, p 198.

26 Trinh, 1989, pp 82–84.

27 Gunning, 1991–92, p 199.

28 *Ibid*, p 193.

29 Bulbeck, 1998, p 84.

contradiction but she offers three strategic tools for its creation. Bulbeck has explained these concisely as, first, 'understanding the cultural pressures which created "us" the self'; secondly, 'looking at ourselves as others might see us'; and thirdly, 'seeing the other as she sees herself in her own cultural context'.[30]

While this methodology cannot be followed here in what is essentially a recording of secondary sources, it does inform the presentation of histories of women, *waqf* property, and the trust. I attempt to walk my own 'tightrope of connection, distance and power',[31] without, I hope, placing 'the margin at the service of the centre'.[32] This is a course which necessarily may lead into ambiguity and contradiction. In the following section, the seeming affiliation between *awqaf* and trusts will be assessed. It will be suggested that Islamic perspectives on the trust can disturb the received history of the textbook and classroom. Before moving the discussion to the documentary evidence of women in the Islamic world who pursued their economic interests in court, I will refer briefly to a different encounter between the trust and *waqf* as a direct consequence of the colonial engagement. It will be argued that the Islamic law of *waqf* endowment was enframed within the western orientalist gaze and, thereby, repressed. Finally, it will be questioned whether the depiction of positive images of Muslim women, in both the particular case of *waqf* endowment or more generally, can be subversive to the power of Orientalism.

AN ISLAMIC THEORY OF TRUSTS

As noted by a number of modern commentators, the *waqf*, on the surface, shares most of its essential characteristics with the trust and its predecessor the *use*; in particular, the division between 'administration' and 'beneficial enjoyment' of property. Henry Cattan, for instance, writing in 1955, regarded the trust as analogous to the *waqf*, describing their similarities as 'striking'.[33] In his own more recent analysis, which is reliant on Cattan's work, Avini has argued that: '... both institutions shared the same structure – the *waqif* is analogous to the person making the *enfeoffment* (settlor); the *mutawalli* is the same as the *feoffee to uses* (trustee); and the beneficiaries [*mustahiqq*, pl *mustahiqqun*] (both present and future) exist in both institutions.'[34]

Moreover, there is, at least superficially, a likeness between *awqaf* and trusts in the distinction between *waqf ahli*, the family endowment, and *waqf*

---

30 Bulbeck, 1998, p 84.
31 *Ibid*, p 221.
32 Gandhi, 1998, p 84, referring to Spivak, 1993.
33 Cattan, 1955, p 212.
34 Avini, 1996, p 1161.

khairi, the charitable endowment. He suggests that the difference between the two types of endowment is not unlike the distinction between public and private trusts, although whether the ideologically loaded (and gendered) western private/public paradigm can be imposed on Islamic legal and cultural space is questionable.[35] However, Cattan suggests that an assessment of the remaining differences between the trust and the *waqf* only serves to confirm their 'close similarity', 'based upon the same legal device of divestment or renunciation of ownership of property'.[36] It has been argued that a crucial difference between the two concepts is that the trustee becomes the legal owner of property held upon trust, while the *mutawalli* does not. Cattan addresses this by pointing to the practical realities of the two situations and suggests that the role of both *mutawalli* and trustee is to administer the property on behalf of the beneficiaries. Another apparent difference relates to duration, since one of the basic rules relating to both classes of *waqf* is that the property must be dedicated in perpetuity. Private trusts are subject to the rule against perpetuities, but as Cattan points out, the trust in its earlier form, the use, could be made in perpetuity.

There are some even more surprising ways in which the technical rules concerning *waqf* endowment and the trust seem to coincide. For instance, Islamic law makes provision for the situation where a charitable purpose has become extinct or disappeared, in which case the benefit of the *waqf* is applied to another charitable purpose, in a manner which bears some resemblance to the doctrine of *cy-près* in the English law of trusts. Cattan points to certain differences in this area, for the *waqf* is, by its very nature, dedicated to charity and may be reapplied without the 'close scrutiny of the settlor's intention'[37] required in the context of a trust. Indeed, where the trust and the *waqf* do clearly part company is in the fact that 'in legal theory at least', the latter has 'maintained its connection with the religious precept of charity', despite the fact that 'in many cases property has been dedicated as *waqf* to escape taxation ... or out of fear of the prodigality of [the *waqif's*] children or for reasons unconnected with charity'.[38] This is the case as much for a so called family *waqf* as one devoted entirely to a public charitable purpose. Srivastava has recently commented that 'the maxim that "charity begins at home" was for the first time enunciated by Islam', in that it 'enjoined that to help oneself, one's dependants and other relatives was also an act of piety'.[39]

Orthodox trust textbooks rarely make reference to the *waqf*, but where they do it is in the context of a search for the origins of the trust. There is a line of

---

35 See, eg, the discussion, in another context, in El Guindi, 1999, pp 77–82, of the different meanings of 'privacy' in western and Islamic contexts.

36 Cattan, 1995, p 212.

37 *Ibid*, p 211.

38 *Ibid*, p 205.

39 Srivastava, 1998, p 5.

argument which reflects Maitland's frequently quoted view that the development of the trust idea is 'the greatest and most distinctive achievement performed by Englishmen in the field of jurisprudence'.[40] In the context of a discussion concerning the 1984 Hague Convention on the Law Applicable to Trusts and on their Recognition, for instance, Goodhart adopts this kind of 'optimistic imperialism' in making the following observation: 'It is at least possible that the trust will in the 21st century join those other English inventions, such as football and the steam engine, which have swept the world.'[41] However, as is suggested by the quote which opened this chapter, there are academics, such as Moffat, who take a somewhat different stance on the 'invention' of the trust, or, in its earlier manifestation, the use.[42] Moffat refers to articles by Avini and Herman in a 1996 edition of the Tulane Law Review, in support of his 'allegation' that the 'source' of the trust may lie in Islamic law. Avini makes a rather more complex and subtle argument about the 'origins' of the use/trust than is perhaps evident from Moffat's brief comments. He acknowledges that the trust, the Roman *fideicommissum*, the *Salic salmannus* and the *waqf* all evolved to mitigate deficiencies arising from rigidity in positive law regarding the ownership and devolution of property in their respective spheres,[43] but suggests that 'just because these institutions

40 See, eg, Hayton, 1998, p 2.

41 Goodhart, 1996, p 259. Maitland, 1936, p 23, himself stated that '[o]f all the exploits of Equity ... the invention and development of the trust ... seems to us almost essential to civilisation and yet there is nothing quite like it in foreign law'.

42 It is rare for the *waqf* to be mentioned even in discussions about the origins of the trust. Hayton, 1998, p 11, eg, argues that equity and the trust were largely shaped by the fact that the Chancellor, who was the King's closest adviser, was 'an ecclesiastic usually learned in Roman law and canon law ... [and] it is likely that he was influenced by the Roman *fiducia* and *fidei commissum*. Herman, 1996, pp 2252–53, provides a useful recent summary of the different interpretations of possible origins for the use: 'Francis Bacon suggested that the use had originated in the Roman *fideicommissum*' and 'William Blackstone charted a path for later historians by crediting the use to clerical adaptation' of this Roman legal concept. He continues: 'Deviating from Blackstone's path, Justice Oliver Wendell Holmes suggested that the use had originated in the Germanic *Salman* or *Treuhand*'. However, Herman does footnote, p 2250, fn 25, the possibility that the use owed its inspiration to the *waqf*. Redgewell, 1999, p 9, argues that 'equity' is not exclusive to the common law, but that the trust is to 'be found flourishing in jurisdictions exposed to and/or borrowing from this system'. However, like Moffat, she records, p 9, fn 4, the possibility that 'the trust concept may be traced back to similar Roman (*fidei commissum*), medieval German (*salman*) and Islamic (*waqf*) concepts', citing Fratcher, WF, 'Trusts', Chapter 11 of Vol VI (Property and Trust) of the *International Encyclopedia of Comparative Law*, 1973, The Hague, Paris, Tübingen: Martinus Nijhoff, in support of this contention.

43 The established view is that the origins of trust lay in attempts to avoid the strict common law rule of primogeniture in relation to land and in the avoidance of taxation. In Maitland's words: 'In the case of land every germ of testamentary power has been ruthlessly stamped out in the 12th century. But the Englishman would like to leave his land by will. He would like to provide for the weal [sic] of his sinful soul, and he would like to provide for his daughters and younger sons. This is the root of the matter. But further, it is to be observed that the law is hard upon him at the hour of death, more especially if he is one of the great. If he leaves an heir of full age, there is a relevium to be paid to the lord. If he leaves an heir under age, the lord may take the profits of [cont]

addressed similar needs in the law does not mean that they shared a common ancestry'.[44] Avini argues that it may be more helpful to think in terms of a 'convergent evolution',[45] rather than to search for the 'source' of the trust; similarities between these different legal institutions being attributable to parallel but independent developments which would 'avoid conjectural findings of causation based on superficial similarities in structure'.[46]

However, Avini does conclude that, if there was an external model for the English trust, he concurs with the Islamic theory that the *waqf* was the greatest influence upon the trust, having been 'imported to England by Franciscan friars ... in the 13th century'.[47] The similarities in 'purpose, theory and structure' are such, he argues, that the *waqf* and the use 'are almost identical institutions'. For Cattan, looking through the lens of Islamic law, 'there is no doubt that the *waqf* is the earlier of the two institutions' leading 'naturally ... to an inquiry as to whether the English trust was derived from the Islamic *waqf*'.[48]

Furthermore, both commentators point to a 'historical proximity' between the *waqf* and the trust. The *waqf* was fully established as a widely used legal device in the Middle East by the 13th century; indeed, Avini suggests that it was at the height of its popularity. He adheres to the belief that it was 'the

---

43 [cont] the land, perhaps for 20 years, and may sell the marriage of the heir. And then if there is no heir, the land falls back ("escheats") to the lord for good and all': Fisher, 1911, p 335. The 'family *waqf*' provided an opportunity to circumvent Islamic inheritance law: 'It is well known that Islamic inheritance law imposes compulsory rules for the distribution of property; bequests may not exceed one-third of the estate and may not be made in favor of a legal heir without the consent of the other heirs. These rules, however, are situated within a larger, more flexible Islamic inheritance system that allows a proprietor to transmit his/her property to his/her desired "heirs" in whatever quantities she/he wishes by means of an *inter vivos* transaction of which one example is the family *waqf* ...': Reiter, 1995, p 174. The *waqf* was used quite widely by non-Muslims who were subject to Islamic law, although any endowment had to be compatible with Islam. Avini, 1996, p 1155, fn 132, suggests that, in the 11th and 12th centuries, the threat of government confiscation may have been a major motivation for many *waqf*: 'Anyone who wished to protect his property against the plots of the powerful or against confiscation for the benefit of the State – a common practice [later] in the Ottoman Empire – had no other way open to him except to proclaim his immovable property – houses, or shops, or factories, such as flour mills, soapworks, limekilns, and oil or sugar factories – as *waqf* foundations for the benefit of mosques or schools, and so ensure to his descendants the income from the property, or at least part of it,' quoting from Granott, A, *The Land System in Palestine*, 1952, p 130. As suggested earlier, tax avoidance may have influenced *waqf* endowment. Eg, in Egypt, *waqf* land was free of tax in the 17th and 18th centuries and was taxed at very low rates in the early 19th century: see Tucker, 1985, p 29.

44 Avini, 1996, p 1141.

45 *Ibid*, p 1141, draws an analogy with the idea of a convergent evolution in biology which is used to describe 'the phenomenon in which geographically separated and unrelated species evolve almost identical adaptations as a result of similar environmental conditions rather than common ancestors'.

46 *Ibid*, p 1142.

47 *Ibid*, p 1159.

48 Cattan, 1955, p 213.

stifling legal environment of 13th century feudal England which was the motivating force behind the trust'[49] and that there were widespread possibilities for cultural exchange between England and the Middle East during this historical period. Avini, drawing heavily upon Cattan's analysis, argues that even those theorists who see the origins of the use in the *Salmannus* or *fideicommissum* are agreed that the concept of the use was firmly established in 13th century England by the Franciscan Friars[50] who were very active in the Middle East at this time.[51] In addition, Avini suggests that:

> [T]he Islamic contribution, by way of returning Crusaders, to the 13th century 'European Awakening' is widely accepted ... Evidence of this Eastern influence can be found not only in a range of disciplines such as medicine, philosophy, and mathematics, but also in the structure of learning institutions such as the English Inns of Court or the 1264 Statutes of Merton College, generally considered to mark the founding of the modern college system.[52]

More recently, trusts and *awqaf* have been implicitly joined together in discussions about intergenerational equity and trusts. The theory is of a 'planetary trust' in which the earth and its resources are held for all members of the human species, including past, present and future generations. It represents a novel approach to global environmental problems and articulates the principle of sustainable development. Each generation has planetary obligations to conserve both natural and cultural resources, in trust, for future generations, but each generation also enjoys planetary rights from a beneficial interest in their legacy from previous generations. This theory of intergenerational equity was developed by Weiss,[53] who likened the planetary trust to charitable trusts. Several aspects of charitable trusts, including the absence of 'temporal limitations' and the requirement for the trust to be of benefit to the community, were deemed useful to the concept of a planetary trust. As Redgewell has argued, 'most writing on intergenerational issues has

---

49   Avini, 1996, p 1163.

50   This is certainly the view taken by Maitland, who emphasised the growth of the order during the 13th century and their need, due to their strict vow of poverty, for a legal device which would permit the beneficial occupancy of land, without ownership of that land. Herman, 1996, pp 2254–55, comments that Maitland's own evidence suggested 'the presence of uses in England well before the Franciscans had come to England in substantial numbers' and '[f]or the sake of accuracy, perhaps Maitland should have said that the Franciscans gave momentum to the use, a device by the 13th century already well known to the church'.

51   Avini, 1996, p 1159, notes, like Cattan, that 'Saint Francis himself spent parts of 1219 and 1220 AD in Islamic territory'.

52   Makdisi, 1985, has suggested that the Islamic college of law, consisting of a mosque and an inn, was the paradigm for the Inns of Court. He contends that crusaders, particularly the Knights Templars who were in Jerusalem from 1120 to the end of the 13th century and the Hospitallers, were both familiar with the Islamic colleges and influential in the development of the Inns of Court. Gaudiosi, 1988, has also found strong similarities between contemporary *waqf* instruments and the 1264 Statutes of Merton College, Oxford.

53   Weiss, 1988.

come from the North and not from the South, and ... inevitably reflects a Western cultural context';[54] however, Weiss emphasised her view that this notion of intergenerational equity was universal, arguing that:

> Philosophers from diverse cultural traditions have recognized that we are trustees or stewards of the natural environment. The fundamental thesis that we have obligations to conserve the planet for future generations and rights to have access to its benefits is deeply rooted in the diverse legal traditions of the international community. There are roots in the common and the civil law traditions, in Islamic law, in African customary law, and in Asian non-theistic traditions.[55]

There is no suggestion that Weiss had in mind the particular mechanism of the *waqf*; indeed, she makes reference to a more general feature of Islamic law which regards natural resources as an inheritance from God which is the right and privilege of the whole community of believers, who should make good use of these resources in a manner which does not damage them for future generations. Nevertheless, the *waqf khairi*, in which property is permanently reserved for a charitable purpose, has clear links to both charitable trusts and Weiss's notion of intergenerational equity.

THE *WAQF* IN TRUST

The colonial engagement produced different encounters between legal cultures, which were almost the literal opposite of the Islamic theory of the origins of the trust presented by Cattan and, to a lesser extent, Avini, amounting to participation by the trust in the occupation of another legal culture. Syed Ameer Ali in the Tagore Law Lectures of 1884 wrote in the opening section of his 'law relating to *Wakf*' that: '[T]he doctrine of trusts has been recognized and enforced in the *Mohammedan* system from the earliest times ... its origin is traced to the Prophet.'[56] His lectures then progressed with a description of *waqf* endowment in a format identical to a standard trust textbook, which would be instantly recognisable to any current English law student, from the creation of the trust and its complete constitution, to the '*cy-près*' doctrine in *awqaf*. In the process the writing moves, seemingly almost at random, into and out of the language of trusts, as in the following passage on classification:

> Trusts in the Mohammedan system are called *wakfs*, and may for the sake of convenience be divided under three heads, viz, public, quasi-public and private ... *Wakf* ... for public works of utility or charitable trusts are regarded as

---

54   Redgewell, 1999, p 99.

55   Weiss, 1988, p 18.

56   It is worth noting in this context that the book was called 'The Law Relating to Gifts, Trusts and Testamentary Dispositions among the Mohammedans ...'.

public *wakfs*. All other trusts are treated as private. Of course there is no specific designation for private trusts. But all wakfs are created in one category ... however, there is a large body of trusts which without being public trusts, partakes something of that character, I have thought it expedient to include them under the head of quasi-public *wakf* ...[57]

It is suggested that the slippage in this passage between trusts and *waqfs* is not 'innocent', but evidence for the effects of what Strawson has termed legal orientalism. He contends that law may be located in the cultural sphere and 'as such is contested', arguing further that as legal culture became 'an object of colonisation' it had 'to be conquered'.[58] Just as territory was conquered through military and political manoeuvres, so Islamic law was mastered through repetitive representations as 'decadent', 'defective', 'incomplete' and 'corrupt'.[59] This legal orientalism is 'secreted' in works on Islamic law in English texts, where the de-legitimised legal system 'has its mirror image in the representation of European law as a complete, established and definite legal system, legitimate in all respects'.[60]

Here, the message is that *awqaf* are to be viewed through trusts and it is the Islamic legal mechanism which is Other. It reflects a process whereby Islamic law was reshaped during the 19th century, as it was penetrated by European law in the name of modernisation. The law of *waqf* endowment and its attendant legal concepts are legitimated through their cradling by the trust. Islamic law is, therefore, captured and possessed, just as the 'physical artefacts of other cultures appear in museums and exhibitions'.[61] This replication in legal culture of colonial power relationships is such that even the writings of a non-westerner, such as Syed Amir Ali, take place on the terrain of legal orientalism. This pattern has survived into the postcolonial period, with articles in English where *awqaf* both become trusts and are slotted into a hierarchy of legal cultures. Marsot, for instance, in the preface to her recent discussion of women's economic activity in 18th century Egypt, relates the following: 'The *Qu'ran* states that Muslim women are legal heirs and must therefore inherit, yet we find in some Muslim countries when it comes to land, women were cut out of such a share in the inheritance, belying the religious directives. One method of cutting out women was to turn property into trust, or *mortmain*, known as *waqf*, and exclude females from a share in it.'[62]

Strawson argues that: '[I]n order to release Islamic law from the colonial exhibition we are obliged to demolish the walls of legal orientalism.'[63]

---

57 Ali, 1885, pp 178–79. Note the use of the term *wakfs* to describe *awqaf*.
58 Strawson, 1996, p 28.
59 *Ibid*, p 22–23.
60 *Ibid*, p 23.
61 *Ibid*, p 40.
62 Marsot, 1996, p 35.
63 *Ibid*, Strawson, p 41.

Disturbing established western histories of equity and trusts is unlikely to make a contribution to the demolition work: at best, it may draw attention to 'narrow provincialism masquerading as universalism'[64] or make visible what was repressed. Engaging with histories of Muslim women and property is fraught with even more difficulty, for a variety of reasons, including the fact that within the 'orientalist lineage' Islamic law has 'largely been seen as a branch of history'.[65] Nevertheless, the tightrope will be walked, albeit in the certainty of 'failure'.

EXPERIENCING *WAQF* ENDOWMENT

Muslim women, as already stated, have fixed rights of inheritance, although in smaller shares than their male counterparts. Jennings, in his research, presented in 1975, into the Ottoman judicial records of the *Sharia* court in Kayseri during the 17th century, found women to be property holders of considerable importance. He refers to the view held by many 'Arabists and anthropologists' which suggests that 'Muslim women never really gained possession of what they were entitled to, either being excluded from the division by stronger male heirs or relieved of what they did get by domineering husbands'.[66] However, Jennings argues that, in Kayseri, the records show women actively seeking the intervention of the courts to defend their rights, often to establish that she was the owner of property as against her neighbour, a member of her family or her husband. Moreover, the frequency with which women bought and sold both land and buildings suggests that they accumulated great wealth. His analysis is that: 'Where an Islamic inheritance was practiced and where a strong court system guaranteed the implementation of these legal divisions, women property holders might well be nearly as numerous as men.'[67]

Gerber, who again looked at the position of women in a 17th century Anatolian city, in this case Bursa, argues that the court records show women in a very different light from that projected in Orientalist fantasies. However, he admits that simply because the court records demonstrate that the Islamic law of inheritance was applied in accordance with the law, does not provide 'definitive proof that women did actually inherit'.[68] Nevertheless, he suggests that the women of Bursa appeared in court in person and pleaded many cases quite freely, suggesting that their ability to enforce the law of inheritance was not merely theoretical. It is fairly clear that many Muslim women have also,

---

64 Strawson, 1996, p 3.
65 *Ibid*, p 12.
66 Jennings, 1975, p 98.
67 *Ibid*.
68 Gerber, 1980, p 232.

over successive centuries, acquired property at the time of marriage. Looking at urban women in Syria and Palestine in the 17th and 18th century, Tucker, for instance, suggests that '[t]he gendered transfers of property that accompanied marriage were strictly regulated. The bride, but not the groom, was to be endowed by her husband's family through the *mahr*; and by her own family through the *jihaz*. In supporting her right to these endowments, and to full control of them, the *muftis* endorsed the idea that a woman should enter marriage as an empowered individual.'[69]

Interestingly, Tucker comments further that estate records in Nablus, Palestine during the 18th and early 19th century indicate that the level of dower amongst the middle and upper classes represented approximately 15–20% of a woman's estate upon death. This suggests that women either had other sources of wealth or were successful investors. However, she points to the fact that a further source of wealth for women arose from beneficial interests in *waqf* properties. In her study of peasant and urban lower class women in 19th century Egypt, Tucker suggests that 'many founders of *waqfs*, both male and female, appear to have used the institution, in part, to provide specifically for female heirs whose claims on the inheritance would normally be weaker than those of men.'[70]

However, women have also been active founders of *awqaf* and, as Roded has argued, there have been 'provocative findings on the ownership and management of property by women'[71] as a consequence of studying deeds of endowment. There were some very famous endowments by women of high rank involving the sponsoring of monumental public works. One of the most famous was Hurrem, or Khurrem, the wife of the Ottoman Sultan Suleyman the Lawmaker, who endowed major philanthropic institutions in her own name in Mecca, Medina, Jerusalem, Edirne and Istanbul. 'The earliest of these, the Istanbul complex, constructed between 1537 and 1539, consisted of a

---

69 Tucker, 1998, p 57. She does warn against overemphasising the importance of dower and points to the fact that the courts of the time upheld the practice of 'lending' or 'sharing' of bridal trousseaus, by which means the bride's family retained some control over her property.

70 Tucker, 1985, p 95. Tucker notes also that the terms of a *waqfiyah* may also serve to disinherit women and gives an example of a founder who specified that the income from a *waqf* should pass only through his male descendants 'and never the female'. Roded, 1999, p 143, states that: 'Establishment of family *waqfs* has been regarded as one of the major vehicles for disenfranchising women from their legal *Quaranic* share inheritances. Some studies support this contention; others have found explicit discriminatory clauses to be rare, but the outcome of the distribution of benefits favoured by men in the long run; and still others have found clearer attempts to make provisions for daughters in endowments.' Baer, 1969, in his analysis of *awqaf* documents registered in 1546 in Istanbul, records that only in four out of a sample of 500 were women explicitly excluded from any part of the income from a *waqf*. He suggests that, at later periods in some other geographical areas, the exclusion of daughters and female descendants from the benefit of *awqaf* following marriage was the norm.

71 Roded, 1999, p 142.

mosque, a religious college, a soup kitchen, a hospital and a primary school.'[72] Tucker points out in her study of Egypt that, although the majority of *awqaf* were established by women of the ruling or commercial elite, 'women of the artisanal class' also endowed property.[73] Marsot, who was also concerned with the position in Egypt, points to the chaotic and decentralised nature of the system of government in the 18th century, in which there was much infighting in the ruling class. In a situation where male mortality amongst the ruling class was high, property appears to have been turned over to women, through *waqf* endowment, to 'prevent it being confiscated or simply taken over' should their male relatives or husband die. She suggests that 'such a pattern was not limited to elite women, for we find that women of all strata owned property; bought, sold and exchanged property; and endowed it at will'.[74]

Baer discovered that more than one-third of all founders of *awqaf* in mid-16th century Istanbul were women, but as he also states:

> What is the significance of [that] fact ... It shows, no doubt, that women were property holders, a fact which has been pointed out for various Islamic societies and should be reiterated here. It should be stressed that this certainly was not the case in many other civilisations, including many Western societies. The question is whether it also disproves the view of the subservient role of women in traditional Islamic society, and whether it shows that women played a considerably greater role in the economy of the Ottoman Empire than has generally been believed.[75]

He notes that women's *awqaf* were 'not only fewer and smaller', but they 'lacked almost completely the asset considered most important – land'[76] and he has an interesting stance on the control of *awqaf*.

It is certainly the case that women did, unlike their contemporaries in England, administer and manage their *waqf* property, with some women, some of the time, serving as *mutawallis*. Tucker, in her study of 19th century Egypt, concludes that women frequently acted as the administrators of *awqaf*, receiving, as did most of those who held this position, about 10% of the total income. She argues that since '*waqf* administration involved a number of possible business transactions, including the keeping up or renting of the ... property, the overseeing of the income, the supervising or repairs to the endowed mosque or school ...', it is evidence of 'the perception of women as independent legal actors with requisite skills and knowledge'.[77]

---

72 Pierce, 1993, p 199. She suggests that the nature of power in the Ottoman ruling class during the 16th century was such that monumental building by female members of the dynasty was an established feature. See, also, Roded, 1999, p 142.

73 Tucker, 1985, p 96.

74 Marsot, 1996, p 37.

75 Baer, 1983, p 10.

76 *Ibid*, p 13.

77 *Ibid*, Tucker, p 96.

However, according to Roded, Baer, looking at 16th century Istanbul, suggests that women were less prominent as managers of endowments than as founders and even 'female founders designated men as managers in 75% of ... cases'.[78] Baer points out that 'even *awqaf* which were administered in the first instance by women usually passed into the hands of male'[79] *mutawallis*, in part because religious officials were designated to take on the administrative role at a later stage and these were men. Baer's overall conclusion is that:

> [T]he women of 16th century Istanbul established *evkaf* to safeguard their property and its income against interference and control by their husbands or guardians or by their husbands' families. Nevertheless, in the long run, the *waqf* served to recycle property in the sense that property which had fallen into the hands of women by inheritance or otherwise gradually returned to male beneficiaries and to the control of male managers. Thus, the *waqf* actually weakened the economic position of women as a group.[80]

Ahmed also warns against the scholarly establishment 'especially in the West' too 'enthusiastically' hailing 'the documentary evidence showing that women inherited and owned property and vigorously pursuing their economic interests, even in court'.[81] While she acknowledges that the evidence undoubtedly undermines western stereotypes about Muslim women, she is also of the view that '[a]reas of the economy in which wealth might be aggressively acquired were by and large closed to women', unless they inherited wealth, meaning that their relationship to property was 'derivative and marginal'.[82] It is very obviously the case that it would be wrong to essentialise women in a diverse set of historical circumstances and geographical settings. In relation to Egyptian women of the 19th century, for instance, Tucker argues that: '... for a peasant trader of the Delta, a petty trader in Cairo, and a member of the palace *harim*, the bonds of womanhood undoubtedly paled before the vast separations, in experience and interest, created by class and environment.'[83] Women's roles no doubt took on quite different dimensions within different epochs, different social situations and so on.

Marsot raises an interesting point in this regard. She argues, unlike Tucker, that there was major change in women's position in Egypt between the 18th century and the 19th century. As trade was extended with Europe, to the degree that by the last third of the 19th century, there were 68,000 European merchants in Egypt, the status of elite and middle class women declined. In

---

78 Roded, 1999, p 143.
79 Baer, 1983, p 14.
80 *Ibid*, p 27.
81 Ahmed, 1992, p 111.
82 *Ibid*, p 112.
83 Tucker, 1985, p 5.

the 18th century to conduct business they had to deal through a male, but, crucially, the documentation registered her legal existence as the active participant; he was merely a conduit. The arrival of European institutions, banks, insurance companies and the stock exchange, imported a different kind of ideology which did not acknowledge the legal existence of women. Any woman still had to operate through a male, but he was not her agent and she lost her legal personhood: a further example of the diffusion, not uncontested, but nevertheless firmly present, of 19th century English legal culture into colonised space.

Nevertheless, it is necessary to question whether much of this history amounts to little more than a species of what Spivak regards as 'reverse ethnocentrism'.[84] The point was well made by Young, who compared it to reverse sexism:

> If the man/woman duality as it is currently constituted is simply inverted, then, as many feminists have pointed out, the constitution of 'woman' is still determined according to the terms of the original opposition. In a similar way, those who evoke the 'nativist' position through a nostalgia for a lost or repressed culture idealize the possibility of that lost origin being recoverable in all its former plenitude without allowing for the fact that the figure of the lost origin, the 'other' that the coloniser has repressed, has itself been constructed in terms of the coloniser's own self-image.[85]

The same doubts could be raised both about the story of the 'lost origins' of the trust presented in the previous section and the undermining of western stereotypes of Muslim women. Replacing a stereotype with 'authentic' information about Muslim women and their relations to property does not shatter the power of Orientalism. In her recent discussion of western women's narratives of the harem, and their deployment in critiques of Said's Orientalism, Yegenoglu suggests that such 'simple' reversals 'retain the very structure and the force and violence through which opposites are construed as opposites'.[86] What happens is a reduction of the 'power of Orientalism to a mere constellation of "distorted" representations ... [preventing] us from grasping the more subtle Orientalizing operations of Orientalism which construe difference in a particular way'.[87] She emphasises that it is not a matter of distinguishing a 'distorted' Orient from the 'real' Orient, thereby missing that the 'power of Orientalism exceeds the negativity of images'.[88]

However, it is perhaps the complicated patterns and unevenness of the histories discussed which suggest a fresh outlook upon the history of women, equity, and trusts, without collapsing into simple surprise that the Orientalist

---

84 Spivak, 1985, p 121.
85 Young, 1990, p 168.
86 Yegenoglu, 1998, p 87.
87 *Ibid*, p 86.
88 *Ibid*, p 87.

fantasy of passive, secluded and resourceless Muslim women is disrupted by these new women's histories. Women's rights to property, whether in the form of inheritance or as beneficiaries of *awqaf*, were 'brought forward in some periods and pushed into the background in others'.[89] The *waqf*, like the trust, played a complex part in women's lives. Shatzmiller has suggested that 'male domination was never complete in propertied families' and that 'this calls into question the characterisation of the Muslim family as "patriarchal"'.[90] She suggests that it points to 'the need for a new social, cultural and economic explanation of the nature of the Muslim family'.[91] In fact, it probably reinforces the need for new explanations of both western and Muslim families and the place that law plays in the constitution of familial relations. If nothing else, this exploration of the *waqf* is a reminder of the need, which Spring identified, to debunk simplistic notions of equity as the saviour of women and to associate all that is associated with the common law as regressive and oppressive.

Strawson has argued that reading legal cultures is not a matter of making space for excluded voices, for such a process is based on the untenable assumption that 'we possess a discourse which can engage with the excluded'.[92] What I have attempted here is not a 'reading', but a contribution towards 'ground clearing', which is, in turn, an important part of beginning to disrupt the power of western legal discourse, including equity and trusts. Such ground clearing is necessary if the debate about such issues as intergenerational equity and the planetary trust is to be meaningful and provide any challenge to the colonialisms of the past and the present.

---

89 Marsot, 1996, p 33.
90 Shatzmiller, 1995, p 219.
91 *Ibid*, p 219.
92 Strawson, 1996, p 40.

CHAPTER 4

UNDERSTANDING EQUITY'S SECRET UNDERSTANDINGS

Susan Scott-Hunt

Secrecy about the ownership of property is an abiding theme within equity. Whether defined by constituent 'things' or the ability to act autonomously or command the compliance of others, property is a form of power, and, as such, is a 'crucial indicator of the balance of power between women and men'.[1] From women's perspective, the theme of secrecy about property has particular resonance, because of the social and historical necessity for women to hide (or have hidden) their power over property and the way men have used secrecy about power over property to control women's choices.

This chapter will explore the theme of secrecy in equity, focusing mainly on secret and semi-secret trusts. First, the role of secrecy in the historical development of the trust from the 'use' will be examined, an account being given of the early recognition of secret and semi-secret trusts and their uses. Secondly, characteristics of secret and semi-secret trusts will be described in order to provide a context in which to analyse the concept of 'personal' or equitable fraud, the supposed basis of such trusts, and to notice the debate about their doctrinal classification. The discussion will focus on the character of equitable fraud as reflected in the language used by courts to describe it and by would be makers of secret trusts to describe their motivations. Thirdly, the theme of secrecy will be explored to a lesser extent elsewhere in equity, including in the *donatio mortis causa*, and in proprietary estoppel.[2] The doctrinal and practical connections between the places in equity where the theme of secrecy can be heard will be investigated and the impact upon women of equitable devices and remedies which recognise and effectuate secrecy will be assessed. Where equity effectuates secrecy, it sometimes appears to create conceptual anomalies. It will be argued that the existence of such anomalies may bring advantages, not only to some women in some situations, but to equity's ability to respond flexibly and, above all, pragmatically, to a variety of situations.

There are two types of secret trust. In the first, the fully secret trust, the property is given to the apparent beneficiary as an absolute interest, although, in secret, she acquiesces with the testator or donor that she will hold it on certain trusts. In the other, the semi-secret trust, it is apparent on the face of the

---

1   Hirschon, 1984, p 1.
2   Mutual wills bear some similarity to secret trusts, but are distinguished by being contractual and *inter vivos*. They will not be discussed in this chapter.

will (or transfer) that the beneficiary or transferee is a mere trustee, but the nature of the trusts upon which she holds is not disclosed or not fully disclosed. The basis of secret trusts is said to be that equity will not allow a statute (the Wills Act 1837) to be used as an instrument of fraud but, as will be discussed, the nature of the fraud has never been clear. A theory that such trusts operate 'outside the will' has emerged, but the inconsistency of this view with policy about succession on death gives rise to conceptual difficulties within property law.

Sheridan, in a 1951 article in the Law Quarterly Review, describes secret trusts as a 'remarkable product of equity jurisdiction' and as an area 'rich in strange distinctions'.[3] In a modern law syllabus, secret and semi-secret trusts are, arguably, not as important to providing a sound and contemporary understanding of modern trusts as many other parts of trust law. It is right to give way, say, to exploring the uses of the 'new model' constructive trusts, the use of trusts in commercial transactions or charitable trusts. Thus, for some time on some syllabi, secret and semi-secret trusts have been relegated as an optional extra. A few of the popular student texts give them short shrift.[4] Some of us are, however, unhappy about abandoning the study of secret and semi-secret trusts. Why? It is, of course, partly because of the 'rich and strange distinctions' they involve. However, it is also partly because they present the potential for narratives involving intrigue, perhaps even illicitness. We like the stories of secrecy and intrigue. Our students like them. One aspect of the intrigue which we, as teachers, play upon, especially in devising hypothetical problem questions for examinations, is the scenario of the secret trust used to hide property provided for 'a mistress and illegitimate children'. The scenario is historically real enough; the secret trust (actually semi-secret trust) case perhaps most easily recalled is a 'mistress' case, *Blackwell v Blackwell*,[5] but the historical significance of the secret trust for a 'secret mistress' scenario is not particularly great.

SECRET STIRRINGS

In the beginning, all trusts were secret trusts. The desire for secrecy was a key reason for the development and evolution of the trust from the medieval use.[6]

---

3 Sheridan, 1951, p 314.

4 See Hudson, 1999, pp 141–43; Todd, 2000, pp 246–49; Hayton and Marshall, 1996, pp 92–104; but see Hanbury and Martin, 1997, pp 143–63.

5 [1929] AC 318.

6 Holdsworth, 1945, Vol 4, p 420. Holdsworth tells us that the earliest trace of the 'use' in English law was in the middle of the 14th century and the use of the 'use' in testamentary dispositions developed rapidly from then onwards, so that it was, by the 15th century, quite well established.

Key characteristics of what modern trust law would recognise as situations giving rise to a secret trust appear in the first stirrings of equity. Holdsworth tells us that it was not uncommon for an *inter vivos* conveyance of land to *feoffees* to be made on the understanding that they held to the use of the *feoffor* until he gave them further directions.[7] The uses to which medieval *feoffees* were held were sometimes declared orally. A deathbed parole *feoffment* of a will of land was possible.[8] Occasionally, a medieval will referred to another document in which uses were more fully declared.[9] A principal aspect of the flexibility or usefulness of the use, what Moffat describes as its ability to perform a variety of 'tricks', arose from the fact that uses 'made secret conveyancing of land possible, whereas at common law a transfer of seisin had to take place by public act'.[10] Uses, and the secrecy they allowed about the real ownership of land, abetted the evasion of feudal incidents, increased the range of dispositions available to the tenant, enabled land to be looked after in the tenant's absence and frustrated creditors.[11]

Most uses were of land. Occupation, in general, disclosed the interest of the *feoffor* or *cestui que* trust, as the case might be. However, in the case of an absentee owner, the lack of express declaration of a use in his favour did, in fact, hide ownership. The solution was to create a rule of law; that the use resulted to the *feoffor*[12] if not expressly declared unless there was a conveyance for value. The essential idea that, when one person *enfeoffed* another without consideration, a use resulted by operation of law to the *feoffor*, thus sprang from the development of the distinction between gratuitous and non-gratuitous promises, between gift and contract. In regard to this early conceptual separation, which marks the very birthplace of the trust, Holdsworth quotes Bacon, saying that 'purchases were things notorious and trusts were things secret'.[13]

As modern trust law would recognise them, the secret and the semi-secret trust only appear after the Statute of Frauds 1644. However, the circumstance of the secret trust existed long before then. A 16th century case, *Rookwood*,[14] is of interest. It is a contract case, but the situation was similar to that of the secret trust. A testator who had three sons proposed to charge his lands with an annuity in favour of his younger sons for life, but the eldest prevailed upon

---

7 Holdsworth, 1945, p 423.

8 *Ibid*, p 422, fn 5.

9 *Ibid*, p 422, fn 9.

10 Moffat, 1999, p 27.

11 *Ibid*, pp 27–28.

12 'The recognition of this "resulting" use, perhaps as early as 1465, confirms how usual it had become for *feoffments* to be made on secret or undisclosed trusts, or to perform the *feoffor's* will generally.' Baker, 1990, p 287.

13 Holdsworth, 1945, p 424.

14 (1589) Cro Eliz 164. See, also, Sheridan, 1951, p 314 for a fuller account of the origins of secret and semi-secret trusts.

him not to charge the land, promising both father and brothers that he would pay the annuity. After the death of the father, he refused to do so. There was, because of the promise, of course, no necessity to find anything but contract. There was no fear of fraud because the younger sons, in fact, knew about the promise. Their knowledge was not necessary to contract, although the promise was. Absent the promise, the factual circumstances are secret trust circumstances; the elder son is given a beneficial interest under the will or intestacy. In fact, he has agreed to hold subject to the benefit to the brothers.

Rookwood was a century before what was arguably the first recognition by Chancery of a secret trust. *Thynn v Thynn*,[15] decided in 1684, involved another son prevailing upon his father, who had made his wife executrix, to make a new will naming the son executor instead. The court's decision holding that the son held for the mother was based on fraud – for the first time. A few years later, in *Devenish v Baines*,[16] where a wife was nominated successor to lands on condition that she hold in part for the plaintiff, fraud was again the basis for enforcement. *Sellack v Harris*[17] involved a secret trust arising on intestacy. An elder son dutifully made a deathbed promise to his father that he would hold lands the father had purchased with a younger son's money for the younger son. Fraud was a basis for enforcement by the younger son when his brother was not so willing to do so following their father's death. In *Whitton v Russell*[18] fraud, or the possibility of fraud, was again held to be the necessary ingredient. *Moss v Cooper*[19] can perhaps claim to have brought a general statement of the accepted modern principle of the secret trust. That case also recognised the possibility of a secret trust existing, whether or not the undertaking of secret trust precedes or follows the making of the will. Next, in *Jones v Badley*,[20] decided a year before the House of Lords recognition of secret trusts in *McCormick v Grogan*,[21] Lord Cairns made the first statement of principle which would today would be recognised as describing secret trusts:

> [A] person, knowing that a testator, in making a disposition in his favour, intends it to be applied for purposes other than of his own benefit, either expressly promises, or by silence implies, that he will carry out the testator's intention into effect, and the property is left to him on the strength of that promise or undertaking.

What were the origins of the semi-secret trust? It has come to be accepted[22] that there is a juridical distinction between secret and semi-secret trusts, but

---

15 (1684) 1 Vern 296.
16 (1689) Prec Ch 3.
17 (1708) 2 Eq Ca Ab 46.
18 (1739) 1 Atk 448.
19 (1861) J & H 352.
20 (1868) LR 3 Ch App 362.
21 (1869) LR 4 HL 82.
22 Sheridan, 1951, p 324.

the factual situations that give rise to both types of trust are similar and, not at all surprisingly, their historical development was concurrent. Between *McCormick v Grogan* and the House of Lords' decision in *Blackwell v Blackwell* recognising it, there was considerable discussion as to the validity of this second type of secret trust. According to Snell,[23] Lord Jeffreys LC has some claim to paternity. In *Crook v Brooking* (1688),[24] property was left by will 'on such uses as the testator had declared' to the legatees. As the uses were proved to have been declared (by a letter written by one semi-secret trustee to the other), the obligation of trust arose. Another early case was *Pring v Pring*,[25] but there, the trustees made an undertaking 'for a remembrance over and above their costs and charges'. It was not clear from the will what had been undertaken by the trustees (one of whom denied the trust). The report of the case does not say whether the testator made the declaration before or after he made the will or both. In *Podmore v Gunning*,[26] a testator gave property to his wife 'having a perfect confidence that she will act up to those views which I have communicated to her'. In other words, the communication was made previously. *Johnson v Ball*,[27] a much later case, is really the first case where the main point of analysis is that the trustee is informed of the objects after the will has been made.

Moffat quotes Coke as saying that there were 'two inventors of uses; fear and fraud',[28] and this is, in some degree, seen in the use of secret trusts from their early recognition through the Victorian era and in contemporary case law. Once equity began to indulge secrecy, even from early times, the circumstances of its employment or attempted employment were wide and motivations were, naturally, various. *Crook v Brooking*,[29] for instance, was a case of a secret trust for a married daughter, the clear object of which was to keep the money (from her father) away from the husband/son-in-law. Much later, *Podmore v Gunning* (1836)[30] involved an allegation that the deceased's wife was secret trustee for the 'natural' daughters of her deceased husband. *Re Huxtable*[31] was about a semi-secret trust for charitable purposes. *Re Fleetwood*[32] involved the attempted use of a semi-secret trust by a wealthy testatrix.

---

23   Snell, 1990, p 106.
24   (1688) 2 Vern 50.
25   (1689) 2 Vern 99.
26   (1836) 7 Sim 644.
27   (1851) 5 De G & Sm 85.
28   Moffat, 1999, p 27.
29   (1688) 2 Vern 50.
30   (1836) 7 Sim 644.
31   [1902] 2 Ch 793.
32   (1880) 15 Ch D 594.

As mentioned earlier, the secret trust for a 'secret mistress scenario' is, if not a myth, at least an anecdote often exaggerated in its telling. It is also mainly confined to the Victorian era. There are a few notable (and entertaining) 'secret mistress' cases besides *Blackwell*: amongst them is *Johnson v Ball*,[33] where the trust tragically failed. At one time, it was suggested by Sheridan that the 'mistress' trust was the only type of secret trust for which a practical use remained.[34] However, since the enactment of the Inheritance (Provision for Family and Dependants) Act 1975, the mistress has acquired a qualification, provided she is dependent. She is qualified to have the court exercise its discretion in her favour in redistributing property passing under a will or on intestacy. Indeed, the provision was styled a 'mistress's charter' by contemporary newspapers.[35] Green's 1988 article on the Act[36] describes how the dependency test employed by the Act significantly circumscribes its impact. Such circumscription, Green argues, is an inevitable product of courts' timidity and vulnerability to confusion and technicality when straying too far from the anchor of classical liberalism, whose values include respect for the sanctity of private property and testamentary freedom. It might be thought that the family provision legislation renders secret trusts for mistresses legally obsolete, or that they are socially obsolete in any case. However, *Gold v Hill*,[37] discussed below, is a surprising modern 'mistress' case, in which the 'myth' of the secret trust for the 'secret mistress' is clearly echoed.

Not surprisingly, secret trusts worked or failed to work in some cases for the interests of particular women and in some cases against the interests of particular women. In the 'secret mistress' cases, it worked for the 'mistress' and against the wife. The inevitable difficulty in assessing the history of the use of the secret trust by women and ways that its use affected women is that,

33 (1851) 5 De G & Sm 85.

34 Sheridan reduces the uses of secret trusts to three: the mistress/illegitimate child scenario; the undertaking by intestate successors to benefit other family members (which he thought was a constructive trust); and oral trusts to avoid the *Mortmain* restrictions. Since the last is no longer relevant and the second is subsumed by the constructive trust, the first is the problem, says Sheridan, for the policy of the Wills Act 1837 which 'tries to provide for the [interests of] evidence without making allowances for [the desire of the testator for] secrecy. Sheridan's solution (or one of them) was to advocate registration of written communications but limit who could see the register.

35 Green, 1988, p 195. A wife, whether dependent or not, though not given a forced shared under the Act, was entitled, at the discretion of the court to sue for provision at death equivalent to that available for divorce. One proponent of the amendments, Lord Mansfield, had stated that the '[b]readwinner is morally obliged to share the loaf that he has been free to earn'. It should be noted that the Law Reform (Succession) Act 1995, s 2, inserted a new s 1A into the 1975 Act – an amendment recommended by the Law Commission – as a consequence of which a heterosexual cohabiting partner of the deceased, provided the couple have lived together as husband and wife for a period of at least two years immediately preceding the death, may apply for discretionary provision from the deceased's estate without establishing dependency.

36 Green, 1988, p 188.

37 [1999] 1 FLR 54.

as noted elsewhere in this collection, women were rarely actors in legal cases. Moreover, Stretton's comprehensive and fascinating study of ordinary women of Tudor and Stuart England asserting their rights before the Court of Requests[38] notwithstanding, the cases in which the principles about secret trusts were fretted out predominantly involved men and only occasionally featured women of high social status and wealth. This is true also of the relatively few post Victorian secret trust cases, but the 1970s produced two notable secret trust cases: *Re Snowden*[39] and *Ottaway v Norman*.[40] These two modern secret trust cases, together with *Gold v Hill*,[41] a case from the High Court in which principles 'analogous to' secret trusts were recognised, will be examined closely below. As it happens, all three cases involved or affected particular women.

THE DOCTRINAL BASIS OF SECRET
AND SEMI-SECRET TRUSTS

Controversy and confusion surround the doctrinal basis of secret and semi-secret trusts. It is desirable to begin with a basic outline of the features of secret and semi-secret trusts in order to have a context in which to examine the concept of 'personal' or equitable fraud, the principle upon which, according to the orthodoxy, their features are based. It is convenient to examine the characteristics of fully secret trusts first and then to look separately at the characteristics of semi-secret trusts.

Every testamentary disposition is required to be executed and attested as a will or codicil[42] (and every *inter vivos* disposition of a trust interest is required to be in writing).[43] However, the law will not enforce the formality requirement where an apparent donee would be able to claim a beneficial interest but, in fact, has promised to hold such interest for someone else. Where a testator either makes a will or does not revoke[44] a disposition in a will on the faith of an express promise by the donee that she will carry out the testator's intentions, equity will admit extrinsic evidence[45] of the testator's intention and of the communication of that intention to, and acquiescence by, the apparent donee. Thus, the essential elements of the fully secret trust are: an

---

38 Stretton, 1998, p 3. Stretton refers to Cioni's work on women in the Court of Chancery: see Cioni, 1985.
39 [1979] 2 All ER 172.
40 [1971] 3 All ER 1325.
41 [1999] 1 FLR 54.
42 Wills Act 1837, s 9.
43 Law of Property Act 1925, s 53.
44 This occurred in *Tharp v Tharp* [1916] 1 Ch 142.
45 Extrinsic evidence is evidence outside the will, but not contradicting it.

intention of the donor to subject the primary donee to an obligation in favour of a secondary donee; the communication of that intention to the primary donee; and the acceptance of that obligation by the primary donee, either expressly or tacitly.[46] The timing of communication and acceptance are important. They affect validity; communication and acceptance must be in the lifetime of the testator.[47]

Where the property is given to more than one donee, on an undertaking of one of them to hold it on trust for some particular person or object, whether the interest of the other donee is bound by the trust depends on the time when the understanding was given. It will also depend upon whether the gift is to the donees as joint tenant or tenants in common. Both donees are bound if the undertaking was entered into by or on behalf of both before or at the time of the execution of the will. This is so, even though it was given without the knowledge or consent of the other donee, but the other is not bound if it is entered into after the will has been executed. The fact that the gift is to donees as tenants in common strengthens the case that the other is not bound, and this, of course, is only material where the understanding or undertaking was given before or at the time of the execution of the will.

In situations of semi-secret trusts, property is given by will to persons upon trusts referred to in, but not defined by, the will.[48] The trustees cannot take beneficially and the trustees hold the property either for the secret beneficiaries or, if the trusts fail, for those entitled to the residue or on intestacy.[49] The trustees hold as 'semi-secret trustees' for the secret beneficiary if the trusts are described in the will as having been defined and communicated to the trustees prior to or contemporaneously with the will.[50] It must also be proved that they were so defined and so communicated to some, even though not to all, of the 'semi-secret trustees'.

Although the received account[51] is that the doctrine of secret trusts originated on the basis of not allowing a statute (the Wills Act 1837)[52] to be used as an engine of fraud, the doctrine has in fact been applied in many cases where no real fraud is possible. Moreover, as will be discussed further below,

---

46 A donee accepts the obligation not only either orally or in writing but also when silently acquiescing in it when the intention of the testator is communicated to him, *Paine v Hall* (1812) 18 Ves 475; *Lomax v Ripley* (1855) 3 Sm & G 73.

47 See *Re Stead, Witham v Andrew* [1900] 1 Ch 237; *Re Keen* [1937] Ch D 236. For a discussion of *Re Keen* and *Re Stead*, see Perrins, 1972, p 225; and Holdsworth, 1937, p 501.

48 At one time there was identification between the doctrine of incorporation by reference and semi-secret trusts, but this theory has been abandoned. See Martin, 1997, p 143.

49 *Sellack v Harris* (1708) 5 Eq Ca Ab 46 is an example of a secret trust upon intestacy and *Re Gardner* [1920] 2 Ch 523 is an example of a partial intestacy.

50 See, generally, Perrins, 1972, p 228.

51 For the received account of the doctrinal basis of secret trusts, see Hayton and Marshall, 1996, p 92; and Oakley, 1997, p 245.

52 *Ibid*, Oakley, p 244.

the version of the fraud theory which can account for the recognition of secret trusts cannot normally account for semi-secret trusts.[53] Some have argued that this is unsatisfactory and even 'contrary to principle'.[54] It may be more satisfactory to say that the basis of secret trust is the 'simple principle of enforcing the equitable obligations binding a man's conscience'.[55]

The cases are unclear about the nature of the personal fraud said to be the basis for enforcement.[56] Where there is nothing in the will disclosing any trust, it is said to be the element of 'personal fraud' that gives the court jurisdiction. Why do the courts call this fraud 'personal'? What is 'personal' about it that is not 'personal' about other frauds? Is it 'personal' fraud because the context is usually (though not always) that of a personal relationship, a relationship of friendship? Is it personal fraud because the person perpetuating the fraud benefits personally? Lord Hatherley does suggest in *McCormick v Grogan* that the problem is that the secret trustee might profit 'by his own personal fraud'. It is unclear in other judicial statements whether the problem is that the secret trustee would himself profit wrongly, whether the would-be secret beneficiary is in danger of being cheated or whether the testator will have been misled. All three effects are possible simultaneously. Which is the primary concern upon which equity's intervention is based?

The communication to and acceptance by the donee is said to create a personal obligation, but to whom is it an obligation? The obligation ceases altogether on the death of the donee in the lifetime of the testator. In such circumstances, the secret beneficiary will have no claim against the testator's estate or any person entitled to an interest under the will or upon intestacy. The outcome is the same if the trustee renounces.[57] So, the personal obligation does not seem to be to the beneficiary. Such an outcome would suggest that the obligation (and therefore the 'personal fraud') springs from the relationship between the legatee and the testator – at least that this is primary.

---

53 Oakley, 1997, p 246.

54 *Ibid*, p 261.

55 Snell, 1990, p 110. See, also, Viscount Sumner's account in *Blackwell v Blackwell* [1929] AC 318.

56 See Oakley, 1997, p 245: 'There has been considerable judicial disagreement as to the nature of the fraud. Some judges have found this fraud in the ability of the intended trustee to take the property beneficially if evidence of the terms of the trust is not admitted. Others have instead found it in the consequential failure to observe the intentions of the testator and the consequential destruction of the beneficial interest arising under the trust.'

57 *Per* Cozens-Hardy LJ in *Re Maddock* [1902] 2 Ch 220, p 231, but see Buckmaster LJ in *Blackwell v Blackwell* [1929] AC 318, p 328.

PERSONAL FRAUD AND THE
LANGUAGE OF MALE FRIENDSHIP

Between the early cases involving secret trusts discussed previously and the Victorian cases, culminating in the House of Lords' recognition of secret trusts in *McCormick v Grogan*, there is a dearth of cases. *McCormick v Grogan* has, as a result, become the case that is seen to consolidate the principles according to which such trusts are recognised. The facts of the case present a paradigm secret trust situation, even though it was held that there was no secret trust created. The discussion casts some light on the nature of what the court means by personal fraud. The court's laboured discussion of the expectations and relationship of the testator and the proposed secret trustee betrays a view of the values of male friendship, honour and faithfulness which is relevant to assessing the willingness of equity to value and effectuate secrecy, sacrificing transparency and accountability.

Abraham Walker Craig, the wealthy Belfast linen merchant, with whose will the case was concerned, died unmarried, leaving several relatives and appearing to leave 'the whole of [his] property, both real and personal, to [his] most sincere and valued friend, Mr William Grogan, of Wellington Place, Belfast'. The will appointed Grogan sole executor. A few hours before his death from cholera, Craig had sent for Mr Grogan and communicated to him the fact of having made a will leaving all his property to Grogan. To Grogan's ambiguous response, 'Is that right?', Craig replied 'It shall be no other way'. The testator then told Grogan where the will and an explanatory letter were kept. In the letter, the testator explained that he had done what he had done in order to prevent squabbling amongst his family and friends as to the division of his substantial property. The letter said that the testator 'thought it best to invest the whole [of his property] in your hands ... well knowing you will carry out my intentions to the best of your ability'. The letter then set out details about the desired destinations of various amounts of money. However, the letter also stated: 'I do not wish you to act strictly to the foregoing instruction, but leave it entirely to your own good judgment to do as you think I would if living, and as the parties are deserving.' It is worth quoting further from the letter in order to notice the nature of the language used to describe the relationship between the testator and the would be secret trustee – or at least the apparent attitude of the testator towards that relationship and, implicitly, the values it reflects. The letter further discloses the testator's desire for secrecy as an implicit feature or advantage of honourable friendship as follows: '[I]t is not my wish that you should say anything about this document [so that] there cannot be any fault found with you by any of the parties should you decide not to act in strict accordance with it. The only excuse I can offer for imposing such trouble upon you is that I would if required have undertaken a similar task for you.'

Mr Grogan made a few gifts from the property – but not to Mr McCormick. Then, conceiving himself to be left the property absolutely, Grogan decided not to make any further gifts. McCormick sued for a declaration of the trusts. The trial court declared a trust. The Court of Appeal reversed. The House of Lords, dismissing the appeal, sought to circumscribe 'within proper limits' the operation of the doctrine of secret trusts, a doctrine that the House recognised 'has long been established in Equity'. Lord Westbury states in *McCormick* that the doctrine rests upon 'a sound foundation with reference to the jurisdiction of Courts of Equity to interpose in all cases of fraud'.[58] The jurisdiction does not have, necessarily, anything to do with the Wills Act 1837 (or the Statute of Frauds 1644, which the judgments hardly mention).

The judgment describes the character of the fraud as 'personal fraud':

> [T]he jurisdiction which is invoked here by the Appellant ... is a jurisdiction by which a Court of Equity, proceeding on the ground of fraud, converts the party who has committed it into a trustee for the party who is injured by that fraud. Now, being a jurisdiction founded on a personal fraud, it is incumbent on the Court to see that a fraud, *malus animus*, is proved by the clearest and most indisputable evidence.

Examining the conversation between Mr Grogan and Mr Craig and the letter left by the latter for the former, the House of Lords was unable to say that Mr Grogan had acted *malo animo*. Grogan had not acted in such a way as to show distinctly that he knew the testator was beguiled and deceived. He had not betrayed that bond of friendship, he had not made and then betrayed an undertaking motivated by such friendship. The House of Lords reaches this conclusion by analysing Grogan's behaviour as not showing 'complicity'[59] in getting the will made. Grogan had acted 'honestly', said Lord Hatherley. He had not in any way brought about the state of things. '[U]pon being left for half and hour with his dying friend he was informed, for the first time, of his having left him his whole property, and his first impression, like that of an honest man, was "is the thing right?" In reply to which, he is told that it must necessarily be so.' Grogan's behaviour, says the court:

> Upon finding himself placed in a position which is in no way of his own seeking, and finding this letter of his friend, he has, to the best of his judgment, carried those instructions to effect, with the desire, doubtless, of doing that which he would think it right and reasonable to do, though under no possible legal obligation to effectuate intentions which were not properly and legally conveyed to him.

The intention of the testator was to persuade Grogan (voluntarily, but without any legal obligation, the court concludes) to create himself as a 'second self'

---

58   (1969) LR 4 HL 82, p 88.
59   *Ibid*, p 93.

for Craig. Grogan had not let his friend down because, the court says, Craig had clearly contemplated the possibility of Grogan not making any of the gifts. Grogan, in fact, deciding not to do so, was, therefore, not a betrayal of friendship. It is interesting that the court gives little weight to the fact that Grogan distributed some of the money.[60]

Blackwell v Blackwell is the cardinal 1929 decision of the House of Lords which recognised the semi-secret trust. Blackwell's deserted widow and son sued his male friends and semi-secret trustees for a declaration that there was no valid trust of a legacy given to the trustees 'for the purposes indicated by me to them'. The purposes were to provide for Blackwell's long time 'mistress' and 'natural' child. The testator gave detailed oral instructions to one of the trustees, followed by a signed confirmatory memorandum, naming and giving information about the beneficiaries. The House explains that Blackwell had been ill for several weeks and the court notes that he was 'much concerned as to how he should make provision for the woman and her child without disclosing all the circumstances in his will'. He 'expressed his anxiety to his friends' and they agreed to act as trustees.

McCormick v Grogan did not govern the situation. As Lord Buckminster stated: 'the real difficulty lies in considering whether the fact that the will itself made plain that the gift is fiduciary destroys the principle upon which oral evidence has been admitted to show the nature of the gift purporting to be absolute and beneficial.' It was urged, as had been stated in *McCormick*, that the underlying principle was that the legatee cannot himself profit by his own fraud, a principle that did not apply where the legatee's interest is patently fiduciary. Indeed, as discussed above, Lord Hatherley LC had pointedly supported this position in the *McCormick* case.[61]

In *Blackwell*, however, Lord Buckmaster reasoned that, in either case (secret or semi-secret), the real beneficiary is equally defrauded and, more centrally, the 'faith on which the testator relied is equally betrayed'. Buckmaster considered there was no difficulty in this, saying 'the personal benefit of the legatee cannot be the sole determining factor in considering the admissibility of the evidence'. How, in the semi-secret trust situations, is faith 'personally' betrayed? There can be no *malus animus* on the trustee's part. There is only a frustration of expectations, yet the court still labels the fraud as 'personal' in the semi-secret trust situation.

By not allowing the purpose of the promise to be frustrated, the reasoning in *Blackwell* amounts to a recognition of the 'simple principle of enforcing the

---

60 *Ottaway v Norman* [1971] 3 All ER 1325.

61 See *McCormick v Grogan* (1969) LR 4 HL 82, p 89. Lord Hatherley had stated in *McCormick* that, as secret trusts allow a 'wide departure from the policy of the Statute of Frauds' they should only be recognised 'in clear cases of fraud ... cases in which the court has been persuaded that there has been a fraudulent inducement held out on the part of the apparent beneficiary in order to lead the testator to confide to him the duty which he undertook to perform'.

equitable obligations binding a man's conscience'[62] within a friendship. The powerful and classical (though problematic) concept of 'the intention of the testator' seems, in this analysis, to be left to one side.[63] Is this because the court is uncomfortable with the intention of secrecy and so must justify the effectuation of secrecy by clothing it in the moral cloak of faithfulness within friendship? Why should the undertaking be sanctified, be given such a powerful effect, be allowed to displace transparency and potentially to defeat the expectations of (usually) the spouse and next of kin? Do they reflect values which male courts react to protect on the basis of an emotional response to an experience of male bonds of friendship? If so, are such values, or have such values been, at odds, in practical terms, with distributive justice within families[64] or other personal relationships? The historical context of the Victorian secret trust and semi-secret trust cases, and the language used to describe the interaction between testator and legatee, suggests that one reason the promise is given such effect is that it is a promise between men. Moreover, it is about a man's perceived right to control other people through disposition or potential disposition of property. Such activity by Victorian men was an activity which, implicitly, men are fit to do and which it is proper for them to do according to their own judgment.[65] Transfer of such judgment is the business of men. An abiding characteristic of the bond between the testator and the trustee is a motivation to keep secret, power over property. The secret exercise of power or the exercise of secret power is a paramount value exhibited by secret trusts and semi-secret trusts. It is a value that historically operated from the context of patriarchy.[66]

EQUITY'S INTERPOSITION

The beneficiary under a secret trust is said to take dehors the will and not under it. What, then, is the relationship between the Wills Act 1837 and the

---

62 Are the equitable obligations that bind a man's conscience the same as bind a woman's? See the arguments in Hobby, Chapter 11, and Dunn, Chapter 9, in this volume, regarding the different styles and concerns of women as employees (in whistleblowing cases), and as charitable trustees.

63 Oakley, 1997, p 245, writing on constructive trusts, criticises the 'failure' of Lord Buckmaster's analysis in *Blackwell v Blackwell* 'to observe the intentions of the testator and the destruction of the beneficial interest', saying that it is 'deceptively simple' and 'completely circular'. Only when, contrary to the Wills Act, the terms of trust are admitted, can the testator's wishes or intentions be the terms of the trust and can those entitled be the beneficiaries. The justification for admitting the evidence is only possible after the evidence is admitted.

64 See, generally, Green, 1988. See, also, Smart and Brophy, 1988, p 10.

65 'Men have been constituted as beings who can govern (or protect) themselves, and if a man can govern himself, then he also has the requisite capacity to govern others': Pateman, 1998, p 249.

66 See Smart, 1989, pp 85–88 for a general discussion on law and patriarchy.

secret trust? Fleming[67] suggested that even though the trust is outside the will, it is dependent and conditional upon it.[68] In respect of fully secret trusts, the beneficial and absolute gift will pass to the legatee in accordance with the will. However, Fleming argues[69] that having permitted him to take under the testamentary instrument, at law, equity then interposes itself and compels him to apply it in accordance with the trust arising by reason of his undertaking.[70]

The view of Viscount Sumner in *Blackwell v Blackwell* was that secret trusts operate wholly outside the will or intestacy. Oakley's view is that this is the only principle capable of explaining both secret and semi-secret trusts. If the trusts operate wholly outside the will or intestacy, probate rules are inapplicable; there is then no problem with the introduction of oral evidence to prove the trust because trust law has no problem with oral evidence. Oakley concludes that failure to observe the testator's intentions ('personal fraud') is, therefore, not a justification for either secret or semi-secret trusts. Enforcement is 'dependent upon fraud only to the extent that the basic duty of trustees to carry out their obligations as such is dependent on general equitable principles'.[71] Moffat, however, while recognising the pragmatism of the *dehors* the will solution, seems to question whether it can be reconciled with equitable principles or the policy of the Wills Act 1837.[72]

As much controversy as has attended the question of the doctrinal justification for secret and semi-secret trusts has attended their classification. It is not intended to provide a detailed account of the debate, but a summary of it may be useful. Moffat says that the balance of academic opinion is that both secret and semi-secret trusts are express trusts.[73] In both cases, they are the product of the testator's act, whether this act is called a 'declaration' or not. They are both then constituted by the transfer of the property to the trustee and therefore not imposed by the court. Oakley is amongst those arguing that

---

67 Fleming, 1947, p 28.

68 Since equity does not interpose until the will takes effect, it is argued, the trust is dependent upon, but is not part of, the testamentary instrument. This argument puts paid to the confusing aberrant basis, suggested in both some secret and semi-secret trust cases, that the trust was incorporated into the will.

69 Fleming, 1947, p 28.

70 Further, as *ibid*, p 29 explains, '[s]ince equity imposes its power at the moment when the interest passing under the will has reached the legatee, an attempted communication after the death of the testator is altogether nugatory'. This explains why, as discussed previously, communication and acceptance of the trust prior to the time of the property devolving to the legatee at law are essential to its validity in equity. It also follows that a memorandum prepared by the testator but not communicated to the legatee in the testator's lifetime cannot be admitted. See *Wallgrave v Tebbs* (1855) 2 K & J 313. On the other hand, the tender of a letter to the legatee in the testator's lifetime, even though with a request not to open it until after death, amounts to sufficient communication and acceptance of the trust. The trustee had the means of knowing the terms of the trust. See *Re Boyes, Boyes v Carrit* (1849) 16 Sim 476.

71 Oakley, 1997, p 249.

72 Moffat, 1999, p 119, fn 4.

73 *Ibid*, p 119.

they are both express trusts and, indeed, that as such they are subject to s 53(1) of the Law of Property Act 1925.[74] Sheridan, however (writing half a century ago), argued that they are juridically distinct.[75] The secret trust, he said, is a constructive trust. The semi-secret trust has to be an express trust; it is expressly created.[76] Like other constructive trusts, they arise where, by a representation, a person obtains property which it would be inequitable for him to keep. (In this respect, the will is irrelevant.) While most secret trusts arise in the context of a testamentary disposition, it:

> ... makes no difference to the rule whether the instrument of transfer is testamentary or an inter vivos conveyance or by operation of law. In any case where a person obtains property by fraud or by the abuse of a fiduciary position, he is bound to hold the property on trust for the person with the best equity. The fact that the transaction is secret does not make it different in principle. It is but one illustration of the broad principle of constructive trust.[77]

In respect of semi-secret trusts, Sheridan's view was that they are express trusts, but that the question then arises whether or not the nomination of the beneficiary is a 'testamentary operation'.[78] His conclusion about the classification of semi-secret trusts is that they are 'a strange third institution ... an express trust partaking of some of the rules of constructive trust'.[79]

USEFUL SECRETS: MODERN SECRET TRUSTS CASES

The tangled controversy surrounding the whole doctrinal basis and classification of secret and semi-secret trusts has not led courts of equity to eschew them. Nor has it led to their merger into a broad principle of constructive trust, remedial or 'institutional'. While there are fewer cases of secret trusts involving secrecy within personal relationships, the theory of secret trust is still occasionally useful. *Gold v Hill* provides some indication of modern courts' willingness to use the 'hook' provided by the secret trust situation in analogous contexts. There is also some indication that the secret trust has moved now into the commercial sphere.

Moffat contrasts the two significant modern secret trust cases, *Re Snowden* with *Ottaway v Norman*.[80] *Re Snowden* can perhaps be seen as a modern

---

74 Law of Property Act 1925, s 53(1)(b) requires that creation of a trust be manifested and proved in writing.

75 Sheridan, 1951, p 324. Austin seems to have agreed. See Finn, 1985, p 196.

76 See Oakley's discussion of Hayton's view that fully secret trusts are constructive, 1997, p 261, fn 73.

77 Sheridan, 1951, p 324.

78 Sheridan points out that Holdsworth did not think that it was.

79 Sheridan says also that they partake of some of the rules of incorporation.

80 Moffat, 1999, p 129.

McCormick v Grogan, in which the testatrix was a wealthy woman, like Abraham Walker Craig, unable to decide how to provide for a range of near and distant relations, who attempted to constitute her older brother, Bert, a 'second self'. Six days before her death, she made her brother her residuary legatee, but the brother died six days after her own death, leaving his entire estate to his son. The written records of the testatrix's vacillations consisted of a number of attendance notes prepared by her solicitors, at least one of which reflected a conversation between the testatrix and the brother. One of the notes stated:

> She thought the easiest way would be to leave the legacies to her nephews and nieces and others of different amounts to suit their needs and her wishes for them, and for what was left to be divided ... between nephews and nieces equally. She said she would like the residue left to ... Bert and he could see everybody and look after the division for her. She turned to him and said, 'You would see to it for me wouldn't you Bert'. He replied, 'Of course, dear, if you want me to'.

Two later affidavits recorded that the testatrix had said that her brother 'would know what to do' and that he had agreed 'to deal with everything for her' and that he 'was perfectly aware of how [she] wished him to distribute the money'. Megarry VC, quoting at length from the judgment of Christian LJ in the Court of Appeals in *McCormick*, decided that the testatrix had not imposed a trust obligation on her brother:

> The picture which seems to me to emerge from the evidence is of a testatrix who for long had been worrying about how to divide her residue and who was still undecided ... She therefore left her residue to ... her trusted brother, more wealthy than she and a little older ... I cannot see any real evidence that she intended the sanction to be the authority of a court of justice and not merely the moral conscience of her brother. I therefore hold that her brother took the residue free from any trust.

Megarry's attention to the fact that Bert was both older and wealthier than the testatrix provokes the question of whether it would have made a difference if he was poorer, younger – or female. Moffat queries whether the result of the case might have been different if Bert had survived the testatrix longer and had sued for directions.[81] A more productive issue concerns whether there was a stronger indication of intention to create a secret trust in *Ottaway v Norman* than in *Re Snowden*. The testator in *Ottaway*, a widower, had lived as man and wife with Miss Hodges for 30 years. He had a son by his marriage in whose presence he told Miss Hodges that he would leave the bungalow (in which they both lived) to her for life, but that she should leave it to the son on her death. Miss Hodges seems to have agreed to the arrangement and, following the testator's death, she made her own will consistently with it. Later, she became friendly with Norman and his wife, fell out with the son

---

81 Moffat, 1999, p 133, fn 4.

over proposed alterations to the bungalow, and changed her will to favour the Normans. The Court of Appeal (Brightman J) recognised the creation of a secret trust, a binding obligation on Miss Hodges, notwithstanding that there was evidence the testator considered and rejected the option of setting up an express trust (because he had complete confidence that she would do as told).

Two aspects of *Ottaway* are crucial to the difference of the result in that case and in *Re Snowden*. One, of course, is that there was more direct evidence of what the testator wished the destination of the real property to be (though there was much less certainty about the subject matter of other property, furniture and fittings, which the court also found fell into the secret trust). The other difference is that, unlike the nieces and nephews of the testatrix in *Re Snowden*, Ottaway's son relied on the understanding; it was not secret from him. The court, however, does not discuss the son's reliance.

In *Gold v Hill* (1999),[82] the deceased nominated Mr Gold as beneficiary under an employment-related insurance policy. Later, in a conversation over drinks before dinner at a hotel, the deceased told Gold of the nomination and that he should use the proceeds of the policy to look after the deceased's 'mistress' and children. There was conflicting evidence of the date of the conversation. Moreover, the deceased had, in making the nomination of Gold as beneficiary, described Gold's relationship to him as his 'executor', although the executor of the deceased's previously prepared will was, in fact, Mr Hill. During the conversation, the deceased told Gold that he was going to Nigeria (on somewhat risky oil exploration work), that his firm was arranging very substantial insurance and that he had made Gold the beneficiary of this insurance. The deceased then said: 'If anything happens to me you will have to sort things out – you know what to do – look after Carol [the 'mistress'] and the kids. Don't let that bitch [the wife] get anything.' The High Court found that Gold held the proceeds of the insurance policy as a constructive trustee for the mistress and children, *on analogy with the law relating to secret trusts*:

> [T]his is a useful analogy. The nomination, like a testamentary disposition, does not transfer or create an interest until death. It is consistent with the principle in *Blackwell v Blackwell* that the nominee should take under the rules of the policy, but then be required to 'apply it as the court of conscience directs and so, to give effect to the wishes of the testator'. Such doubts as there may be in the case of testamentary dispositions, as to the effectiveness of an intention communicated after the execution of the will, appear to be derived from the particular rules applying to wills. There is no reason why they should create similar difficulties in the case of nominations. Since the nomination has no effect until the time of death, it should be sufficient that the nature of the trust is sufficiently communicated prior to that time.

It is natural to wonder whether the court in *Gold v Hill* was willing to be persuaded by the analogy to the principles of secret trusts simply because the

---

82   [1999] 1 FLR 54.

situation in that case involved a 'mistress'. The conversation between the two male friends took place in a hotel bar, not a Victorian men's club, and the mistress was hardly a secret one in *Gold v Hill*. The use of the 'analogy' by the court suggests the power of the secret trust for a 'secret mistress' myth retains its vitality in our modern legal culture.

DONATIO MORTIS CAUSA AND PROPRIETARY ESTOPPEL

Donationes mortis causa, like secret trusts, can amount to informal wills and can be secret, though in neither case is secrecy between the donor and donee a necessary circumstance. A valid *donatio mortis causa* must satisfy three requirements: the property must be 'given' in contemplation (though not necessarily in expectation) of impending death; it must be conditional in the sense that it becomes absolute only upon death; and there must be delivery of the subject matter or the essential *indicia* of title (the manifestation of which will vary according to the character of the property). These requirements make the donatio a 'hybrid'[83] creature; it is neither *inter vivos* nor testamentary in nature.[84] Dominion over the subject matter must be transferred prior to death but absolute title only transfers at death.

The recognition by equity of the *donatio mortis causa* 'raises important questions of policy about succession on death'[85] because, like secret trusts, *donationes mortis causa* are obviously susceptible to fraud. The persistence and, indeed, the recent significant extension of the doctrine, in *Sen v Headley*[86] and *Woodard v Woodard*[87] are remarkable. The court in *Sen v Headley* recognised a *donatio* of a valuable London house, the main asset of the deceased. The donee was the deceased's companion and housekeeper and dominion was transferred when the donor slipped the keys into the donee's handbag. In *Woodard v Woodard*, a *donatio* of an Austin Metro was recognised where the keys to the car were given. The element of delivery sets *donatio* apart from secret trusts because, where there is very strong evidence of delivery, evidence of intention is strong. However, as argued by Borkowski and others,[88] the persistence of the doctrine may be explained by the very usefulness of *donationes* in circumventing the statutory formalities. *Donationes mortis causa*

---

83 Borkowski, 1999, p 3.
84 It is a 'singular form of gift of an amphibious', according to Buckley J in *Re Beaumont* [1902] 1 Ch 889, p 892. The *donatio mortis causa* has also been described as a *sui generis* category of property dealing, 'being neither completely *inter vivos* nor completely testamentary': Rickett [1989] Conv 184, p 189.
85 Borkowski, 1999, p 3.
86 [1991] 2 All ER 636.
87 [1995] 3 All ER 980.
88 Borkowski, 1999, p 3.

and secret trusts are legal institutions which 'recognise a deep felt need of mankind'.[89] This need is indeed very deeply felt; it is the need for secrecy.

Re Basham[90] was a case in which the plaintiff relied upon the principle commonly known as proprietary estoppel. Unlike the doctrine of secret trust, proprietary estoppel requires that the party claiming the property demonstrate detrimental reliance upon an understanding or belief encouraged by another as to her present or prospective ownership of property. This means that, unlike in the circumstance of secret trusts, the understanding cannot be secret from the person claiming the beneficial interest. The plaintiff in *Re Basham* was the stepdaughter of the deceased. There was abundant evidence that her stepfather had led her to understand that she would inherit his cottage upon his death, but he died intestate. In a judgment upholding the plaintiff's claim, Edward Nugee QC described the circumstances of proprietary estoppel as 'a species of constructive trust' based upon unconscionable reliance on legal rights,[91] and drew attention to the relationship between proprietary estoppel and secret trusts. Both doctrines involve the 'vesting of property in [a beneficiary] in the faith of and understanding that it will be dealt with in a particular manner'. In a secret or semi-secret trust case, the understanding is with the trustee. In proprietary estoppel, it may be between the ultimate beneficial owner and the donor.

'PIGEON HOLING' ANOMALIES OR BROAD PRINCIPLES?

The increasing overlap[92] between proprietary estoppel and the 'common intention constructive trust' has led to the claim that the distinction between them is 'illusory' and to inevitable calls for the recognition of a broad basic principle of unconscionability in English law.[93] Moffat describes the overlap as follows:

> There are indeed strong similarities between constructive trusts (at least of the 'expressed but informal agreement' type) and proprietary estoppel: the requirements of an agreement, arrangement or understanding that has been relied on to the plaintiff's detriment are mirrored in the requirements of assurance, reliance and detriment necessary for estoppel.[94]

---

89   Borkowski, 1999, p 3, quoting Baker, 'Unreliable assumptions in the modern law of negligence' (1993) 109 LQR 19.

90   [1987] 2 FLR 264.

91   [1987] 2 FLR 269. It was said that constructive trusts were used 'to prevent a person relying on his legal rights where it would be unconscionable for him to do so'.

92   See Lord Bridge in *Lloyds Bank v Rosset* [1990] 1 All ER 1111. In such a case, a 'constructive trust or proprietary estoppel arises'. See Moffat, 1999, p 473.

93   See Oakley, 1997, p 76; and Hayton and Marshall, 1996, p 373. '[I]t is time that the courts and counsel moved beyond pigeon holing circumstances into constructive trusts and equitable estoppels and concentrated upon the basic principle of unconscionability underlying both doctrines.'

94   *Ibid*, Moffat, p 473.

It has been suggested, however, that the two are distinguished by the extent of detrimental reliance.[95] Hayton has argued against the pigeon holing[96] of circumstances in which there is reliance on an understanding as to proprietary rights. A broad principle of unconscionability might enable courts to take into account the ways in which women in particular have (as the 'common intention' situations show) detrimentally relied upon such 'understandings'. On the other hand, broad principles foster broad judicial discretion. As is argued elsewhere in this collection, women are not necessarily benefited by the exercise of discretion. In some areas, codification has served women's interests better.[97] A broad principle of the remedial constructive trust may not serve women's interests because it sacrifices the proprietary rights basis of trusts.[98]

Where do the secret understandings in the context of which equity acts in secret and semi-secret trust situations figure in terms of the potential shift towards assimilation into broad principles? Despite the fact that secrecy can, and has, assisted particular women's interests, from women's perspective, the effectuation of secrecy in the law of property may understandably be viewed with a general suspicion. At the same time, where 'no single pattern of recovery predominates',[99] where the fabric of the law remains willing to accommodate doctrinally anomalous devices such as secret and semi-secret trusts and *donationes mortis causa*, equity retains the advantage of a pragmatic, yet principled, response to women's interests.

---

95 Browne-Wilkinson VC in *Grant v Edwards* [1986] Ch 688.
96 Moffat, 1999, p 474; and Hayton [1990] Conv 370, p 378.
97 See Hobby, Chapter 11, in this volume.
98 See Bottomley, Chapter 12, in this volume.
99 Moffat, 1999, p 475.

CHAPTER 5

WEAVING ALONG THE BORDERS: PUBLIC AND PRIVATE, WOMEN AND BANKS

Kate Green and Hilary Lim

... this blurring of boundaries, the mobilisation of intimacy and kinship for commercial purposes ... causes the problem for legal analysis in many cases involving third party guarantees.[1]

INTRODUCTION

Feminist interest in the legal and practical ramifications of the nook by the hearth, in legal terms the 'family home', as security for debt, particularly business debt, is considerable.[2] A typical story in this area of law goes like this: a man and a woman agree to live together, with or without the ties of marriage, and a family home is bought. His business gets into difficulties and he decides to take out a loan to keep him going over a hard time. Sometimes, however, the loan is less innocent: he may say it is for business purposes, but it may be to pay gambling debts, or for a holiday, and/or it might be for a sum much greater than he has told his domestic partner. The bank manager,[3] from experience, refuses to lend to him unless the woman with whom he shares the house agrees to sign the mortgage deed or to act as surety for his loan. This assumption of liability for a partner's debts has become widely known as 'emotionally' or 'sexually' transmitted debt.[4] Such debt is, of course, not limited to wives or female cohabitees, and the cases below illustrate this. However, we are choosing to focus on the positions of women who become sureties for a man's debt, since such cases are in the majority.

In most cases, of course, the loan is repaid and the business, and family income and family home, continue unchanged. However, if the loan is not repaid, the bank naturally seeks enforcement, and this means a forced sale of the land to repay the debt. The woman then is faced with not only the loss of her (partner's) income, but also the loss of her home. Many women who have signed such agreements and are trying to save their homes seek to rely upon either of two equitable doctrines: undue influence and misrepresentation. The

---

1 O'Donnell and Johnstone, 1997, p 47.
2 See, eg, Mackenzie, 1996; and de Than and Scoular, Chapters 10 and 6, in this volume.
3 We include in the word 'bank' also building societies and other lending institutions.
4 See Baron, 1995; and Fehlberg, 1994, 1996 and 1997.

rules about these doctrines have a very long history,[5] but a large number of such cases have come to court in the last two decades. As Lord Browne-Wilkinson commented in the House of Lords in the *O'Brien* case:

> The large number of cases of this type coming before the courts in recent years reflects the rapid changes in social attitudes and the distribution of wealth which has recently occurred. Wealth is now more widely spread. Moreover, a high proportion of privately owned wealth is invested in the family home. Because of the recognition of the equality of the sexes, the majority of matrimonial homes are now in the joint names of both spouses ... in order to raise finance for the business enterprise of one or other of the spouses, the jointly owned home has become a main source of security. The provision of such security requires the consent of both spouses.[6]

In relation to the doctrine of misrepresentation, a woman may argue, for instance, that her partner lied to her about the loan; in the famous case of *Barclays Bank v O'Brien*,[7] the husband told his wife that the loan in question was for less than half the actual amount. Lord Browne-Wilkinson, in another House of Lords' decision of the same year, *CIBC plc v Pitt*, defined misrepresentation as 'a species of fraud ... which prevents the wronged party from bringing a free will and properly informed mind to bear on the proposed transaction'.[8]

Alternatively, the woman may argue that she did not really consent, but acted under the man's undue influence. This is an elusive doctrine that resists 'attempts to pin it down'.[9] Recently, it has been stated that 'importunity and pressure, if carried to the point at which the complainant can no longer exercise a will of her own, amounts to undue influence, but pressure is neither always necessary nor always sufficient'.[10] There are two classes of undue influence: first, actual undue influence, where it is affirmatively proven on the evidence; and, secondly, presumed undue influence.[11] In the majority of decided cases, although not all, the person providing the surety has relied upon the second type, presumed undue influence.

This second class is divided into two categories. In the first, referred to in case law as category A, undue influence is presumed due to the existence of a special relationship, involving trust and reliance, such as religious superior and inferior, doctor and patient, or solicitor and client. It is well established

---

5   O'Donnell and Johnstone, 1997, pp 28–30, suggest that equity's whole intervention into unconscientious dealings has its roots in anti-semitism.

6   [1994] 1 AC 180, p 188.

7   *Ibid*.

8   [1994] 1 AC 200, p 208.

9   Birks and Chin, 1997, p 57.

10 *Royal Bank of Scotland v Etridge (No 2) and Other Appeals* [1998] 4 All ER 705, p 712F.

11 See *Bank of Credit and Commerce International SA v Aboody* [1990] 1 QB 923. This classification was adopted in *O'Brien* [1994] 1 AC 180.

that the list of special relationships does not include parents and children or husbands and wives.[12] Rejection of the idea that wives enjoy a 'special equity' arising out of the marital tie lies, according to the courts, in societal recognition of 'equality of the sexes'. The second of these two categories, usually known as category B, arises where a relationship, on the facts of the particular case, justifies the court in applying the same presumption because 'the complainant generally reposed trust and confidence in the wrongdoer'.[13] Lord Browne-Wilkinson explained in *O'Brien* that, while there is no presumption of undue influence as between husband and wife, 'many cases may well fall into ... Class 2(B) because [a] wife demonstrates that she placed trust and confidence in her husband in relation to financial affairs'.[14]

In the context of emotionally transmitted debt, therefore, there are in effect a number of ways in which the mortgage can be set aside as far as the surety is concerned, either wholly or in part. It is the role of the judges to decide whether the signature of the woman has been fairly obtained. The really decisive question is not, of course, whether the surety can set aside the transaction against the borrower, but whether a third party, particularly (for our purposes) the lender, will have to bear the loss.[15] This depends on whether this third party had actual or constructive notice about the wrong committed by the borrower. Constructive notice arises where the lender is 'put on inquiry' because of facts suggesting that the transaction was not in her interest and may depend upon whether she was, herself, 'on the face of it', benefiting from the loan.

It is in this way that most of the recent cases end up as a conflict between the surety and the bank. In practice, it is likely that all parties contributed to some degree towards the crisis, but their responsibility for it is not equal; the borrower is most likely to bear the greatest share of responsibility, the bank and the surety being less to blame. When the judges come to decide whether the bank had (constructive) notice of the borrower's wrongdoing, therefore, they are choosing between two relatively innocent victims.

It has frequently been pointed out that it is easy to detect a creditor-sympathetic approach on the part of the judiciary in the case law on emotionally transmitted debt, and this approach has been subjected to feminist critique on a number of grounds. It has, for example, been argued that the judges have failed 'to recognise the reality of gendered power

---

12 This was confirmed in *O'Brien* [1994] 1 AC 180.

13 *Ibid*.

14 *Ibid*, p 190.

15 In rare cases, the mortgagee may be deemed to owe a direct duty to the mortgagor, on the basis that the transaction amounts to an unconscionable bargain, but this is not readily found in the English courts. See *Credit Lyonnais Bank Nederland NV v Burch* [1997] 1 All ER 144, but as an illustration of the strict limits placed upon this principle, see *Portman Building Society v Dusangh and Others* (2000) (transcript: Smith Bernal); and *Barclays Bank plc v Coleman and Another* [2000] 1 All ER 385.

imbalance'.[16] Linked to this is the idea that the nature of decision making in the home, particularly about incurring secured debt, is obscured. Its details are invisible to law since it takes place in the private domain where law has no business to enter and no capacity to understand. However, these critiques are only a part of the story.

Our aim is to examine these cases in the context of the public-private divide, but rather than concentrating solely on the problems of the 'private', we seek to problematise also the 'public' realm. We argue, as have many others, that the curtain between public and private is ragged and shifting so that the private sphere is endlessly permeated by public values; further, we contend here that the public sphere is also permeable by the private. The family home is not simply private, and the bank is not simply public. In any discussion about protecting sureties who acted in the private and are being punished according to public values, the degree to which the bank also may have acted according to private values must also be taken into account.

'THERE SHE WEAVES BY NIGHT AND DAY'[17]

We approach the public-private divide as a dynamic, tangled aspect of the western world; for us, the two domains are always interconnecting, always in tension. Actions within the home are traditionally viewed through the curtain of the private sphere – thus, much is hidden, and what is exposed is only partial and, therefore, distorted. Understanding 'what they did and why' within the family home is limited by this curtain; some of these things perhaps can never be understood by strangers, but the whole area is more obscured so long as the weaving of the private itself is not noticed, for boundaries between private and public are not solid walls but, at most, curtains of thought, woven from racist, capitalist and patriarchal abstraction.

It is important to stress that, in our approach, the borders between public and private are never still and never finished – they are like a web, always 'floating wide'. The idea of the family, and the family home, is not the same across the whole population, and it changes over time, and each family itself also has its own different stages. Within the family home, women are also different from one another, and different at different times of their lives. In addition, like the family or women, the law is not fixed either: where private and public meet in cases concerning the family home, changing tensions and contradictions are clearly visible as time passes.

16 Kaye, 1997, p 55.
17 Tennyson.

The feminist story goes that women originated weaving, and the cloth (the curtain) was then turned around against them, folding them away from the 'real' world of men, the spaces of money and power. Thus, weaving can be used to symbolise the world of men and how they have used women.[18] Penelope of Greek legend is a typical weaver in the books written by men – staying faithful to her husband and keeping unwanted suitors away by hiding behind her dutiful weaving and unweaving: she weaves in his service and also unweaves in loyalty to him. There are many others too. Our favourite is Tennyson's *Lady of Shalott*,[19] alone in her solitary tower, 'imbowered' in a 'silent isle':

> There she weaves by night and day
> A magic web with colours gay ...
>
> And moving thro' a mirror clear
>
> That hangs before her all the year,
> Shadows of the world appear ...

She can only see the world through the window, but can never stand at the window where the exterior and interior worlds meet, until she breaks the spell by looking directly at a man and the town beyond him, and then:

> Out flew the web and floated wide
> The mirror crack'd from side to side
> 'The curse is come upon me!' cried
> The Lady of Shalott.

The penalty in the poem is her death – a dire warning to women to keep their gaze averted from the real world, to stay in their place. A woman who enters

---

18 Plant, 1995, p 60, relying on Irigaray, in Freudian terms, says: 'Weaving imitates the concealment of the womb: the Greek hystera; the Latin matrix ... Woman is veiled ... she sews herself up with her own veils, but they are also her camouflage. The cloth and veils are hers to wear: it is through weaving that she is known, and behind which she hides. This is a concealment on which man insists: this is denial of matter which has made culture – and his technologies – possible.'

19 The Lady of Shalott has been painted repeatedly, usually either 'embowered in her tower' or in her boat, particularly by the pre-Raphaelites and artists who were inspired by them. William Holman Hunt, John William Waterhouse and Sidney Harold Meteyard painted her, for instance. Nelson, 1979, has pointed out that the Waterhouse and Meteyard paintings show the 'embowered woman's erotic appeal ... suggested by the fact that both women stretch to relieve muscles cramped from long and tedious hours of weaving', a semi-reclining figure depicted in luxurious surroundings. The nature of these paintings is undoubtedly connected to the most obvious trope of Orientalism, the harem. William Holman Hunt described himself as having 'oriental mania'. The Orient was, however, a fantasy; see Landow, 1982. Elizabeth Siddal, who was married to Dante Gabriel Rossetti, drew the Lady of Shalott in a way in which we prefer to think of her. Nelson, 1979, describes the drawing thus: '... looking over her shoulder through the window into the exterior world as the web bursts and the mirror cracks in an austere room with a bare wooden floor.' Nelson comments that 'Siddal seems to define her by what she does, whereas Waterhouse defines the Lady by her room appointments and her romantic longings and Meteyard defines her as a sensual being whose whole existence centers upon erotic desires'.

the public world cannot go on living – at least, living as a woman, for, if she comes into the world, she must die or pass as a man. However, in the margins of the poem there is more than just the Lady in her tower. The river encircles her island, and the fields and the town lie nearby: in her mirror, she sees the workers and travellers, hears their music, and they hear hers. In addition, in order for the curse to work, there must at least be visitors to this tower, to enable her to go on weaving. The focus on the private tends to obscure the way in which the two worlds are not separate, but inevitably interwoven.

AN OLD PARADIGM; THE PUBLIC/PRIVATE DIVIDE

> Simply to move into the world, without planting one's roots there, and with no protection for one's belonging to oneself, is a mode of being in the world that men want for women. To enter the world, that world at that time, is a way of accepting a place and role that the world of men has provided: men reserve the whole world to themselves, and assign to women a nook by the hearth. But then this nook becomes a space that is impenetrable to the motives of the world, a hearth of one's own.[20]

Engaging with the ideology of the public and the private as material and metaphorical spaces involves, as Davidoff writes, 'grappling with [a] ... complicated web of structures, meanings, and behaviours' working on 'a number of different levels':[21]

> ... public and private are not (and never have been) 'conceptual absolutes' but a minefield of 'huge rhetorical potential' ... which have ... had powerful material and experiential consequences in terms of formal institutions, organizational forms, financial systems, familial and kinship patterns, as well as in language. In short they have become a basic part of the way our whole social and psychic worlds are ordered, but an order that is constantly shifting, being made and remade.[22]

It has been argued that 'the "public" and the "private" rarely confront each other so starkly'[23] as in this field of emotionally transmitted debt, where private actions in the family home are being judged by public values – rationality over altruism, competition over co-operation, individual over community, men over women. For example, Kaye argues that '[w]hen the law considers the arrangement it is in the context of a public dispute between the bank and the woman (and possibly her male partner).[24] She points to the Australian Law Reform Commission's observation that 'a woman who signs a

---

20 Cavarero, 1995, p 18.
21 Davidoff, 1998, p 165.
22 *Ibid*, p 165.
23 Oldham, 1995, p 104, quoted by Kaye, 1997, p 37.
24 *Ibid*, Kaye, p 37.

guarantee as a result of a "private" relationship may not be well served by a law that only deals with "public" commercial dealings'.[25] The border between public and private 'distorts a more complex reality'[26] and '... can be used as a shifting boundary by the socially powerful as a means of protecting their own interests ... [and] rendering disadvantage of the less powerful invisible'.[27] The public-private dichotomy is not a mere statement of difference: the difference matters because the public is economically and politically more important than the private.

Understanding 'what happens' behind the veil of the private family home is supposed to be hard to grasp in public terms. By definition, the public set of values and assumptions about human nature offers the only understanding of the world we – you, our distant readers and us – can share as strangers; we rely on notions of individual autonomy and hierarchy because that is how we are supposed to communicate as strangers. The same is true for the judges: the only values supposedly shared between them and the people facing one another in court are those of the public world. They have made no promises to care for one another, no shared history of trust and dependency and no dream of a common future, so the assumptions in this world of strangers must be those of the market place. Therefore, if a case emerges out of the family home into the public world, the judges have to apply a law based on public values of rationality, individuality and self-interest to actions which took place in the private; they have to judge 'the tenderest exchanges of a common law courtship'[28] by the formal rules made for strangers. While men's speech and actions can thus appear transparent to the law, the speech and actions of women tend to be rendered private and unknowable.

There is also a taken-for-granted link between the idea of privacy in political terms and the idea of a private space in physical or geographical terms. To treat public and private spheres as if they were actual spaces – as most writers in practice do – creates unnecessary confusion when they are applied to a 'real' house. It solidifies the abstraction into bricks and mortar in the mind of the reader and this, too, reinforces the tendency to see the family home as an 'undifferentiated unit'[29] beyond the public world. A further effect of this is, of course, to reinforce the silent isle inhabited by proper women.

Undoubtedly, Fehlberg's well known empirical research,[30] together with a series of key articles by the same author, has been inspirational to feminist commentators in this field.[31] Fehlberg defines the public-private divide as: a

25   Australian Law Reform Commission, 1994, p 206, quoted in Kaye, 1997, p 37.
26   Fehlberg, 1997, p 271.
27   *Ibid*, p 15.
28   Waite J in *Hammond v Mitchell* [1991] 1 WLR 1127, p 1139.
29   Jackson and Moore, 1995, p 2,
30   Fehlberg, 1997.
31   Fehlberg, 1994; 1995; 1996.

'division of the world into a strictly limited "public sphere" which is appropriate for regulation either by the state or the market, and a "private sphere" which is unregulated'[32] and left alone. The law is based on the culture of the public realm; its rules govern the relationships of strangers who are in competition with one another over limited resources. The subject of the law is the rational, self-interested individual and, to this extent, land law is 'men's law'. The family home, on the other hand, is taken to be the site – beyond any other – where the values of co-operation, trust and interdependence operate, separated off from the harsh world beyond the garden gate; if there is any law here, it is 'women's law'.

Fehlberg argues further that 'it is against ... a typical background lack of information about the transaction, lack of clear communication by professionals and a sense of intimidation experienced by sureties in the presence of professionals, that the current operation of the law in this area should be considered'.[33] This conclusion was drawn from her discussion of the nature of power in the family and the effects this had upon women's individual decisions to guarantee the debts of their partners. The fact that women earn, on average, less than men, take a greater share of responsibility for day to day management of the home, thereby working longer hours for less return, ensure that most men will enjoy greater economic and social freedom, status and sense of worth.[34] Pahl also contends that the 'key issue is the link between money and power, which is as real inside the household as it is outside it'.[35] The general picture that emerges from Fehlberg's research is that 'where household income is low the finances are likely to be controlled and managed by the wife. At higher income levels the husband is likely to control finances, especially if he is the only earner, though he will usually delegate management of part of the household income to his wife.'[36]

As far as the woman's 'agreement' to using the house as security is concerned, Fehlberg quotes, for instance, a typical wife's response: 'The issue of choice never crossed my mind ... It was just assumed that I'd sign. It was natural to do so.'[37] This is so even where the woman is clear that her signature might, in the end, mean the loss of her home: 'In reality there is very little one is able to do ... They would stop [my husband's] business from trading, our

---

32 Fehlberg, 1997, p 15.

33 Fehlberg, 1996, p 685.

34 Evidence for this continuing inequality is provided by Charles, 1995, p 108, who shows that the public primacy of (men's) paid work appears to make it ideologically necessary for women to provide a meal which fits his tastes and which is prepared for a time which suits him. Charles shows that, still, '[t]he main meal of the day [is] eaten at a time which [fits] with men's hours of work, usually in the evening' and this again reinforces the importance of the position of the breadwinner.

35 Pahl, 1995, p 37.

36 Pahl, 1989, p 168.

37 Fehlberg, 1996, p 689.

income would disappear, and we would have no means of support.'[38] Sometimes, of course, the woman's 'consent' will be the result of overt intimidation and violence, as in the recent case where a wife said: 'He liked to intimidate me – he used to slap me and pull my hair.'[39] Sometimes, the 'agreement' may not arise from 'any imbalance of power between the parties, or, even, the vulnerability of one to exploitation because of emotional involvement', but it may be a 'reflection of no more or less than the trust and confidence each has in the other'.[40] Another very real response to the use of the home as security against debt is the feeling that: 'It will never happen; it's just signing a piece of paper.' This may well be the view of both women and men faced with the decision to-sign-or-not-to-sign. Such an attitude might possibly lie at the root of the 'primary defence' raised in one recent case by a couple who had given personal guarantees for loans for a company of which the husband was a director, running into millions of pounds. The defence was that 'the guarantees were given for comfort only and were not intended to be enforced'.[41] These remarks indicate a particular kind of 'decision making' that does not fit easily with received views of rational self-interested behaviour on the part of the autonomous individual.

However, we do not simply see the 'family home', within the ideology of the public-private divide, as a place where everyone is irrational, and that this intimate space is oppressed by the public – or that men (and banks) necessarily oppress women. To focus solely on the private tends to locate altruism, love and interdependence, equality and sharing in the home, but in reality, many family members are in competition with one another, while many contracting partners in the business world enjoy long term relationships of trust.[42] Rather, we see the family home as a point of intensity where public and private cultures meet. The curtain between the two is inherently not only shifting, but permeable, for physical and imaginary resources continuously pass from public to private and back again. Goods produced to a greater or lesser extent according to either set of values or assumptions, public or private, circulate endlessly, just as they do through the Lady of Shalott's tower. Many women are involved in homeworking, particularly in garment

---

38 Fehlberg, 1996, p 694.

39 *Bank of Credit and Commerce International SA (In Liquidation) v Hussain and Another* [1999] All ER (D) 1442. She admitted to signing many documents during her marriage, but said that she didn't 'want to have anything to do with it', that 'she was unhappy doing it' and 'never read any documents', but '[w]hen he told me to sign things I did'.

40 *Garcia v National Australia Bank Ltd* (1998) 72 ALJR 1243, p 1246.

41 *Habib Bank Ltd v Jaffer and Another* (2000) (transcript: Smith Bernal). The judges are not oblivious to the important questions about the way in which decisions in the family are made. Eg, Lord Browne-Wilkinson based his judgment in *O'Brien* [1994] 1 AC 180, pp 190–91, to a large extent upon the fact that sexual and emotional ties between the parties 'provide a ready weapon for undue influence' because a woman's true wishes can easily be overborne because of her 'fear of destroying or damaging a wider relationship between her and her husband if she opposes his wishes'.

42 The point is made in discussions about relational theories of contract: Pohjonen, 2000.

manufacture and the production of decorations, cards and so forth. They may clean in other people's homes. Increasingly, more professional and academic jobs are being performed, with the aid of the computer, either wholly or partially in the home. The 'family business', too, ostensibly located in the public and operating according to its values, may also slide between the public-private divide. As Alcorso, in the course of a discussion about a small business sector in Australia, remarks: in this field, 'a clear-cut opposition between the work/family, public/private ... dualities does not exist'.[43]

The clearest example of this circulation is the way in which the home is now usually bought both for 'private occupation' and 'public investment', a mixture of self-interest and altruism. Homes moved inexorably into the marketplace in late 20th century England in a process of commodification which placed an emphasis upon 'exchange value benefits (investment value and capital gains)' such that housing is no longer 'regarded as an engine for social improvement', but a 'consumer good' like any other.[44] Further, 'housing choice and decisions to change dwellings are not just decisions about consumption or choice ... they involve decisions about investment, about using income available once essential needs have been met, about maximising net income and about return on savings'.[45] There may be many other 'reasons' for purchase too. For example, Thompson identified a number of themes about 'home' in conversations with 'migrant' women in Australia that were connected to home ownership. These were: 'home as a site of power in an alien Anglo culture; home as atonement for the pain of migration; and home as a symbol of success in a new society.'[46] The 'lack' which consumer goods like the home can 'fill' (at least temporarily) is a profound and complex product of contemporary forces.[47] Home ownership can be seen as a location where shared desire and individual calculation operate in harness; it is a product of them both, working together in multiple and interrelated ways.

The family home is, therefore, not 'a place beyond', but a place fully engaged with the values of both public and private spheres, one of many sites produced by the tension between the forces of public and private values. Approaches which focus on the family home as the private place tend to obscure the fact that the home is not the only place where public and private meet. Further, people themselves shuttle about between the two domains, and

---

43 Alcorso, 1993, p 98.

44 Madigan and Munro, 1990, p 29. Pawley, 1978, p 143, has argued that 'the evolution of consumer societies ... has transformed the meaning of home ownership and re-ordered the benefits which flow from it. Today [1978] a political majority of the population in Britain enjoys advantages which once belonged to a tiny minority, and the advantages themselves have changed from an assembly of privileges into a supply of products.'

45 Forrest and Murie, 1995, p 59.

46 Thompson, 1994, p 33, quoted in O'Donnell and Johnstone, 1997, p 100.

47 Deleuze and Guattari see 'desire' itself not as a natural product of family life, but as the product of the arrangement of the whole of society, with the family merely acting as 'the Oedipal machine': Goodchild, 1996, pp 100–05, 126.

may at any moment be acting according to public values based on rationality as well as on private values arising out of intimacy and dependency. In our analysis, therefore, the forces of public and private endlessly encounter one another both in specific locations and in the meanings human actors give to what they do.

WIVES AND BANK LOANS

A 'peculiar vulnerability'[48]

The two judgments of the House of Lords, *O'Brien* and *Pitt*, were delivered on the same day in 1994 by an identical group of Law Lords.[49] They have been subjected to in-depth analysis and extensive quotation, both by the judiciary and academics, but it is useful to summarise the facts and judicial reasoning in each case for they are illustrative both of the operation of the two equitable doctrines and difficulties surrounding emotionally transmitted debt. In *O'Brien*, the family home was a house in Farnham, Surrey, jointly owned by husband and wife, subject to a £25,000 mortgage. He was involved in a company which got into difficulties in 1987, eventually agreeing with the bank to extend his (existing bank) loan to £135,000 on the security of his house; he told his wife it was less than half this amount. She, his joint proprietor, had to be brought in to act as a guarantor for the loan. The bank manager sent a note to the local branch, advising the manager that there should be an interview where the couple were to be told the size of the loan and its terms, and that if there were any doubts, they should seek legal advice. However, these instructions, which conformed to the 1992 Banks' Code of Practice, were not followed. Mrs O'Brien was not told the effects of the documents and no one suggested she might take independent advice. She did not read anything, but simply signed it all, and was not given a copy afterwards.

When the company got into further difficulties, the husband could not repay the loan and the bank commenced possession proceedings for the house. Mrs O'Brien, in an effort to save her home, initially argued that the bank was bound by the undue influence and misrepresentation exercised by her husband. However, when the case reached the House of Lords, the undue influence claim was not being pursued.[50] It was held that the key to the issue

---

48 Bigwood, 1996, p 509.
49 Lord Browne-Wilkinson delivered both unanimous opinions.
50 It was rejected by the trial judge and in the Court of Appeal. The Court of Appeal decided that the bank was bound by her rights, but only to the extent that the loan exceeded the amount her husband had told her: she was still bound by the 'real' £60,000 surety agreement. The likely result of this would be that the home would still have to be sold, to raise the money to pay the husband's debt and the £60,000 she guaranteed out of her share of the proceeds; however, the rest of her share was her own.

was the doctrine of notice, that is, whether the bank ought to have inquired about the relationship and taken steps to minimise the likelihood of a successful claim of undue influence or misrepresentation. In doing so, they were clear that the family home needed to be capable of being used as security for a loan. They had to hold the balance fairly between, on the one hand, the vulnerability of the wife who relies implicitly on her husband, and, on the other hand, the practical problems of financial institutions.[51] It was important in their view that the family home should not become 'economically sterile'.[52] The bank was deemed to have sufficient notice of the dangers of the situation. Steps should have been taken by the lender to ensure that these dangers were minimised (as in the letter sent to bank's branch and the Code of Practice). Since the bank had failed to take 'reasonable steps', it was bound by her right to have the transaction set aside, although subject to the £60,000 that she knew about.

Lord Browne-Wilkinson set out guidance for cases such as these in future.[53] To summarise the key points in the decision: they were, first, that '[a] wife who has been induced to stand as surety for her husband's debts by his undue influence, misrepresentation or some other legal wrong has an equity as against him to set aside that transaction'.[54] Secondly, 'a creditor is put on inquiry when a wife offers to stand surety for her husband's debts ... [where] the transaction is not to the financial advantage of the wife' and 'there is a substantial risk' that, in procuring the wife's assent, 'the husband has committed a legal or equitable wrong'[55] such as undue influence or misrepresentation. Finally, 'unless the creditor who is put on inquiry takes reasonable steps to satisfy himself that the wife's agreement to stand surety has been properly obtained, the creditor will have constructive notice of the wife's rights'.[56] On this final point, Browne-Wilkinson LJ envisaged that a lender who wished to avoid being fixed with constructive notice, would arrange a personal interview for the wife 'with a representative of the creditor at which she is told the extent of her liability as surety, warned of the risk she is running and urged to take independent legal advice'.[57] He added that there may be 'exceptional cases' where additional information available to the lender might 'render the presence of undue influence not only possible but probable', where 'reasonable steps' would consist of an insistence 'that the wife is separately advised'.[58]

---

51 *O'Brien* [1994] 1 AC 180, p 197.

52 *Ibid,* p 188.

53 The failure of many banks to anticipate the guidelines may have led to many of the difficult Court of Appeal cases in the aftermath of *O'Brien.*

54 *O'Brien* [1994] 1 AC 180, p 195 .

55 *Ibid,* p 196.

56 *Ibid.*

57 *Ibid.*

58 *Ibid,* p 197.

In the second decision, *Pitt*, the facts were slightly different. Mr and Mrs Pitt, again, were joint owners of their home (her name having been added to the title some years after the purchase) in a London suburb, and it was subject to a building society mortgage. The value of the house at the time of the loan was about £250,000. The husband was keen to 'improve their standard of living' by speculation on the stock exchange and wanted to use their home as security to raise money for this. She was very reluctant and 'he embarked on a course of conduct putting pressure on Mrs Pitt which the trial judge held amounted to actual undue influence. In consequence, Mrs Pitt agreed to the suggestion'.[59] Her husband arranged a mortgage of £150,000 with the mortgage company. The latter was a subsidiary of Canadian Imperial Bank of Commerce and the mortgage was indicative of the globalisation of the British mortgage business in the late 1980s.[60] The loan was stated to be for paying off their existing mortgage and to purchase a holiday home.

For a short time, the husband's gambling proved extremely successful, but in the 1987 crash, he lost everything and possession proceedings began in late 1990. By July 1992, the total sum owing had risen, with interest, to £219,000, and this now exceeded the value of the house, which had fallen in the land market crisis. Mrs Pitt claimed undue influence and misrepresentation, arguing that her spouse had not only unfairly pressured her, but had used the loan, without informing her, for speculation beyond his original plans, and this made their home more vulnerable. The courts all agreed that she had been unduly influenced in signing the joint mortgage agreement. However, this did not necessarily mean that the bank was also bound. The House of Lords said that 'there was nothing to indicate to the plaintiff [mortgage company] that this was anything more than a normal advance to a husband and wife for their joint benefit'.[61] Between the two innocent victims of the lying husband, the bank and the wife, the bank won, the difference between this and *O'Brien* being that, on the face of it, in the latter case the wife was guaranteeing her husband's debts, while here, she was, on the face of it, getting her share of a joint loan to repay the existing mortgage and buy a second home. The message was that merely being a husband and wife (or cohabitees with emotional and sexual ties) is not sufficient on its own to put the lender on inquiry. There must be something more to suggest to the lender that the transaction is not directly in the wife's interest.

Perhaps if the story had ended there, our conclusion would have been that these two cases show that, for the judges, the home is not simply a private space, but one which can be both public and private depending on the situation. Women are not automatically imprisoned in a magic tower, for the judges are clear that the social recognition of women's equality rules out any

---

59   *Pitt* [1994] 1 AC 200, p 205.
60   See discussion below, pp 103–05.
61   *Pitt* [1994] 1 AC 200, p 211.

automatic privileging of them simply as wives or cohabitees. Nevertheless, because women can be subject to special pressures in the home, a relationship of cohabitation must be viewed with suspicion by lenders unless the woman appears to them as a real 'partner' in the deal. The law thus recognises women operating in public and private spheres and, to this extent, it facilitates a greater freedom for them, permitting them, when necessary, to rely on the oppressions of their imprisonment and at other times to leave it. Like the Lady of Shalott, if they leave the tower, they 'die' as (stereotypical) women and must act as rational, autonomous individuals. If they do not enter on a level playing field because of power imbalances in the private realm, only then does the law seek to protect them.

It does appear from the facts of *Pitt*, and general research on decisions in families, that Mrs Pitt did suffer as much, or more, at the hands of her husband as Mrs O'Brien did from Mr O'Brien, who won her case at least in part. However, the House of Lords held that she was not protected because the bank should only be bound by the man's wrongdoing in family cases if it ought, on the face of the deal, to have smelled oppression. It hardly seems fair on Mrs Pitt. However, if the only alternative is for all married women automatically to be 'protected' by being treated as vulnerable to oppression – and safely confined to their silent towers – we might accept that the woman should not win against the bank. In the end, we would rather be constructed as a person who can move in and out of private and public roles than as one who inevitably needs the particular tenderness of equity. We do not want always to be victims:

> A principle which accords to *all* married women a 'special equity' based on their supposed need for protection rests upon a stereotype of wives to which this court should give no endorsement. All persons of full capacity, including married women, should ordinarily conform to commercial transactions which they enter unless statute or judicial law affords relief ... it is offensive to the status of women today to suggest that all married women, as such, are needful of special protection supported by a legal presumption in their favour.[62]

The stigma of dependency at the beginning of the 21st century should not be doubted. Fraser and Gordon have argued that:

> With all legal and political dependency now illegitimate and with wives' economic dependency now contested, there is no longer any self-evidently 'good' adult dependency in postindustrial society. Rather, all dependency is suspect, and independence is enjoined by everyone. Independence, however, remains identified with wage labour. Everyone is expected to 'work' and to be 'self-supporting'. Any adult not perceived as a worker shoulders a heavier burden of self-justification.

---

62 *Garcia v National Australia Bank Ltd* (1998) 72 ALJR 1243, p 1258, Kirby J quoting Stephen J in *Gronow v Gronow* (1979) 144 CLR 513. The latter was commenting upon the presumption that a young child should be in the custody of its mother.

> With the formal dismantling of coverture and Jim Crow, it has become possible to claim that equality of opportunity exists and that individual merit determines outcomes ... postindustrial society appears to some conservatives and liberals to have eliminated every social-structural basis of dependency. Whatever dependency remains, therefore, can be interpreted as the fault of individuals.[63]

It is hardly surprising, therefore, that when the High Court of Australia in *Garcia* upheld the 'special protection' principle, one writer, Elizabeth Stone, should include in the title to her case commentary that famous 19th century litany, 'Infants, lunatics and married women'.[64]

This is the story that might have been, had *O'Brien* and *Pitt* been the end of the 'surge'[65] of case law, but it was not.

Recent developments

A seemingly never ending stream of cases, described by at least one writer as a 'flood',[66] followed the decisions in *O'Brien* and *Pitt*, involving not just husbands, wives, ex-husbands, ex-wives, partners and cohabitees, but also parents guaranteeing business loans for their children. In one situation, an employee's mortgage was providing security for a loan to her employer.[67] Pressures from the volume of cases have, according to one author, resulted in 'increasing signs of instability'[68] in the law and the judicial formulation, adopted in *O'Brien* and *Pitt* to deal with these cases, has proven 'problematic in its application'.[69] Decisions have, on balance, been overwhelmingly in favour of the banks[70] and it is difficult to avoid the conclusion that the Court of Appeal is wriggling to avoid *O'Brien's* more radical implications. A market-oriented approach, designed to limit the burdens upon banks, dominates.

The important questions raised in these cases are twofold: first, in what circumstances will the lender have constructive notice of the undue influence or misrepresentation; and, secondly, what steps can the lender employ to negate such notice? In the process of answering the first question, a number of courts have been concerned also to discover the exact meaning and extent of

---

63 Fraser and Gordon, 1997, p 36.

64 Stone, 1999.

65 Draper, 1999, p 176.

66 Dunn, 1995, p 326.

67 *Credit Lyonnais Bank Nederland NV v Burch* [1997] 1 All ER 144.

68 Tjio, 1997, p 10.

69 Fehlberg, 1997, p 15.

70 *Credit Lyonnais Bank Nederland NV v Burch* [1997] 1 All ER 144 is the most notable exception, although see *Bank of Cyprus (London) Ltd v Markou and Another* [1999] 2 All ER 707.

'manifest disadvantage' as a necessary ingredient in a case of presumed undue influence.

In the 1998 Court of Appeal decision in *Royal Bank of Scotland v Etridge (No 2)*,[71] Stuart-Smith LJ reviewed and attempted to rationalise the post-*O'Brien* case law. On the requirement that the transaction should be to the manifest disadvantage of the complainant, he expressed the view that '[i]t has been widely criticised'.[72] In a more recent Court of Appeal decision, Nourse LJ acknowledged that it was necessary to establish manifest disadvantage in any claim of presumed undue influence. However, he called for a re-examination of a concept which 'was difficult to apply' and upon which 'the authorities have now got into a very unsatisfactory state'.[73] He added that he had 'no disposition to enlarge its significance' and while it must be 'clear and obvious' it need not 'be large or even medium-sized'.[74]

A more important aspect of *Etridge (No 2)* was the detailed consideration given to the 'reasonable steps' regime, which led Giliker to conclude that 'the balance has tipped in the bank's favour'. Giliker concludes that, 'five years on' from *O'Brien*, 'the real issue is no longer one of balancing the interests of the bank and surety, but the interests of the surety/bank and solicitor'.[75] This view is based upon Stuart-Smith LJ's statement in *Etridge (No 2)* that 'there is a consistent line of authority' establishing the following:

> Where the wife deals with the bank through a solicitor, whether acting for her alone or for her and her husband, the bank is not ordinarily put on inquiry. The bank is entitled to assume that the solicitor has considered whether there is sufficient conflict of interest to make it necessary for him to advise her to obtain independent legal advice ... When giving advice to the wife the solicitor is acting exclusively as her solicitor ... It makes no difference whether he is unconnected with the husband or the wife ... or is also the husband's solicitor ... or that he has agreed to act in a ministerial capacity as the bank's agent at completion. Whoever introduces the solicitor to the wife and asks him to advise her, and whoever is responsible for his fees, the bank is entitled to expect the solicitor to regard himself as owing a duty to the wife alone when giving her advice ... If the solicitor accepts the bank's instructions to advise the wife, he still acts as her solicitor and not the bank's solicitor when he interviews her. [In addition t]he bank is entitled to rely on the fact that the solicitor undertook the task of explaining the transaction to the wife as showing that he considered himself to be sufficiently independent for this purpose ... [and t]he bank is not required to question the solicitor's independence ... or the sufficiency of the advice.[76]

---

71 *Royal Bank of Scotland v Etridge (No 2) and Other Appeals* [1998] 4 All ER 705.

72 *Ibid*, p 712.

73 *Barclays Bank v Coleman and Another* [2000] 1 All ER 385, p 396.

74 *Ibid*, p 399.

75 Giliker, 1990, p 613.

76 *Royal Bank of Scotland v Etridge (No 2) and Other Appeals* [1998] 4 All ER 705, pp 720–21.

As stated in a subsequent decision, the 'whole basis of the decision in *Etridge*, so far as lenders are concerned, is that they are entitled to expect a professional person to have done his job properly unless they know or have reason to believe that he has not done so'.[77] Not surprisingly, Giliker and a number of other commentators have predicted that litigation in the future will 'target solicitors'.[78] We have come a long way from Brown Wilkinson LJ's notion that 'reasonable steps' would involve a private interview at which the lender would advise the surety of the risks in, and implications of, the transaction. According to Stuart-Smith LJ, such an interview was 'not adopted in any of the cases before us', although it was 'fair to say they [were] all concerned with transactions which pre-dated *O'Brien*'.[79] The banks had, rather, 'contented themselves' with the requirement that the wife obtain independent legal advice and operated within the confines of their then existing Code of Practice.

Since the decision in 1998, the principles set out in *Etridge (No 2)* have been applied, to take just one example, in defeating the arguments raised by a woman in an action by a bank for possession of a flat registered in both her own and her husband's names. In *Bank of Credit and Commerce SA (In Liquidation) v Hussain and Another,*[80] the wife had executed a charge over the flat and signed an earlier guarantee to secure the liabilities of a company in which both parties to the marriage were interested, as shareholders and directors. The court established that the transactions were manifestly to her financial disadvantage and she signed them because of a catalogue of 'physical and emotional humiliation' inflicted upon her by the husband.[81] The advice she was given, from a legal executive,[82] took place in the presence of her husband and was, in the judge's words, not 'adequate to render inoperative the actual undue influence present'. In the case of the signing of the guarantee, it was the finding of the court that her meeting with the solicitor would not have been 'long enough for any meaningful advice (as opposed to information)'. The bank, it was said, with reference to *Etridge (No 2)*, 'was not obliged to inquire into the nature of the advice which those solicitors had thought proper to give, and its failure to require any kind of

---

77 *Royal Bank of Scotland v Rattan* (1999) (transcript: Smith Bernal).

78 Giliker, 1990, p 613. The Court of Appeal decision in *Kenyon Brown v Desmond Banks and Co* [1999] 1 All ER (D) 1270 may represent one of the first cases where a wife entering into an emotionally transmitted debt transaction was successful in establishing a breach of duty by her solicitor.

79 *Royal Bank of Scotland v Etridge (No 2) and Other Appeals* [1998] 4 All ER 705, p 719.

80 *Bank of Credit and Commerce International SA (In Liquidation) v Hussain and Another* [1999] All ER (D) 1442.

81 According to Hart J, she 'lived in fear' of her husband, with whom 'life was only tolerable if she did his bidding'.

82 On the particular point that a legal executive may give 'independent legal advice' in this context, see the decision of the Court of Appeal in *Barclays Bank v Coleman* [2000] 1 All ER 385, p 401.

certification that proper advice had been given was irrelevant'. Nor did the 'fact that the solicitors were also retained by the Bank to report on title and attend to completion and registration ... alter the position'.

The legal discourse emerging from this case law has raised judicial concern, both inside and outside the court room. Millet LJ, for instance, stated that the situation in England 'is foreign to the traditional approach of a court of equity and is manifestly failing to give adequate protection to the wife or cohabitant who acts as surety'.[83] He was particularly concerned by the 'ritual reliance on legal advice' which was a consequence of the 'reasonable steps' regime confirmed in *Etridge (No 2)*. Millet LJ also argued that any assumption 'that the surety has received adequate legal advice' is one that 'the bank almost always knows to be false'.[84] O'Sullivan has also argued that, in this area, 'the banks are entitled to expect, and indeed to rely on, conduct from a solicitor which is highly unlikely to be acceptable elsewhere in the law'.[85] In support of this contention she referred to the dissenting judgment of Hobhouse LJ in *Banco Exterior Internacional SA v Mann*[86] as evidence of judicial unease with this state of affairs.

The more recent statements of Clarke LJ in *Woolwich plc v Gomm*[87] and another are also pertinent. In this case, a woman had executed a mortgage over her home in favour of the bank, which was not to her financial advantage, because she was under the presumed undue influence of her former husband. She was described by the Court of Appeal as 'being of vulnerable disposition',[88] 'malleable in the hands of her unscrupulous former husband', and 'in need of firm independent advice to save her – and the children – from the financial machinations of [her] dishonest' ex-husband. Clarke LJ admitted to 'doubt' concerning the conclusion that the bank should prevail. He expressed 'sympathy' for her and admitted to a 'sinking feeling' that she did not get the advice from the solicitor which she so clearly needed. His judgment concluded with a question: 'Is it not high time that ... solicitors did a little more for their clients than mindlessly mechanical conveyancing?'

There is, no doubt, work to be done on this shift of focus from banks to solicitors. However, we wish to explore another aspect of the ragged boundaries between public and private. We want to explore whether it is inevitably the case that the interaction between lenders and sureties, and lenders and debtors, occurs predominantly in the public sphere according to values associated with the marketplace.

---

83   Millet, 1998, p 220.

84   *Ibid.*

85   O'Sullivan, 2000, p 100.

86   [1995] 1 All ER 936.

87   *Woolwich plc v Gomm and Another* [1999] All ER (D) 877.

88   She had been diagnosed as a schizophrenic, although her condition had stabilised by the relevant period of time.

BANKS AND BANK LOANS

The image of the bank in the 21st century

In 1979, Lord Denning said, in *Williams and Glyn's Bank v Boland and Another*:

> If a bank is to do its duty, in the society in which we live, it should recognise the integrity of the matrimonial home ... We shall not give monied might priority over social justice.[89]

The 'Big Bang' of 1986 and increased financial deregulation in Britain drew global (foreign) finance capital into the City of London, thus destroying some traditional British sense of being 'at home with its own money'.[90] High street banks, insurance companies and building societies are increasingly turning into identical remotely controlled conduits through which 'foreign' capital enters our lives. In the last quarter century, the increasing importance of 'global finance' and 'virtual money' has dominated the imaginations of some theorists, many of whom enjoy the frisson of the 'invasion' of this money, resonating, as it does, with some deep western fear of invasion by foreign bodies. Stanley, for instance, writes of the 'modern city' as 'dominated by the existential, the transient and the provisional', a 'site of transitory events, movements and memories'.[91] This postmodern, postcapital city is an unknowable and expanding rhizome, with no centre; its model is 1980s Los Angeles, where successive geographies of class and racial divisions create an apparently never ending landscape of alienation and violence.

From this standpoint, the 'home' financial market has been taken over by offshore financial game players, dominating the city just as their big buildings are increasingly dominating the physical landscape. The danger is that such writers themselves are caught up in the tornado and, like Dorothy, end up in the mythical Land of Oz. In fact, of course, the London Stock Exchange has never been the exclusive home of British money.[92] However, the view of the city as the temporary stopping place of uncontrollable gales of non-existent money gusting about global space, a virtual and exploding cash till, with all reality uprooted in the hyperreal circulation of empty signs, does have importance.

---

89 *Williams and Glyn's Bank Ltd v Boland and Another; Williams and Glyn's Bank Ltd v Brown and Another* [1979] 2 All ER 697, CA, p 706.

90 Budd and Whimster, 1992.

91 Stanley, 1996, p 6.

92 Leyshon and Thrift, 1997, p 26.

These fears interconnect with suspicions about the non-productive nature of 'money made out of money', for money now seems to be separated from land, industry and all understanding of reality.[93] In the new virtual space and time of money, new financial constructions are being developed 'at breakneck speed',[94] like the buildings in which they are traded. An important example (and especially relevant to mortgages) is the development of securitisation, which is 'the process in which pools of individual loans or receivables are packaged, underwritten and distributed to investors in the form of securities'.[95] In this way, '[g]lobal finance has the literal power to conjure profits from its own transactions devoid of the messiness of a real economy'.[96] The process began in the US in the early 1970s, and, for companies eager to expand the UK mortgage market, with its 'large and extremely stable market, superb arrears and default record', was seen as an 'obvious choice' because it 'had been operated as a cosy cartel by the building societies'.[97] The breakthrough into the UK mortgage market began in the mid-1980s. By 1988, over 8% of new mortgage loans were securitised.[98]

The electronic movement of virtual money can be seen as the effect, as well as the cause, of the increased circulation of credit and the concomitant dematerialisation of value and the alienation of money from things and people. Capital and information – money and social surveillance and control – flow together in this new urban jungle:

> Today we can see larger and larger areas of Western cities and countryside being transformed into either manageable risk zones, or managed fun ones, through both technological and political developments. Insurance companies regularly designate certain cities, and even areas of cities, as well as individuals, as high-risk, and therefore high-premium; commodifying abnormalities in both space and people's bodies in an ever increasing web of control.[99]

The history of money may be a history of 'increasing dematerialisation'[100] and the history of mortgages one of increasing distance between the mortgagor and the lender(s). Nevertheless, the 'material' of money, land and human relationships remains. The money involved in mortgages is increasingly 'virtual', but the effect of mortgages is still 'real'. Moreover, the society of risk

---

93 Stanley, 1996, p 77, quotes several examples, including Kroker and Cooke: '... money is caught in the grand cancellation of the sign of political economy. It finds itself homeless and constantly put to flight. It is abandoning the "worthless" world of contemporary capitalism'.

94 Thrift, 1996, p 217.

95 Bonsall, 1990, p 2.

96 Budd and Whimster, 1992, p 20.

97 *Ibid*, Bonsall, pp 3 and 5.

98 *Ibid*, p 9.

99 Shurmer, Smith and Hannam, 1994, p 294.

100 Leyshon and Thrift, 1997, p 21.

is, at the same time, a society of trust. As Simmel pointed out, money both separates us from real things by replacing them and also requires an increasing trust amongst people; money can 'only be sustained by social relationships of some depth'.[101]

The monied might of a faceless institution operating according to the alien rhythms of global markets presents one picture of lending institutions. Reading the case of *Portman Building Society v Dusangh and Others*[102] seems to confirm this. There, a 72 year old retired man, with 'poor English' and a very low income, granted a 25 year mortgage, for 75% of the value of his property, negotiated through an agent, to a building society, albeit with his son's guarantee. Simon Brown LJ, in the Court of Appeal, described this as 'commercially unwise', if not 'morally culpable', and noted that, in agreeing to the mortgage, the building society did not follow its own procedures, thereby failing to discover the borrower's illiteracy and poor understanding of English.[103] Ward LJ did suggest that, if one wished to make assumptions in favour of Mr Dusangh, it could be said that 'the building society in those heady days of rising property prices was lending money almost irresponsibly'. A view of 'monied might' which may be reinforced through suspicion of global finance. However, another picture of 'the bank' emerges from other recent case law on emotionally transmitted debt.

There's more than one kind of bank

Some of the cases demonstrate the ways in which 'intimacy', 'mutuality' and 'kinship' may spill over – in some not necessarily immediately obvious ways – into the public context of banking. The 'public' world in which banks and other lenders operate is not simply ruled by the values of self-interested individuals contracting at arm's length. For some people, the bank is an extension of home and kin, and some banks have been working to create such a niche for themselves in particular high streets. Two recent cases can be shown to illustrate this.

First, in *Bank of Cyprus (London) Ltd v Markou and Another*,[104] the bank manager, a Mr Christalides, issued an 'invitation' to Mr Markou to move his company account to the bank. John Jarvis QC states the following:

---

101 Leyshon and Thrift, 1997, p 37.

102 (2000) (transcript: Smith Bernal).

103 Mr Dusangh Senior was, however, unsuccessful in his appeal. He was unable to demonstrate that the bargain was unconscionable. The Court of Appeal did not think that the transaction was such as to 'shock the conscience of the court', but could be explained on the grounds of the affection Mr Dusangh felt for his son. The money was used as part of the purchase price for a supermarket which was not a success. Crucial evidence was that Mr Dusangh had been advised by a solicitor.

104 [1999] 2 All ER 707, p 709. As the court noted, Palmers Green is an area with a large Greek Cypriot community.

In 1989, Mr Markou met Mr Christalides. Mr Christalides was the manager of the Palmers Green branch of the bank and had been manager of that bank for a number of years. He is a very experienced banker. I have no doubt that Mr Christalides was keen to attract members of the Cypriot community to bank with the bank and one only has to look, as I did, at the register of customers to see the vast majority of customers at the bank are of Cypriot origin.[105]

On 12 June 1989, Mrs Markou signed both a guarantee for a loan from the bank to a business run by her husband, although she was its company secretary, and a legal charge over the family home as security for their liabilities to the bank. She signed the documents at the bank in the presence of Mrs Savlangas, the Assistant Manager. The discussion between Mrs Savlangas and Mrs Markou 'involved family, children, vitamins and foods',[106] but not anything about the risk being run by Mrs Markou, the extent of her liability as surety and so on.

In the second, very different case of *Bank of Credit and Commerce International SA (In Liquidation) v Hussain and Another*,[107] where the debts of the defendants' company amounted to nearly £400,000, it was recorded by Hart J in relation to the husband's relations with the bank that: '... he was very well known to senior management [and] ... according to its internal credit information summary, he was perceived to be a man of independent means (respectable, trustworthy and a man of considerable means) who was considered to be "able to withstand any unexpected losses that may be encountered".' One witness also claimed that 'it was well known within the Bank in 1986/1987 that the [husband] had a playboy reputation' and the willingness to lend to his company was 'a result of a decision high up in the Bank to develop and exploit the Bhutto connection'. The latter point referred to the fact that the wife, Sanam Bhutto Hussain, was the youngest daughter of the late Zulfiqhar Ali Bhutto, the former Prime Minister of Pakistan.

Such cases are not unique, but the 'domestication' of the public world has been subjected to very little research. O'Donnell and Johnstone have argued that 'existing patterns of lending opportunities and forms of outcomes of credit transactions are not a natural consequence of some abstract concept such as a 'credit market' or 'freedom of contract'.[108] They point out, for instance, that borrowers within some communities will prefer to use informal finance networks, rather than banks. They quote a small business survey carried out in Sydney that showed that Asian-born entrepreneurs, particularly women, were more likely than other groups to use family and friends as their

---

105 *Bank of Cyprus (London) Ltd v Markou and Another* [1999] 2 All ER 707, p 720.

106 Incidentally, the judge found for Mrs Markou, because the bank was 'put on inquiry' and had not taken 'reasonable steps' to avoid being 'infected' with the undue influence and misrepresentation exercised by Mr Markou over his wife.

107 [1999] All ER (D) 1442.

108 O'Donnell and Johnstone, 1997, pp 49–50, quoting Ramsay, 1995, p 178.

major source of business finance.[109] It is also argued by them that banks and building societies were sidestepped because, particularly prior to banking deregulation, it was difficult for many 'migrants' to obtain loans.

Herbert and Kempson's research, *Credit Use and Ethnic Minorities*, which consisted of 'three case studies' into 'a Bangladeshi and a Pakistani community in Oldham' and an 'African Caribbean community' in Brixton recorded some quite similar findings. They found amongst the Pakistani families, for instance, a considerable reliance on 'the informal sector'. Many respondents with strong religious beliefs abstained from using commercial credit because it was in conflict with Islamic teachings. Borrowing from banks for the purpose of providing capital for business was seen by many as relatively acceptable. Twelve out of 15 families who talked to the researchers had also obtained mortgages to purchase houses and home ownership was high within the whole community at 79%. However, many in this community perceived the high street banks to be racist in their dealings with Pakistanis and Asians in general. One respondent, Jahangir, who had been refused a loan to extend his business, stated: '[T]he forms of credit that are available to Pakistanis from the high street are limited. The high street lenders put you through a microscope if your origins are Pakistani and then they refuse. They don't believe that their money is safe and will be paid back. And when you talk to them they speak to you as though you are stupid.'[110]

One way of coping with this perceived racism 'was to open accounts with the local branch of a bank of Pakistani origin'.[111] In Herbert and Kempson's research, almost one half of the households banked with United Bank. Jahangir, for instance, 'was recommended by a friend' to join the bank, from which he obtained the loan to expand his business. He said: '[M]y friend took me to the [United] bank, the manager was a friend of his. He is now a good friend of mine. He has also given me overdraft facility [*sic*] which comes in handy. I am much happier at the United Bank because I can speak to people in my own language; I can speak to the manager at short notice; the atmosphere is Pakistani. I have most of my family banking at the same branch. I have recommended this bank to everyone I know.'[112] The manager at the local branch of United Bank told researchers that his relationship was 'closer' to the Pakistani community than the high street banks.[113]

---

109 O'Donnell and Johnstone, 1997, p 51, quoting Collins *et al*, 1995, p 159.

110 Herbert and Kempson, 1996, p 49. According to Herbert and Kempson, similar sentiments were expressed in research conducted by Deakins *et al*, 1994.

111 Herbert and Kempson, 1996, p 50.

112 *Ibid*.

113 Members of the Bangladeshi community did not turn to their 'own bank', although there was a branch of the Sonali bank in Manchester. 'According to one of the "community leaders", fewer than a quarter of Bangladeshi households have access to a car and it is too far and too expensive for residents of Oldham to travel to [cont]

Thus, we would argue that there is more than one kind of bank. Global finance does not necessarily always and everywhere dominate the high street. This ambiguity in the activities of banks perhaps goes some way to explain the ambivalent attitude of the judiciary, who seem to favour the banks as against sureties and at the same time to express their regret for what is happening.

CONCLUSION

Any discussion of the 'family home' as security for debt must in some way take account of the interweaving of public and private, including the 'private' actions of public financial institutions. It is undoubtedly the case, as Fehlberg contends, that relations between bank and borrower, or bank and guarantor, take place predominantly in the public universe. Equally, it is the case that the public and private overlap in surprising, even unpredictable, ways. The patterns of the weave are constantly changing, the cloth billows and falls in a myriad of creases.

Kaye's critique of the case law on emotionally transmitted debt was written some three years ago, before the most recent decisions. Given her views on the law's emphasis on 'provision of information, rather than addressing inequality',[114] it is likely that she would share the judicial unease we referred to earlier when judges decide in favour of the lenders and against the sureties. She sees in this equity's – a woman not past the age of childbearing – final abandonment of her sisters. We have argued elsewhere that we do not see 'the common law as Jung's masculine subject, who has a female soul, his anima, in equity, still capable of child-bearing',[115] but we do not, therefore, necessarily dismiss her broader conclusions.

Kaye suggests that there is a way forward. She identifies 'a need for an automatic presumption of influence' in relationships such as husband and wife and cohabitees based on the recognition in *O'Brien* of the risk of 'one

---

113 [cont] Manchester by public transport': Herbert and Kempson, 1996, p 77. However, it was fairly common in the Bangladeshi community to borrow from high street banks. Several respondents reported using 'go-betweens', to whom they paid a commission, who would arrange the loan on their behalf 'because their English was poor and because they did not "know the ropes"', p 76. Amongst the African Caribbean community, however, there were also perceptions of racism amongst the high street banks. However, one respondent, a law student, spoke of what he regarded as the benefits of the faceless, automated banking system: 'It doesn't make any difference what colour you are 'cos when it goes in the computer it doesn't identify what colour you are. I mean when you fill in the form it doesn't ask if you are from the Caribbean or if you are Chinese or whatever ... If you have a full time job and you haven't got any judgments against your name you should get credit ... I have lived in Brixton and I have had so much credit available to me over the past five or six years. It just depends on someone's status', p 22.

114 Kaye, 1997, p 55.

115 Green, 1996, p 102; and Lim, 1996, p 146–47.

cohabitee exploiting the emotional involvement and trust of the other'.[116] Further, she argues that the extension of the presumption to both genders avoids the stigma of a 'special equity' for wives but 'any rebuttal of the presumption for women would expressly consider women's systemic inequality'.[117] Any stranger to the relationship, such as a lender, which seeks to rebut the presumption would need to show that 'they have taken material steps to redress any power difference in the relationship'.[118]

We take the view that this more generous approach allows for a greater appreciation of the blurred boundaries, the warp and weft, of public and private around the family home. However, any proposed solution to the problem must also take into account the fact that there is more than one kind of bank–client relationship. There are, of course, imbalances of power, but just as sureties should be enabled to shuttle as safely as possible from public to private, so too must the banks be permitted to enter relationships based, at least in part, upon private values. Women should not have to choose between imprisonment in the tower or passing as a man – between an invisible dependency and the headline 'Girl found dead in the water'. At the same time, banks must also be enabled to choose to operate on a more intimate level, to be more than merely monied might.

More generally, we would argue that, in any legal analysis which relies on the notion of public and private, and public and private values, it is not enough to focus only on one side of the dichotomy. Any discussion of legal decision making in which the private world seems to enter public space, must also consider the effects on public institutions which may act on the basis of kinship, intimacy and mutuality.

---

116 Kaye, 1997, p 47.
117 *Ibid.*
118 *Ibid.*

CHAPTER 6

THE REVIVAL OF EQUITABLE DOCTRINE IN SCOTS LAW – A SPACE FOR GENDER CONCERNS?

Jane Scoular

The position of equity in Scots law is an uncertain one. In contrast to the formalised system which developed south of the border, equity's presence in Scots jurisprudence, with the exception of uncontroversial and discrete areas such as the *nobile officium*, has been fraught with instability and neglect.[1] Despite this chequered history, interest in equitable principle has been awakened in recent years in the civil domain.

This chapter will focus on the case of *Smith v Bank of Scotland*,[2] which has played an important part in this revival. In this judgment, the House of Lords creatively utilised the doctrine of good faith in order to reduce a standard security in a matrimonial home/business context. The decision received a very cold response from academic circles. Many Scots commentators have expressed a fear of the Scots system being engulfed by English legal concepts and an accompanying aversion to granting women special protection.[3] In examining these arguments, the chapter outlines the implications of the resort to equitable principles for women and others who fall outside the mercantile frame. In *Smith*, fixed legal categories of challenge proved particularly insensitive to this empirically significant context. Contract's mercantile ideology and attendant construction of subjects as wealth maximising, autonomous agents was unable to accommodate a different discourse, which is often uncomfortably termed altruism, or recognise the relationship of interdependence which gives rise to this situation, often characterised as 'sexually or emotionally transmitted debt'.[4] It was the equitable doctrine of good faith which provided a space for this woman's narrative and sought to achieve justice by placing a duty to redistribute information on the bank allowing welfarist considerations to steep into Scots law.[5]

While this is a just decision, dependent very much on Lord Clyde's creative and sympathetic judgment, the present author examines the factors

---

1   Discussed below, p 112.

2   1997 SC (HL) 111.

3   Good faith was introduced to avoid the difficulties of implanting the device of constructive notice into Scots law. Many commentators, however, do not welcome this development, viewed as an unnecessary extension and contrary to established authority: McGregor, 1998 and Thomson, 1997.

4   Kaye, 1997, p 35.

5   See, generally, Trebilock, 1993.

which inform the operation of equitable principles. In warning against uncritical collusion with communitarian norms which do not offer a multiplicity of values, essential to a feminist strategy, I argue in conclusion that contractual norms may ironically offer the strategic values to empower as opposed to merely protect.

EQUITABLE DOCTRINE IN SCOTS LAW

Equity has several distinguishable meanings, as natural law, as fairness or justice, as flexibility and discretion opposed to rules of strict law, and as a body of principles distinct from those of law administered by separate courts.[6]

It is certainly the case that, in contrast to its pivotal position in English legal principle, equity in Scotland, with some exceptions, has an almost ethereal existence. Certainly, it is the case that, north of the border, there is no system of equitable doctrine as in England, where, even if 'fusion' is complete, the subject can still command singular attention due to its historical evolution as a separate court and distinct body of rules. By contrast, the absence of equitable rights and remedies as distinct from those legal in the Scots system and the failure to develop a distinctive forum of the Chancellor or develop any remedial jurisdiction, would lead some observers to conclude that there is no trace of equity in Scots law.[7] However, this is not entirely accurate. There is tangible evidence of equitable doctrine in certain proscribed areas, most evidently in the *nobile officium* of the High Court of Justiciary and Court of Session. The *nobile officium* can be petitioned if injustice would result by way of a strict application of law or where a case involves an exceptional and unrecognised legal scenario. It is, however, exercised only in very proscribed circumstances, either in analogous cases or by way of established precedent. Therefore, equity's role is very much circumscribed and controlled, operating in an established and uncontroversial manner with any unruly flexibility being colonised by the familiar operation of precedent.

Outwith this secure area, there is the view by many in the Scots legal tradition that, if one were to focus on equity not as simply a system, but also its meaning as a general philosophical concept, then it is possible to conclude, as Walker, that 'Scotland has never known equity but has long had equity in her system'.[8] The historical development of Scots law as a mixed system, of both common and civil tradition, borrowing from Roman and English law, has

---

6   Walker, 1997, p 462.
7   In addition, there are no textbooks; with one rather antiquated exception, Kames, 1760, to aid this study of this area, it is not a recognised rubric in the classification of cases and it is not an area given prominence in terms of academic scrutiny or study.
8   Walker, 1954, p 105.

meant equitable considerations are the cornerstones of many legal principles which fuel Scots law. Many doctrines have been modified by equity with boundaries very much blended and in a sense the fusion which the Judicature Acts achieved south of the border has always characterised equity's place in Scots legal tradition.

The notion that principles of equity have permeated Scottish jurisprudence means that equitable principles have become entangled with common law rules and their influence in most spheres, save the above noted exceptions, are often difficult to discern. As Walker notes: 'Scottish courts have always administered an undivided system of law and equity' and there is '[c]onsequently ... practically no question of the arbitrary exercise of a jurisdiction founded on principles of equity'.[9]

GOOD FAITH IN SCOTS LAW

For the most part, then, equity is intertwined with legal doctrine, making it impossible to see equity laid bare and examine its composition and texture. Recently, however, equitable consideration has been disentangled from common law rules.

Smith concerned the enforceability of a standard security granted by a wife in respect of her husband's business debts. This case caused quite stir in Scots legal circles, as the House of Lords departed from established contractual principles and utilised the doctrine of good faith in order to facilitate the reduction of the security. Lord Clyde's brief mention of the latent Scots doctrine of good faith served to obviate many of the difficulties encountered by strict application of contract law. This device was utilised in the absence of the English equitable notion of constructive notice, reflecting the Scots preference for general principle over equitable construction. Not only does this doctrine bring norms of justice and fairness into contract law, but it provides relief for a group of women who occupy an empirically significant position of inferior bargaining strength in the security context. In this sense, it could be described as creating a space for women, within a regime of contract law which was inflexible and insensitive to their position.

---

9   Walker, 1994, p 108.

THE SYMPATHETIC JUDGMENT AND
THE CASE OF *SMITH v BANK OF SCOTLAND*

The Outer House: *Mumford and Smith v Bank of Scotland*[10]

This case began as a joint action by Kathleen Smith and Elizabeth Mumford, taken against the Bank of Scotland. The two women had entered into cautionary contracts with the bank, agreeing to grant a standard security over their matrimonial home, which each owned jointly with their spouses, in return for an overdraft being facilitated for their husbands businesses. Both claimed that they had entered into the agreements as a result of false reassurances made by their husbands which blinded them to the full extent of the obligation which they had entered into.

The pursuers' case appeared problematic. Counsel could not point to any Scots authority in which the actions of a third party were held to be attributable to the creditor in the present circumstances. As Gretton states, Scots law in this context has always been 'robust', parties are assumed to consent to what they sign in the absence of any recognised grounds of challenge.[11] However, less than a year prior to the Scots women's actions, the House of Lords in England had found in favour of a wife in comparable circumstances. Thus, in the absence of Scots *dictum*, counsel reached across the border and sought to rely upon the leading case of *Barclays Bank v O'Brien*.[12]

In this leading decision, once again, a mortgage agreement was entered into for the purpose of securing an advance to cover a husband's business debts. And once again, the female guarantor claimed that, as a result of her spouse's misrepresentation, she was ignorant as to the full extent of her contractual obligation. In their opinion, the Lords held that the relationship, being one in which a party has reposed trust and confidence in the other, was one in which there was a substantial risk of wrongdoing, of agreements being secured by way of misrepresentation or undue influence.[13] Consequently, where the surety stood in such a relationship to the principal debtor, and the agreement was 'on its face' not in her financial interest, then a duty of inquiry arose on the part of the bank to ensure that consent had validly been obtained. The duty could be fulfilled by advising the client to obtain independent advice or by explaining the consequences of the realisation of the security. A bank (and this was the case for Barclays Bank) who failed in this duty was deemed

---

10 1994 SC 618; 1994 SLT 1288; 1994 SCLR 856.
11 Gretton, 1997, p 195, see, eg, *Royal Bank of Scotland v Purvis* 1990 SLT 262.
12 [1994] 1 AC 180.
13 *Ibid, per* Lord Browne-Wilkinson, p 196.

to have constructive notice of the fraud which had occurred.[14] Mrs O'Brien was, for this reason, relieved of her obligations to the bank.

The *O'Brien* judgment thus proved attractive and was lifted by counsel for the pursuers. The action in the Outer House proceeded directly upon the basis of 'constructive notice'. Counsel argued that the relationships between the two women, Kathleen Smith and Elizabeth Mumford, and their respective husbands were analogous to that in *O'Brien* and, as such, were those in which there was a 'substantial risk of wrong-doing'. Counsel averred in both cases that it was the husband who assumed the position of financial manager in each relationship and, as a result of this, both women deferred to their partner's judgment when monetary decisions had to be made. Adhering to the *O'Brien* judgment meant that, due to the close relationships and the fact that the transactions were not in the financial interests of the cautioners, the bank had a duty to 'take reasonable steps' to ensure that the apparently disadvantaged party's valid agreement had been given. The pursuers concluded that the absence of any such inquiry furnished the Bank of Scotland with constructive notice of the fraud and that this would therefore enable the security to be reduced.

In dismissing the claim in the Outer House, Lord Johnston found: 'No authority in Scotland outwith the context of agency where constructive notice can be inferred in the mind of a person wholly ignorant of the ... [existence of a] misrepresentation by the husband, simply because of surrounding circumstances.'[15] In rejecting counsel's claim that the English test should apply in Scotland, he stated: 'I am not prepared against the background of long established Scots authorities ... to import such a presumption into the law of Scotland' and, in distancing himself further from *O'Brien*, commented that it 'accords to the law of England as regards English equitable principles'.[16]

First Division: *Mumford v Bank of Scotland; Smith v Bank of Scotland*[17]

In reclaiming to the First Division, the case was re-framed in order to appear more consistent with, and palatable to, Scots law. Counsel downplayed the notion of constructive knowledge and focused instead upon the argument that the circumstances were such as to put the creditor on inquiry and failing to do so, therefore, resulted in bad faith on the part of the bank.

---

14 An important feature of the decision is that it is not necessary to demonstrate manifest disadvantage; this emanates from *O'Brien's* sister case, *CIBC Mortgages plc v Pitt* [1994] 1 AC 200.

15 *Per* Lord Johnson, p 1291H.

16 1994 SLT 1288, p 1291J–K.

17 1996 SLT 392.

This approach was not favoured by the court, which clearly stated that Scots law does not share English law's presumption of wrongdoing. Lord President Hope, delivering the opinion of the court on behalf of himself, Lord Abernethy, and Lord Weir, found no Scots authority which 'has recognised that a presumption of undue influence can arise in a question with a third party'.[18] Anything short of actual knowledge could not create a duty of inquiry; the bank, therefore, could not be acting in bad faith by failing to exercise such a duty.[19]

Smith v Bank of Scotland[20]

Mrs Mumford dropped out after the First Division hearing, leaving Smith alone to appeal to the House of Lords. The bench consisted of Lords Goff, Lloyd, Hoffman, Jauncey and Clyde. Lord Clyde gave the leading judgment, approved by the three English judges, in support of the appeal.[21]

Lord Clyde's judgment begins with a recognition that established authority clearly states that the duties incumbent upon a cautioner only extends as far as his own interests. The only deviations from the rule occur where there is fraud and where 'the creditor knowingly misleads the cautioner'; in this situation, Clyde specifies his representations must be 'full and fair'.[22] He also affirms that the case before him did not fall into any of the following recognised exceptions to that rule; where the cautioner has been acting as an agent for the debtor,[23] has participated in the fraud,[24] a gratuitous benefit has been obtained as a result of the fraud[25] or, finally, where the fraud which takes place is so extreme, for example veering into extortion, that it vitiates *consensus in idem*.[26]

---

18 1996 SLT 392, *per* LP Hope, p 398D.

19 The earlier case of *Helen McCabe v Skipton Building Society* 1994 Inner House Cases concerned an analogous situation where a husband's misrepresentations could not have a bearing on a fraudulently obtained security agreement between a woman and a bank.

20 1997 SC (HL) 111.

21 Lord Jauncey, 1997 SC (HL) 111, p 115F–G, however, also delivered a rather novel opinion. It begins as, and on the whole is, a dissenting speech, which loses confidence, abandons ship and, in its conclusion, supports the majority. Lord Jauncey's scepticism mirrors the earlier courts' opinions and stems from his adherence to the 'principles of Scots law alone'. However, he turns away from them when recognising 'that your Lordships do not share my difficulties' and in his appreciation of 'the practical advantages of applying the same law to identical transactions in both jurisdictions'.

22 Lord Clyde, 1997 SC (HL) 111, p 117I, referring to Gloag and Irvine, 1897, pp 706 and 713.

23 *Mair v Rio Grande Rubber Estates Ltd* 1913 SC (HL) 74.

24 *Falconer v North of Scotland Banking Co* (1836) 1 M 704.

25 *Clydesdale Bank v Paul* (1877) 4 R 626.

26 *Trustees Savings Bank v Balloch* 1983 SLT 240.

Despite the authorities being pitted against him, Lord Clyde perceived himself to be in the same position to that in which the House of Lords found themselves in *O'Brien*, when they consciously sought to extend the law in England. With this as impetus, Lord Clyde felt confident to make 'a corresponding extension ... to the law of Scotland'.[27] To do so, he had to be creative; constructive notice, the device utilised in *O'Brien* for such a purpose, was not at Clyde's disposal, it being identified as 'a development of the principles of equity' and, therefore, inconsistent with Scots principle.[28] Lord Clyde had to strain somewhat to accommodate Smith and managed this by unpicking the common factor which unites these exceptions: 'Lying behind these examples of situations where the creditor is obliged to take steps in the interest of the cautioner is the basic element of good faith.'[29] In this context, the principle of good faith required that 'there must be perfect fairness of representation on part of the creditor in the constitution of the contract'.[30]

The duty to act in good faith was deemed to arise where circumstances 'lead a reasonable man to believe that owing to the personal relationship between the debtor and the proposed cautioner the latter's consent may not be fully informed or freely given'.[31] In order to meet this standard, Clyde directed: 'As part of that same good faith ... it seems to me reasonable to expect that there should also be a duty in particular circumstances to give the potential cautioner certain advice.' The actions of the Bank of Scotland, in failing to advise the cautioner of the consequences of the transaction or advise her to take independent advice, fell short of perfect fairness and consequently the appeal succeeded.[32]

Lord Clyde's attempt to satisfy the perceived broad policy considerations of the two close jurisdictions and to ensure that principles of caution and surety correspond, has not been warmly received in his homeland. The two main strands of this critique, the departure from Scots common law and the misplaced concern for women signing guarantees, form the basis of my inquiry into good faith in Scots law, as it opens up question of norms, equality and protection which are a theme of this collection.

---

27 *Per* Lord Clyde, 1997 SC (HL) 111, p 121A.

28 Interestingly, there is a distancing from English equitable doctrine, which is viewed by Scots commentators as being artificial: McKendrick, 1996, p 219 and Dickson, 1998, p 41. Yet the invocation of good faith could generously be described as creative rather than contrived: see below.

29 *Per* Lord Clyde, 1997 SC (HL) 111, p 118C.

30 *Rodgers Builders v Fawdry* (1950) SC 483, *Trade Development Bank v Haig* (1983) SLT 510; both cases were referred to in terms of confirming this broad principle of good faith in contract.

31 *Per* Lord Clyde, 1997 SC (HL) 111, p 121H.

32 It should be noted that the House of Lords' decision in *Smith* was on a debate point and, at the time of writing, the case has returned to court for proof.

Good faith in Scots law

Smith was greeted with hostility in the initial commentaries; many writers accused the House of Lords of sullying the Scots legal tradition in its importation of foreign, English legal concepts and concurred with the Court of Session's rejection of the action.[33] Disdain has been expressed at what is perceived to be blatant judicial law making.[34] Many writers shared LP Hope's view, expressed in the First Division hearing, that if the law was deemed to be lacking then it should be matter for the Law Commission to consider reform, rather than the courts engaging in what is described by McGregor as 'a conspicuous exercise in judicial activism'.[35] The House of Lords are accused of 'violence inflicted on established principles' and Lord Clyde particularly of 'identify[ing] a result which he considered to be attractive and then scouring the authorities to find a basis for the result'.[36] Good faith, as Thomson observes, is 'the forensic rabbit let out on this occasion'.[37]

The position of this doctrine in Scots law is very much disputed: its presence, like that of equity, is opaque. Any flurry into the annals of Scots law shows that little attention has been paid to it over the centuries. Recent groundwork, which has been carried out in preparation for the unified European code in contract, noted: 'There is also an underlying principle of good faith in the Scottish law of contract, although it is difficult to find a clear and comprehensive statement of it.'[38] The development of Scots law as a mixed system would explain the vestiges of civilian tradition[39] yet, with the exception of the work of Kames and Bankton,[40] there is no detailed account in either the texts of our institutional writers or their modern counterparts. Where it does feature, a distinction in approach is evident; Bankton and Bell view it to be a unifying principle in contract[41] while Kames restricts the notion of *bona fides* to particular settings.[42] More modern writers[43] are noticeably vague, though many would appear to support the idea that good faith is a general and 'animating principle' in contract.[44] Just quite what that means is currently occupying the attention of Scots jurisprudence. Awoken by Smith's

---

33 This case is mentioned briefly in Belcher, 2000, p 44. The writer, however, does detail the role of good faith in the decision.

34 Gretton, 1997, p 195.

35 McGregor, 1998, p 90.

36 1997 SC (HL) 111, p 193.

37 Thomson, 1997, p 124.

38 Lando and Beale, 1995, p 58.

39 MacQueen, 1999, p 7.

40 Forte, 1999, p 76–79.

41 Bankton, 1751–53, para 1.11.65; Bell, 1839, para 13.

42 Kames, 1778, p 194.

43 Gloag, 1929, p 400; Smith, 1962, pp 297–98; and Gow, 1964, p 73.

44 *Ibid*, Gloag, p 73.

very animated use of the doctrine of good faith, previous dormancy has now been overtaken by a flurry of scholarship which is beginning to contest, evaluate and map the position of good faith in Scots law.[45]

Contemporary writers are divided on the issue. Those who support its introduction recognise that self-pursuit must be tempered by justice and welcome the imposition of community values on contracting parties; Forte, for example, describes it as 'restor[ing] a necessary equilibrium'.[46] It is a doctrine which, if one looks closely, runs through many grounds of challenge and its increasing recognition would certainly help clarify the artificiality which surrounds error in particular.[47] In any case, it is pointed out by many that the introduction of good faith in Smith prefixes what many predict as a full scale adoption through codification.[48]

Animosity to the good faith doctrine is based not only in scepticism over its legacy in Scots law, but also concern as to its liberal tendencies. Thomson argues against a general principle of good faith, preferring Scots common law doctrines, which, he states, achieve similar objectives.[49] In areas where doctrine is inadequate, any interference with this freedom of contract has to be justified, either to protect a particularly vulnerable group in society (he cites the legislative framework to protect consumers), or to prevent distortions of the market as a result of monopolies. In all other cases, freedom of contract is seen to be consonant with the norms present economic conditions of capitalism demand. This focus on subjective positions of the parties should only apply in these specific conditions,[50] and as a general principle would undermine contract doctrine: 'It is amorphous, complex and at variance with the cultural values which have moulded the current law ... it is not the function of a system of private law to compel persons to act in an altruistic manner ... To do so, would be to remove the edge of competition and self-interest which are also human values and which have created the wealth upon which our society currently depends.'[51]

---

45 Forte, 1999, is a most useful development in this area in her attempt to begin an assessment and critical analysis of the good faith doctrine.

46 *Ibid*, p 98.

47 See Woolman, 1986; and Thomson, 1992. *Steuarts Trs v Hart* (1875) 3 R 192 has long recognised good faith as the motivating principle.

48 This mirrors the debate in England which is similarly divided between those who view good faith as a distraction and interference with contract principle, and those who see it as a necessary limitation to excessive self-interest or as an instrument of welfare. See, generally, Beatson and Friedman, 1995 and Brownsword, Hird and Howells, 1999.

49 Thomson, 1999, pp 63–76.

50 Such special circumstances would not extend to cases such as *Smith*, as outlined below.

51 Thomson, 1999, p 76. Similar hostility is present in some English commentators' reaction to the notion of a general principle of good faith: 'Better to leave an occasional widow penniless by the harsh application of the law ... than take in pitiful strays such as good faith ... for these strays carry the lice that will infect us all': Forte, 1999, p 99, quoting from White and Summers, 1995, p 85.

Gender trouble

Many of the criticisms of *Smith* restate the Court of Session's view that there is no presumption of undue influence in Scots law in transactions between spouses and that, consequently, a surety wife such as Mrs Smith would not require special protection. Underlying this conviction is a view that the law has a misplaced concern for gender equality in this context. Thomson, in support of the earlier decision, states, for example: '... this is a sensible result given a married woman's economic and social position in the late 20th century ... any other result would be patronising to wives, presupposing them to be so dependent and/or deferential to their husbands that they are incapable of safeguarding their own financial interests.'[52] McGregor concludes that this result gives the strong impression that women cannot read or understand or take steps to understand documents and can hide this ignorance behind their spouse. Such views, she states are 'reflective of the economic relations between spouses in the last rather than current century'.[53]

Sexually and emotionally transmitted debt

It is tempting to counter these broad assertions as to the apparent advanced position of women's social position with figures on domestic labour, pay, poverty, childcare and domestic violence, which clearly reflect an inequality, marginalisation and vulnerability undiminished by the passage of time.[54] The previous statements, while well intended, are more aspirational than real and echo the failures of the liberal legal tradition. In this schema, equality is viewed as a formal rather than a substantive issue, which detaches subjects from their historical position and the complexities of their gender. A substantive approach, on the other hand, argues for a more responsive legal forum which can hear multiple voices and needs.

In addition, there are more complex and particular nuances to the situation Mrs Smith faced.[55] The case involves the interplay between the private world of intimate relations and the public world of commercial contracts. This private sphere, although not unregulated, as a crude public/private

---

52 Thomson, 1997, p 124. He also talks, p 125, of a misplaced concern for married women. Dunlop, 1997, p 468, asks: Why should a husband be more likely to use undue influence towards a wife than parent towards a child?

53 McGregor, 1998, p 93.

54 See, generally, Engender, 1997, 1998–99, 2000, which documents women's position in Scotland and, of course, the vast body of feminist scholarship which continues to demonstrate women's material inequality.

55 The phenomenon of 'sexually' or 'emotionally transmitted debt' is well documented in feminist work and by important empirical studies. This work has only been briefly mentioned in a small number of Scots commentaries and its implications not studied in any depth.

distinction may suggest,[56] involves negotiations, bargains and agreements which are informal and outwith the reach of contract law. Feminist theory has, over the years, raised concern at the way in which public/private spheres and norms in different ways operate to define and delimit many women's lives. Participation in public life remains fragmented for many women who remain the primary caretakers of children and carry out the majority of work in the domestic sphere. Fehlberg's empirical work shows this is 'particularly [so] in middle and higher income households [where] women are less likely to have financial control and responsibility if they do not earn an income'.[57] A factor which compounds this is that women's earning ability is often interrupted and reduced as the roles of motherhood and home-maker take prominence in their lives. Lack of State support often enforces dependency on a partner, all of which can mean a significant proportion of women are less likely to participate in public business matters than they are in the business of 'running the home'. Consequently, many women have less experience and knowledge of commercial matters, resulting in patterns of decision making often split along gendered lines; with women deferring to male authority or, in a less sinister manner, trusting male experience in commercial matters.[58] This is particularly the case if the woman's life is demarcated by the role of homemaker or mother.[59]

The surety/cautionary situation involves the overlap between the private world of intimate relations and the public world of commercial contracts. An 'agreement' is hatched between the spouses in the domestic sphere but played out in the public sphere, as the cautionary contract introduces the third party, leaving law with the difficult task of negotiating the uneasy boundaries between public/private and commerce and intimate relations. This entrance to the public sphere for private reasons demonstrates that it is not simply women's exclusion in a domestic sphere which is the problem, but rather the fact that the surety wife is 'both in and out' and between norms. Prior to the cases of *O'Brien* and *Smith*, courts in the UK favoured a traditional contractual analysis which prevented any inquiry into this incomparable duality. The agreement between spouses was considered private and not recognised as

---

56 Feminist scholarship has increasingly questioned the original stark divide between public and private spheres: Olsen, 1983; Pateman, 1989; Lacey, 1993; and Thornton, 1995. Eg, domestic relationships are not exclusively private, as they can also be located in the public discourses of family law, fiscal and public policy, demonstrating that the public–private dualism is more complex than originally espoused by feminists. Indeed, as this chapter demonstrates, women in the context of sexually transmitted debt or emotionally transmitted debt, traverse both domains, reinforcing the recognised constant blurrings and shifting of position; see Fehlberg, 1997, p 15.

57 See, generally, *ibid*, Fehlberg, Chapter 2.

58 Indeed, in *O'Brien*, the House of Lords recognised that in many families 'the wife follows her husband's advice on business matters without independent thought', *per* Lord Browne-Wilkinson [1994] 1 AC 180, p 188F.

59 Fehlberg, 1997, p 11.

binding by courts,[60] but as the third party enters into the frame, financial dealings move from unregulated incidents of domestic life to the public domain where the law of contract applies its norms. These norms rely on objective standards which proscribe that parties are bound by what they sign in the absence of a recognised ground of challenge.

The norms of the commercial and market sphere, from which women have traditionally been absent, govern and interpret women's experience. For these reasons, sexually transmitted debt was coined by Australian feminists, to describe the flight of those who prejudice their own property rights in order to secure finance for partners' businesses.[61]

As more and more cases of this nature appeared before the courts of law in the UK, the notion of sexually transmitted debt gained ascendancy.[62] The cause of this outbreak can be adduced if one considers the context in which strong economic growth and government policy encouraged individual entrepreneurs – only to be interrupted by a period of political and economic recession. This had a significant impact on surety wives and partners who commonly provided their family home as security for their partner's business debts, the home, in most cases, being a couple's largest financial asset.[63] It is this economic climate and the gravity of home repossession that accounts for the significant increase in litigation in 1990s.[64]

---

60 *Balfour v Balfour* [1919] 2 KB 571. Agreements between those in emotional relationships 'are not made with seals and sealing wax but by natural love and affection which counts for so little in these cold courts', p 579. This approach, however, is increasingly being challenged, particularly in the context of cohabitation contracts: see, generally, Kingdom and Wightman, 2000.

61 Howell, 1994, p 93, following on from the Women and Credit Task Force, 1990.

62 Emotionally transmitted debt is now regarded as a more apt term to describe not simply a sexual tie but rather the emotional bond that operates to motivate an individual to take on debts of others in signing a guarantee. Lord Clyde himself, 1997 SC (HL) 111, p 122A–B, was adamant that the category of relationship in Smith should not be closed: 'Given the range of circumstances in which persons may be prepared or prevailed upon to act as cautioners it seems to me to be unwise to make any more precise formulations but to leave the matter to the application of common sense to the circumstance.' Fehlberg, 1997, p 4 refers to the English cases of *Lloyds Bank v Bundy* [1975] 1 QB 326, CA; *Avon Finance Co Ltd v Bridger* [1985] 2 All ER 281, CA, in relation to surety parents. Reported cases on surety husbands are rare; however, there is one recent case involving a husband providing security for a business run by his wife, daughter and son-in-law, who successfully appealed and had the order set aside on the basis of his wife's undue influence: see *Barclays Bank v Rivett* [1999] 1 FLR 730. Fehlberg notes two similar instances worldwide: *Money v Wespac Banking Corp* (1988) ASC 55–664 (Fed Crt of Aust) and *Manulife v Conlin* (1994) 20 OR (3d) 499, CA. Nevertheless, women are particularly susceptible and statistically are more likely to provide surety in the context of private relationships for various, often interrelated, reasons. Fehlberg, 1997, p 4, notes: 'The sexual or potentially sexual relationship which exists between couples, especially spouses, involves assumptions about shared interests and lives, played out against a cultural history of male dominance over women.' These complex cultural histories do not hold for these other relations. I have, therefore, some reservations that, in order to be inclusive, the term emotional does not capture the dynamics of the sexual.

63 In addition to its emotional value, it may also provide a home not only for the parties, but also for their children.

64 Fehlberg, 1997, p 1.

Normative values

Yet, the legal system was not anxious to diagnose or treat the symptoms of sexually transmitted debt. In earlier decisions, the woman's apparent choice to sign away her home stands on its own, as the signature of a self-interested individual. Priority was given to women's autonomous decision to take on debts of others in the law's shortsighted desire to treat women equally and not to offer special treatment based on status. The framework of formal equality and focus on an abstract view of the free will of the contracting agents detaches judgment from social circumstances, thus concealing the unequal bargaining power in these situations. Patriarchy's predilection for abstract rationality and self-regard characterises the traditional model of contract. Parties meet on 'equal' terms at arm's length in order to maximise their own autonomous interests. This was very much the philosophy behind the earlier courts' decisions and the aforementioned academic support. A case such as *Smith*, where a party has acted in a manner which could not be characterised as autonomous or wealth maximising, was clearly hard to comprehend under this schema. As Goodrich notes:

> The dominant doctrinal model of contract within modernity has been narrowly obsessed with commodity markets and fantasies of legal certainty engendering commercial security. The gender characteristics of such a market are aligned to representations of an acquisitive and antagonistic individuality and corresponding legal personality. Typifications of the contracting subject have, in general, been variously officious and calculating, rationalistic and aloof, competitive, cold and disjunctive.[65]

The relationship between women and men in this context has a real bearing on any consideration as to whether consent is freely given. Classic and modern contract law constructs legal persons as 'free and equal owners of commodities, all similarly equipped to engage in transactions which will redound to our personal advantage'.[66] A Scots law which follows the classical tradition and values autonomy above fails to recognise that voluntary decisions are not in all cases made by an individual with the aim of maximising their own wealth. Writers such as Trebilock argue that, in important instances, this is not the case and that autonomy and welfare can be antagonistic.[67] 'The Limits of Freedom of Contract' become clear when, as he notes, autonomy and welfare diverge. Hadfield relies on this work to describe 'the feminist dilemma of choice': where choice may promote a woman's autonomy, but yet diminish her welfare at the same time.[68] Autonomy,

---

65 Goodrich, 1996, p 44.

66 Naffine, 1990, p 73.

67 Trebilock, 1993.

68 Common examples in feminist literature are the prostitution contract and surrogacy agreement: Hadfield, 1996; and Pateman, 1988.

accordingly, can only be valued according to: 'The opportunities available to the individual, the legal treatment of initial consent in light of a change in an individual's assessment of her well-being and her capacity to identify and pursue results that are in her self-interest.'[69] Prostitution contracts and surrogacy agreements are commonly cited as illustrative of this dilemma and the surety situation would also appear to confirm this observation. Legal measures, therefore, in order to effect any real change, must begin to facilitate the convergence of these parallel values.

Law, however, has traditionally automatically assumed that a party's signing of the contract represents the protection of her self-interest. Additionally, spouses are likely to encounter real difficulty in meeting the objective requirements of established grounds of challenge. As Fehlberg notes: '[I]t is a complex series of practical and emotional motivations and the interdependence of surety with debtor interests'; this makes traditional grounds of challenge impervious to these complexities. Few defences reflect their subjective experience; an objective approach finds it difficult to locate 'subtle and insidious emotional pressure'[70] which can be understood, perhaps, only within the context of the particular relationship. Doctrines such as undue influence and misrepresentation require a pursuer to establish a publicly recognised legal wrong. This narrow categorisation limits the scope for private issues, where parties, not obviously vulnerable, may nonetheless act as a result of subtle and insidious emotional pressure. Such pressure falls short of a legal wrong and the rigidity of legal categories stifles the material reality and ordering of intimate relations.

It is in this restrictive atmosphere that equity in England, and equitable doctrine in Scotland, has made space for women's narratives. As MacQueen notes in relation to good faith in Scotland: '[As their c]ontext is not fixed or static ... general principles allow innovation in response to social conditions.'[71] Attuned to substantive equality needs, as opposed to formal limitations, equitable considerations offer a responsiveness sorely lacking in

---

69 Hadfield, 1995, p 323; and see, generally, Trebilock, 1993, pp 78–163.

70 Fehlberg, 1997, p 33. There was the additional obstacle that courts, in England, until the case of *CIBC Mortgages v Pitt* [1994] 1 AC 200, HL, required the transaction to be to the woman's 'manifest disadvantage'. This is judged in purely financial terms and women's interests are, as Fehlberg notes, p 20, 'often lumped [together] with their husband's'. Her economic dependence is regarded as an advantage and at no point is her contribution in the home off-set against the benefit of the income from the business. This assumption still informs the opposition to relief in cases of sexually transmitted debt. This view, that wealth is shared between partners, is not borne out by empirical study, as Fehlberg has shown, p 84, 'even where a benefit is technically available, underlying power relations may dictate distribution'. This is particularly the case when the marriage or partnership disintegrates, or where any direct benefit amounts simply 'to staving off the apparently inevitable repossession of the marital home', p 14; see *National Westminster Bank v Morgan* [1985] 1 AC 686, HL.

71 MacQueen, p 7.

legal doctrine.[72] It is tempting, at this point, in recognising equity's sensitivity, to equate and merge its norms with those whom it serves to protect; to welcome it as the champion of women as it cuts through a contractual order which, in this instance, is particularly neglectful of women's material position.

Indeed, this feminisation of equity is all too familiar to English lawyers. Mackenzie, for instance, observes that in much of the literature 'equity ... is frequently marginalised as elusive, uncertain, irrational, subjective, quintessentially feminine'.[73] This is in contrast to a common law which is 'purportedly authoritative as precedent-based, rational, objective and certain'. The relationship between these two strands of law is often characterised as 'tempestuous'.[74]

My misgivings are centred round two main concerns, somewhat interrelated. First, there is danger even in metaphorically naturalising certain constructions of women which then operate as a trope, reinforcing traditional models of femininity. This concern is shared by other feminists who do not want to reproduce the rhetoric of earlier equity cases where women are characterised as victims, dependent wholly on their husband and needing to be rescued from 'softhearted and soft-headed loyalties by equitable intervention'.[75]

Secondly, I want to question to what extent equity can 'mitigate [against] the structural inequalities from which women suffer without reproducing models of dependency'.[76] I will return to this point in conclusion, but want first to deal with the question of alternate norms, and their ability, if adopted uncritically, to collude with stereotypes of femininity which are particularly pernicious.

FRAGMENTATION OF CONTRACT LAW

This quest for alternate values is shared by critical scholars who have embarked upon a project to fragment the classical contract model. 'Attacks' upon its integrity have centred upon the following truisms: its unitary nature, defined by clear rules of general application; its 'over-arching ideology' of

---

72 The constant tension in law re-emerges between the traditional view of cases as mere opportunities for 'the application of pre-existing rules and principles' and critical approaches which see them as 'the occasion ... for judicial decision' and as opportunities to move towards justice: Thomson, 1991, p 75. The latter tends to be favoured by feminists who are particularly concerned about the way in which precedent operates to reproduce inequality.

73 Mackenzie, 1996, p 158.

74 Maitland, 1932, p 11.

75 Mackenzie, 1996, p 166.

76 Bottomley, 1993, p 58.

freedom of contract which does not account for situations outwith the one-off mercantile frame or concern itself with promoting fairness in the market. As an antidote, greater emphasis has been placed on alternate norms in order to addresses some of the limitations of orthodox contract theory; the work on reliance pioneered by Atiyah and the more recent focus on good faith being prime examples.[77] Ian Macneil's work is particularly relevant, providing what has been described as 'a virtual rehabilitation of contract' focusing on the importance of trust and solidarity in long term relationships.[78]

Macneil's typology of discrete transactions and relational contracts has attracted much feminist interest. Discrete contracts describe the situation where the parties' only connection is the transaction itself, which, when completed, leaves the parties as disparate as before. Relational contracts involve long term relationships, where parties are connected to each other through the long term agreement which is very much determined by norms of trust, altruism, co-operation, preservation of relationship, and harmonious settlement of disputes.[79] Macneil argues that relational contracts do not adhere to the idea of a single moment of agreement. Unlike discrete transactions where free will is exercised in isolation, in a long term context it emerges through the relationship. From this perspective, focusing solely on the original agreement misses 'obligations which emerge from the interaction of the parties as their relationship evolves'.[80] In addition, parties cannot be simply defined as wealth-maximising individuals; interests of the other party also feature as a motivating factor.

MULTIPLE VALUES

Macneil's focus on relational contracts would seem to provide a hospitable framework for feminists attempting to disrupt dominant norms of contract.[81] While certainly offering a parallel description of contract law's inability to be context-specific, it should noted that it also applies to a different context. In moving from mere description to strategy, we must be vigilant and not rush in to uncritically adopt into a long term intimate context norms which apply to long term commercial transactions. This is a pit into which significant and oft-quoted feminist work has already fallen.

---

77 Atiyah, 1979, 1986; Beatson and Friedman, 1995; and Brownsword, Hird and Howells, 1999.

78 Wightman, 2000, p 101. These values are of particular interest to those involved in the recent revival of interest in cohabitation contracts; see Kingdom and Wightman, 2000.

79 Macneil, 1978, 1980. Note, however, that Macneil's approach has been criticised as being 'both overinclusive and underinclusive'; see Eisenberg, 1995, who offers a more sophisticated analysis of Macneil's discrete/relational typology.

80 *Ibid*, Wightman, p 103.

81 I am not in any sense dismissing this important work out of hand. It may be useful in other contexts; eg, the aforementioned cohabitation context.

I am thinking, in particular, of the work of Mary Jo Frug, which is often cited uncritically as a major work in the deconstruction of contracts.[82] Frug set out to offer a gendered analysis of two significant schools of contractual scholarship; the Law and Economics movement, with particular reference to the work of Posner, and the relational work of writers such as Macneil.[83] The conceptual limitations of this work stem from Frug's construction of unbending, paradigmatic oppositions between 'forms of argument which value abstractness, certainty in the application of rules', which are cast as stereotypically male, and 'response to context, a decentering of agreement, a concern for fairness of outcome', characterised as female.[84]

This is a debate which, as Brown notes, lends itself to masculine/feminine casting. She refers specifically to the 'high octane' value of Posnerian masculinity '... built on the "stranger" mode of the one-off, arm's length, atomistic, discrete transaction' and the corresponding feminisation of Macneil's work, with its focus on 'the relational subtext in contract law' and commitment to preserving ongoing relationships.[85] Brown warns against reaching elementary conclusions: '[The] temptation to read the debate in terms of the well worn master opposition ... to [view] classic contract doctrine as merely the application of classic liberal theory to be opposed to the sentimental virtues ... with the feminine on the side of the nascent counter-principles against the dominance of the discrete transaction, and the ideology of freedom and classic individualism.'[86]

Macneil's thesis denotes the importance of the contractual community in which the party's interactions take place: '... social context of the parties generates many of the norms which apply to their contract.'[87] Radical critiques, such as his, emphasise the importance of relationality in the analysis of contract and see it as capable of being informed by norms of a more progressive nature: '... the shift from contract as commerce to contract as relationality facilitates a shift from norms of self-interest and competitiveness and towards norms of altruism and co-operation.'[88] Diversity appears to be achieved as contracts 'need no longer be read as creating exclusively commercial obligations, not predominantly in terms of the intention and consent of the parties and the validity of the clauses'.[89]

---

82 Frug, 1992.
83 Macneil, 1978, Posner, 1992.
84 Wightman, 2000, p 103.
85 Brown, 1996, p 12.
86 *Ibid*, p 14.
87 *Ibid*, Wightman, p 103.
88 As Brown, 1996, notes: 'For [Macneil], the courts represent the pathology of contract law, not its norms; what happens when things go wrong, not when they go right.' Macneil then, p 12, looks to settled business, where contracts, he argues, are underpinned by more relational norms, such as reciprocity and solidarity.
89 Kingdom, 2000, p 5.

Yet, the appeal of community offers something of a poisoned chalice. As many feminists have come to recognise: 'Pluralistic and fragmented solutions have not been their typical form.'[90] Brown's particular concern centres on Macneil's uncritical promotion of informal norms, where she points out that the language of unspoken agreements, gentlemen's agreements, making deals, 'have, far from being alien to masculinity, been its greatest standby'.[91] This is a scepticism that I share. Communitarian values, while aptly describing the situation faced by women in sexually transmitted debt cases, are norms which do little to wrench women out of this position. Care must be taken not to venerate or descend into 'a mush of altruism'[92] where we essentialise ethics of community, caring, nurturing and self-sacrifice as female or to fuse self-reliance and autonomy as male.[93] Communitarian norms, if promoted alongside traditional individualistic norms, may offer a breadth and pluralism in contract. The ability to appropriate a multiplicity of models is essential to feminist strategy, if we are to 'move from debates imbued with absolutism' and 'embrace ambiguity and complexity'.[94] By polarising contract and relation, more liberating aspects of contractual doctrine are lost and subtle, contingent strategies cannot be formulated.[95]

In examining to what extent doctrine such as good faith and equity can offer a multiplicity of values, many feminist commentaries complain that equitable doctrine, while attempting to protect the weak, has done little to empower the party in the marginalised position.[96] I will conclude by arguing that good faith and equity may actually require the service of contractual norms to facilitate empowerment and this can be seen particularly in the context of independent advice. A multiplicity of values are thus vital in any conceptualisation of good faith, and this is what feminist influence on the doctrine must seek to achieve.

---

90 See, generally, Young, 1990; and Frazer and Lacey, 1993.

91 Brown, 1996, p 14. This is the effect when, as Brown points out, p 12, 'law is replaced not only by custom but by corporate regimes of governance'.

92 Wightman, 1996, p 43. Even the more circumscribed account of relational contracts, 'as a shared means of pursuing self-interest', when used in this context fuses women's self-interest to that of her partner in a manner which conceals material inequalities and disparities in decision making.

93 Kingdom, 2000, p 8. In any case, as Fehlberg's research demonstrates, p 269: 'The implicit stereotype of willing self-sacrifice often evidenced in the case law [is] clearly at odds with the accounts of sureties,' many of whom were extremely unhappy at the burden they had to endure for the sake of the business.

94 Bottomley, 1993, p 66.

95 Quoting Grosz, 1989, Bottomley, 2000, p 56, notes that: 'Unlike truth, whose value is eternal, strategy remains provisional; its relevance and value depend on what it is able to achieve, on its utility in organising means towards ends.'

96 Mackenzie, 1996, p 168; and see, generally, Hadfield, 1996.

EMPOWERMENT – INDEPENDENT ADVICE

Reforms which have been proposed to remedy this situation have included banning or imposing certain legislative restrictions on granting a security over the family home.[97] It is, however, unlikely that such restrictions would be favoured in the British context, where judicial and governmental support has been expressed in favour of maintaining this form of security.[98] This type of policy would also be hostage to claims of paternalism and, interestingly, when interviewed, sureties themselves favoured improved advice and assistance rather than radical restriction.[99]

This is presently the form that protection takes in both Scotland and England, with good faith requiring banks to offer independent advice. Although this duty is hardly revolutionary to the banking world,[100] advice has failed to be proscribed in the spirit of *O'Brien* and *Smith* and, in subsequent, cases ostensible rather than actual protection is evident.[101] Legal advice has often been particularly mechanical, with courts assuming any advice was 'honest and competent', and this applied even when the solicitor was chosen by her husband and he attended the interview.[102]

The practical result is that there has been an overwhelming recourse to legal advice in the surety context. Responsibility has shifted from large financial institutions to legal firms and their indemnity insurance. The Court

---

97 Fehlberg, 1997, pp 73–75, suggests this version of 'homestead legislation', currently in force in New Zealand, Canada and parts of the US, where the family home is protected from claims up to a specified sum.

98 *O'Brien* [1994] 1 AC 180, p 196.

99 Indeed, the present 'all or nothing situation' means that if a court were to find a contract to be tainted with bad faith then it is struck down with no facility to negotiate on more equal terms: Fehlberg, 1997, p 71. This simply reinforces the charge of over-protection. Reform should consider greater flexibility, which enables this limited class of non-commercial, potential cautioners to take control in negotiations.

100 As Forte, 1999, comments, this is not an unduly onerous duty for banks who already had reasonable standards of practice, encouraging oral warnings and advocating independent advice; Banking Code 1998, para 3.14.

101 This dissatisfaction has been echoed in the Court of Appeal's assessment that intended protection has been illusory in cases where advice has been merely perfunctory: *Royal Bank of Scotland v Etridge (No 2)* [1998] 4 All ER 705, p 711.

102 *Midland Bank plc v Massey* [1995] 1 All ER 129 and *Banco Exterior Internacional SA v Mann* [1995] 1 All ER 936. *Etridge (No 2)* [1998] 4 All ER 705 can be seen as a step in the right direction, in that it examines the substance, rather than the form, of legal advice. The case raises the question of whether the solicitors have access to all relevant documents in order to be able to advise their clients and, as Gretton, 1999, p 54, remarks, whether the form of their practising certificate renders them suitably qualified to advise. The requirement for more information, while certainly assisting in cases of misrepresentation, is not particularly well suited to cases of undue pressure. In these circumstances, the problem is not information imbalance, but 'the inability to bring an independent mind to the wisdom of entering into the transaction'. It is in this context that a more onerous task of advising clients and inquiring into the circumstances of the relationship is important, if power differentials are to be addressed in any way by the legal advice.

of Appeal, in the case of *Royal Bank of Scotland v Etridge (No 2)*,[103] not only acknowledges this practice, but sets up even more stringent standards for the legal profession to perform in extinguishing this obligation. This includes more detailed examination of the proposed agreement, in certain circumstances ascertaining the stability of the marriage, judging whether pressure has been applied and making calls on the financial merits of the transaction.[104] While I agree with Gretton that a more equitable division of responsibility is appropriate, the proposals do go some way towards addressing the bargaining powers of parties and empowering women. If coupled with private meetings, increased access to all relevant information,[105] ensuring lenders take responsibility for independent financial advice, guidelines to assist solicitors in advising, not just explaining, the legal effect of documents and cooling off periods,[106] these reforms could not only remedy many wives' vulnerabilities, but also encourage 'sureties to consider their own commercial self-interest.'[107]

The construction Gretton applies to *Etridge* of '[s]urety wives ... with two barrels to their shotguns',[108] aimed at the bank and now the law firm, is unhelpful and reminiscent of the 'woman scorned' clichés.[109] His conclusion that 'solicitors prepared to advise "surety wives" are solicitors with a death wish'[110] casts the woman as "the problem" to be avoided when, in fact, the difficulty is the banks' shirking of responsibility, protecting themselves rather than dealing with the issue of the abuse of bargaining power. Law requires the co-operation of financial institutions to help engender a more equitable regime of security in this context. This ties in well with Trebilock's solution to conflicts between autonomy and welfare. Rather than choosing between the two, he argues: 'law should rely on different institutions to vindicate different values.' Thus, autonomy can still guide the private ordering of agreements, but simultaneously the welfare of weaker parties can be protected through the 'regulation of contractual terms, distribution policies and government

---

103 [1998] 4 All ER 705.

104 *Ibid*, pp 715, 717; Gretton, 1999, p 54.

105 Fehlberg, 1997, p 276. Information as to the creditworthiness and potential liabilities of the company is particularly important where security is being provided for an ailing business. Fehlberg also makes the point that sharing information in this way can instil trust and confidence and encourage a shared approach to future decision making.

106 Gretton questions the appropriateness of questioning the 'state of relationship'. Fehlberg's study, 1997, however, points to the interrelationship between the health of the emotional and commercial partnership.

107 *Ibid*, Fehlberg, p 282, does not overemphasise law's ability to transform this situation and points to extra-legal measures such as the use of community education and trained financial counsellors.

108 Gretton, 1999, p 55.

109 A similar stereotyping is evident in Cretney, 1992.

110 Gretton, 1999.

investment'.[111] This reliance on other institutions recognises that we should not over-estimate law's ability to remedy social inequality single-handedly. The requirement that banks, with the aid of the profession, endeavour to promote a more self-interested approach to contractual undertakings is not, in any case, arduous, mirroring the norms that banks set themselves.[112] The difference is that the legal system must be concerned that such advice be more than perfunctory if inequality is to be addressed in any real sense and material change is to be effected.

CONCLUSION

The Scots legal system is not alone in hiding behind legal principle to avoid addressing the difficult and complex question of inequality. The absence of a system of equity has meant that narrow and inadequately drawn grounds have, for a long time, staved off any detailed or socially responsive inquiry into the complex issues of substantive inequality. The insensitivity of legal rules was apparent in the case of *Smith*, where, in order to facilitate relief, the court had to move outwith the contractual frame. The House of Lords' resuscitation of the latent doctrine of good faith in Scots law is controversial. Some have cast doubt on the legitimacy of the doctrine, preferring to retreat to the familiar 'truisms' of Scots law and the classical contract model with its promotion of contractual freedom and what could be termed rampant individualism. Yet, the recognition of this doctrine signals an increasing flexibility and willingness on the part of the legal system to begin to examine the complex interplay of public and private norms and the gendered nature of decision making and control in certain family relationships.

Nevertheless, protectionist views are not without cause. The position of the good faith doctrine in Scots contract law is nebulous. Forte describes it as 'like the wind; we cannot see it, but feel its force'.[113] Staying clear of the metaphysical, good faith may be better understood as a discretionary device, inherent to the administration of justice. Its ability to facilitate flexible, sympathetic judgments and accommodate distributive outcomes makes it a welcome addition to a constrictive contractual order. In the particular context of sexually transmitted debt, its introduction has created a space for different narratives, previously incoherent, in the dominant contractual discourse. Feminist scholarship, informed by women's experience, uncovers alternate motivations such as care, interdependence and altruism, previously absent from official reports.

---

111 See, generally, Trebilock, 1993.
112 Banking Code 1998, s 3.14.
113 Forte, 1999, p 101.

Caution must be exercised not to over-determine and present these alternate norms as manifestations of a distinctive 'female voice'. In a similar manner, care must also be taken not to make an easy assimilation between equity and these norms. It may be tempting to ally equity and equitable principle with the plight of women and cast them both as 'brothers (or sisters) in arms', against the brutish force of the present contractual regime. Such dualisms, however, have proved over-determinate and unproductive in an evolved feminist strategy.

Values associated with the feminine, such as care, altruism and trust, may to some extent describe the situation women experience in this context, but are not those which the operation of good faith should valorise. Similarly, scholarship on relational contracts, although descriptively familiar, when applied to this context, is in fact strategically impotent. It is, ironically, contract's norms of self-interest and autonomy which are most useful in wrenching women from these inferior bargaining positions.

Equitable doctrine, then, as it develops in Scots law, must preserve its ability to accommodate a multiplicity of norms. This may prove to be a challenge as it is inevitably captured and becomes expressed in rules, but this preservation is essential if equitable doctrine is to adequately respond to the complexities and contradictory effects of power in the 21st century.

CHAPTER 7

PROPERTY RIGHTS FOR HOME-SHARERS: EQUITY VERSUS A LEGISLATIVE FRAMEWORK?

Simone Wong

At the breakdown of a marriage or a relationship between cohabitants, one significant issue that often arises relates to the distribution of the parties' assets and, more particularly, their respective rights over the family home. Whilst the courts are given powers to adjust the property rights of spouses at the breakdown of marriage,[1] the powers do not extend to cohabitants or other parties in a domestic relationship. In the absence of legal co-ownership in the property, these parties will have to rely on contract law, property law and trusts principles to establish an equitable interest in the said property.[2] The use of trusts principles, especially the common intention constructive trust, has been subject to much criticism as an effective method of resolving family property disputes. This is partly owing to the narrow interpretation that subsequent courts have given to the criteria laid down by Lord Bridge in *Lloyds Bank v Rosset*[3] for establishing the existence of the requisite 'common intention' so as to ground a proprietary claim.[4] One of the key criticisms of Rosset is its focus on direct financial contributions, thereby exposing the test to gender bias. The approach is formulated and interpreted by the courts in a manner that tends to mask the effects of sexual division of labour in relationships and, consequently, to discriminate against female claimants.[5] The test ignores how, in a domestic relationship, the woman generally remains the partner who is primarily responsible for the care of the family and the home. This will, in turn, affect both the ability of most women to participate in the labour market and their economic resources.[6] Consequently, an approach that focuses on direct financial contributions and downplays the significance of indirect non-financial contributions places women at a disadvantage.

---

1   See Matrimonial Causes Act 1973, s 28(3).
2   These include spouses whose marriage has not broken down and thus fall outside the scope of the Matrimonial Causes Act 1973, s 28(3).
3   [1991] 1 AC 107.
4   There has been a plethora of literature pointing out the limitations of the common intention approach in resolving family property disputes. See, eg, Bottomley, 1993, p 56; Eekelaar, 1987, p 93; Halliwell, 1991, p 550; Glover and Todd, 1996, p 325; Lawson, 1996, p 218; and Wong, 1998, p 369.
5   Neave, 1991a, p 14; Flynn and Lawson, 1995, p 105; *ibid*, Wong; and *ibid*, Halliwell.
6   *Ibid*, Wong, p 373.

Questions have been raised about how rights of family members over the family home may be better dealt with and in a less discriminatory manner. Given the forthcoming consultation paper by the Law Commission on the rights of home-sharers, these questions are clearly of significance and will require further consideration.[7] A significant aspect of the Law Commission's forthcoming consultation paper is its reference to 'home-sharers'. This suggests that the potential reform that may be recommended may not be limited merely to spouses, cohabitants or family members. It may extend to include other domestic relationships where the parties are neither related to each other by family or marriage, nor in a sexual relationship. There is the further possibility of the Law Commission recommending a legislative framework to avoid the injustices or inadequacies of the current legal principles governing this area, particularly its failure to give adequate weight to indirect financial and non-financial contributions. This raises the important question of whether legislation is indeed desirable for the resolution of family property disputes. The article will focus on the development of equitable doctrines in comparison with a legislative framework. A key question raised is whether legislation will indeed provide a basis for the resolution of family property disputes that is less gender-biased than that currently provided by the equitable doctrines. For the purposes of the discussion, I shall be drawing on the experiences of the New South Wales courts in applying the Property (Relationships) Act (PRA) 1984. The original Act, the *De Facto* Relationships Act (DFRA) 1984, was limited to *de facto* relationships between heterosexual couples.[8] The DFRA 1984 has since been amended by the Property (Relationships) Legislation Amendment Act 1999 to read as the PRA 1984 and to apply to a wider class of relationships.[9]

The chapter is divided into three sections. The first section will examine the various equitable principles that are currently used in England and three other Commonwealth jurisdictions, namely Australia, Canada and New Zealand, in the resolution of family property disputes. In this section, I will argue that the English courts should move towards a remedial approach, as this will facilitate the analysis shifting away from ownership as a starting point. In doing so, this will enable the courts to move away from a narrow interpretation of the types of contribution that will qualify in providing relief to a claimant. It will provide the courts with greater flexibility in terms of the range of remedies that may be granted to the claimant. In the following section, I shall be looking at the provisions of the DFRA 1984 and the way in which the Act defines the scope of the courts' discretionary powers to make

---

7   The Law Commission in 1995 commenced the present review into the property rights of home-sharers. The consultation paper was initially due to be published in late 1999 but is now expected to be published some time in 2001.

8   See the DFRA 1984, s 4.

9   Property (Relationships) Legislation Amendment Act 1999, Sched 1, para 2.

orders for adjustment of property rights. The section will further consider the extent to which the DFRA 1984 has been amended by the PRA 1984.

In the third section, I shall be considering the way in which the New South Wales' courts have interpreted and applied their statutory powers under the PRA 1984 and the role of the equitable principles within this legislative framework. In doing so, there are several issues that I am particularly concerned with. First, I would like to examine whether the exercise of the courts' discretion under these statutory provisions is premised on a principled basis upon which property adjustment orders may be made. I will argue that there appears to be little distinction between the way in which the courts are, in practice, exercising their discretion under certain equitable principles, more particularly unjust enrichment, and the PRA 1984. This is, therefore, an undesirable approach as it is likely to lead to greater confusion. It will lead to the creation of a jurisprudence that fails to distinguish between equitable principles and those underpinning the statute. Secondly, it is necessary to consider whether the legislative provisions succeed in providing a more gender-neutral way of enabling parties to a domestic relationship to establish a proprietary claim. In exploring these issues, I will argue that legislation may provide statutory recognition of indirect financial and non-financial contributions. In doing so, it will resolve some of the difficulties raised in the application of equitable principles such as the common intention constructive trust. It may further empower the courts to make property adjustment orders that are similar in some ways to the adjustive powers of the courts under the marital provisions. At a practical level, it may not, however, provide female claimants with a framework that is completely gender-neutral. Legislation may further be at the expense of doctrinal clarity and legal certainty.

EQUITY'S RESPONSE TO THE HOME-SHARERS' DILEMMA

Under English law, an equitable principle commonly relied upon by home-sharers to ground a proprietary claim over the family home is the common intention constructive trust. This approach requires the establishment of two elements: a common intention between the parties to share the property; and the detrimental reliance of the claimant on the common intention.[10] The common intention to share may be express or, in the absence of such an intention, it may be inferred from the conduct of the parties. The conduct from which an inference may be drawn has, however, been limited to the direct financial contributions of the claimant towards the acquisition of the property. In doing so, it has been argued that the common intention approach is gender-biased in two principal ways. First, it fails to take into account the economic

---

10   See *Lloyds Bank v Rosset* [1991] 1 AC 107.

inequality between men and women, which directly affects their ability to acquire assets.[11] Secondly, the approach fails to take into account the effects of sexual division of labour and its impact on women's economic position.[12] An examination of the approaches taken by other Commonwealth jurisdictions, such as Australia, New Zealand and Canada, points to the development of a variety of equitable principles as alternatives to the common intention approach.[13] The Australian courts have applied the doctrine of unconscionability in cases where the domestic relationship may be analogous to a joint venture.[14] In Canada, the courts have adopted a restitutionary approach based on notions of *unjust enrichment*.[15] The New Zealand courts have, on the other hand, based their approach on the 'reasonable expectations' of the parties to the relationship.[16]

A common thread emerges from these three Commonwealth approaches, that is, the courts have all moved towards a remedial approach in dealing with family property disputes. In cases where the courts have granted a proprietary remedy, it has been acknowledged that the remedy is purely remedial in nature. The imposition of a constructive trust is not premised on any pre-existing proprietary interest that the claimant may have over the property. It is imposed on the basis that, in the circumstances of the case, it would be unconscionable not to grant a proprietary remedy to the claimant. However, not all the approaches taken by the Commonwealth jurisdictions have succeeded in eradicating the gender bias in the equitable principles. In focusing on the establishment of some kind of joint endeavour between the parties, the unconscionability approach continues to emphasise the significance of financial contributions.[17] This is replicated in the need for some

---

11 Wong, 1998; Neave, 1991b; and Lawson, 1996. For further discussion on the weaker economic position of women in relation to the financial arrangements and allocation of resources within domestic relationships, see Pahl, 1989; Pahl, 1990, p 119; and Pahl and Vogler, 1994, p 263.

12 For a more detailed discussion on how sexual division of labour continues to affect the earning capacity and hence the economic position of women, see *ibid*, Wong.

13 See Gardner, 1993, p 263; *ibid*, Wong.

14 *Muschinski v Dodds* (1985) 160 CLR 583; *Baumgartner v Baumgartner* (1987) 164 CLR 137. The analogy to a joint endeavour may be made through the pooling of financial resources towards the parties' relationship.

15 *Pettkus v Becker* (1980) 117 DLR (3d) 257; *Sorochan v Sorochan* (1986) 29 DLR (4th) 1; *Peter v Beblow* (1993) 101 DLR (4th) 621. The approach requires the establishment of three elements: an enrichment of the defendant; a corresponding deprivation of the claimant; and an absence of a juristic reason for the defendant's enrichment.

16 *Gillies v Keogh* (1989) 2 NZLR 327; *Lankow v Rose* (1995) 1 NZLR 277. Under this approach, the claimant needs to establish four essential elements: that contributions, whether direct or indirect, have been made towards the acquisition, preservation or enhancement of the defendant's assets or property; that the claimant had expected an interest in such assets or property; that such expectations were reasonable in the circumstances; and that the defendant should reasonably be expected to give the claimant an interest.

17 Wong, 1998; and Neave, 1991b, p 185.

form of pooling of financial resources by the parties. In the absence of any evidence of some financial contributions having been made to the parties' joint relationship, the courts are unlikely to grant a proprietary remedy to the claimant.[18]

Although the reasonable expectations approach is willing to take account of both financial and non-financial contributions, it remains gender-biased in two ways. First, the approach requires the courts to balance the contributions made by the claimant against the benefits received. Although there is no requirement that the contributions be by way of direct financial contributions, a proprietary remedy will only be granted if the contributions manifestly exceed the benefits received. There must further be some causal relationship between the contributions and the property in issue. In the case of a female claimant whose contributions are mainly domestic (non-financial) in nature, a consequence of a conservative valuation of such contributions against the benefits she has received will mean that the courts are less likely to intervene. The second aspect of the gender bias is found in the ability of the other partner to expressly 'opt out' of any sharing intent. Here again, the continued assumption of a domestic role in the relationship will place the female claimant at a disadvantage and may disable her from making adequate financial contributions. Given that women continue to be principally responsible for the care of the home and family and that they are generally in a weaker economic position, the reasonable expectations approach will equally discriminate against female claimants as in the common intention approach.

Simon Gardner has raised the possibility of adopting an unjust enrichment approach to the resolution of family property disputes in the English context.[19] More recently, John Dewar has argued that there would be greater clarity in the law relating to the family home if the analysis shifted away from ownership as the starting point and focused instead on identifying the types of rights that family members may actually need in relation to the family home.[20] This shift away from ownership is particularly significant for female claimants. It enables the courts to break away from its present preoccupation with direct financial contributions towards the acquisition of the property, as this is inextricably linked to the issue of ownership.[21] It has been argued that the unjust enrichment approach may facilitate this shift in emphasis. The

---

18 See cases like *Tory v Jones* (1990) DFC #95–095, *Public Trustee v Kukula* (1990) 14 Fam LR 97 and *Bryson v Bryant* (1992) 29 NSWLR 188, which illustrate how the lack of financial contributions to the parties' joint relationship will be fatal to a claim for a proprietary remedy.

19 Gardner, 1993.

20 Dewar, 1998, pp 327–55.

21 This is reflected in the continued perception in English law of the constructive trust being institutional in nature, where the declaration of the trust is seen merely as vindicating the pre-existing proprietary interest of the claimant.

attractiveness of the unjust enrichment approach as an alternative to the common intention approach lies in its willingness to take into account a wider range of contributions, relationships and available remedies.[22]

The unjust enrichment approach taken by the Canadian courts illustrates a greater willingness than the other three approaches to take into consideration both the financial and non-financial contributions of the claimant as being incontrovertible benefits for the purposes of establishing an unjust enrichment. This is particularly significant in cases where the non-financial contributions outweigh the financial ones. This is, further, a more realistic acknowledgment of the domestic arrangements in most familial relationships.[23] Welstead observes that most familial relationships operate as common enterprises where each member contributes in accordance with his or her abilities and resources, and the needs of the other members of the family.[24] Upon the breakdown of the relationship, any rights over the property should accord with the contributions made, be they financial or non-financial. In doing so, Welstead argues that the approach is less susceptible to accusations of gender bias, since the approach allows for the greater recognition of indirect contributions such as domestic services.[25]

Notwithstanding that the unjust enrichment approach does require the establishment of an enrichment that is unjust, the approach differs from the reasonable expectations approach in several ways. In the reasonable expectations approach, the contributions must, in some way, be made towards the property in issue, whether in terms of its acquisition, preservation or enhancement. A clear proprietary nexus between the contributions and the property must be established in order to justify granting a remedy to the claimant. In contrast, the Canadian courts tend to take a less restrictive approach towards the requisite proprietary link in domestic cases. This is owing to the fact that, unlike commercial cases, the acceptance of risk in domestic relationships is generally absent.[26] Although the courts have noted that some proprietary link is required to justify the imposition of a constructive trust, the proprietary nexus appears more easily satisfied through the establishment of the claimant's reasonable expectation of an interest as a result of her contributions and the presumptions raised in her favour stemming from the nature of the parties' relationship.[27] Thirdly, unlike the ability of the defendant expressly to opt out of a sharing intent in the

---

22 For a more detailed discussion, see Wong, 1999, p 47.
23 Welstead, 1987, p 151.
24 *Ibid*.
25 This approach further avoids the difficulties of the common intention and unconscionability approaches, that is, the constraints of the need for financial contributions to the relationship to ground a claim.
26 Paccioco, 1989, p 315.
27 Scane, 1991, p 260.

reasonable expectations approach, the Canadian courts have indicated that expressing such an intent may not necessarily suffice in treating the continued provision of contributions by the claimant as being purely 'voluntary'. Hence, a restitutionary remedy will not automatically be excluded.[28]

In adopting a remedial approach, the unjust enrichment approach has the added advantage of giving the courts greater discretion as to the more appropriate remedy to be awarded to the claimant. The establishment of an unjust enrichment does not automatically confer on the claimant a proprietary interest in the family home. The grant of a proprietary remedy through the imposition of a constructive trust will depend on the particular facts of each case and whether the circumstances justify the granting of a proprietary remedy to reverse the unjust enrichment of the defendant.[29] The courts may, on the other hand, award the claimant some other form of remedy such as a monetary award. The imposition of the constructive trust is remedial and purely a discretionary response from the courts. The approach, therefore, provides a more flexible method of considering the various rights that parties may have over the family home at the breakdown of the relationship and for providing for those rights, without necessarily using ownership as the starting point of the analysis.

A LEGISLATIVE FRAMEWORK:
THE NEW SOUTH WALES MODEL

Under s 14 of the DFRA 1984, parties to a *de facto* relationship that falls within the scope of the Act may make an application to the court for the adjustment of interests with respect to the property of the parties to the relationship or either of them. The PRA 1984 was amended to apply to a more widely defined class of relationships, namely, de facto relationships as well as domestic relationships. The DFRA 1984 was based on a model prepared by the New South Wales Law Reform Commission in its report in 1983.[30] The Law Reform Commission had, at that time, observed that the existing injustice or inadequacy of the law in dealing with family property disputes were owing to:

> ... the concentration of existing law on the common intention of the parties and on direct financial contributions to the acquisition of assets. Specifically, the law fails to give sufficient recognition to two kinds of contribution to a *de facto* relationship: indirect financial and non-financial contributions by one partner to the acquisition, conservation or improvement of assets, such as

---

28 *Sorochan v Sorochan* (1986) 29 DLR (4th) 1.

29 *LAC Minerals Ltd v International Corona Resources Ltd* (1989) 61 DLR (4th) 14.

30 Law Reform Commission Report, No 36 of 1983.

contributions to the family's household expenses which assist the other partner to acquire assets in his or her own name; and financial and non-financial contributions by one partner to the welfare of the other partner or the children of the relationship, including contributions made in the capacity of homemaker and parent.[31]

The Law Reform Commission went on to recommend that the courts should, therefore, be entitled to take into account a wider range of contributions by either party to a *de facto* relationship towards the acquisition, conservation or improvement of assets and the welfare of the other partner or the family generally. Moreover, the Commission proposed a model for legislation that would enable the courts to examine the specific areas of law to determine whether there were inadequacies or injustices and the type of remedial action required.[32] The Commission then specified the contributions to be taken into account as being those referred to in s 20(1)(a) and (b) of the DFRA 1984. It was of the opinion that the contributions referred to in paras (a) and (b), taken together, would ensure that a wide range of contributions would be taken into account by the court when determining the appropriate order to make.[33] Thus, the effect of the proposed legislation was to provide the court with the requisite statutory power to make an order for the adjustment of the interests of *de facto* partners to the extent that their contributions make it 'just and equitable' to do so.

THE *DE FACTO* RELATIONSHIPS ACT 1984

There are several significant aspects of the DFRA 1984. First, indirect financial and non-financial contributions are, for the first time, given statutory recognition in New South Wales. Secondly, the courts are given the statutory power to, inter alia, make orders for the adjustment of interests with respect to the property of *de facto* partners or either of them.[34] The prerequisites for

---

31 Law Reform Commission Report, No 36 of 1983, para 7.53.

32 The Law Reform Commission identified four possible remedies or models for legislation: see para 5.41 *et seq* of the report. However, the Commission rejected equating *de facto* relationships with marriages (para 5.57); that relief should be based on dependence (para 5.58); and equating '*de facto* relationships with marriages for certain purposes' (para 5.61).

33 *Ibid*, paras 7.44–7.46. These should include contributions such as direct financial contributions to the acquisition or improvement of property; physical labour in connection with the home or a business; payments towards household expenses; assistance in increasing the earning capacity of the other party (eg, supporting that party while he or she undertakes a course); the provision of housekeeping or nursing services; and contributions in the form of caring for children.

34 DFRA 1984, s 14(1) provides that a *de facto* partner may apply to the court for the adjustment of interests of property belonging to the *de facto* partners or either of them or for the granting of maintenance, or both. Section 3(1) defines *de facto* partners as a man and woman living together as husband and wife in a *bona fide* domestic basis although not married to each other.

making such an order for adjustment include, *inter alia*, the existence of a *de facto* relationship for a period of not less than two years, or where the requisite period of cohabitation is not satisfied, the parties have a child.[35] In addition, the court must be satisfied that the claimant has made substantial contributions of the kind referred to in s 20(1)(a) or (b) for which (s)he would not otherwise be adequately compensated if no order for adjustment is made and that this will result in a serious injustice to the claimant.[36] The courts' statutory power to make orders for the adjustment of property interests may be exercised where it seems just and equitable to do so.

The DFRA 1984 provides no clear definition of what 'just and equitable' means, but some guidance is given on the matters that the court should take into account when deciding whether or not to make an order. Section 20(1) states that, in determining whether to make an order for adjustment, the court should make an order that seems just and equitable, having regard to the contributions specified in paras (a) and (b). The relevant contributions have to fall into one of two categories: financial and non-financial contributions. The contributions referred to in para (a) cover financial and non-financial contributions made by the claimant which have contributed, directly or indirectly, to the acquisition, conservation or improvement of any property of the parties or either of them, or to the financial resources of the parties or either of them. Paragraph (b) contributions, on the other hand, focus on non-financial contributions made by the claimant in the capacity of homemaker or parent, to the welfare of the other partner or the family constituted by the parties. In giving statutory recognition to indirect financial and non-financial contributions, the approach taken in the DFRA 1984, to a large extent, avoids the practical difficulties faced by claimants under the common intention approach which continues to place greater significance on direct financial contributions for getting the claim off the ground.[37]

THE PROPERTY (RELATIONSHIPS) ACT 1984

The DFRA 1984 is novel in that it not only confers on the courts adjustive powers that are, to some extent, similar to those under marital provisions, but also gives statutory recognition to non-financial contributions, particularly domestic services, as qualifying contributions. One clear limitation of the DFRA 1984 is that it is restricted to *de facto* relationships between heterosexual

---

35 See DFRA 1984, s 17(1).
36 See *ibid*, s 17(2)(b)(i).
37 See *Lloyds Bank v Rosset* [1991] 1 AC 107.

gender - based discrepancy that doesn't affect
Feminist Perspectives on Equity and Trusts _Same-sex_
relats.

couples.[38] It does not extend to a wider range of relationships such as same-sex couples and other forms of domestic sharing, for example by parent and child, or siblings.[39] Consequently, the aim of the Property (Relationships) Legislation Amendment Act 1999 is, *inter alia*, to rectify this limitation of the DFRA 1984 so that the Act would apply to parties to relationships of a more widely defined class.[40] This is reflected by the new PRA 1984 being extended to 'domestic relationships' within the meaning of the Act. Beyond that, there is little change to the scope of the courts' discretionary powers. The PRA 1984 basically retains the wording of essential sections.[41]

The new s 5(1) defines a domestic relationship as either a *de facto* relationship[42] or a 'close personal relationship' between two adult persons, whether or not they are related by family, who are living together, and one or each of them provides the other with 'domestic support and personal care'.[43] A *de facto* relationship is, however, re-defined as one between two adult persons living together as a couple and who are not married to one another or related by family.[44] Unlike the old s 3(1), there is no reference to the sex of the *de facto* partners in the new s 4. Thus, the adjustive powers of the courts under the PRA 1984 now extend to same-sex couples. The new s 4(2) further

---

38 This is reflected in the express reference in s 3(1) to a *de facto* relationship being one between a man and a woman living together in *bona fide* domestic basis without being married.

39 After the enactment of the DFRA 1984, there was strong lobbying by minority pressure groups such as the Gay and Lesbian Rights Lobby to confer on same-sex couples the same property rights as then existing for those in married and heterosexual *de facto* relationships.

40 As far back as the 1988 election, the coalition opposition had promised to introduce such a Bill, but never did so. In the 1995 election, the Australian Labor Party made a similar promise, but did little to fulfil that promise after coming into power. Due to the government's inactivity on the issue, a private member's Bill – the Significant Personal Relationships Bill – was introduced into the New South Wales Parliament in September 1997. The said Bill did not, however, get past the second-reading stage. Subsequently, in June 1998, another private member's Bill – the *De Facto* Relationships Amendment Bill – was introduced by the Australian Democrats into the New South Wales Parliament but that Bill was referred to the Standing Committee on Social Issues for a full inquiry. Before the Standing Committee could report on the said Bill, the Government, in response to minority group pressure, introduced its own Property (Relationships) Legislation Amendment Bill.

41 For the purposes of this chapter, see PRA 1984, ss 14, 17 and 20(1)(a) and (b).

42 See *ibid*, s 5(1)(a).

43 See *ibid*, s 5(1)(b). The section, however, excludes any relationship where the provision of domestic support and personal care is for a fee or reward, or on behalf of another person or organisation such as a charitable or benevolent organisation, or a government or government agency: s 5(2)(a) and (b).

44 See *ibid*, s 4.

provides guidance to the courts on the type of matters that may be relevant in determining the existence of a *de facto* relationship between the parties.[45]

'Domestic relationships', by its very definition, is capable of encompassing a wider range of relationships, both familial[46] and non-familial. The definition suggests that there are three criteria that must be satisfied in order for a claimant to have *locus standi* to make an application under s 14 of the PRA 1984. The first is the establishment of a 'close personal relationship'. Unfortunately, unlike the new s 4(2), where some guidance is given on the relevant matters that a court may taken into consideration in determining whether a *de facto* relationship exists, little guidance is given in s 5 as to what is actually meant by a 'close personal relationship' and what factors are deemed relevant to warrant labelling a particular relationship as being a 'close personal' one. Would the matters listed in s 4(2) be equally applicable to the assessment of whether a relationship is a close personal one? Arguably not, since s 5(1)(b) makes it explicit that a close personal relationship is one other than a marriage or a *de facto* relationship. Yet, to a large extent, questions such as the duration of the relationship, whether there is the presence of a sexual or non-sexual relationship, the level of financial dependence or interdependence of the parties (which may be reflected in the provision of domestic support and personal care), and the presence of children may be equally pertinent to the issue of the existence of a close personal relationship.

The second criterion is that the parties must be living together. This criterion may arguably be less problematic, in that it suggests that some form of sharing of a domestic household, but not necessarily the existence of a sexual relationship, is a relevant factor. More crucially, the third criterion that a claimant will need to satisfy is the provision of 'domestic support and personal care'. The emphasis appears to be on caring relationships, but the PRA 1984 is silent on the definition of these terms. It is unclear what the criteria are by which a party is deemed to provide sufficient domestic care and personal support so as to fall within the scope of the Act. This raises issues as to both the qualitative and quantitative aspects of the provision of 'domestic support and personal care'.

---

45   The relevant matters are: the length of the parties' relationship; the nature and extent of common residence; whether or not a sexual relationship exists; the degree of financial dependence or interdependence, and any arrangements for financial support, between the parties; the ownership, use and acquisition of property; the degree of mutual commitment to a shared life; the care and support of children; the performance of household duties; and the reputation and public aspects of the relationship. But s 4(3) is quick to point out that this is not intended to be in any way an exhaustive list. The court is entitled to have regard to other matters as may seem appropriate to the court in the circumstances of the case.

46   See PRA 1984, s 5A.

THE APPLICATION OF THE PRA 1984 AND EQUITY'S ROLE WITHIN A LEGISLATIVE FRAMEWORK

Whilst the DFRA 1984, and now the PRA 1984, provide the courts with the discretion to make orders for adjustment where it seems 'just and equitable', much debate has emerged regarding the appropriate test for the exercise of the courts' discretion.[47] This raises three issues. The first touches on the question of the exact scope of the courts' discretion under the Act. The second is the principles underpinning the exercise of that discretion. The third focuses on the relationship between equitable principles and the courts' discretion. The case law evinces some consensus on certain key aspects of the courts' discretion under s 20(1). There is, for example, a general acceptance of the four-stage process established by Powell J in *D v McA*[48] for determining whether an order for adjustment should be made. The first step is to identify and value the assets of the parties. The next is to determine whether contributions like those referred to in s 20(1)(a) and (b) have been made by each of the parties. Thirdly, the court has to determine whether the claimant's contributions have already been sufficiently recognised and compensated for during the relationship. Finally, the court has to decide what order should be made so that the claimant's contributions will be sufficiently recognised and compensated.

Powell J further observes that, despite the similarity between s 79 of the Family Law Act 1975[49] and s 20(1) of the DFRA 1984, there are significant differences between these two provisions.[50] One significant difference is that the range of matters that may be taken into account under s 20(1) when determining whether there should be an order, and what order for adjustment is to be made, is much narrower than that permitted under s 79.[51] Powell J puts these differences down to two reasons: that s 20(1) is a response to the criticisms made about the injustices that arise as a result of applying orthodox legal and equitable principles in resolving property disputes between *de facto* partners; and that, whilst the DFRA 1984 is intended to remedy some of these

---

47 Given that the wording of s 20(1) has been basically retained in the PRA 1984, the case law relating to that section is still relevant and helpful in providing guidance on its construction.

48 (1986) 11 Fam LR 214.

49 The Family Law Act 1975 is limited to parties to a marriage and s 79 governs the adjustive powers of the court with respect to the property of the parties to a marriage or either of them.

50 (1986) 11 Fam LR 214, p 228.

51 See s 79(4) and, more particularly, s 79(4)(e), which provides that the court may take into account the matters referred to in s 75(2). That section provides a list of matters reflecting the needs of the claimant that the court may take into account in determining whether to make an adjustive order. In addition, s 75(2)(o) provides the court with relatively wide discretion to take into account 'any fact or circumstance which, in the opinion of the court, the justice of the case requires to be taken into account'.

injustices, it is not Parliament's intention to place *de facto* relationships on a par with marriages.[52] When evaluating the non-financial contributions of a *de facto* partner, particularly contributions as homemaker and parent, the courts have conceded that such contributions should not be regarded as being in some way inferior to the corresponding contributions of a spouse.[53] Nor would it be suggested that an appropriate way of valuing such contributions is by reference to the wages applicable to a domestic servant or any other commercial provider of similar services or benefits.[54] The courts have acknowledged that it is important to give full and proper value to the contributions of the kind referred to in s 20(1)(b) and that they should not be treated in a token way.[55] There is, however, no assumption that equal division is the appropriate form of, or the starting point for, the adjustment of property interests.[56]

The exercise of judicial discretion under s 20(1) raises two principal issues. First, the courts have to grapple with the exact meaning and effect of s 20(1). This issue focuses on the matters of which the court should take account in determining whether an order for adjustment should be made. The second issue is the application of the section, on its true construction, to the facts and circumstances of each case. The focus here is on what order the court should make that seems to it to be 'just and equitable' in the circumstances of the case. The conflict lies principally in the construction of s 20(1), and the practical difficulties underlying this are demonstrated by the fact that two conflicting lines of authority have emerged.[57] In *Dwyer v Kaljo*,[58] Handley JA states that the purpose of s 20(1) is to empower the courts to make an order for adjustment as seems 'just and equitable' to the courts. In construing the scope of this judicial discretion, Handley JA takes the view that, although adequate compensation is central to s 17(2)(b)(i), the power conferred by s 20(1) goes further. The section is not limited to providing adequate compensation. It confers on the courts a power to remedy an injustice that the claimant would otherwise suffer because of either his or her reasonable reliance on the relationship (the reliance interest), or his or her reasonable expectations from the relationship (the expectation interest). He further states that the section authorises the making of orders that will restore to the claimant benefits that

---

52   (1986) 11 Fam LR 214, p 228.
53   *Black v Black* (1991) 15 Fam LR 109.
54   *Ibid.*
55   *Green v Robinson* (1995) 18 Fam LR 594.
56   *Mallett v Mallett* (1984) 9 Fam LR 449.
57   *Dwyer v Kaljo* (1992) 15 Fam LR 645; cf *Wallace v Stanford* (1995) 19 Fam LR 430. It should be noted that, in *Dwyer v Kaljo*, Handley JA and Priestley JA formed the majority, with Mahoney JA dissenting; whereas, in *Wallace v Stanford*, Mahoney JA and Sheller JA formed the majority, with Handley JA dissenting.
58   (1992) 15 Fam LR 645.

* While not downgrading dom-services of unmarried partner, Parl's intention is not to put DF rels on a par w/ marr. So no presump. to equal divis.

have been conferred on the other partner during the relationship or their value (the restitution interest).[59]

Handley JA does recognise that the courts' discretion is not unfettered and an order for adjustment must satisfy the 'just and equitable' criteria. However, he distinguishes 'just' and 'equitable' on the grounds that 'just' means that relief is not limited to situations where it would only be granted on equitable grounds under the general law. According to Handley JA, s 20(1) suggests that, although equitable considerations may be applied by analogy, the section goes further than these considerations.[60] This points to a broader approach where the court is not limited to making adjustment orders that are merely compensatory in nature. The approach taken by the majority suggests that s 20(1) empowers the court to make adjustment orders based not only on equitable considerations, but also on the reliance or expectation interest of the claimant or on restitutionary grounds.[61] The test for determining the exercise of the court's discretion rests squarely on the words 'just and equitable' as opposed to the contributions referred to in s 20(1)(a) and (b). In determining this, the matters referred to in paras (a) and (b) are merely factors, among others, that the court may or shall take into account.

However, in *Wallace v Stanford*,[62] a narrower construction of s 20(1) is taken by the majority, that is, the proper test for determining what is 'just and equitable' must be confined to looking at the matters referred to in paras (a) and (b). Mahoney JA maintains the position, taken in his dissenting judgment in *Dwyer v Kaljo*, that the discretion given is not as broad as to allow the court to take into account any other matter which it would otherwise consider in deciding what seems just and equitable. He bases his narrower construction of the scope of the courts' jurisdiction on three reasons.[63] First, the terms of s 20(1) are plain in that regard is to be given to the specified contributions. There is no mention in that section that, in addition to those contributions, reference may be made to other matters. Secondly, Mahoney JA draws support for this narrower view from the Law Reform Commission's recommendation that the court be entitled to take into account a wide range of contributions and that the contributions 'to be taken into account' are those referred to in s 20(1)(a) and (b).[64] The proposed legislation was intended to have the effect of 'adjusting the interests of the partners in the property' to the extent that the contributions made by the parties make it just and equitable to do so.[65]

---

59 (1992) 15 Fam LR 645, p 660.

60 This implies that a court may make not only compensatory orders, but also orders for equitable compensation to the claimant.

61 (1992) 15 Fam LR 645, p 660.

62 (1995) 19 Fam LR 430.

63 *Ibid*, p 436.

64 *Op cit*, fn 33.

65 (1995) 19 Fam LR 430, pp 438–39.

Thirdly, Mahoney JA observes that the DFRA 1984 reflects not only Parliament's recognition of the existing mischief noted by the Law Reform Commission, but also its determination of the extent to and the manner in which this mischief is to be adjusted. The purpose of the DFRA 1984 is, therefore, to provide a basis upon which the court could adjust property interests by taking the property from one *de facto* partner and giving it to the other. In that respect, Mahoney JA states that the 1984 Act reflects Parliament's adoption of the Law Reform Commission's proposal to grant discretionary powers of adjustment to the courts. However, this discretion is limited to the considerations specified in s 20(1)(a) and (b).[66] Thus, the proper test for determining whether it is 'just and equitable' for the court to make an order must be determined by reference only to those contributions.[67]

In an attempt to resolve the conflicting approaches taken in *Dwyer v Kaljo* and *Wallace v Stanford*, a five member Bench of the New South Wales Court of Appeal was specially constituted to hear *Evans v Marmont*.[68] By a three to two split, the majority[69] stated its preference for the narrower approach taken in *Wallace v Stanford*. On the question of the exercise of judicial discretion, Gleeson CJ and McLelland CJ stated that the essential test is on the contributions provision rather than on what is 'just and equitable'. Both Chief Justices drew support for this conclusion from 'the language and structure of [the DFRA 1984], and upon the legislative purpose as it emerges from the terms of the Act and the history of the legislation'.[70] They observe that there has been an omission in s 20(1) of provisions similar to those found in s 75(2)(o) of the Family Law Act 1975, which entitles the court to take into account, alongside the factors referred to in paras (a) and (b), 'any fact or circumstance which, in the opinion of the court, the justice of the case requires to be taken into account'.[71] The grammatical structure of s 20(1) thus suggests that the contributions in paras (a) and (b) are focal points upon which the discretionary judgment of what is just and equitable must be made. They are fundamental rather than merely matters to be taken into account amongst any other relevant matters. Notwithstanding this, Gleeson CJ and McLelland CJ do concede that, in deciding what seems just and equitable, the evaluation of the contributions will ordinarily have to be made in the context of the nature and incidents of the parties' relationship as a whole.[72] This reasoning was,

---

66 (1995) 19 Fam LR 430, p 439.

67 *Ibid*, p 440.

68 (1997) 21 Fam LR 760.

69 Gleeson CJ and McLelland CJ in equity, with Meagher JA concurring except on the matter of the quantum to be awarded to the claimant.

70 (1997) 21 Fam LR 760, p 767.

71 *Ibid*, p 768.

72 Eg, the needs and means of the parties to the relationship, the length of the relationship, promises or expectations of marriage and lost opportunities of the parties.

however, criticised by Mason P as being rather circuitous, in that the court appears to be 'letting in by the back door the cat they had thrown out the front'.[73]

In addition, both Chief Justices reject the wider approach taken by Handley JA, in that reference to 'just and equitable' empowers the court to compensate the claimant for her reliance or expectation interests.[74] Reference to paras 7.43 and 7.44 of the Law Commission Report indicates that this is not the intention of the section but, instead, it is to enable the courts to give adequate recognition to the indirect financial and non-financial contributions of the claimant, non-recognition of which permits one partner to be enriched at the expense of the other partner. Notwithstanding the adoption of this narrower interpretation of the scope of s 20(1), there is implicit acknowledgment that the aim of the section is to prevent the unjust enrichment of the other party to the relationship in terms of the contributions, direct and indirect, made by the claimant towards either the assets or financial resources of the other party or to his welfare and/or the welfare of the family constituted by them.

This 'true construction' of s 20(1) raises the crucial question of the exact relationship between equitable doctrines such as unjust enrichment and the principles underpinning the exercise of judicial discretion under s 20(1). On the one hand, the judges appear to go to some length to distinguish the application of the legislative framework from purely equitable principles. On the other hand, usage of phrases such as 'just and equitable' in the legislation has not been helpful in making the distinction clear. This lack of clarity is reflected in both the qualitative and quantitative aspects of the adjustments orders made by the courts in all these cases. Although the courts have conceded that there is no presumption of an equal share as a starting point, the cases fail to make clear the exact basis upon which the courts have determined the extent of the awards to be made to the claimants.[75] To a large extent, there is a strong sense

---

73 (1997) 21 Fam LR 760, p 776.

74 According to Gleeson CJ and McLelland CJ, this would mean a major shift in focus and would seem to be importing, by analogy, principles under which equity would award compensation for the breach of equitable duties. There does not, however, appear to be a rejection of the relevance of the claimant's restitutionary interest.

75 This is reflected in the cases where, in deciding the quantum of the order to be made, the judges have referred to matters such as the parties' intention, whether the contributions were being made towards their joint lives and whether an injustice would be suffered if no adequate compensation and recognition is given to contributions made. These matters are all reminiscent of equitable doctrines such as the common intention constructive trust, unconscionability, and unjust enrichment.

that the judges have approached the issue from a compensation perspective.[76] The inquiry focuses on whether the claimant has made any contributions of the types referred to in paras (a) and (b) and, if so, whether these contributions have been adequately recognised and compensated during the relationship. In doing so, this line of inquiry bears a strong resemblance to the search for an incontrovertible benefit to the defendant and the corresponding deprivation to the plaintiff in the unjust enrichment analysis.

Reference to 'just and equitable' in the statutory provisions appears to involve the courts in the same evaluative exercise as the 'absence of juristic reason' requirement for determining whether the enrichment has been unjust. In both situations, there is great similarity in the process and the objective of the inquiry, that is, to decide whether there has been an unjust enrichment of the defendant at the claimant's expense, and whether and if so what remedy ought to be awarded to reverse that enrichment. Hence, it is difficult to tease out from the cases whether there is any real, as opposed to apparent, differences between the statutory and the unjust enrichment approaches. There are, arguably, two main differences. First, in the legislative framework, indirect contributions are given clear statutory recognition as being qualifying factors in determining the issue of enrichment. However, adequate recognition of these contributions can be achieved even without statutory intervention, as can be seen in the unjust enrichment approach.[77] Secondly, the courts are given powers to adjust property interests despite any pre-existing proprietary interest in any particular asset. This may be the more significant of the two differences. Whilst there must be some nexus between the contributions and the parties' relationship, there need not be a (proprietary) nexus between the contributions and any specific asset that is made subject to an order for adjustment. Notwithstanding this, the remedial approach adopted in the unjust enrichment analysis indicates sufficient flexibility for the appropriate proprietary nexus to be established through the presumptive role played by the parties' reasonable expectations.[78] Moreover, the unjust enrichment approach provides the possibility of a proprietary

---

76 See Sifris, 1998, p 179. Sifris identifies five different approaches that the courts have taken in these cases. She, however, argues that only two approaches have since been endorsed by *Evans v Marmont*: the narrower 'contributions approach' adopted by Meagher JA; and the broader version of that approach adopted by Gleeson CJ and McLelland CJ which incorporates elements of the 'adequate compensation approach' taken in *D v McA*. In either case, there are similarities between the 'contributions approach' and 'adequate compensation approach', in that compensation in respect of contributions is central to both approaches.

77 *Pettkus v Becker* (1980) 117 DLR (3d) 257; *Sorochan v Sorochan* (1986) 29 DLR (4th) 1; *Peter v Beblow* (1993) 101 DLR (4th) 621.

78 See pp 137–39, above.

remedy, even in the absence of any pre-existing proprietary interest in a particular asset.[79] Thus, the differences between the legislative provisions and the application of equitable doctrines such as unjust enrichment may be more apparent than real.

CONCLUSION

The introduction of a legislative framework along the lines of the PRA 1984 will, no doubt, resolve some of the difficulties presently faced by claimants relying on equitable principles in the resolution of family property disputes. In particular, problems relating to the recognition of indirect contributions, especially non-financial contributions, and the power to the courts to adjust property interests without the need to call upon mechanisms such as the constructive trust, are directly addressed by the legislation. Statutory reform may provide solutions in the short term but, in the long run, the consequences may be less beneficial. First, in giving statutory recognition to indirect non-financial contributions, a legislative framework may, to some extent, address the problem of gender bias that is symptomatic of certain equitable principles such as the common intention constructive trust and unconscionability. As to a total eradication of gender bias, it remains unclear whether legislation will be more successful. Although the New South Wales judges have affirmed that indirect non-financial contributions should not be marginalised and treated in a token way, a problem remains in that the evaluation of such contributions remains susceptible to value judgment by the judiciary. A conservative valuation of the contributions made by a claimant who has undertaken a purely domestic role in the relationship may result in the judges finding that her contributions have been sufficiently recognised and compensated for during the relationship. However, as illustrated by the unjust enrichment approach taken by the Canadian courts, the judges are capable of taking a more gender-neutral approach, wherein appropriate recognition may be given to such contributions, even without the need for statutory intervention. The Canadian courts have indicated their willingness to treat domestic contributions as being incontrovertible benefits.

Secondly, in taking a compensation approach that focuses on contributions made, there is considerable overlap between the way the judges go about exercising their judicial discretion under s 20 and in the unjust enrichment approach. This may result in the emergence of a jurisprudence which fudges the application of unjust enrichment and the principles underpinning the legislative framework. This is particularly so if the courts become increasingly

---

79 *LAC Minerals v International Corona Resources* (1989) 61 DLR (4th) 14. See, also, Paccioco, 1991; Scane, 1989; and Wong, 1998.

receptive to the imposition of a remedial constructive trust as one possible remedy for reversing an unjust enrichment. The only difference may be more technical than legal, in that a claimant may opt for the legislative framework when the criteria are met,[80] but would otherwise need to resort to the equitable principles where they are not. Whilst the New South Wales' legislation is well intentioned, it illustrates the dangers, as well as difficulties, of legislating in a sensitive and tricky area such as property rights for home-sharers.[81] Thus, if legislative reforms are to be tabled for England and Wales, the proposed legislation should take on board the sort of difficulties that have emerged from the PRA 1984. We would need to go back to basic principles and, more particularly, consider carefully what the objectives of the proposed legislation are and how these objectives may be practicably achieved.

---

80 Eg, the parties must have lived together in a domestic relationship for at least two years (see PRA 1984, s 17(1)), and the application must be made within two years of the cessation of the relationship (see s 18(1)).

81 It should be noted that, in September 1999, the Attorney General of New South Wales requested the Law Reform Commission to conduct a full review of the PRA 1984. The Law Reform Commission's terms of reference were to inquire into and report on the operation of the PRA 1984 with particular regard to, *inter alia*, the effectiveness of s 20 in bringing about just and equitable adjustments of the parties' respective rights, and the process of decision making or determination of rights. The Law Reform Commission's Discussion Paper is expected to be published later in 2000.

CHAPTER 8

GOVERNING FROM A DISTANCE: THE SIGNIFICANCE OF THE CAPITAL INCOME DISTINCTION IN TRUSTS

Malcolm Voyce

What struck me with great force on reading Judith Wright's *The Generations of Men* was the account of how her grandfather, Albert Wright,[1] spent his evenings on his remote property in the 1850s going over and over his financial accounts. This may not strike us as unusual, as it is an activity that we all might do, but the desperation of Albert Wright's activity, threatened as he was with drought and bank foreclosure, hit me with particular force. Albert Wright's pastoral activities were typical of the era of 'settler capitalism'[2] or of colonial liberalism. This pastoral expansion was funded in the heyday of British imperial investment in Australia.

Only later, after reading Carnegie's work on pastoral accounting, and his description of the role that financial reporting systems played in pastoral development, did I fully appreciate the importance of accounting practices in rural Australia.[3] In a sense, Wright's nightly activities over his sums encouraged me to think (like Miller) of the linkages or interdependencies between the practices and rationalities of accounting, on the one hand, and the State, on the other.[4]

My purpose in this chapter is to develop earlier ideas[5] of how accounting and legal practices as forms of *inscriptions* help structure relationships and provide a means for the State to 'governance at a distance'.[6] This expression enables me to show how a particular view of the decentred State rules through a diversity of structures in heterogeneous ways to regulate the lives of individuals.[7] In this sense, the work of Foucault and his notion of *governmentality*[8] was attractive, as he argues that power does not necessarily reside in the centralised government or the State, but in the everyday practices in civil society. Such practices include those of semi-private agencies like workhouses, asylums, prisons and social welfare agencies. In this sense, the State is involved in the private sphere through a multitude of agencies and

---

1   Wright, 1998.
2   Denoon, 1983, interprets 'settler capitalism' to describe 'a mode of production' in settler societies in the southern hemisphere during the 19th century and up to 1914.
3   Carnegie, 1994.
4   I follow Rose and Miller, 1992, in adopting this term from Latour, 1986.
5   Voyce, 1996.
6   I follow Rose and Miller, 1992, in adopting this term from Latour, 1987.
7   Miller and Rose, 1990.
8   Foucault, 1991.

techniques, some of which may only be associated loosely with the origins of the State.[9]

This chapter will outline the importance of classification of land (property/estates/tenure) and will examine in greater detail how the specific deployment of the capital/income division in trusts operated with other discourses to reinforce the marginalisation of the role of women. To achieve this, I develop the concept of 'governance' to show that the State does not have a 'unity', 'individuality' or 'rigorous functionality' which controls the population by directly enforceable edicts which are implemented in the provinces.[10] Neither is the State controlled and tugged by the logic of class or the mode of production.[11] Rather, I argue that the State rules via a set of technologies which, in the particular context of this case, involve fundamental technical processes such as accountancy practices and the distinctions inherent within law, such as the capital income distinction.

I will examine three facets of what I describe as liberalism. First, I see government as a problematising activity, in that it imposes obligations on rulers in terms of the problems it seeks to address.[12] Secondly, I note that the programmatic aspects of government have been called political rationalities.[13] By their very nature, political rationalities are highly abstract and set out the objectives of government. Consistent with my decentred view of the State I view these rationalities as also emanating or circulating at a local level as a product of local power centres. Thus, unlike Rose and Miller, I include in my view of political rationalities dominant popular discourses. I accept that these rationalities may not necessarily be abstract, but may be contradictory or diffuse in nature. This approach allows me not to see ideologies as always being determinative at a local site, but allows for local agency or resistance. Thirdly, I envisage liberalism as a form of governance requiring not so much a confrontation between the governor and the governed, but a constant and often invisible reshaping of the taken for granted freedom of subjects.[14] Fourthly, as I have indicated, government also consists of technologies of government. Technologies of government are widely diverse and include mundane as well as sophisticated mechanisms. They include techniques of notation, computation and calculation; procedures of examination and assessment; the invention of devices such as surveys and presentational forms such as tables; the standardisation of systems for training and the inculcation of habits; the inauguration of professional specialisms and vocabularies;

---

9   Miller and Rose, 1990.
10   McNay, 1994, p 118.
11   Corrigan and Sayer, 1985, p 7.
12   Rose and Miller, 1992, p 181.
13   Miller and Rose, 1990.
14   Foucault, 1991; and Kendall 1997.

building design and architectural forms.[15] Importantly for my purposes, I include in this list (as suggested by Miller and Rose) legal classifications and accountancy practices.

These technologies are important because they enable 'government at a distance' and do not rely on close 'physical proximity of the governed to ensure efficiency'.[16] The forms of techniques I enumerate in this chapter enable *fidelity* or confidence of outcome to be obtained over a distance. Fidelity emerges when assemblages of heterogeneous elements such as legal taxonomies and procedures are used, as this enables previously unreliable actions to be prescribed and made regular and observable. In this sense, law talks of fidelity techniques.[17] By this process, domains of the self become visible, their bodies legible. New domains of the self become problematised as space for governance; inscriptions can be compared and analysed. However, more importantly, when subjects are acted upon and habits instilled, a subject's 'progress' can be measured. Humans become calculable, the individual is constituted as an effect and object of knowledge, and their bodies are worked on to increase their economic or non-economic 'productivity'.[18]

My task here is to show how discourses act in close alliance with technical devices established by accountancy practices. This chapter accepts the link between capitalism and accountancy. By transforming assets into abstract values and by expressing quantitatively the results of business activities, double-entry book-keeping clarified the aims of business and provided a rational basis on which capitalists could choose the directions of their investments. It allowed the possible separation of the business firm from its owners and, hence, the growth of the limited liability company.[19]

I also build on some recent research on accounting which argues that accounting practices may be regarded as social and institutional practices which are intrinsic to and constitutive of social relations, rather than as being derivative or secondary. According to this research, accountancy is seen not only as a technology capable of acting on individuals and amounting to a social practice, but furthermore, as a social practice which can constitute and reconstitute the economic domain.[20]

With regard to accountancy, three aspects are noted. First, I will argue that accounting techniques, through the administration of estates, shape widowhood, via the practice of granting widows income rather than capital. Secondly, the spread of accountancy practices saw the advent of an obligation

---

15 Miller and Rose, 1990, p 8.

16 Kendall, 1977.

17 Law, 1986.

18 Foucault, 1977a, p 192; and McWhorter, 1989.

19 Sombert, 1924.

20 Miller, 1994; and Hopwood and Miller, 1994.

to account through the maintenance of records pertaining to resources. Thus, accounting records have traditionally provided evidence of an accountor's stewardship of the owners' resources. As I will note, this is particularly relevant in the taxation and death duties context. Thirdly, whilst I do not expand on this point, it may be noted that accounting practices assist pastoral communities by lubricating barter in isolated settlements and thus assisting pastoral expansion.[21]

This approach allows me to show how technologies, together with classifications within land law, such as the object/subject distinction,[22] the notion of estates and tenure, and trusts, were not neutral, but involved political visions. I take it as established that the epistemologies within these dichotomies were fundamental to colonial liberalism.[23] I have shown elsewhere how the political constructions behind these classifications reinforced the marginalisation of women.[24]

TRUSTS AND THE DEVELOPMENT OF SETTLER CAPITALISM IN AUSTRALIA

I have referred to the existence of classifications in law. Elsewhere[25] I have shown how developments within liberal legal thinking allowed for the development of notions of mastery of self and of objects/land. Davies argues that paradigms of identity in law, property and personality emphasise delimitation and exclusion of others. This knowledge, she argued, was constituted at a distance: a knowledge that relied on making something an object of thought.[26]

Over the course of time, English law developed a system of classification of interests in land. It was intrinsic to the structure of medieval land law that it regarded the king as holding the underlying title to land, as he had originally granted it on terms of a grant that derived from the largesse of the Crown. In

---

21 Carnegie, 1994.

22 I draw here on Alexander, 1987, pp 305–36, who argues that 'categorical ordering', developed in late 19th century thought, created the process of deferring boundaries within which substantive legal concepts could operate.

23 For a review of the debate on capitalism and private property, see Rubin and Sugarman, 1984.

24 Voyce, 1996. See the change in census figures to disguise women's works on farms, the cases from the Industrial Wage Commission which saw the male as the breadwinner and the female as a dependant, and the treatment of war widows: Deacon, 1985; Blackmore, 1994.

25 *Ibid*, Voyce. Ideas of property were developed upon notions from William of Ockham, who distinguished the difference between the faculty 'of using a thing' from the right to a thing: Tierney, 1988.

26 Davies, 1994.

this sense it was not clear what, if anything, an individual 'owned'. The answer to this conundrum was the 'doctrine of estates' or an abstract entity called *the estate in land* which was interposed between the tenant and his land. Thus, a tenant owned not the land itself, but the conceptual estate. Gray writes that, by this ingenious compromise, English law resolved the contradiction between theory and reality in the ownership of land.[27] By a further device, a dimension of time was introduced into the description of the terms enjoyed by the 'tenant'. Each tenant was given a 'temporal slice' as regards the period of time they might enjoy their estate. By yet another abstract notion, the law came (in almost a mathematical abstraction) to recognise different rights to different slices of time. The 'future estate' created a right to something perceived as existing in the present, co-existent with a right for a present estate.[28]

In the recent *Wik* judgment, Brennan CJ observed that, as found in Australia:

> The English system of private ownership of estates held of the Crown rests on 'two fundamental doctrines in the law of real property' namely, the doctrine of tenure and the doctrine of estates ... By the interlocking doctrines of tenure and estates, the land law provides for the orderly enjoyment in succession of any parcel of land. The doctrine of tenure creates a single devolving chain of title and the doctrine of estates provides for the enjoyment of land during successive periods. The doctrine of tenure (with its incident of escheat) and estates ensure that no land in which the Crown has granted an interest is ever without a legal owner.[29]

This fairly standard explanation of tenure, estates and successive interests for my purposes needs to be supplemented by an explanation of trusts. The essence of a trust is that it splits the facets of property ownership. The trustee is the legal owner of property and the real or beneficial owner is the beneficiary. Thus, the essential feature of a trust is that the formal or 'titular interest' in the property is vested in a nominee (or trustee), whose duty it is to protect the beneficial enjoyment of the person or persons who holds the beneficial interest under the trust. Trusts are versatile devices, because the founder of the trust can play a range of tricks with three particular aspects of property ownership: nominal title, benefit, and control.[30]

Legal doctrine is not neutral, in the sense that it has instrumental aspects. The liberal idea of property distinguishes between legal subjects (persons), who are equal before the law, and objects which can be owned (things), and conceptualised as being distinct from them. Subjects are formally equal, but

---

27 Gray, 1996.

28 *Ibid*, p 247.

29 *Wik Peoples v Queensland* (1996) ALR 141, p 156.

30 Moffat, Bean and Dewar, 1994, p 5.

the distribution of assets is not.[31] In particular, the founder or settlor of the trust[32] generally may not interfere with the trust at his will. The trustee may control the property in his discretion. While the trust property may float in suspension, it is nevertheless controlled by those who exercise power. Once the trust is executed, the settlor is out of the picture, only the deed itself speaks.

The trust device makes it clear who owns property. This is explicitly recognised by law. In this way, the trust enables the concentration and preservation of capital and the power and security of those who have legal ownership.[33]

Cotterrell argues that the legal doctrine of property is important not only for what it expresses, but also for its silences. He says that in the trust realm, the notion of property avoids certain features of social life. In particular, he argues that the idea of private power is banished. Thus, the device of the trust, initially developed to protect the property of knights on crusades, later made it possible for English law to recognise many forms of property ownership without attracting the technical and ideological conflicts implicated in the doctrine of corporate personality in continental legal systems.[34] In essence, the trust device and the subsequent development of the life estates enable those who have control (the trustees) to exert private power or, to use Hale's term, 'private government'.[35] To illustrate the role of trusts, I discuss several forms it took in rural societies, namely, the strict settlement in England in the 19th century, and recent usages of trusts in rural Australia. It has been said of strict settlements that:

> There is nothing, perhaps, in the institutions of modern Europe which comes so near to an *imperium in imperio* [an empire within an empire] as the settlement of a great English estate. The settler is a kind of absolute lawgiver for two generations; his will suspends for that time the operation of the common law of the land and substitutes for it an elaborate constitution of his own making.

> The trustees of a family settlement are something like the constitutional safeguards of a complex political system; their presence is, in ordinary circumstances, hardly perceived, but they hold great powers in reserve, which may be used with effect on an emergency.[36]

Wealthy families in England developed over the centuries a particular form of the trust device, called the strict settlement, to keep family property intact in

---

31 Cotterrell, 1987.

32 The controller of the trust is usually the trustee, but in some forms of trust, settlors may retain some control as advisory trustees.

33 Cotterrell, 1987, p 85.

34 Maitland, 1936.

35 Duxbury, 1990.

36 Pollock, 1896, p 117.

the hands of successive oldest sons. Its principal aim was to inhibit any disposal of family estates by the heirs out of the family. The strict settlement has been simply described as a complicated series of life estates which could be set up at any one time, but the most common event leading to its creation was the coming of age of the eldest son. Generally, there had to be a resettlement in every generation if the constraints on disposal were to be maintained.[37] Every substantial landowner in the 18th and 19th century in England was subject to strong pressure from the landowning class to adopt strict settlement, as a means of controlling land estates and guaranteeing the political position of the 'landed estate' class in the country.[38] By the end of the 17th century, a fairly standard form of strict settlement had evolved at the hands of eminent conveyancers and was endorsed by the courts. This form of conveyance survived until the beginning of the 20th century, when death duties led to its demise and lack of effectiveness.

Strict settlements made a significant contribution to the consolidation and preservation of wealth and power of the landowning classes of England. By the mid-18th century, such devices had been imposed on up to half, or perhaps even three-quarters of English land.[39] New families could obtain access to this class through the purchase of land, which was difficult given the limited number of hereditary titles available. The only means to buy new land were to mortgage existing properties or to arrange for an advantageous marriage to a wealthy heir. As a buttress against the possibility of family ownership of land the strict settlement was a line of defence against short-sighted sales by an heir or heiress.[40]

It has not been my intention to outline the law of strict settlement. Rather, it is to show how the concept of the trust was a semi-autonomous device or a facilitative law[41] which enabled trustees to utilise a form of family arrangement to act as a property holding vehicle.[42] In this context, we should note how lawyers, as sustainers both of middle class ideologies and their supporting values, invent new categories of ideas on trusts in response to specific socio-economic problems.[43]

Australia, for a variety of reasons, never used strict settlements.[44] Historians have indicated the reasons for this: there existed vestiges of moral economy imported by the convicts; resentment over the treatment of labour in

---

37 It is not my intention here to outline in great detail the strict settlement. For references, see Baker, 1990, pp 335–36; and Rubin and Sugarman, 1984.

38 Chesterman, 1984, p 130.

39 *Ibid*, p 130.

40 Mingay, 1977; Spring, 1990, 1993; Pottage, 1998.

41 Sugarman and Rubin, 1984.

42 Fricke and Strauss, 1964, pp 103–04.

43 Sugarman, 1993.

44 Atherton, 1993, pp 103–06.

the era of industrial capitalism; the suspicion of efforts to reproduce English social relations; and the scorn that was heaped on efforts to establish a 'bunyip aristocracy'. English dynastic notions of property were foreign to Australian soil. While the colonial gentry had prospered and retained substantial political power, it did not successfully transplant, on the whole, the British 'customs of patronage and deference in such an uncongenial soil'.[45] In short, colonial aristocracy was on the defensive, and governors of States had to take into account popular sentiment, such as the needs of squatters' access to land. While ownership of rural land in Britain was consolidated in a few hands and continued to be the social and political base of the dominant classes, the opposite was generally true in Australia, in that land was freely available. In essence, property was a commodity.

The above may be a partial explanation of why the strict settlement was not employed in Australia. To date, at least, historians have not suggested other reasons. Since the founding of Australia, the formal device of strict settlement has been extremely rare. Greater use was made of life estates set up with a trust in a will and trusts under the Settled Land Acts. Such arrangements are usually called trusts rather than settlements, and are governed by the various State Trustee Acts. In effect, the universal form of trust and the power politics behind it were remodelled in a different form through life estate trusts and family trusts. In effect, then, we may recast Pollock's observation, cited above, that while trusts did not act as constitutional safeguards in the English sense, they did allow trustees to hold great powers in reserve, not only to be used in emergency, but as vehicles for the enforcement of trustee autocratic power.[46]

The advantage of family trusts (whether *inter vivos*, testamentary trusts or life estates) is usually seen as to minimise tax. However, the other advantage is that they enable protection of the estate against what may be seen as the extravagant claims of widows/widowers or infant children. They also protect the estate against the possibility of 'family property' being threatened by the consequences of divorce. Most legal practitioners claim that family trusts are set up when relationships are stable and the reason for setting up trusts is to minimise income taxation. Kennedy argues: '... it is rare for a trust instrument to be designed for the purpose of defeating the property provisions of the Family Law Act.'[47] With increased pressure for profits and competition, the legal profession is ever seeking new products to sell. In addition to the well known tax minimisation reasons, solicitors advocate the use of trusts to help 'retain the farm in the family' or 'keep the business in the family' or, in effect, to help retain the lion's share of the property for the male. Many practitioners understand that awarding a 'fair', or at least reasonable share, of the farm or

---

45 McIntyre, 1985.
46 Pollock, 1896, p 117.
47 Kennedy, 1996.

business to a female will ruin the chances of male continuity of the farm or business. The role of lawyers is not merely to sell a particular product. Legal products are not neutral, but have ideological consequences. Legal advice, therefore, 'retails ideology' and fits clients into a particular view of social life.[48] Thus, farming relationships or business families are moulded by the very technical apparatus lawyers choose to sell.

Given the perception that life estates are problematic and with the rising rate of divorce, solicitors have recently stressed the need for family trusts. Family trusts have also become attractive as they may (in some States) be set up in the rural context without the payment of stamp duty. Solicitors in Western Australia have become especially aggressive in selling family trusts on the basis that it will 'save' the family farm and 'protect the estate against daughter-in-laws'. Normally it is the male in the family who consults the lawyer. Male lawyers who make up the majority of lawyers in rural areas readily appreciate the needs of men and the fears of men in 'losing their farms'. At the same time, women in rural areas find it difficult to find a woman solicitor and one who does not make 'value judgments about women based on personal values'.[49]

THE ROLE OF LIFE ESTATES

In the traditional approach, often called a 'reciprocal will', the husband and wife create life estates for the benefit of their survivor. A life estate in the estate planning context is usually created through a will.[50] Thus, the person who makes a will may go on buying and selling property upon the death of the will-maker. A life estate is created in favour of the grantee (the surviving spouse).[51] The essential feature of a life estate in its most common form is that the surviving spouse receives an interest in the property as a life tenant, but that interest determines (ends) on his or her death.[52]

---

48 Sugarman, 1993, p 291.

49 Australian Law Reform Commission, 1994.

50 Butt, 1996, says that, in modern Australian property law, the life estate occurs predominantly as the creation of a will. Life estates may, however, be created *inter vivos*.

51 There are two varieties of life estate. The estate for the life of the grantee ('an ordinary life estate') and the estate for the life of another ('an estate *per autre vie*'): *ibid*, Butt, p 133.

52 A life estate could determine on the happening of any specified event such as death of the life tenant, remarriage, entering into a *de facto* relationship or the happening of some other event such as children reaching 25 years. In particular circumstances, the life estate can be extinguished by an agreement between the life tenant and the remaindermen; see the rule in *Saunders v Vautier* (1841) Beav 115. See *ibid*, Butt, p 133.

The time-honoured role of a life estate[53] has three advantages. The first is that the life estate enables the surviving spouse to have the benefits of the estate during his or her lifetime, while the freehold land or the capital is preserved for the children. The second advantage is that creating a life estate ensures the land is kept in the family for the next generation. The third advantage, for the surviving second spouse with the remainder interest preserved for children of a former marriage, is that it balances the interests of that spouse against the need to benefit the children of an earlier marriage. Life estates may be inappropriate in some cases, such as where it is appropriate to make beneficiaries the masters of their own destinies, or where the assets (such as personal chattels) do not lend themselves to ongoing trusts, or where the amount set aside is insufficient having regard to the costs involved.

The restrictive rules of life estates frustrate the life tenant in various ways. First, depending on how a life estate is set up, the life tenant may only receive the income from the life estate and may not be able to utilise the capital of the estate as different needs arise. Secondly, the life tenant, who normally receives the income from the estate, may suffer from the growth of inflation, and consequently from a depreciating income. Thirdly, the life tenant, where there is the customary obligation to repair in the life tenancy, is usually subject to an obligation to maintain and repair. Such a covenant in law imposes restrictions on the way the life tenant may treat the land, so that the interests of successive beneficiaries are not depreciated. The usage of a life estate in a will is one of many strategies adopted by will-makers to restrict the life tenant. Others include restrictions on residence and clauses in restraint of marriage.[54]

Although some advisers still recommend them as being suitable in particular circumstances, life estates are increasingly falling out of favour. Three problems are seen to follow from the adoption of life estates. First, the creation of life estates is seen to have unpredictable adverse capital gains taxation implications as the law is unclear in this area. Secondly, it now may be regarded as unwise for a will maker to leave a life estate to his/her surviving spouse.[55] Many advisers advise against the use of life estates, as they may be seen as inadequate maintenance at the instigation of a surviving spouse's claim for further provision under Testator's Family Maintenance legislation. De Groot argues that, in adverse circumstances, a surviving spouse may be awarded a judgment giving him or her all of the life estate.[56] Thirdly, there is the problem of conclusively demarcating what constitutes income and

---

53 The term 'estate' denotes the right of seisin (possession) to the land. An estate is a 'thing' separate from the land itself. This is possible because, under feudal theory, the tenant does not own the land, he holds it from his lord, but he does own the estate in his land.

54 Rowland and Tamsitt, 1994, p 210.

55 *Ibid*, p 208.

56 De Groot and Nickel, 1993, p 64.

what constitutes capital. While this problem may be overcome, with the provision of a clause in the will to apportion capital and income, the problem of family tension may remain.

Under the rules of trusts as regards life estates, there are differing rights and responsibilities for the co-owners or successive beneficiaries. A life tenant is entitled, during the continuance of the life estate, to possession and enjoyment of the asset. Upon the death of the life tenant, the remainderman is entitled to the property. For instance, as the duration of the life estate is uncertain, the law encourages the life tenant to cultivate the land by giving the life tenant a right to emblements. Under the law of *emblements*, remaindermen can enter the life estate after it has come to an end and reap the crops that the life tenant has sown. The rule on emblements only applies to crops which are ready to harvest within 12 months, but does not extend to the right to pick fruit from trees.[57]

A life tenant is liable for 'voluntary waste',[58] or to some positive act of injury to the property that diminishes its value for the person next in line to receive it. However, a tenant is not liable for 'permissive waste', which involves passively allowing the property to fall into disrepair, unless the deed creating the life tenancy imposes an obligation to repair.[59] The law of waste provides an inadequate basis for the proposed adjustment of life tenants and remaindermen. Thus, without a specific clause to cover repair, a life tenant is not accountable if the house or farm falls into a dilapidated condition or is left uncultivated.[60] Where the life estate is money, the life tenant is entitled to the interest from the money. Thus, should a life estate consist of annuities, they must be apportioned between capital and income.[61]

A considerable body of law exists concerning the obligation of the life tenant to keep the land and buildings in reasonable repair. Well drafted wills detail who is responsible for outgoings. It is a well established principle that the life tenant must maintain the same value of stock of trade as the life tenant received. Moreover, all outgoings of a recurrent nature (such as rates and income taxes) which relate broadly to the property and benefit of the life

---

57 Butt, 1996.

58 See *Re Cartwright, Avis v Newman* (1889) 41 Ch D 352. A tenant is not liable for permissive waste. He or she may accordingly allow the property to deteriorate and the court will have no jurisdiction to interfere or make an order charging the cost of the repairs against capital, see *Re De Teislsier's Settled Estates* [1893] 1 CLD 153; *Poweys v Blagrave* [1854] 69 ER 210. The trustees cannot interfere with the possession of a life tenant merely because he or she fails to keep the property in repair unless he or she is committing voluntary waste, that is, the state of disrepair that arises from acts of commission by the life tenant, not acts of omission.

59 *Ibid*, Butt, p 144.

60 *Ibid*.

61 Ford and Lee, 1995, pp 1120–230 argue that such annuities should be apportioned according to the rule in *Re Chesterfield's Trusts* (1883) 24 Ch D 643.

tenant must be paid out of income, while those outgoings which benefit the estate as a whole (such as investment advice) must be borne by the capital.[62]

The widow/er may need a certain standard of living, but may be saddled with repair covenants. This may be highly unfair if a widow/er has extensive property to be maintained. A separate fund may be established for this purpose on farms or businesses where surviving spouses have maintenance obligations. It is also advisable for the trustees to have powers to sell an existing property and, if necessary, purchase another.

Upon acceptance of the office of trustee, a trustee is subject to a variety of imperative or facilitative duties which compel or allow a trustee to act in certain ways. In the administration of an estate, a trustee is bound to refrain from acting in such a way as to favour one class of beneficiaries at the expense of another. This duty is most pertinent when there are beneficial interests in succession. In this context, the trustees must not favour either the life tenant or the remainderman at the expense of the other. The generally accepted principle is that the life tenant receives the income from investments while the remainderman receives the capital. The idea is that the life tenant can live off the proceeds of the investments while the corpus is protected and reserved for the remainderman.[63]

A 'capital/income problem' eventuates when payments arise to be paid to support the life tenant or after the death of the life tenant when the estate is wound up. The problem for trustees is to determine whether those payments are capital or income and, accordingly, go to remainderman or life tenant respectively (or their respective estates). The problem is really exacerbated by the conflict of needs between the successive beneficiaries; the life tenant wants income, and the remainderman wants maximum capital growth.

In most cases where trustees are set up in the will to carry on businesses, the rights of the life tenant and remainderman for income and capital respectively will be set out in the terms of the will.[64] In modern times, it is thought advisable to invest a trustee with a proper discretion and to acknowledge the right of the trustee to exercise that discretion. The trustee, it is argued, should be given a broad discretion to determine capital and income. Such clauses should also contain powers to stock or restock and purchase additional lands out of income or capital. However, if the trust instrument

---

62 Moffat, Bean and Dewar, 1994, p 373.

63 A recent reformulation of the balancing of capital and income was discussed in *Nestlé v National Westminster Bank plc* [1993] 1 WLR 1261. In this case, Hoffman J saw the approach of modern portfolio theory as being a desirable investment strategy for trustees; see Ford and Lee, 1995, p 1037; Dalpont and Chambers, 1996; Waters, 1984; and Gover, 1933.

64 See the precedent suggested in Rowland and Tamsitt, 1994, p 288. An appropriately drawn clause will also negative the rule in *Howe v Earl Dartmouth* (1802) 7 Ves 137 that wasting reversionary or hazardous assets be converted.

contains no express provisions, the trustees will have to determine what is to be distributed as income and what is capital.[65] The problem, however, has been that in the past, this type of clause has not always been inserted into wills.

The origin of the concept of income and capital derives from ideas of agricultural economy from Europe and was developed by lawyers during the 18th century. In a predominantly agricultural economy, income was regarded as the annual harvest and capital was the land.[66] Income was regarded as arising from a purposeful activity, such as farming, and occurred fairly regularly with the passage of the seasons. Income was seen to be like an annual harvest, as it was given off or separated by a fixed source and became available for consumption without depletion of the source.[67] This principle can be seen in *Hassell v Perpetual Executors Trustees and Agency Co Ltd*,[68] where a farmer left the income of his estate to his wife for her lifetime, stipulating that on her death the capital was to go to residuary legatees. The farmer died on 26 September 1950. Included in his estate was a large number of sheep which were shorn shortly after his death. The wool was sold for £20,095 in November 1950. The court held that the whole sum was income to which the life tenant was entitled.

The full court held:

> The reason why the proceeds of wool shorn and lambs dropped are brought into the accounts of a business as revenue items is to be found in the character in which wool and the lambs come into existence as independent subjects of property. They come into existence, by severance in the case of wool and by birth in the case of lambs, as produce of the sheep from which they are derived, and, like crops of grain and fruit, they belong to that class of produce which is periodically detached and radically recurs: they are, by their very nature, a profit.[69]

This case illustrates that certain objects (here, sheep or stock) are regarded as capital and other objects (wool, in this case) are income. By contrast casual, sporadic or unexpected gains or gifts did not fit the concept of income as they appeared to be the result of good luck. Lacking a continuing source such as a farm business, they could not be expected to occur at regular intervals. A provident man would therefore regard them differently from income, so, consequently, they would not be available for ordinary consumption. Capital gains, on the other hand, thus included all unexpected receipts.[70]

The origin of the concept of the distinction between capital and income can be traced back to the practice of entailing landed estates in 18th century

---

65 Ford and Lee, 1990.

66 Flower, 1974, p 86.

67 Stratchen, 1910.

68 (1952) 86 CLR 513.

69 *Ibid*, pp 523–24.

70 Seltzer, 1951, p 25.

England. The courts in the 18th century had to decide the ramifications of this distinction. These courts decided that the income of the estate belonged to the life tenant, but that the life tenant did not have a right to spend the capital. They took the view that the capital was the land and the income was the annual harvest because the life tenant could dispose of the annual harvest without affecting the physical existence of the land.[71]

Over the next 200 years, subsequent to the development of strict settlement, different forms of wealth developed, such as securities and bonds.[72] The courts applied the same principles to these as they had to land. Thus, the factor to be maintained was the bond itself, not the money value. The rise and fall of the bond in the market did not change the character of the bond. Under this view, should the bond be sold (perhaps at a profit), the entire proceeds of the sale retained the character of the original capital assets, as did any assets acquired with the money; any increase in the value was capital. The life tenant had no right to the increase. Capital gains were, therefore, ignored.[73]

We can see that the legal concept of capital is fundamentally different from that adopted by economists. An economist would view capital as the total value of assets in hand. A legal approach, however, treats the capital asset as a *res* or a 'thing'. Under this line of reasoning, lawyers would ignore the capital gain, while an economist would treat the capital gain as income.[74] Hirsch writes that generally accepted accounting principles treat increases in wealth as income. He argues that it does not matter whether the income derives from normal profits or from inflation. The book value of new animals, for instance, is treated as profit.[75] The application of an economic concept rather than a legal one requires regular revaluations of all the assets of the estate. This involves considerable work and provides endless opportunities for dispute between life tenants and remaindermen. It requires detailed accounting records on the changing value of each asset. The *res* concept can be applied with a clear-cut distinction between capital and income and can be applied with elementary accounting records, as only a list of the physical assets is required.[76]

The transference to Australia of this legal concept on capital and income had important implications. Early records clearly show that these accounting practices were insisted on by banks; accountants/solicitors employed as trustees of estates deployed this notion of capital and income in a flexible

---

71 Flower, 1974, p 85; and Seltzer, 1951.
72 Langbein, 1988.
73 Flower, 1974, p 86.
74 *Ibid*, p 87.
75 Hirsch, 1983, p 615.
76 Flower, 1974, p 86.

fashion.[77] Carnegie argues that accounting in Britain had reached a certain stage in its development by 1836 and that the spread of colonisation accountancy practices played a specific role in the development of the colony.[78]

Early historical records from Victoria suggest that, by 1900, pastoral families began to keep some form of personal financial records showing annual profits and the movements of stock, stores and shearing records.[79] These practices were developed locally before any governmental requirements such as those laid down by death duties. When double entry book-keeping requirements were imposed, some properties kept on working with the old system of accounts. It was only in 1893, according to Bridges, that the first farm accountancy system was published by Musson in the *Agricultural Gazette of NSW*.[80] This work by Musson prescribed how pastoralists should keep accounts to ascertain whether they were making a profit or a loss.[81] In 1900, Vigars published the first Australian book concerned with farm accounts called *Station Book-keeping*.[82] Carrying on from the long boom in the 1870s–80s, pastoralists continued to borrow large sums to finance land acquisitions to erect homesteads.[83] At the same time, the land tax of 1877, on estates in excess of 640 acres, saw increasingly regulatory regimes put in place.[84] By the turn of the century, professional accountants began to sell their services.[85] Pastoralists began to employ their services and implement accrual-based double entry accounting systems with an emphasis on periodic production of profit and loss accounts and balance sheets. Frequently, accountants successfully sold these services to pastoralists on the basis that such services were needed for the determination and collection of death duties.[86] By the 1870s, following the pressure of statutory requirements and the pressure of banks, it had therefore become necessary for pastoralists to employ accountants.[87]

The duties of trustees as regards life estates have already been indicated. It is clear that, from 1900, the accounting professions were involved in estate management and saw it as a fruitful area of work. After the introduction of death duties, accountants were also involved in deceased estates, as they were

---

77 Carnegie, 1993.

78 *Ibid.*

79 Carnegie, 1995.

80 Musson, 1893, quoted in Bridges, 1975.

81 Carnegie, 1993.

82 Vigars, 1914.

83 Carnegie, 1995, p 19; Bailey, 1966, pp 78–84.

84 For a discussion of the introduction of death duties and income tax in Australia, see Smith, 1993 and Carnegie, 1994, p 43.

85 Davidson, 1978, p 111; Chua and Poullaos, 1998.

86 Carnegie, 1995, p 13.

87 *Ibid*, p 23.

required to produce valuations for probate.[88] The necessity of valuing assets and liabilities to help collect government revenue provided a convenient and reliable means for professional accountants to implement double entry accrual-based accounting systems to replace the personalised ledgers previously kept by station owners.[89]

In an article in the *Public Accountant* entitled 'The accounts of sheep stations managed by trustee' in 1922, Hungerford argues that it is impossible to be sure that apportionment between capital and income is correct.[90] Hungerford details the various types of ledger which farmers utilised, such as cash books covering stores, petty cash, wages, shearing and paddock holdings. He recommended that, where the station is controlled by trustees, the appropriate books should be kept in the public accountant's office.[91] As regards stock valuations, he states that these are done annually, as the information is needed for tax purposes. In particular, the article describes the accounts of stations run by trustees. Hungerford argues that:

> Where an accountant's services are most often called in is where the estate is settled in trust for the tenant for life, with remainder to others. He should be particularly on his guard in making up the accounts, against adjusting them too much in favour of the tenant for life. The temptation to do so is very great. The tenant for life is on the spot, and expresses himself vigorously if he conceives himself injured, and his hostility might be injurious to an accountant's professional success. On the other hand the remainderman is absent, perhaps unascertained, and as the injury to him is comparatively remote he does not trouble to enquire about it at once. Moreover, his silence is not acquiescence, as it might be in the case of a tenant for life. He need not complain until he comes into his kingdom.

> Consequently an accountant should make it a point of professional honour to protect the remainderman. He should decide in his favour when there is a doubt. In doing so he will only discharge his duty to his real employer – the trustee. If the tenant for life is over-paid he may die before it is discovered, and the trustee will have no power to readjust the accounts out of the future income. When the tenant for life is a married woman, restrained from anticipation, the trustee nearly always has to recoup out of his own pocket, an expenditure from which he derived no benefit. The court is very chary of removing the restraint for the purpose of repaying the trustee.[92]

The implication is that a trustee would lean in favour of a remainderman against the interests of a life tenant (usually a woman, since women tend to outlive men). I suggest that this apportionment practice acted to the

---

88 Carnegie, 1994, p 240.

89 *Ibid*, pp 241 and 268; Carnegie, 1993, pp 210 and 216; and Oehr, 1899.

90 Hungerford, 1922, p 296.

91 *Ibid*, p 280.

92 *Ibid*, p 301.

detriment of the life tenant in favour of the interests of the son, who in most cases stood to receive the life estate on the death of the life tenant.

I have suggested that, at the turn of the century, farmers were increasingly forced to adopt accounting procedures. The imposition of accounting practices on pastoralists to make them submit information for government levy purposes required an obligation by farmers to collect and record certain types of information.[93] Economic development involved the progressive development of measures to assess the performances of each sector in terms of economic efficiency and production.

Carnegie reports that the pastoral pioneers in the Western Districts in Victoria came from Scotland, where they were educated. These settlers carried with them important accounting insights gained from the Scottish Enlightenment. Carnegie argues that those pioneers brought with them practical texts.[94] My argument is that book-keeping style represented an inscription and that book-keeping as an *inscription* provided for the possibility of 'action at a distance', thereby helping to implement the requirements of colonial capitalism. Carnegie argues that professional accountants took their skills to be of great importance and that the correctness of their accounts was accepted as a version of the truth in court.[95] Audit certificate statements early in this century focused on the correctness of accounts being examined in court. As recollected by Brentnall,[96] the following dialogue between a judge and Brentnall (an accountant) occurred:

Judge: Mr Brentnall, are you prepared to stake your reputation as an accountant upon the accuracy of your statements as set forth in your report?

Mr Brentnall: Yes, your Honour.

Judge: Then I have no further comment to make – the case is closed.

In later years, we see the acceptance of accountancy records, and the apportionment made by trustees, in a series of cases up to the High Court case of *McBride v Hudson*.[97]

Academic accountancy literature carried the debate on the virtues or otherwise of the two main approaches inherent in the capital/income debate

---

93 Carnegie, 1994.

94 *Ibid*, p 286; and Mepham, 1998.

95 *Ibid*, Carnegie, p 284.

96 Brentnall, 1938.

97 (1963) 107 CLR 604. For earlier cases, see *Thornley v Boyd* (1925) 36 CLR 526 and *Ritchie v Trustees, Executors and Agency Co Ltd* (1951) 84 CLR 553.

as regards taxation.[98] In the taxation context 'lawyers did not wish to appear to pronounce on business practices and thereby give guidance to accountants'.[99] However, case law, as regards trustees and their duties for the administration of estates, and the particular application of capital and income as regards the life tenant and remainderman, took a different perspective compared with accountants and economists. Furthermore, as my case analysis shows, courts endorsed a particular interpretation of the income/capital division in rural Australia.

I have referred to the body of law that states that trustees should allocate receipts or payments to either an income or capital account. The decision on how to allocate such funds produced a considerable number of cases where trustees sought court rulings on how an allocation should be made or where a beneficiary challenged an allocation made.[100] How payments should be apportioned in station properties as between life tenant and remainderman has been said to involve, in the words of the leading text, 'special considerations'. Such problems, argues Jacobs, arise from the buying and selling of stock, natural increment and the unexpected problems of drought, fire and flood.[101] The particular problem in the 'station cases' is the propriety of the use of profits (income) to buy further stock and the retention of natural increment of stock to the detriment of the life tenants.[102]

Why a distinction should be drawn between pastoral cases and any other industry is not adequately explained in the cases. Arguing against the existence of such a dichotomy, Kitto said, in 1930, that there should be no distinction between pastoral cases and any other industry. 'The contention is unsound that the general rule does not apply to pastoral industry in New South Wales as a drought is normal in this State.' Secondly, Kitto argued that a life tenant is not an insurer and there was no rule in ordinary trust law that a loss should be replaced out of the income of the remaining investments.[103]

From the literature available on rural accountancy[104] as well as from the legal cases on life estates, I suggest annual (seasonal) or periodic valuations were made of stock to show stock losses and increases. Receipts were

---

98 See Lee, 1994, for an outline of the debate within accounting circles which he identifies as two alternative capital maintenance approaches – that is, maintenance based on capital defined in terms either of a specific monetary attribute, such as the money unit or the purchasing power unit (financial capital); or a specific attribute of the reporting entity's physical asset structure such as its physical units or operating capacity (physical capital).

99 *Ibid.*

100 Ford and Lee, 1990.

101 Meagher and Gummow, 1993.

102 *Ibid*, p 540; Ryde, Rainsford and Arnott, 1928.

103 Kitto, in a submission for the life tenants in *Union Trustee v Eckford* (1930) 31 (SR) NSW 92, p 97.

104 See Vigars, 1914 and the review of accountancy literature by Bridges, 1975.

apportioned between life tenant and remainderman by the trustees, in some cases on an *ad hoc* basis, with no rigid rules of income and capital, and in some cases according to settled legal principles.[105] Information on apportionment practices indicates a tendency towards the remainderman. This tendency might not necessarily indicate a bias towards the male farming son, who might be the remainderman, since the trustee might also be considering the interests of daughters who might also be remaindermen. I will later show how courts endorsed this practice by the rule of 'prudent management'. This approach, as Hungerford suggested, worked well for the interests of a remainderman, as the property could be built up to increase the value of his interest.[106] It was only natural, therefore, given family strife over estates, that this informal system would be contested in the courts. I therefore examine the cases.

The cases on station properties are confusing, but two broad lines of authority are discernible. The first line of authority establishes that a life tenant is only entitled to what the ordinary course of prudent management allows. The second line of authority established that the life tenant cannot demand an annual evaluation of the stock and a yearly distribution based on this procedure.[107] For instance, in *McIntyre v McIntyre*,[108] a testator created a trust out of three cattle stations for the benefit of his family. After his death, the trustees had wide powers of management including powers to stock up, restock and purchase additional lands out of income. At the death of the testator, the stations were considerably understocked, so the trustees, in the ordinary course of prudent management, stocked up the stations, partly by prudent management and partly by purchasing new stock. As a consequence of these investments in new stock, the life tenants had received no income. The court held that the trustees had an absolute discretion under the terms of the will to determine what was capital and income. Therefore, the life tenant was deemed to have received all their due and consequently the sale of the stock belonged to the remaindermen. The court held that, in the case where the testator directs that the income is paid to a life tenant, the latter is only entitled to receive in any one year the amount which is available in the ordinary prudent management of that business during the course of that which was available for distribution as cash. As Harvey remarked:

> That is strictly the net income of the business and because there are still remaining in the business unsold assets, which if they had been realised during the year in question would have gone to swell the account of profits, it does not seem to me to follow that a life tenant during that particular year is entitled to anything in respect of such unsold assets.[109]

---

105 Carnegie, 1994, pp 142, 147 and 170; and Hungerford, 1922.
106 Hungerford, 1922.
107 Meagher and Gummow, 1993, p 541.
108 (1914) 15 SR (NSW) 45.
109 *Per* Harvey J in *ibid*, pp 48–49.

This case reveals how widely drawn clauses may give power to trustees to determine capital and income.[110] It also shows that the trustees' prudent management gives them wide scope to favour the interests of the remainderman.

This line of cases seems to have met with disapproval from the High Court in *McBride v Hudson*.[111] In that case, the testator, Norman McBride, owned a grazing property in South Australia. During his illness in the war, he had found it difficult to get adequate labour, as his son was engaged in war service. Seasonal conditions had been bad, so, as a consequence of these factors, the farm was run down in stock to a carrying level of 1,850 sheep. The testator by will left the property to the his widow, Helda McBride, and his son, John McBride, in common during the lifetime of the widow, with remainder to John and his sister, Molly Hudson. The will directed the trustees to continue the pastoral business and directed that the profits should be shared during the wife's lifetime to his wife and son in equal shares (less the son's managing expenses). After the death of the wife, the farm was to be sold and the proceeds divided in equal shares between his son and his daughter, Molly Hudson, equally.

By the time the testator's widow died (11 years after the testator's death), the sheep numbered 4,346. During this period, the life tenant went without income so that the estate might be built up. The trustees attempted to apportion the increase in sheep to corpus so they would be inherited by the remainderman. Those who stood to receive the widow's interest argued that the increase in sheep was an unrealised profit which was built up at the expense of the life tenant and, accordingly, should be available to the widow's estate. The remaindermen contended that the increase was capital, and should be given to them. The trustee's livestock trading account for each year, between the death of the testator and the death of the widow, showed the stock in hand at the end of each year and their value, set against the costs of the station, to reveal book profits for every year.[112] These accounts were prepared after the death of the widow. Molly Hudson claimed a half share of the increase of the livestock up to the widow's death.

The High Court ruled that, while these accounts had been compiled in this fashion, the trustee must be taken to intend the profits to be ascertained according to the relevant business activity. The court held it was, therefore, open to the trustees to determine the appropriate method of accounting relevant to station properties. The testator, as a person conversant with the

---

110 See Meagher and Gummow, 1993, pp 529–40.

111 *McBride v Hudson* (1963) 107 CLR 604.

112 See *ibid*, Meagher and Gummow, p 542.

manner in which pastoral businesses were generally carried on, had to be taken to have intended that the trustees adopted the normal rural practice.[113] As there was nothing in the will to indicate to the testator how profits should be ascertained, it must be taken that he assumed that the accounts would be ascertained by the conventional method in the industry, including what income should be distributed at any time. Following this approach, the court held that the increase of sheep belonged to capital and there was no justification for a claim by the life tenant for book profits. The consequence was that the proceeds of the increase of the sheep went to the remainderman instead of the life tenant.

The approach of the High Court sits curiously with the annual harvest theory and a decision a year later by the High Court decided that surplus tin should be profit for the life tenant (*Kelly v Perpetual Trustees Ltd*).[114] Further, in an important sense *McBride v Hudson*[115] rejects any method of calculation, preferring the matter to be resolved by the intention of the testator. The result of this approach is that the court endorses the practice of farmers within established discourses of domesticity and the sexual division of labour. The implications are that pastoral trustees may utilise their discretions here to make full use of the legal distinctions between life tenant and remainder to the advantage of the remainderman. Should later decisions follow the *McBride* approach and regard, in the absence of express provisions, stock increases as capital for the remaindermen, this will decrease the living standard of the life tenant. Thus, where wills are drawn widely to give powers to the trustees to apportion capital and income in a discretionary manner, the general rule is that a trustee may increase stock from the time of carrying capacity and that seasonal expectations render this prudent. The rule is that this provision comes out of income. This rule works to the detriment of the life tenant.[116] Generally, then, as long as the trustee favouring a remainderman can argue that he or she is acting prudently and not building up stock to favour the remainderman, the remainderman's interest will be advanced.[117]

---

113 (1963) 107 CLR 604, *per* Taylor J, p 623, but see the statements by Dixon CJ, Taylor and Menzies JJ in *Kelly v Perpetual Trustees Co Ltd* (1963) 109 CLR 258, pp 269–70.

114 See the critique in Meagher and Gummow, 1993.

115 *McBride v Hudson* (1963) 107 CLR 604.

116 See *ibid*, p 625; *McIntyre v McIntyre* (1914) 15 SR (NSW) 45; *Porter v Porter* (1930) 31 SR (NSW) 115; and Allen, 1942, p 203.

117 *Porter v Porter* (1930) 31 SR (NSW) 115, p 124.

AFTER-THOUGHTS ON 'RULING FROM A DISTANCE': LIBERALISM AND FREEDOM

Towards a final version of this chapter it occurred to me that I must clarify a possible misconception. This is that classificatory mechanisms within law once formulated within imperial law automatically resulted in a certain outcome in the periphery of the empire. This approach would conceive of law as being socially determinative. Rather, I prefer to see laws as shaping the possibilities of life. An alternative (also mistaken) reading of this chapter might suppose that graziers were enmeshed in dominant ideology and merely carrying out their prescribed role as pastoralist capitalists. My concern is to give consideration to the resistance or 'the fighting back against domination'.[118] This orientation then gives consideration to the voluntary or self-reflective characteristics of the self and the way liberal rationalities work through the conduct of the autonomous self.[119]

Settlers to Australia in the 18th and 19th centuries, owing to the economic transition in Britain, possessed a variety of attitudes towards central government and social hierarchy. mcintyre has argued that some settlers held robust ideas of self-autonomy and suspicion towards the class establishment, while some accepted the legitimate authority of society. Martin has likewise shown, in his critique of the debate over a hereditary upper chamber in New South Wales in the 1850s, how those who provided the leadership of radical movements had little in common with the older established landed families and their more conservative views.[120]

The vehicles of rural family enterprise were the trust[121] and the company. These facilitative devices enabled families to carry out their family operations which coincided with imperial ambitions. At the time, British capital saw Australian colonies as a site for investment.[122] In this process, the role of the trust was important, as it allowed capital accumulation at a local level with a convenient means of self-governance.

---

118 Drinkwater, 1992.

119 On the question of Foucault and resistance, see Hunt and Wickham, 1994, p 17; Callinicos, 1989, p 87; and Dean and Hindess, 1998, pp 16–17.

120 Martin, 1986, p 51.

121 The history of trust law in Australia has not been written. The English law on trusts was first adopted in 1830 in New South Wales. In 1849 and 1852, the Trust Acts were amended. The last amendment was concerned with the duties of trustees as it appeared that the earlier legislation might have been deficient in estimating deceit. It extended, with the 1898 Act, the range of trustee investments. I am grateful to Patrick McCormack for this information.

122 Goodwin, 1974; and Ville, 1996.

While I have argued that the capital income distinction worked to support the interests of remaindermen and, by implication, the long term interests of pastoralism, it was not necessarily a forgone conclusion that this result was necessarily uncontested given the richness of family politics.[123] I have not been able to locate archival records for evidence of the richness of family dramas fought out between trustees and beneficiaries.[124] However, a survey of cases between 1825 and 1933[125] reveals the tensions between trustees and beneficiaries. While, in trust law, the beneficial ownership rests with the beneficiaries, in fact, the trustees have a high degree of control over the parties involved in a family trust through exercise of the legal ownership. Cases litigated in this period show the frequency of disputes over whether or not widows should receive the trust property absolutely or merely as a life estate.[126] Other issues involve the degree to which the widow must repair the property,[127] support the children,[128] or whether the widow should lose the estate on remarriage. Likewise, children frequently attacked the trustee for more maintenance, greater investment on improvements, or on the basis that they should have continued funding from the estate despite their forisfamiliation.[129]

These cases show the attempts of trustees to rule authoritatively over family affairs. In some cases, the trustee was also a beneficiary, so the trustee may have been looking after his/her long term interest in the property alongside other beneficiaries. Likewise, some children (perhaps daughters) may have pursued their own interests in litigation by asking for capital to be considered income, or by being silent in the knowledge that their interests were being fulfilled by their brothers' or sisters' legal proceedings. The widow, in most of these cases involving life estates, was castigated as a problem for legal discourse. She was regarded as restricting the smooth transition of the estate. Alternatively, she might have realised that she was receiving unfair treatment, but have been happy in the interests of the greater good of the family to 'go along' with the situation.

---

123 Different historians have described the unequal power structure in the rural area in the 19th century, with its frequent male abuse, improvidence, drunkenness and violence: Grimshaw, 1986; and Evans, 1992, p 202.

124 However, Carnegie, 1994 and Atherton, 1988, amongst others, provide an indication of the struggles involved between men and women over estates.

125 *Australian Digest*, 1940.

126 Eg, *Butterworths v Butterworths* [1916] SALR 180.

127 Eg, *O'Donnell v Perpetual Trustees* (1917) 127 SR (NSW) 547.

128 Chambers 19 VLR 1893; *Dutton v Dutton* [1892] 19 VLR 57.

129 *Holdsworth v Holdsworth* (1932) 33 SR (NSW) 34. This case establishes the right for a son to receive maintenance does not end when he leaves the family but the forisfamiliation principle applies when a daughter leaves the family, *per* Long Innes J, p 46.

CONCLUSION

Up to the end of the 1880s, pastoralism used informal ad hoc procedures of farm recording based on needs as they arose. However, with the advent of accountancy firms promoting their services and the rise of pastoral lending, farmers adopted accountancy practices, necessitated by the developing tax system and death duties, to meet the requirements of their banks and, where appropriate, to assist in the administration of rural estates. By the end of the 19th century, dissatisfied litigants contested apportionments of receipts between life tenant and remainderman in the courts. In this respect, case law in Australia regarding the general administration of estates clearly followed English precedent in the context of the trustees' duty in the application of capital and income. Trustees administering estates applied this principle in general on the basis of the 'annual harvest' theory, that annual increases should be received by the life tenant.[130] However, in the rural context in Australia, the courts adopted rulings consistent with the interests of 'settler capitalism'. In effect, this created a new dichotomy/approach that put the interests of the remainderman first, namely, that the division of minimal support for a widow against the interests of the remainderman should be maintained. This outcome reflected the interests of male continuity of farming and that farming was regarded as a male occupation. Women as life tenants were regarded as merely the conduit between male generations.[131]

The courts have achieved this position in two stages: first, the 'early cases' endorsed the 'prudent management' approach, thus giving the advantage to the remainderman; secondly, through the *McBride v Hudson* approach which, by implicitly rejecting the endorsement of any specific form of accountancy practice, refers, in the absence of a specific instruction, to current practice as being authoritative. As most forms of local accounting are utilised to endorse the interests of the remainderman, the outcome in both stages was identical. Thus, while the annual harvest approach may not be followed, the ability of trustees to utilise the power of the office of trustee to its full potential, and the division of the estate into two temporal halves (life tenant and remainderman), operates to the advantage of the remainderman.

With the achievement of statehood in Australia, British imperial interests were faced with the problem of long distance control.[132] Australian colonies with stable State governments which were committed to a fully fledged market system were seen as good investments for pastoralism and for minerals and, hence, a suitable destination where capital might flow.[133]

---

130 Allen and Reynolds, 1942.
131 Voyce, 1996.
132 Connell and Irving, 1992, pp 108–09.
133 Ville, 1996.

Imposed English notions of law had a clear epistemological basis resting on a set of classifications which were fundamental to the security of *laissez faire* capitalism.[134] These classifications or technologies of government concerning the ownership of property and the classifications in trusts (life estates, and the capital/income division) were imbricated in a form of economy that allowed the State to run and be ruled itself. My argument is that these classifications or technologies had prescriptive effects, in that accountancy practices inscribed pastoralists, rendering them subject to the observation and control of pastoral banks. These technologies were embedded with, or coincided with, political rationalities concerning the dependency of women which constructed women as unproductive.[135] In other words, the rationalities were embedded with a substantial political or social correlation.[136]

---

134 Okoth-Ogendo, 1979.
135 Voyce, 1993, 1993b.
136 Miller, 1994.

CHAPTER 9

TRUSTING IN THE PRUDENT WOMAN OF BUSINESS: RISK, RECONCILIATION AND THE TRUSTEES' STANDARD OF CARE ON INVESTMENT

Alison Dunn

Reviews of trust law in the last decade have highlighted the need for attention to be paid to reform of trustees' investment powers.[1] The Lord Chancellor, Lord Irvine, for example, recently acknowledged that the archaic nature of trust law had meant that the law relating to trustee powers and duties had not kept pace with the roles of trusts in modern society.[2] Much of the attention has focused, rightly, on the outdated Trustee Investments Act 1961, and to the need for trustees to be able to undertake investments in a range of securities once considered too risky to countenance.

Less attention has been paid to the duty of care which attends trustees in their investment concerns. According to a line of 19th century case law, including the House of Lords' decisions in *Speight v Gaunt*[3] and *Learoyd v Whiteley*,[4] the standard of care for trustees who exercise powers of investment is that of the ordinary prudent man of business. Although reform seeks to codify this duty into a statutory rule,[5] few have been mindful of how it affects female trustees.

This chapter seeks, in part, to redress that balance. It examines how the trustees' duty of care as fashioned through the prudent man rule applies to female trustees, and questions whether further reform is necessary. This chapter also endeavours to highlight the fact that female trustees are a neglected area of feminist discourse, and one rich for future research.

The structure of this chapter falls into three parts. The first considers the traditional role of trusteeship and examines the prevalence of female trustees in a contemporary sample of 'public' trusts. Secondly, the question is raised whether women have a distinctive approach to their office of trusteeship, and this is considered by drawing analogies to the literature covering female styles of management. There is some evidence from this literature that women bring gender-specific approaches to their decision making, including financial management. The final section of this chapter examines the development and

---

1   See, *inter alia*, Law Reform Committee, 1982: HM Treasury, 1996; Law Commission 1997; and Law Commission, 1999.

2   The point was made by Lord Irvine in his introduction to the Trustee Bill's second reading in the House of Lords: *Hansard*, HL Deb, Vol 1804, col 373, 14 April 2000.

3   (1883) 9 App Cas 1.

4   (1887) 12 App Cas 727.

5   Trustee Bill, cl 1, discussed below.

reform of the trustees' duty of care as it relates to their investment powers. The point to be made is that the language in which the duty of care has been cast, though ostensibly objective, can conceal a position which is exclusive of women and which therefore fails to take into account female management style.

THE TRADITIONAL BOUNDS OF TRUSTEESHIP

Traditional understandings and explanations of trusteeship emphasise the trustees' role as protectors of the interests of the trust's third party beneficiaries.[6] The construct of this mien has placed upon trustees the impression of carer, guardian and steward. A primary aspect of the trustees' moral and legal obligations is to take into their care trust property and, as equity's caretakers, trustees are charged with responsibility, supervision and disinterested concern. In the past, passage to trusteeship was most usually gained by those connected closely to family fortunes, either wholly as a family member or, often more integrally, as the family's legal, medical, financial or spiritual advisor.[7] The custodian role undertaken by these trustees lay little beyond that of an overseer. Today, however, this is no longer necessarily the case. Just as equity's environment has moved beyond the hearth to the heart of commerce,[8] so trustees have eschewed their traditional lineage and moved from being members of the settlor's family to those more squarely based within the corporate milieu.[9] Contemporary trusts increasingly function along corporate bases, both through their exercise and in the composition of their trustee membership. Present day trustees tend to be drawn exclusively from the professional classes, and their role has ostensibly burgeoned into a more executive style. Trusteeship in the 21st century, then, is one of a carer constructed in the language of managerialism.

Despite the guardianship role of trusteeship, there is a general lack of literature on the prevalence and appointment of women trustees, though ample on women in the workforce, women as company directors and women in management.[10] Trusteeship seems to have fallen outside established critiques of women and the labour market, perhaps because for traditional feminist discourse the polarity identified above is problematic. Trusteeship's

6 For a summary of the arguments on the origin of the trust and its predecessor, the use, see Potter, 1931, pp 82–84.

7 See Gardner, 1990, pp 172–74; and Law Reform Committee, 1982, para 2.13.

8 See Millet, 1995, p 36; Millet, 1998; and Mason 1994.

9 See *Nestlé v National Westminster Bank plc* [1994] 1 All ER 118, p 139, *per* Leggatt LJ, on the development of the trust from Victorian times.

10 For an introduction to women and the labour market see, *inter alia*, Witz, 1997; Wajcman, 1998, pp 32–33, which provides statistics on women in management; and see, also, literature cited in footnotes below.

context within the guardianship mould sits oddly with its more managerial outlook, and the juxtaposition of the conventional female care stereotype and the archetypal masculinity of the corporate domain does not neatly fit within the extensive debate concerning labour's gendered landscape.

Moreover, this tension is evidenced not simply in the nature of the trustees' role, but also in the context of their appointment and employment. Since trusteeship is open, at least theoretically, to both the professional and the unprofessional, and since it is an office which operates on an infrequent basis and is part time in the loosest sense of the term, it should cut across the boundaries and barriers that commonly bar women's access to the labour market. Given the evidence on gender barriers, glass ceilings and the sexual contract,[11] and given the theories on women's exclusion through their lack of currency as human capital,[12] the auxiliary nature of trusteeship would seem to make it an ideal avenue for a woman.

In practice, however, it appears that the finding that there is 'no evidence that the glass ceiling is cracking in corporate Britain'[13] applies equally well to the office of trustee. That women have far to go if they are to match the prevalence of male trustees is evident from data on the gender ratio of trustee boards collated by the author from the top 325 grant making trusts in the UK.[14] When considering the data analysed below, it should be borne in mind that it is no more than illustrative. The sample concerns only a very small number of trusts, which are largely charitable trusts, and it is certainly feasible that the constitution of boards trustees of these 'public' trusts will differ from those of private family trusts, or from corporate pension trusts.[15]

Collectively, the top 325 grant making trusts are run by 2,032 trustees. Complete data of trustee gender is available for 1,627 of these trustees, which

11 For one discussion on the gender barriers and the sexual contract, see Wajcman, 1998, Chapter 2.

12 See, eg, Becker, 1985; and Hakim 1995.

13 Gregg and Machin, 1993, p 18.

14 The following data was collated by the author from analysing the trusts listed in Fitzherbert, Addison and Rashman, 1999. This publication is a directory which provides details of the major trusts, including details of trustees. Where the data was unclear as to the gender of the trustees, clarification was sought directly from the individual trusts. Where information was refused or unavailable, the trust has been classified as having fully or partially incomplete data. Complete data was available for 264 of the 325 trusts (81%). Partial data (ie, number of trustees in a trust, but not their gender) was available for 32 of the trusts (10%), and the remaining 29 trusts (9%) had fully incomplete data.

15 It may be that female trustees are more prevalent in trusts of this kind, rather than in private family or pension trusts, because of charity's public nature. Neither the Charity Commission nor the National Council for Voluntary Organisations provides guidance on best practice for the gender balance of trustee boards. In truth, it would be difficult for them to do so, since it is a trust's governing document which will determine the relevant factors for deciding the constitution of the trustee board. The Charity Commission's sole recommendation is that 'trustees be selected for what they can contribute to the charity ... on the basis of their relevant experience and skills': see Charity Commission, 1999, para 9.

represents 264 of the trusts (81%). Within that number, significantly less than one-third are female (436, or 27%), compared with 1,191 (or 73%) who are male (see Figure 1).[16]

Figure 1

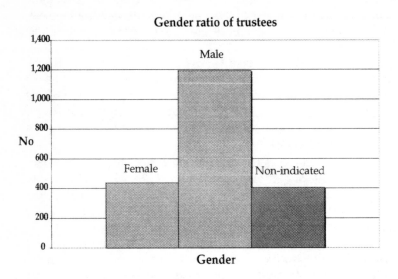

When broken down into the percentage of female/male trustees in individual trusts, it becomes evident that the female trustees are sparsely spread. The trusts analysed in the above sample tended to contain a small proportion rather than a preponderance of female trustees. For example, 30% of the trusts in the sample only had one female trustee.

Figure 2 indicates the percentage of female/male trustees on individual trustee boards. It shows that of the sample's 264 trusts with complete data, 28% had no female trustees. This compares with only one trust (0.4% of the sample) which had no male trustees. Of course, the reverse purport of these figures is that only one trust had a full complement of female trustees, as

---

16 In reality, the bare figures for the overall number of trustees will be less, since one person could be trustee for a number of different trusts, but would be counted separately in each instance. So, a female who was trustee for four trusts would be counted four times, rather than just once. The purpose for this double counting was to provide as accurate a picture as possible regarding the gender ratio of trustees in each individual trust.

compared with 28% of trusts which had an all male trustee board. Between these two extremes, the representation of women on boards of trustees in individual trusts tends to be clustered around the lower end of the scale, peaking at around 40% representation. The boards of trustees of 13.6% of the sample, for example, contained 11–20% of female trustees,[17] and 14% of the boards of trustees were composed of 21–30% of trustees who were female. Of those trusts with both male and female trustees, the most common representation of women was in the 31–40% region.[18] These trusts accounted for one-fifth (20%) of the sample. Only 25 trusts were precisely equal as between female/male trustees on their trustee board. This amounts to less than 10% of the trusts in the sample. As Figure 2 shows, a preponderance of female trustees was rare.

Figure 2

Percentage of female/male trustees on individual boards of trustees

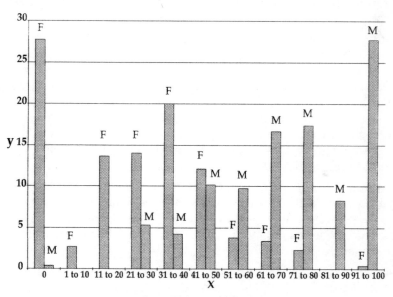

y axis = percentage of trusts
x axis = percentage of female/male trustees

---

17 A common figure was one female trustee among a board of five.
18 A common figure was one female trustee among a board of three, or two female trustees among a board of five.

Given the small sample, these bare figures are no more than illustrative. Nevertheless, they underscore a stark position. Although, theoretically, women should be in an ideal position to take up the office of trustee, in practice it seems that few do so.[19] Whether this is by choice or design is impossible to ascertain from this limited data sample, but it may not be an unrealistic assumption that a glass ceiling operates. Where trustees are drawn from professional and corporate ranks, the barriers of entry into those professions will make the pool from which female trustees can be drawn smaller.[20] In addition, the sacrifices professional women may have already made in terms of time and commitment to their primary employment role, may make them less flexible than their male counterparts in accepting the additional office of trustee. Even for charitable trusts, the fact that more women than men volunteer to work within the organisation does not correlate to their ability to move up through the ranks to positions of management or, where trustees are appointed from within an organisation, to trusteeship. The gender pyramid applies to charities and voluntary bodies as it does to other organisations.[21]

This can be seen directly from the sample analysed, since the majority of the trusts were charities covering a broad range of areas from education and research, social and community welfare through to poverty, health and religion. Encouragingly, there was little evidence to suggest that female trustees were located within, or excluded from, any particular charitable area. There was slight under-representation in medical science, as compared with nursing and general health related causes. But, on the whole, there was little to suggest gender stereotyping of women trustees into so called female issues such as childcare or general welfare.

In terms of leadership on boards of trustees, only 4% of the trusts had a female chair (see Figure 3). This is 40% less than the figure for male chairs. Whilst this may not be a major significance, it could influence the way in which trustee duties are carried out. Women's management style is examined in the next section.

---

19 The extent to which those women in the sample were token female trustees is impossible to ascertain. Many appeared to have some family connection to the trust, or were public figures. On bare figures, 44 of the 436 female trustees were titled. As noted in *op cit*, fn 16, this figure may be smaller, owing to the double counting of trustees.

20 On women in the legal profession, see McGlynn and Graham, 1995; and McGlynn, 1998.

21 See Morris, 1999.

Figure 3

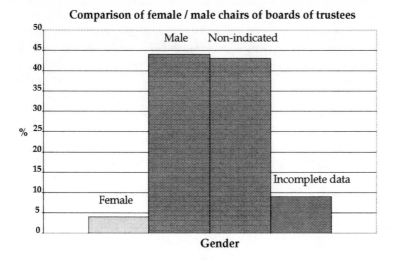

Comparison of female / male chairs of boards of trustees

WOMEN AND MANAGEMENT STYLE

Feminist academics have long researched and debated the question of whether women bring gender-specific approaches to their decision making, and so whether women have a distinctive management style. The literature on this issue is voluminous.[22] At its heart, there is a distinction between 'feminine' techniques of management and women's actual management styles within a male oriented working environment.

The former gives consideration to, and labels, techniques which are gendered female but which are utilised by either sex.[23] These feminine techniques centre upon a transformative and interactive approach to

---

22 On qualities of leaders, see Aldag and Brief, 1981; and Stogdill, 1948. See, also, Chell and Baines, 1998; and the literature cited in the following footnotes.

23 Eg, Wajcman, 1998, p 57, cites a British Institute of Management Report, 1994, which emphasised the currency of relational communication skills in modern day corporate management. Relational communication skills have been traditionally perceived as a feminine quality.

management.[24] This, in turn, is largely non-confrontational, co-operative and inclusive. The so called 'feminine' style is deemed particularly germane to contexts of negotiation and employee-centred management. It is also commonly adopted by managers seeking to show the 'caring face' of an often faceless corporation. In studies, women managers have self-appraised their style and approach to management tasks and decision making in these terms, and consider themselves to be responsive, incorporative, bridge builders, flexible, communicative and enabling.[25] This contrasts sharply with the construct of the male manager stereotype, employing a more purposive, aggressive and directive approach. As Bass and Avolio have shown in their study of male and female managers, though men can adopt a 'feminine' style, where it is used, women surpass them in terms of transformative leadership.[26] A further point, implicit from Loden's research, is that women do not confine their inclusive, collaborative management style to people-centred tasks, but will use it also in areas of standard setting and risk taking.[27]

Although there is, of course, a degree of overlap, often the exercise of management powers by women in the field will not be wholly representative of the techniques of management labelled feminine. Indeed, Wajcman refutes the notion that, in practice, women have an individual management style distinguishable from their male counterparts',[28] principally because 'women's presence in the world of men is conditional on them being willing to modify their behaviour to become more like men'.[29] This need for, and ability of, women to duplicate the prevailing hierarchy is largely true. A woman's ticket to a position of managerial power has traditionally been bought within a male monetary system. The reason for this is hardly surprising. Employees succeed in organisations where they are able to reflect their working environment in a way which is proactive, but non-threatening. As organisational behaviour tends to be gender-specific,[30] it is understandable, if discouraging, that to succeed, women adopt a mimetic guise. Yet, automatons they are not, and it seems more appropriate to say that, just as men can operate a 'pick and mix' approach to management style, choosing more masculine or feminine traits as necessary, so can women (albeit in a more limited framework) accommodate their style to the environment in which they work.

---

24 See Rosener, 1990, where these qualities were debated. See, also, Gilligan, 1982; Wexley and Hunt, 1974; Baird and Bradley, 1979; and Grant, 1988.

25 See the findings of the study of women managers in Grimwood and Popplestone, 1993, pp 108–09, from where these adjectives were drawn. See, also, Wajcman, 1998, p 66; and Alban-Metcalfe and West, 1991.

26 Bass and Avolio, 1993, p 10. The study tested for charisma, inspiration, consideration and intelligence.

27 Loden, 1985; and see Wilson, 1995, p 156; and Davidson and Cooper, 1983.

28 Wajcman, 1998, pp 55–56.

29 *Ibid*, p 8. See, also, the study of women managers in Marshall, 1984.

30 See Wilson, 1995, p 4; and Van Nostrand, 1993.

In investment, too, research suggests that women have a broader based approach than their male counterparts. Levin, for example, has argued that women have a distinctive technique to financial investment, going beyond balance sheets to an objective utilisation of feeling and sentiment in investment choice.[31] A report in 1992, by NOP Corporate and Financial Survey, also found that in financial forecasting, women proved to have a far more prudent approach than men.[32] This is supported by a more recent study of the investment strategies of women entrepreneurs, which found that, whereas men take greater financial risks in business, women tend to be more prudent in seeking expert advice.[33] It is, moreover, interesting that the requirements often specified for entry into the profession of investment banking rank interpersonal skills, creativity, inclusivity and communication skills (the so called 'feminine techniques') alongside, and as highly as, analytic competence.[34] It is, of course, difficult to draw concrete conclusions from these disparate studies, but it seems fair to suggest that women, as do men, bring some gender-specific qualities to financial matters.

As the above analysis indicates, research on women's working style, approach and *modus operandi* tends to focus exclusively on management and leadership, particularly in the fields of commercial business and health management. Although many female and male trustees will be drawn from these professional fields, the literature does not specifically cover trustees, nor their decision making duties and powers. An important distinction is to be made here. Although the trustees' role is dressed up in the language of managerialism, trustees are not in parallel management positions. Trustees do administer, but they are not in the position of selling, buying or marketing products, of general people management or of company survival. They are not primarily concerned with hiring, firing or market position. True, trustees are interested in balance sheets, share prices and profit and loss accounts but,

---

31 The argument is that the knowledge used to determine investment strategies is socially constructed, and so influenced by emotion. Nelson, commenting on Levin, makes the point that emotional construction of knowledge does not preclude more traditional 'objective' strategies of investment choice such as mathematical calculation derived from balance sheet analysis. See Levin, 1995; and Nelson, 1995. Reference to Levin was first found in Gray and Fennell, 1996. On feminist approaches see, also, Ferber and Nelson, 1993.

32 Cited in Wilson, 1995, p 82. NOP retains its surveys for a maximum of three years, and so it has not been possible to check the overall findings in this report. Outside the business environment, it seems that due to social pressures and men's reluctance to surrender decisions to their female partners, women are less likely to take the initiative in their personal financial affairs than are men, see National Savings Press Release 58/98, 4 November 1998.

33 Women Entrepreneurs Study, a Joint Research Project undertaken by Cheskin Research, Santa Clara University's Center for Innovation and Entrepreneurship and The Center for New Futures (January 2000) (available at: www.scu.edu/scu/centers/ scucie/WomenStudy.htm).

34 Eg, *Business and Finance Career Directory* (Detroit, Visible Ink, 1993); *Harvard Business School Career Guide: Finance 1996* (Boston, Mass, Harvard Business School, 1996); *Career Paths in Finance* (www.geocities.com/wallstreet/2529/ibjobs.html).

significantly, their profit making is as steward to third parties. In these circumstances, it is difficult to discern how a manager would directly translate her principal management role into an auxiliary trusteeship position, wholly independent from her everyday working environment.

Superficially more analogous is the position of a company director who owes a duty to company shareholders. But even here, fundamental differences remain.[35] Shareholders' interests lie in company growth and in high investment returns. Implicit to these interests is a demand for risk taking. As is well known, a key function of company directorship is to be entrepreneurial and to increase market share.[36] Trustees, in the main, are stewards acting on behalf of other parties, working within the remit of a settlor's wishes, but thinking exclusively of the beneficiaries' best interests. The beneficiaries' best interests principally lie in fund preservation and inflation-proofed return. In contradistinction to company directors, trusteeship demands more prudence than dynamism. As Leggatt LJ has acknowledged: 'The importance of preservation of a trust fund will always outweigh success in its advancement.'[37] Of course, some trustee boards are established to carry on a business rather than administer a family estate or to protect a beneficiary's pension nest egg. Even so, the level of business risk placed upon these trustees remains balanced by the prudence necessitated for an inflation-proofed market concern.

Albeit that the literature does not specifically cover the situation of trustees, and bearing in mind that women may well use different approaches to trusteeship than they do as managers or in their own financial affairs, nevertheless, some broad themes can be drawn together. These themes arise from feminine style *per se*, and from the location in which women are posited. Techniques labelled 'feminine' give emphasis to inclusiveness and responsiveness, with an accentuation upon 'enabling' as a consequence. In practice, too, placing women in a work environment also underscores their ability to be responsive, particularly from the angle of reflecting hierarchical norms.

Do these themes necessitate a change in the way the law looks at the trustees' duty of care, and the way in which trustees exercise their investment powers for the benefit of the beneficiaries' best interests? To answer that

---

35 For a discussion of the differences between directors' and trustees' duties of care, see Griggs and Lowry, 1997.

36 This function, though relating to the interests of specific shareholders, is also a concern of the national economy which affords another, broader, distinction with the consequences arising from the acts and duties of trustees. See comments in the introductory section of 'The Committee on the Financial Aspects of Corporate Governance, 1992'.

37 *Nestlé v National Westminster Bank plc* [1994] 1 All ER 118, p 142. This case clearly demonstrates that the balance tips more towards prudence than risk.

question, an examination must be made of the trustees' duty of care, its role and purpose, and this will be undertaken in the next section.

HISTORY, DEVELOPMENT AND RATIONALE OF THE DUTY OF CARE

The traditional bounds of trusteeship, as dictated through notions of guardianship and stewardship, have particular ascendancy in the construction of the trustees' duty of care, and the remainder of this chapter will discuss the duty of care in relation to the trustees' investment powers.

Although broached in earlier cases,[38] *Speight v Gaunt*[39] in the 1880s established the trustees' duty of care on investing trust funds. Gaunt, as trustee of the will of John Speight, had employed a stockbroker to undertake investments in three municipal corporations: Leeds, Huddersfield and Halifax. Gaunt had no special knowledge of investments and had employed a broker to undertake the investments on his behalf. The broker was chosen from a firm which had been used regularly by the testator prior his death. In the event, the broker embezzled the trust funds. In questioning whether the actions of Gaunt amounted to a breach of trust, Jessel MR, in the Court of Appeal, relied upon previous authorities which had established that trustees were not to have any higher duty than assignees.[40] He made this point:[41] 'On general principles a trustee ought to conduct the business of the trust in the same manner that an ordinary prudent man of business would conduct his own, and that beyond that there is no liability or obligation on the trustee.' Jessel MR's judgment was accepted upon appeal by the House of Lords;[42] Lord Blackburn reasoned that:[43] '[I]t would be both unreasonable and inexpedient to make a trustee responsible for not being more prudent than ordinary men of business are.'

Three years later, the Court of Appeal in *Learoyd v Whiteley*[44] followed the approach taken in *Speight v Gaunt*. The formulation of the rule provided by Lindley LJ in Learoyd was also endorsed upon appeal by the House of

---

38 Holdsworth, 1922, Vol 5, p 306 notes, eg, the case of *Carew v Peniston* (1637–38) Tothill 136 in which it was stated: 'If the trustee let ... [money] out to supposed able men [though they fail the Court] will not charge the trustee for more than he received.'

39 (1883) 9 App Cas 1.

40 See *Ex p Belchier* (1754) Amb 218; *Bacon v Bacon* (1800) 1 Ves 331; *Massey v Banner* (1820) 1 Jac & W 241; *Clough v Bond* (1838) 3 My & Cr 490.

41 (1883) 22 Ch D 727, pp 739–40.

42 See, in particular, the discussion of Lord Blackburn (1883) 9 App Cas 1, pp 17, 19–20.

43 *Ibid*, p 20.

44 (1886) 33 Ch D 347.

Lords,[45] and is often quoted as the standard to which trustees must adhere. It was Lindley LJ's view that:

> ... the business which the ordinary prudent man is supposed to be conducting for himself, is the business of investing money for the benefit of persons who are to enjoy it at some future time, and not for the sole benefit of the person entitled to the present income. The duty of a trustee is not to take such care only as a prudent man would take if he had only himself to consider; the duty rather is to take such care as an ordinary prudent man would take if he were minded to make an investment for the benefit of other people for whom he felt morally bound to provide.[46]

Thus, upon investment, the trustees are to have an even handed regard to the needs of all the beneficiaries and to the requirements of prudent investment practice.[47] The standard of prudence required dictates that trustees are to avoid investments which are attended with hazard.[48] This is not to say that trustees may not embrace risk in carrying out their investment powers. According to Bacon VC, speaking towards the end of the 19th century, the standard of prudence must not be 'strained' beyond its ordinary meaning,[49] particularly since a level of risk is an inexorable part of investment. Rather, in risk taking, trustees must follow a prudent standard and exercise reasonable care. As North J commented in *Re Medland*:[50] '... the matter must be dealt with by practical men in a practical way. They must consider what is expedient to be done at the time.'

Although the duty of care is not among the 'irreducible core of obligations'[51] concomitant with a trust, nevertheless, this duty to the beneficiaries is paramount.[52] Care, caution and circumspection are the trustees' watchwords. As reference points they are, moreover, located firmly within an objective standard of the prudent man and not, at present, within the subjectivity of judgment trustees may demonstrate in their own affairs.[53]

---

45 (1887) 12 App Cas 727; see, in particular, Lord Halsbury, p 731 and Lord Watson, p 733.

46 (1886) 33 Ch D 347, p 355.

47 See Cotton and Lopes LJJ in the Court of Appeal (1886) 33 Ch D 347, pp 350 and 358 respectively. In *Re Lucking's WT* [1967] 3 All ER 726, there was discussion on the course of action a prudent man would take.

48 *Per* Lord Watson in *Learoyd v Whiteley* (1887) App Cas 727, p 733.

49 In *Re Godfrey* (1883) 23 Ch D 483.

50 (1889) 41 Ch D 476. See, also, Lopes J in *Re Chapman* [1896] 2 Ch 763, p 777. This point was taken up by Lord Goodhart during the Trustee Bill's second reading in the House of Lords, see *Hansard*, HL Deb, Vol 1804, col 381, 14 April 2000.

51 See discussion of Millett LJ in *Armitage v Nurse* [1997] 3 WLR 1046, p 1056.

52 See discussion of Sir Robert Megarry in *Cowan v Scargill* [1985] 1 Ch 270, p 287, and that of Wynn Parry J in *Buttle v Saunders* [1950] 2 Ch 193, p 195. More recently, Lightman J in *Fuller v Evans* [2000] 1 All ER 636, p 638, emphasised that the duty of the trustees to act in the best interests of the beneficiaries operated irrespective of the interests of the settlor.

53 The subjective standard was rejected as leading to exhaustive and meaningless inquiries into trustees' intelligence: see discussion of Lord Watson in *Knox v Mackinnon* (1888) 13 App Cas 753, pp 766–67.

As the judiciary have warned, 'if [a person] likes to undertake the duty of a trustee ... he must be dealt with as an ordinary man of ordinary intelligence',[54] since otherwise, any protection to a beneficiary would be 'illusory and mischievous'.[55] The fact that trustees act honestly in the making of investment decisions and the carrying out of their investment powers will be of little consequence if they fail to reach the objective standard of the ordinary prudent man.[56] Moreover, if the trustees are represented by bodies such as trust corporations, their standard of care is an objective standard based on the professional standard they hold themselves out as possessing.[57]

The extent to which the prudent man of business test formulated in the 19th century is so freely applicable to today's trustees is open to question. It is also open to question whether the 'prudent man' rule is representative of contemporary trustee boards. Although the above analysis of the prevalence of female trustees in a small sample of trusts noted that women are underrepresented on boards of trustees, both as board members and chairs, they are, nevertheless, an important presence.[58] It is certainly arguable that the way in which investment risk, share choice and portfolio management are handled by women, coupled with the present-day nature and demands of trusteeship as compared with that of the 19th century, and the trends in contemporary investment practice, command a different standard of care; that which also takes into account the ordinary prudent woman of business.

In recent years, debate over whether there should be reform of the trustees' investment powers and duty of care has been prevalent in this jurisdiction[59] and in other jurisdictions.[60] On issues of flexibility and portfolio management,

---

54 *Per* Lindley J in *Learoyd v Whiteley* (1886) 33 Ch D 347, pp 350–51. For examples of cases where the standard has been applied, see *Smethurst v Hastings* (1885) 30 Ch D 490; *In Re Olive* (1886) 34 Ch D 70; *Re Clifford's Estate* [1900] 2 Ch 707, 716; and, more recently, *X v A* [2000] 1 All ER 490, pp 494–95.

55 *Per* Lord Macnaghten in *Knox v Mackinnon* (1888) 13 App Cas 753, p 768; Law Reform Committee, 1982, para 2.14.

56 Honest trustees are not required to make good an investment loss if they can show that they have acted prudently: see *In Re Chapman* [1896] 2 Ch 763 p 776, *per* Lindley LJ and *Wight v Olswang* (2000) *The Times*, 18 April. However, as Sir Robert Megarry noted in *Cowan v Scargill* [1985] 1 Ch 270, p 289: 'Honesty and sincerity are not the same as prudence and reasonableness.' Megarry J acknowledged, p 288, that this standard of prudence may mean that trustees have to act dishonourably, citing as an example *Buttle v Saunders* [1950] 2 Ch 193.

57 See Brightman J in *Bartlett v Barclays Bank Trust Co Ltd* [1980] 1 Ch 515, p 534.

58 It may well be that the constitution of the trustee boards of pension trusts alter over time due to the changes made under ss 16–21 of the Pensions Act 1995, which require one-third of the trust's trustees to come from a company's employees.

59 See works cited in *op cit*, fn 1.

60 See, *inter alia*, Palmer, 1986; Committee on the Modernisation of the Trustee Act, 1999; and Manitoba Law Reform Commission, 1999. For a discussion on trustee investment and duty of care in a selection of other jurisdictions, see Finn and Ziegler, 1987; Dal Pont and Chambers, 1996; and Delaney, 1996.

it is an area readily disposed for reform.[61] As the Lord Chancellor, Lord Irvine, recently acknowledged: '... trust law governing the powers and duties of trustees has not kept pace with the evolving social and economic role trusts now fulfil.'[62] The Trustee Bill, currently making its way through the House of Commons, proposes to put on a statutory footing the trustees' duty of care. Clause 1 of the Bill provides that a trustee:[63]

> ... must exercise such care and skill as is reasonable in the circumstances, having regard in particular (a) to any special knowledge or experience that he has or holds himself out as having, and (b) if he acts as trustee in the course of a business or profession, to any special knowledge or experience that it is reasonable to expect of a person acting in the course of that kind of business or profession.

Although this clause is really a codification of the existing common law standard, as is evident from part (a) of the clause, the intended statutory duty of care comprises a subjective as well as an objective element. It dovetails with the Bill's proposals of applying a general power of investment and allows a more wider and flexible approach to trustees in exercising their investment functions.

Whether or not these proposals go far enough in their reform is open to debate, particularly from a feminist viewpoint. It seems that one crucial factor has been overlooked. Innate to trustee investment is a question of care, and that question of care is located within a standard of reasonableness. Though ostensibly objective, the reasonableness standard applied is neither pluralistic nor impartial. Rather, it is drawn from the yardstick of the 'usual course of business'.[64] Here lies the issue for female trustees: constructs of the 'usual course of business' are homogeneous with a male hierarchy. Men's predominance in the rank and file to the upper corridors of corporate society ultimately structures professional codes and prudent business policies, strategies and behaviour. Admittedly, women are a component of this system, but aside from a handful of notable examples who have found the portal in the glass ceiling, they do not, at present, have a sufficient groundswell to make

---

61 For a discussion of investment risk and modern portfolio management see Rizzi, 1975.

62 *Hansard*, HL Deb, Vol 1804, col 373, 14 April 2000.

63 The Trustee Bill seeks to amend the law relating to trustees and to persons having the investment powers of trustees. Clause 1 implements the recommendations in Law Commission, 1999, Pt III. Clause 3 provides for a general power of investment and cll 4 and 5 provide that the trustee when investing must still have regard to standard investment criteria including diversification, investment suitability, and the requisite advice. See Schedules and explanatory notes.

64 See discussion of Lord Watson in *Learoyd v Whiteley* (1887) 12 App Cas 727, p 734. Clearly, the notion of 'the usual course of business' has altered since the late 19th century when *Learoyd* was decided. The pace of change in business terms is legion, and never more so than in the present commercial climate. Even so, the 'usual course of business' test as a standard has not been left behind with its 19th century origins, but would now incorporate and cover more contemporary practices to those which applied at the test's inception.

a serious impact on common business methods. The usual course of business test, which is indelibly male at its core, is exclusionary as a yardstick. One consequence of this is that, in terms of the care provided by trustees to beneficiaries, either generally or specifically in exercise of their investment powers, not all perspectives or approaches are represented.

Moreover, although the proposed new standard of care laid down in the Trustee Bill contains a subjective element which would take account of any special knowledge or experience that the trustee has, it would not appear in reality to pay heed to women's overarching style of management, identified in the preceding section. The reasons for this are twofold. The first is that a trustee's style or approach to investment is different from their experience in the field, and would not seem to fall naturally within the category of 'specialist knowledge'. To take one example, experience may indicate that it would be best to avoid investments in certain companies on the day before a budget is declared, but that experience gained in the field does not attest to individual technique which is to be applied when investments are chosen. Style is not equivalent to experience.

The second reason is that, even if the two were equivalent, analysis of a trustee's experience or special knowledge, though subjective, still takes place within the objective remit of a reasonable standard, the usual course of business test, which does not encompass female style. To explain: questions concerning approach to risk taking are traditionally seen as different from questions concerning the standard of care to be applied.[65] The methods by which trustees consider investment risk, or the methods by which trustees monitor investments, are separate from the standard that they are required to reach when those risks or decisions are taken. The former pertains to strategy, the first stage in the investment process; whereas the latter is concerned with the second stage, the level to be attained when the approach taken at stage one has been employed. That said, despite the division in theory between these stages, the two questions unite in practice. This is because the standard to be attained by the trustees under the usual course of business test is fashioned by prevailing business strategies. That is, it is constructed from an analysis of how trustee decisions are reached. Thus, the 'how' of trustee investment has become normative of the 'what'; that is, the accepted level of risk that should be taken. This is significant because, as noted above, decision making occurs in different ways. Individual trustees have different styles, and an analogy with the management literature would suggest that female/male trustees have distinguishable approaches to matters of investment choice and monitoring. Yet, it is the male approach which predominates and conditions what will ultimately be the usual course of business. Consequently, it also conditions the relevancy of the subjective elements of trustee experience and specialist knowledge, highlighted as important in the Trustee Bill.

65 I am grateful to my colleagues Chris Riley and Ian Dawson for discussion on this point.

If the trustees' present duty of care test excludes female trustees at an objective level, and if the codified duty of care test in the Trustee Bill disregards female trustees through both its objective and subjective elements,[66] does that mean that the trustees' duty of care on investment needs to be recast once more? On the level of equal treatment, the answer must lie in the affirmative. But one needs also to examine this issue in light of whether the test, through its inattention to female management style as an integral part of construct of the 'usual course of business', actually fails to achieve its purpose.

The duty of care placed upon trustees in the context of their investment powers has two principal purposes. The first, clearly, is to protect the beneficiaries of the trust who, not having legal title, are dependent upon the actions of trustees. This fits in neatly with other provisions in trust law which seek to protect beneficiaries from the trustees' vagaries, including their incompetence or bias. There is particular resonance here with the provisions concerning trustees' fiduciary duties, and also with the proprietary nature of equitable remedies for breach of trust which allow beneficiaries an advantage over the trustee's creditors.[67] It also resonates with the judicial inclination against the propriety of clauses in trust documents exempting trustees from liability, unless loss to the trust is caused by their actual fraud.[68]

Conversely, the second purpose of the duty of care is to protect the trustees, or perhaps more appropriately, to protect the office of trusteeship. A duty of care allows for certainty and consistency both for the beneficiaries of a trust, and for those who administer the property.[69] It provides trustees with a concrete threshold from which to proceed. This certainty is concomitant with furnishing trustees with a degree of security in the event of investment failure. A duty of care allows for confidence to be placed in the trustees' actions, not just by beneficiaries, but also by trustees personally. This is often equated with the need to ensure that trusteeship, as a responsible office, remains a legally and financially viable position for those who wish to take it up.

Plainly, the duty of care, as it is currently formulated, has limitations which ultimately work against the test's success in achieving these two purposes. It

---

66 The issue of whether there should be an objective or subjective duty of care, or whether there should be different duty of care tests dependent on the person concerned have been traversed in the context of the duty of care of company directors. See, in particular, Finch, 1992; and Riley 1999.

67 Not to make an unauthorised profit and not to put themselves in a position where the trustee's interests and the interests of the beneficiaries conflict: *Bray v Ford* [1896] AC 44.

68 See discussion of Millett LJ in *Armitage v Nurse* [1997] 3 WLR 1046 and the disquiet expressed in the House of Lords debates that the Trustee Bill omitted to prohibit exemption clauses (*Hansard*, HL Deb, Vol 1804, col 383 (*per* Lord Goodhart), col 392 (*per* Lord Wilberforce), 14 April 2000). Lord Irvine indicated in the same debate (cols 393–94) that this issue is one suitable for investigation by the Law Commission.

69 See discussion of Lord Irvine LC, *Hansard*, HL Deb, Vol 1804, col 373, 14 April 2000.

can, for example, encourage passivity on the part of trustees, and make it difficult for beneficiaries to bring their trustees into account. The case of *Nestlé v National Westminster Bank plc*[70] certainly stands as testament to these two points. Yet it is hard to see how failure to take into account female management style *per se* works against the duty of care's two purposes as identified above. True, the duty can also stifle trustee creativity, or sensitivity, and limits trustees from taking into account broad concerns, such as ethical or socially responsible considerations, when making their investment choice.[71] But that does not work against the beneficiaries' best interests, nor does it open up a trustee to insecurity. So, whilst female trustees may very well take a different stand to their male counterparts on ethical or socially responsible concerns when selecting investments, because the focus of trust law rests solely on financial returns, the difference between female and male style on this issue is not a relevant consideration.

Moreover, as the research on managers has indicated, styles of management are not the sole preserve of either sex.[72] Failure to expressly incorporate a 'feminine style' in the construct of the usual course of business will not exclude the approach taken by all women trustees, and it will not, conversely, recognise all male techniques. In the absence of showing that female trustees protect beneficiaries more prudently than male trustees, it would be difficult to reformulate the duty of care test in a way which would deal with style and prudence in an appropriate manner. This is particularly so when the duty of care test imports a standard drawn from external considerations; those derived from the prevailing philosophy of corporate society.

Ultimately, the standard to be applied to trustees in investment matters is a difficult balancing act. The duty of care should be such that it offers protection for the vulnerable beneficiary by discouraging unwarranted risk taking, but it should also try not to stifle modern investment practice, nor discriminate against the methods by which different trustees carry out their duties and powers. Whether or not female style of management is more protective of beneficiaries is open to question, and is an area rich in potential for future

---

70 [1994] 1 All ER 118. Leggatt LJ (p 142) called the duty of care test an 'undemanding standard of prudence'. See, also, *Wight v Olswang* (2000) *The Times*, 18 April.

71 The duty of care dictates that trustees must act in the best interests of the trusts' beneficiaries. Sir Robert Megarry VC pointed out in *Cowan v Scargill* [1985] 1 Ch 270, pp 286–87, that acting in the best interests of the beneficiaries, in a trust which has the purpose of providing financial benefits, means pursuing the best financial return from investments. This duty of care precludes trustees from investing in an ethical or a socially responsible manner, where the proposed investment, though morally correct, is financially wrong. See, also, *Harries v Church Commissioners for England* [1992] 1 WLR 1241 (a more lenient position for charitable trusts); *Martin v City of Edinburgh DC* 1988 SLT 329 (position in Scotland).

72 See above, text to fn 23ff.

research. But rather than recast the duty of care at this stage, attention would be better placed focusing on the makeup of trustee boards. As analysis of a small group of trusts and trustees shows, female representation is found wanting. The most propitious scenario for trust beneficiaries would seem to be to have a board of trustees pluralistically constituted. The argument should be one for diversity of approaches, rather than homogeneity of standards. How and why, and why not, women are appointed trustees should be our first port of call.[73]

---

73 The author is grateful to Anna Leaker for her research assistance in the area of female investment practice.

CHAPTER 10

EQUITABLE REMEDIES: CYPHER WIVES, WEAK WOMEN AND 'EQUITY'S SPECIAL TENDERNESS'

Claire de Than

... the identification of certain privileged female characteristics may benefit some women, giving them gender pride, but it simultaneously has negative features in that it excludes some, while constraining others' personalities.[1]

If this is so, then the identification of negative female characteristics and their implicit use in creating precedent and statutes must surely be an undesirable phenomenon.

The main focus of this chapter is the extent to which women are treated differently in the grant or denial of equitable remedies, and the potential positive and negative effects of any such differences. In most fields, equity now, generally, treats women as rational and autonomous actors. There are some extreme examples, such as *Clark v Clark*,[2] a divorce case, where the wife was found to be a 'wicked' and 'devious' woman 'of considerable charm and attraction' who so controlled her older husband that she was responsible for all his actions over a period of six years, including his suicide attempt and even his senility. But the field of equitable remedies contains false universalisms and explicit stereotypes[3] of women which, although not always overtly negative in effect, are backward-thinking and in need of dragging into at least the 20th century. Some of the stereotypes are appealing, nostalgic, romanticised and even advantageous to the particular women applicants or defendants, but at the price of reinforcement of those very stereotypes. Many are deliberate or overt, others are hidden assumptions; sometimes seemingly genderless rules may have unexpected differential effects on men and women because of other societal factors. Because the grant of any equitable remedy is discretionary, courts are able to cloak policy decisions and unjustified assumptions behind what appears to be no more than a series of decisions made only on the relevant facts. So, whilst equity has been responsible for the invention and development of some of the most effective remedies available in English courts, many of which have changed the rights and lives of women for the better, 'mainstreaming' and changes in judicial attitude are still necessary.

---

1   Greenberg in Frug, 1992.
2   [1999] 2 FLR 498.
3   For a complex discussion of subjects and subjectivities see Bottomley, 1993.

As Frug argues:

> Law requires all legal claimants to assume a particular posture – a partial identity – in seeking judicial assistance; we must leave aside much of the multiplicity and complexity of our lives in order to engage in legal discourse. Injustice occurs ... when legal rules structure these particular postures in such a way that subordinate groups cannot squeeze into them at all. In these situations, legal rules need to expand the narrow and rigid character of the subject position they impose as a condition of admission to the legal arena.[4]

But, further, sometimes such identities are all too easily ascribed to groups or subgroups of claimants, who may participate in their own stereotyping in order to win a remedy for their own personal injustices. It will be argued in this chapter that, in relation to some equitable remedies, women manage the conjuring trick of simultaneous exclusion and myth-participation. As far as the received wisdom on equity and trusts is concerned, women mainly 'belong' to, or are relevant in, the family home, domestic violence and harassment cases, marriage settlements, fraud (as victims), the long sidelined presumptions of advancement, as convenient extra defendants, and as historical beneficiaries of equity's kindness in providing a remedy where the common law was unhelpful. Images of women as active and actors are rare, and there are relatively few women in the 'leading cases' on equitable remedies. Are there no solo active women who seek equitable remedies unconnected to their family relationships and domestic situations? The concentration of women in certain defined fields of equity limits innovation in legal thinking, structures future cases and legal syllabi, creates legal textbooks and casebooks which may be read as gendered for either a lack of women, or reference to them only in standardised contexts such as injunctions in family law, and stultifies developments in equitable doctrine. Frug, who wrote mainly about images of women in contract law, might have argued that this situation cannot avoid sending messages about women's inferior status to any reader of, for example, an equity and trusts casebook, and, further, that this intrinsically harms the reader. Remedies are not always given to the weak, vulnerable, oppressed, and outwitted, but if a reader concentrates only on those leading cases which have a woman as either party, it would be difficult to believe this. Whereas men appear in a wide variety of roles, weak and powerful, victim and wrongdoer, commercial and private, the situation for women remains pigeonholed and one-sided. Because equitable remedies are so pervasive, of application in almost every legal field, these images may have far reaching effects.

---

4   Frug, 1992, Chapter 2.

RECTIFICATION AND RESCISSION; 'OUTWITTED, DECEIVED AND DUPED' WOMEN AND A LITTLE 'SPECIAL TENDERNESS'

Since other chapters in this book focus upon the *Barclays Bank v O'Brien*[5] scenario and have the space to do it justice, it will not be analysed in detail here. However, a brief reference to the equitable remedies of rectification and rescission, in particular, the setting aside of contracts for mistake, misrepresentation and undue influence, is pertinent and allows the drawing of parallels later. For some time, it appeared that equity would be the duped wife's champion when she was convinced to guarantee her husband's doomed business venture, often by way of a charge on the family home,[6] but recent cases have shown a clear preference for commercial interests over those of the duped. However, the earlier cases remain of interest for the statements and assumptions which they make about the women involved, and even the most recent judicial pronouncements contain echoes of such rhetoric. One statement, in *Cresswell v Potter*,[7] which elaborates equity's ability to overturn transactions due to an inherent unfairness (undue influence and unconscionability are used fairly interchangeably in the cases), is that this will be possible '[w]here a poor ignorant person entered into a disadvantageous transaction (for example, at an undervalue) without any independent legal advice'. Women appear to fit this definition rather well in even quite recent case law. The *Cresswell* case itself abounds with overt and implied statements about women's roles, class divisions as well as gender divisions, and displays the ease with which women are viewed as having victim status. In the judgment of Megarry J (who has already made a number of appearances in this book), being a telephonist was sufficient grounds on which to find the wife 'poor and ignorant', and the idea of a wife transferring property to her husband on divorce was so unusual as to arouse suspicion as to the validity of the transaction. However, in some circumstances, being poor, ignorant and entering into a highly disadvantageous transaction is not enough basis for equity to intervene at all, especially where the most important kind of third party rights, those of banks and other commercial interests, are involved. This is discussed elsewhere in this book. But an interesting comparison may be made with the defendant in *Portman Building Society v Dusangh*,[8] who did satisfy the 'poor and ignorant' test in the eyes of the court, since he was elderly, illiterate and had a very low income. His taking out of a large loan to

---

5   [1994] 1 AC 180.
6   For a more detailed discussion of these cases, see Green and Lim, Chapter 5, and Scoular, Chapter 6, in this volume; see, also, Mackenzie, 1996.
7   [1978] 1 WLR 255.
8   (2000) unreported, 19 April, CA.

fund his son's business venture was also clearly unwise. But, according to Simon Brown LJ, the fact that the building society had failed on several occasions to adhere to its own policy and safeguards as to ensuring that the defendant would be able to make the repayments was not material, since those safeguards exist for the building society's benefit rather than to protect the borrower from making an unwise commitment. Perhaps the result would have been different if the influence had been between husband and wife rather than son and father, since wives are still not viewed as entirely independent of thought or activity in recent judgments.

In *Barclays Bank plc v O'Brien*,[9] Lord Browne-Wilkinson made a number of comments about the reality of married life and the strange mixture of dependency and independence of some modern wives.[10] Further, although he dismissed the previous theory of equity's 'special protection' of wives undertaking surety transactions, he found, instead, that there is a 'special tenderness' for women in this situation so that wives are more likely to establish undue influence than are others: '... the "tenderness" shown by the law to married women is not based on the marriage ceremony but reflects the underlying risk of one cohabitee exploiting the emotional involvement and trust of the other.' Thus, in spite of the general view that *O'Brien* represents a significant narrowing of the defence, it is equally possible to argue that *dicta* in that case show a willingness to expand the categories of relationship in which undue influence may be argued to any which involve close emotional ties. 'Special tenderness', however, is a difficult concept, which contains more than a hint of paternalism. Lord Browne-Wilkinson attributed its existence in part to the courts' recognition of sexual and emotional ties between the parties, making it easier for the wife's will to be overborne, since she fears that their relationship will be damaged if she opposes her husband. This may well be true in many cases, but creates an impression of fearful wives doing their husbands' bidding, but saved by equity on its white charger – hardly a positive image for the end of the 20th century. However, the banks' rights prevail so long as the wife has received separate and independent legal advice as to the effect of the surety transaction in question, and has had the paperwork explained to her by the bank. This case, and its development in subsequent cases,[11] create a doubly unfair situation; there is the appearance of special treatment for a class of 'vulnerables' comprising mainly wives and female cohabitees, yet, when the surface is scratched, there is little chance of

---

9   [1994] 1 AC 180.

10 'Wives' here includes cohabitees, since it is the nature of the relationship rather than the label attached to the parties which triggers the possibility of an undue influence argument: later cases, including *Massey v Midland Bank* [1995] 1 All ER 929, have made it clear that the same principles will apply wherever a relationship is such that one party relies upon the other to deal with financial affairs and places trust and confidence in that party for that purpose.

11 See, eg, *Royal Bank of Scotland v Etridge (No 2)* [1998] 4 All ER 705.

any practical help or financial recompense for those perceived to be so lucky. Arguably, special tenderness is just another way of phrasing the differential treatment and stereotyping which will be seen in other areas of equitable remedy.

INJUNCTIONS: VULNERABLE WOMEN

Injunctions are possibly the most famous and effective child of equity, and have been used increasingly in recent years to provide relief for victims of harassment, domestic violence, stalking and other wrongs previously unaddressed by law. Although each of these harms is now dealt with by statute law, the roots of the statutory change in each case came from innovation by the courts in their application of the power to grant an injunction 'in all cases in which it appears to the court to be just and convenient to do so'.[12] It appears that the House of Lords is now willing to uphold an injunction protecting any legally recognised right, even in novel cases.[13] Further extension is likely in the near future after the Human Rights Act 1998 comes into force, particularly in relation to invasions of privacy which have been hitherto permitted under English law. Whilst innovative thinking to meet new situations is always to be welcomed, it should be noted that, in many of the cases extending the jurisdiction, there is a perception of women as automatically vulnerable; this point will be revisited later.

Innovative injunctions against harassment and stalking

As an example of the use of injunctions to protect individual rights where statute and common law have failed to provide redress, harassment and stalking is apt. Until the mid-1990s, such behaviour would result in legal intervention only if there was physical injury or a breach of another legally recognised right by an act such as trespass or nuisance. Married and cohabiting couples were 'lucky' enough to receive some statutory protection[14] with the ultimate sanction of an ouster injunction to remove a spouse from the matrimonial home,[15] but courts did not seem keen to enforce such draconian orders as ousters.[16] The framework was unnecessarily complicated, with

---

12 Supreme Court Act 1981, s 37(1) and County Courts Act 1984, s 38, restating the previous principles.

13 *Channel Tunnel Group v Balfour Beatty Construction Ltd* [1993] AC 334.

14 Including Domestic Violence and Matrimonial Proceedings Act 1976.

15 Matrimonial Homes Act 1983, ss 1 and 9.

16 Eg, *Khan v Khan* [1995] 2 FLR 221; there must be an intolerable situation and danger in the home before an order will be made.

different authorities governing spouses, former spouses, cohabitees and former cohabitees.[17] None of the statutory schemes was of any use where the parties had never cohabited. In *Khorasandjian v Bush*,[18] the court was faced with a stark choice between ignoring previous authority[19] that there was no existing right upon which basis to grant an injunction restraining harassment and allowing behaviour which was clearly extremely upsetting and potentially harmful to continue unchecked. An 18 year old woman had been the recipient of threats of violence, malicious telephone calls, verbal abuse and finally death threats from a man who had once been her friend. Eventually, he was arrested and served a short term of imprisonment for the threats to kill her. Understandably, the woman applied for a temporary injunction to restrain a stream of abusive telephone calls made to her and members of her family. A county court judge granted the injunction, restraining the defendant from 'using violence to, harassing, pestering or communicating with' the plaintiff in any way. The defendant appealed, contending that the judge had no jurisdiction to restrain the defendant from 'harassing, pestering or communicating with' the plaintiff because those words did not reflect any tort known to the law and an interlocutory (temporary) injunction could only be granted to protect a legal right. The majority of the Court of Appeal found that courts did have power to grant an injunction restraining harassment by telephone calls, since the defendant's behaviour was both an unjustified interference with the use of property, that is, the home, and since further calls would be likely to cause psychiatric injury to the applicant. Viewed as a whole, the defendant's actions were clearly calculated to cause harm, and constituted at least private nuisance.[20] Thus, the court's approach was eminently sensible; given that the defendant's behaviour was serious enough for criminal liability, it would have been ridiculous to deny the applicant a civil remedy designed to back up the findings of the criminal court and to prevent further illegal behaviour.

Building upon that decision, the court in *Burris v Azadani*[21] effectively invented the courts' ability to restrain actual or threatened harassment by injunction where there was no convenient other right, such as trespass or private nuisance, upon which to base the argument. Even in *Khorasandjian v Bush*, the court had been careful to avoid stating that there was any free standing tort of harassment upon which the injunctive relief could be grounded. The present court appears to have refused to believe that equitable

---

17 The Family Law Act 1996 has now erased these distinctions as far as rights of occupation of the family home are concerned.

18 [1993] 3 All ER 669.

19 Eg, *Patel v Patel* [1988] 2 FLR 179.

20 Now, such behaviour would be caught by the Protection from Harassment Act 1997 which restates the courts' power to grant such injunctions but in fact adds little to existing case law, both civil and criminal: see Conaghan, 1996 and 1999.

21 [1995] 4 All ER 802.

relief could not be found for harassment, and was a spur towards legislative reform. It went as far as imposing an exclusion zone around the applicant's house to prevent further acts of harassment. The applicant and her two children had been subject to a campaign of harassment from the defendant, who was eventually given a prison sentence for repeatedly breaching the injunctions granted against him. The defendant appealed, contending that the county court had no jurisdiction to impose an exclusion zone when making a non-molestation order. The Court of Appeal held that it is within the power of either the High Court or a county court to grant injunctions, phrased in wide terms to restrain conduct that is not in itself tortious or otherwise unlawful, whenever it was regarded as necessary for the protection of a plaintiff's legitimate interest. Thus, placing an exclusion zone around the applicant's premises is a permissible and effective method of preventing further harassment and may be ordered so long as the defendant's freedom is not unnecessarily constrained. In the words of Sir Thomas Bingham MR:

> Respect for the freedom of the aggressor should never lead the court to deny necessary protection to the victim. Ordinarily, the victim will be adequately protected by an injunction which restrains the tort which has been or is likely to be committed, whether trespass to the person or to land, interference with goods, harassment, intimidation or as the case may be. But it may be clear on the facts that if the defendant approaches the vicinity of the plaintiff's home he will succumb to the temptation to enter it, or to abuse or harass the plaintiff; or that he may loiter outside the house, watching and besetting it, in a manner which might be highly stressful and disturbing to a plaintiff. In such a situation the court may properly judge that in the plaintiff's interest – and also, but indirectly, the defendant's – a wider measure of restraint is called for.[22]

Thus, it has been the courts, rather than the legislature, which have provided more immediate, effective and practical remedies for prevalent form of distressing behaviour regardless of the relationship between the defendant and victim, and later legislative change has merely built upon the broad jurisdiction carved out by courts on their own initiative and behalf.

However, two other varieties of injunction are not to be heralded as landmark developments in the recognition and enforcement of civil liberties and human rights, particularly the rights of women. Both search orders and freezing orders are designed to safeguard the applicant's interests for a future trial and hence to ensure fairness, but have been applied in a manner which contains implicit negative assumptions about women and simultaneously treats individual rights as secondary to commercial interests. The cases to be discussed in the following two sections can be contrasted against the House of Lords' Practice Direction[23] for both forms of injunction: '[T]he granting of a

---

22 [1995] 4 All ER 802, p 811.
23 28.7.1994.

Mareva [now freezing] injunction or Anton Piller [now search] order is a matter for the discretion of the judge hearing the application. However, it is desirable that a consistent approach should in general be adopted to the form and carrying out of such orders, since they represent serious restrictions on the rights of those persons subjected to them ...'

It will be argued that implicit stereotyping prevents any such consistency and has a serious adverse effect upon the rights of third parties. Both types of injunction have a decisive effect on many difficult cases and can cause great potential harm to the defendant and to third parties. It is time for a more structured rethinking of the rules for both categories of injunction, with greater focus on protecting the rights of all potential third parties and with a distinction between the innocent and those complicit in the alleged wrongdoing.

Search orders: 'lone and vulnerable' women

Search orders, formerly known as Anton Piller orders, undertake the sensible task of prevention of destruction of evidence before trial. Once granted, they permit the search of the defendant's business premises or home and the seizure of items or documents which might be evidence in a future case by the applicant against the defendant. The search will be carried out by solicitors and, if any relevant items are found, they may be removed temporarily, usually only for copying purposes. In order to be of any practical use, such a search must be carried out without giving the defendant an opportunity to prepare the premises to be searched and dispose of the very evidence which the order is designed to preserve; hence, they are obtained without the defendant's knowledge and without giving him a chance to defend his position. So, a series of cases have created forceful judicial guidelines and safeguards for the obtaining and execution of search orders, most of which are sensible and contain neither explicit nor implicit bias. The applicant must show that he has an extremely strong arguable case, including evidence that the defendant has relevant items which he is likely to destroy; searches should only be carried out during working hours; the applicant must give an undertaking in damages to protect the defendant's rights, and so on.[24] However, even a properly executed search is intrusive, invasive if the home is searched, and compromising to both the defendant's rights and those of any third party. Further, not all the safeguards are so easily justifiable: '(1)(b) On an application for an Anton Piller order ... [w]here the premises are likely to be occupied by an unaccompanied woman and the supervising solicitor is a man, at least one of the persons attending on the service of the order should be a woman.'[25]

---

24 See *Universal Thermosensors v Hibben* [1992] 1 WLR 840 for a full list, and the Practice Guidelines cited above.

25 House of Lords Practice Direction 28.7.1994.

The entire framework of search orders and of the safeguards for their enforcement contains an explicit sex differential; women are more vulnerable, particularly when at home alone (which appears to mean without a man, since children and other women do not 'count' in cases such as Hibben (below)), and so must receive special treatment. The identification of women with the home is a long, familiar one, if hardly progressive thinking, and reinforces the image of women as weak and in need of extra protection (from solicitors knocking at the door). Do not all persons have an equal right to sanctity of the home, regardless of sex? Surely every order should be enforced in a manner which shows respect for any individual's home? Further, the particular safeguard is surely of little practical value beyond some 'safety in numbers' argument, and arguably displays yet another stereotype, that female professionals are more caring than male professionals.

The reason behind that particular rule comes from the facts of a famous case, *Universal Thermosensors v Hibben*:[26]

(1) In the present case Mrs Hibben was alone in the house, with her children in bed. She was brought to the door in her night attire at 7.15 am, and told by a stranger knocking at the door that he had a court order requiring her to permit him to enter, that she could take legal advice forthwith, but otherwise she was not permitted to speak to anyone else at all. But how could she get legal advice at that time in the morning? ...

(2) There is a further feature of the situation ... which must never be allowed to occur again. If the order is to be executed at a private house, and it is at all likely that a woman may be in the house alone, the solicitor serving the order must be, or must be accompanied by, a woman. A woman should not be subjected to the alarm of being confronted without warning by a solitary strange man, with no recognisable means of identification, waving some unfamiliar papers and claiming an entitlement to enter her house and, what is more, telling her that she is not allowed to get in touch with anyone (except a lawyer) about what is happening.[27]

The case raises a number of interesting questions which are, unfortunately, unanswered by the official report. Was it the fact that Mrs Hibben was female or rather that she was the only adult in the house which prompted the court to use such strong condemnation? Was it relevant to the decision that there were small children in the house? What would the court's attitude have been to a group of adult women being disturbed by a group of male lawyers at an unsocial hour? It may well be the case that the court's words give a stronger appearance of being based upon sex and assumptions about women than was

26 [1992] 1 WLR 840.
27 *Ibid*, pp 860–61.

intended, but to avoid such a reading would require access to far more detailed judicial argument on the point than was actually made. Distressing as the situation may have been, and clearly undesirable as its repetition is, a man might have been equally distressed, and justifiably so. In view of Art 8 of the European Convention on Human Rights and its First Protocol, which protect the rights to respect for privacy and for family life, and the right to property, respectively, it might be thought that such searches would be viewed with the utmost suspicion and subjected to intense scrutiny. However, existing case law has confirmed that they have an important role to play in modern civil and criminal justice, and it is interference with commercial rather than private interests which has been held to be a breach of the Convention.[28] It remains to be seen how English courts will interpret the ECHR rights after their incorporation into English law in October 2000, but radical change to the existing ECHR interpretation of privacy is extremely unlikely, since the recognition of even a basic right to a private life is beyond the scope of current English law.

In *Lock plc v Beswick*,[29] Hoffman J borrowed a concept from European law to state the best practice on the decision whether to grant a search order; that there must be proportionality between the perceived threat to the applicant's rights and the invasive nature of this particular remedy:

> The more intrusive orders allowing search of premises or vehicles require a careful balance of, on the one hand, the plaintiff's right to recover his property or preserve important evidence against, on the other hand, violation of the privacy of a defendant who has had no opportunity to put his side of the case. The making of an intrusive order *ex parte* is contrary to normal principles of justice and can only be done where there is a paramount need to prevent a denial of justice to the plaintiff. The absolute extremity of the court's power is to permit a search of a defendant's dwelling house, with the humiliation and family distress which that frequently involves.

This would indeed be good practice, but abuses have occurred in both the granting of search orders without strong evidence that they are required, and in the carrying out of these increasingly common injunctions. For example, they can be granted on weak evidence. In *Yousif v Salama*,[30] evidence that the defendant had previously forged a cheque was taken to be sufficient evidence of 'untrustworthiness' that it was probable that he would destroy or interfere with evidence, when arguably, there is no necessary link between those two types of behaviour. Even when the best practice is followed, this test is applied variably and with contradictory results. Invasion of privacy, distress and humiliation seem to be fine as long as the person who is present at the time of

---

28 See *Chappell v UK* [1989] 1 EHRR 543; *Niemietz v Germany* [1992] 16 EHRR 97.
29 [1989] 1 WLR 1268.
30 [1980] 1 WLR 1540.

the search is not an unaccompanied woman, and a female solicitor or legal executive is a cure for all potential abuses.

One field where these contradictions and problems are highlighted is that of the use of search orders in matrimonial cases. There is an immediate paradox: according to *Emmanuel v Emmanuel*[31] it is, and should remain, very difficult to obtain a search order in matrimonial cases; but, contradictorily, matrimonial proceedings where it is thought that one spouse has failed to make truthful disclosure of his/her assets are one of the most common applications of search orders. So, it may be difficult, but it is not uncommon as a last resort (rather than a truly pre-emptive strike). This remedy can be a very powerful tool in achieving fair divorce settlements for the 'weaker party' and, even in modern marriages, that is still usually the woman. In *Emmanuel*, a wife succeeded in obtaining injunctions to search for and copy documents relating to the husband's wrongful sale of two properties which had been awarded to her. Wood J found that, since this husband had shown himself happy to flout the authority of the court, there was 'no doubt that justice in this case' could not 'be achieved without making the present order, and that there' was 'a grave danger that evidence' would 'be removed and destroyed'. He could not 'think that any real harm' would 'be caused to the husband from making the order, as the only documents sought' were 'those which he ought properly to produce and, indeed, ought to have produced in the past'.[32]

However, there appears to be some inconsistency in the cases here, and a useful comparison is *Araghchinchi v Araghchinchi*.[33] In a clean break divorce, the husband was awarded his business, which was valued at around £10,000, but he later sold it for £150,000. The wife and children's original awards were, in fact, entirely swallowed by negative equity and legal costs. Under cross-examination in subsequent family proceedings, the husband admitted that around two-thirds of the proceeds of the sale had been given to his father and a friend, but refused to say what had happened to the remainder. Before appealing against the original divorce award, the wife sought an Anton Piller order and a Mareva injunction in order to protect her position until a reopening of the divorce settlement could occur, and to provide further evidence of her husband's undisclosed means. Ward LJ noted that the defendant husband had concealed matters from the Inland Revenue, had bank accounts in various names, had been sentenced to imprisonment for failure to pay maintenance, was 'devious and dishonest', and that getting information out of him previously had been like pulling teeth. 'This is, unfortunately, yet another of a category of cases which makes its way regularly through the divorce courts, where the court grapples with the dishonest and devious husband determined to conceal has assets and determined to frustrate both

---

31   [1982] 1 WLR 662.
32   *Ibid*, p 676.
33   (1997) unreported, 26 February, CA.

the court and the applicant seeking ancillary relief.' However, the circumstances were not 'exceptional' enough to urge the court to grant the injunctions: 'There is, in my judgment, insufficient evidence to demonstrate that he has destroyed anything at all or that he will so dispose of incriminating documents, such as the passbooks and so on, as would enable the relief to be granted.'[34] The court was of the opinion that the wife's interests could be effectively protected without either form of 'draconian and expensive' order, in spite of the great deal of sympathy which it felt for her. So, sometimes being dishonest, devious and having hidden assets is not sufficient grounds on which to order an injunction. It is strongly arguable that the standards being applied in matrimonial cases are far more stringent than those in commercial cases, with the result that spouses are permitted to indulge in fraudulent behaviour and to defy the court's power even to the extent that criminal sanctions are imposed. But, courts still fail to use some of equity's most effective weapons. Yet, I am not aware of any case where a search order has been refused as against a bank or company simply because that type of commerce is becoming so fraudulent that the present facts would not be exceptional. Would the result in *Araghchinchi* have been the same if the defendant had been a company?

Freezing orders: 'cypher wives' and 'infectious dishonesty'

These injunctions, formerly known as Mareva orders, are awarded to ensure the preservation of assets for trial and, although originally created by case law, are now enshrined within the jurisdiction of s 37 of the Supreme Court Act 1981. Whilst there are many good reasons in favour of the existence of freezing orders (including, paradoxically, the rights of third parties such as beneficiaries behind a trust), it is clear that they will often affect persons other than the immediate defendant. Any freezing order will rely to some extent upon the manner in which third parties behave, particularly in those situations where a large proportion of the defendant's assets are in the custody of a third party. Without any method of control over such third parties, the jurisdiction would, in many cases, be meaningless, but it is strongly arguable that the balance of rights is not always equally weighted. Judges always pay lip service to the protection of the rights of third parties in this field. A typical statement comes from the authoritative case of *Project Development Co Ltd SA v KMK Securities Ltd*,[35] *per* Parker J: 'It is an essential aspect of the jurisdiction to grant Mareva types of injunction that the position of innocent third parties should be fully protected.'

Courts have repeatedly stated their concern for the rights of third parties in this field. However, is there a difference between statements and practice?

---

34 (1997) unreported, 26 February, CA, p 8 of transcript.

35 [1982] 1 WLR 1470.

The concern appears to be variable in extent and effect. In particular, courts have failed to appreciate fully that there is more than one kind of third party;[36] that banks, small businesses and members of the defendant's family require separate treatment; that a distinction should be drawn between innocent custodians of another's property and persons suspected of complicity in the wrongdoing in question; and that very different considerations should apply when freezing the assets of a private individual than should apply when freezing company assets. Thus, wives have been treated as nothing more than a cypher for their husbands, an extra source of assets, on the basis that it has not been established conclusively that assets within their possession do not belong to their husbands, the defendants. Safeguards in practice guidelines include that the order must contain provisions for protection of third parties, but it is arguable that banks receive far more respect and protection than do wives of potential defendants.

In theory, assets can only be frozen if they are in the legal or equitable ownership of the potential defendant, so that assets which appear on their face to belong to a third party should not be included within any injunction unless the court 'has good reason to suppose that they really belong to the defendant'.[37] The mere fact that the third party in question is the defendant's wife has been a good enough reason to presume that the assets are either her husband's, or she is likely to carry out her husband's instructions as to disposition of the property and so is, arguably, a *de facto* trustee.[38] If a wife asserts that assets covered by an injunction are actually hers, the court does not have to accept this assertion and may leave the injunction in place, with the question of ownership to be determined at the full trial (if that ever occurs).[39] It seems that business interests are held in higher regard by courts than the financial rights and independence of wives, since the leading and most cited cases show the courts' reluctance to grant freezing orders where to do so would affect a third party business – for example, by preventing the defendant from fulfilling a contract with that third party company, even where the applicant offers an indemnity.

On the freezing of jointly owned or wife's assets, a case which has been accepted without question or feminist analysis is *Mercantile Group v Aiyela*,[40] where a wife's bank account was frozen in a separate injunction from that against her husband although all proceedings against her had been dropped, and in spite of her protestations that the money was her own. Although there were no more than 'unsubstantiated allegations' against her, the orders were upheld by the Court of Appeal, with Bingham MR stating that:

---

36 See Birks, 1999, pp 539–63 for a reasoned categorisation of the existing case law.

37 *SCF v Masri* [1985] 1 WLR 876.

38 See, eg, *Winter v Marac Australia Ltd* (1986) 6 NSWR 11.

39 *SCF v Masri* [1985] 1 WLR 876.

40 [1993] 3 WLR 1117.

Both principle and authority persuade me that the judges who made these orders did have jurisdiction to make them. I am very pleased to reach that conclusion, for if the jurisdiction did not exist, the armoury of powers available to the court to ensure the effective enforcement of its orders would in my view be seriously deficient. That is in itself a ground for inferring the likely existence of such powers, since it would be surprising if the court lacked power to control wilful evasion of its orders by a judgment debtor acting through even innocent parties. The jurisdiction is of course one to be exercised with caution, restraint and appropriate respect for the legitimate interests of third parties.[41]

Further, in the earlier and also unchallenged case of *SCF Finance Co v Masri*,[42] it was held that, if the defendant has a joint bank account with his wife, the court has discretion to order the freezing of the account in spite of the wife's claim. As in *Mercantile v Aiyela*, the applicant had no arguable cause of action against the wife, who was a true third party; this case also conflicts with much judicial authority that the desire to prevent and punish fraud should not be used to infringe third party rights. The court reasoned that the mere fact that a third party (here a wife) claims that assets over which an injunction is sought belong to that third party is not sufficient to prevent the award of the remedy. Thus, a court in this position may reject the third party's claim and either order that this issue should go to a separate trial before the commencement of the action to be brought by the applicant, or (more commonly) the injunction can be awarded immediately and the issue of true ownership can be left to be decided at the main trial. There are at least two great problems with this reasoning. First, to reject the third party's assertion at this stage can cause irremediable injustice to him and is an obvious interference with his right to property. Secondly, in this case, as in many others, the court presumes that the final trial will sort out any temporary injustices caused to either party, but in fact many such cases never reach a full trial. Many applicants for 'temporary' injunctions, including freezing orders, have absolutely no intention of ever proceeding to a full trial, although a promise to do so is a requirement for gaining the injunction. The injunction will serve their interests well enough on its own and so disadvantage the defendant that there is no need to proceed to a full trial. The requirement imposed by the Practice Direction that an applicant must undertake to pay reasonable costs incurred by third parties[43] and notify them of their right to apply for discharge of the injunction, backed up by an undertaking in damages, is therefore less significant and protective than it might otherwise appear. According to Lloyd LJ in *Masri*, the defendant's use of one cheque signed by a wife was sufficient evidence upon which to presume that he had access to her bank accounts and, therefore, that the money within those accounts belonged to the defendant husband:

---

41 [1993] 3 WLR 1117, p 1124.

42 [1985] 1 WLR 876.

43 See *Project Development Co Ltd SA v KMK Securities Ltd* [1982] 1 WLR 1470.

I can see no reason whatever why the court should be obliged to discharge the injunction on the mere say-so of the third party. If the court were so obliged, then the Mareva jurisdiction would be in danger of being nullified at the whim of the unscrupulous. If a court were not permitted to inquire into a third party's claim, but were bound to accept it at its face value, how could the court be satisfied that any transfer of assets to the third party had occurred before rather than after the injunction?[44]

Lloyd LJ, in *Masri*, based his argument upon cases where both the defendant and the third party were companies, not individuals, and so did not argue that different considerations should apply in those two very different situations. To deny a company access to \$400,000 of its funds may, undeniably, cause problems, but to freeze that sum of the wife's assets is a far greater interference. Although, of course, she would be allowed access to sufficient funds to pay bills and survive, she was not a defendant in either a civil or criminal case yet was, arguably, treated as if she were one. An interesting comparison may be drawn against cases where the third party was a company whose 'legitimate business interests' might be affected: in fact, the courts appear to be much kinder to that class of third party.

In *Oceanica Castelana Armadora SA v Mineralimportexport (Barclays Bank International Ltd Intervening) (The Theotokos)*,[45] it was held that freezing orders had never been intended to interfere with the contractual relationship between a third party and the defendant, and that a bank which held the defendant's frozen funds must not end up in a worse position than other creditors of the defendant. Earlier that same year, in *Galaxia Maritime SA v Mineralimportexport (The Eleftherios)*,[46] it was held that, if the effect of granting an injunction would be to interfere substantially with an innocent third party's freedom of action generally or freedom to trade (perhaps by interfering with his performance of a contract existing between him and the defendant relating to the assets in question), the third party's right to freedom of action and freedom to trade should prevail over the applicant's wish to secure the defendant's assets for himself. Even if the applicant offered to indemnify the third party for any contractual losses, including loss of business and profits, the interference with the third party's rights would be unacceptable; according to Eveleigh J:

> I regard it as absolutely intolerable that the fact that one person has a claim for a debt against another, that third parties should be inconvenienced in this way, not only to affect their freedom of trading but their freedom of action generally speaking ... where the effect of service must lead to interference with the performance of a contract between the third party and the defendant which relates specifically to the assets in question, the right of the third party in

---

44 [1985] 1 WLR 876, p 881.

45 [1983] 2 All ER 65.

46 [1983] 1 All ER 796.

relation to his contract must clearly prevail over the plaintiff's desire to secure the defendant's assets for himself against the day of judgment.[47]

Thus, contractual rights are sacred, yet personal rights are not. In *Polly Peck International plc v Nadir and Others (No 2)*,[48] Lord Donaldson MR stated that the same principles apply in considering whether to freeze assets held by a third party, regardless of the status and identity of that third party, although the principles may have very different results depending upon those factors. Surely the difference in results and the hardship which may be caused requires the application of different rules for banks, companies and private individuals?

To move to a slightly different focus, since the Matrimonial Causes Act 1973, modified statutory freezing orders may be, and often are, used in matrimonial cases to preserve money, chattels, the family home or other property pending a divorce. The statutory version of the injunction may be granted without evidence that otherwise the defendant would dispose of or destroy the property in question.[49] But, ordinary freezing orders may also be used, especially where it is feared that the defendant may move assets out of the jurisdiction; yet the rules have been applied differently in matrimonial cases. In *Ghoth v Ghoth*,[50] the court stated that in no circumstances can a freezing order be granted over all of a party's assets in a matrimonial case, even though every freezing order makes allowance for living expenses. This is because it is unlikely in any divorce that either party would be awarded the whole of the other party's assets, and so, in matrimonial proceedings, any freezing order should operate only over the amount which is the maximum which could realistically be awarded. This is a strange point for the court to make, since there is no apparent reason to distinguish between matrimonial and all other cases here; all freezing orders should be restricted to the maximum realistically achievable by the applicant if successful at a future trial. So, here is another situation where the applicant is trying to achieve the same result as in the above examples, but two more sets of rules are applied by the courts, depending on whether the action is brought under the general freezing order jurisdiction or under family law. If the property which the applicant is seeking to preserve pending divorce proceedings should happen to make its way into the hands of a third party, which principles would the court choose to apply? The situation is unnecessarily complicated, yet still holds the potential for great injustice to third parties and original defendants.

---

47 [1983] 1 All ER 796, p 802.
48 [1992] 4 All ER 769.
49 *Shipman v Shipman* [1991] 1 FLR 250.
50 [1992] 2 All ER 920.

Both freezing and search orders often have a decisive effect upon the case in question and threaten great potential harm to the defendant's rights because they are granted secretly and so may be affected by skewed 'evidence' presented by the applicant. Alternatively, the court may fail to spot a perfect defence which could be raised by the defendant. The existing safeguards need to be restructured to take account of the wide range of parties who may be in possession of the assets or evidence which the applicant seeks to preserve. We appear to have several different and conflicting standards in operation, with respect to the granting of freezing and seizing orders. Women need special safeguards when their homes are searched, but are unlikely to receive effective help when an ex-husband evades payment of the settlement. Wives' personal property is not presumed to be their own unless they so prove and is frozen in circumstances where a third party company would be treated more leniently and arguably with greater respect. It is as if a husband's dishonesty infects his wife automatically, unless she can establish righteous ownership of her own property. If there is evidence that a wife has acted dishonestly and is helping her husband to avoid liability for his wrongdoing, then she should face full liability in her own right. Thus, it is time for some consistency, and reconsideration from first principles, of the rules upon which these specific injunctions depend.

SPECIFIC PERFORMANCE: 'WOMEN WHO ACT LIKE MEN' AND 'STUBBORN WOMEN'

Specific performance of a contract can be an extremely powerful remedy, but has become increasingly difficult to achieve. Thus, some of the discussion in this section will be historical. Yet, public policy has played as much of a part in the granting and denial of specific performance as have the merits of the applicant's case, and some rather old cases which remain authoritative show marked assumptions about women, marriage and the family. Any law student reading a casebook will come across most of the women who appear below. The student may form views about the availability of equitable remedies which are, at least in part, determined by the language used by the judges, the portrayal of the male and female characters in each story and the differing results of those cases. Therefore, the cases merit closer attention than they usually receive.

The first category of cases for comment relates to specific performance of contracts for the sale of land. *Wroth v Tyler*[51] is an example of the interplay between public policy and third party rights in the decision whether or not to grant the equitable remedy of specific performance. Mrs Tyler was extremely

---

51   [1974] Ch 30.

unenthusiastic about a proposed family move to Norfolk and so registered a notice of her rights of occupation of the family home in order to block its sale, a short time before her husband was expecting the sale to be completed. The husband had to withdraw from the purchase of the new house and tried to persuade his wife to cancel her notice, but she refused. The would-be purchasers of the family home then sued for specific performance of the sale contract, but lost for public policy reasons with firm roots in the importance of marriage. The remedy was denied since it would have 'forced' a husband to sue his wife (a third party, since she did not have title to the property) when he did not wish to do so and they were, in fact, still cohabiting. Further, even if the wife's rights to remain in the matrimonial home had been upheld, the legal action would involve a risk of breaking up the family. An argument that specific performance could be ordered subject to the wife's right of occupancy was also rejected on the ground that it would then be possible to evict the defendant and thus separate him from his wife and daughter. According to Megarry J, there were some very old cases where husbands had been compelled by court order to obtain their wives' consent to sale, but, here, the defendant had sufficiently attempted to do so. Although his language is carefully moderated, the image of the wife which emerges is that of a stubborn and duplicitous woman who would do anything to avoid moving home:

> The ultimate truth as between the defendant and his wife I do not know. As the evidence stands, his wife did nothing whatever to warn the plaintiffs that she was not willing to leave the bungalow, but conducted herself so as to lead them to believe that she concurred in the sale. So far as the defendant was concerned, his wife was very cool about the move, and it may well be that the move was one which a strong-willed husband was in effect imposing on a reluctant yet secretive wife. Nevertheless, the consequences of disputes between husband and wife, whether open or concealed, ought not to be visited on innocent purchasers.[52]

Yet, in this case, that is precisely what happened; marriage, even to a stubborn and secretive wife, is more important in some courts' eyes.[53]

In *Patel v Ali*,[54] the court again refused to grant specific performance of the contract, but showed far greater sympathy for the position of this wife, who was neither stubborn nor secretive. In fact, her circumstances were extreme: she had bone cancer (which resulted in amputation of her leg), three young children and a bankrupt and less than helpful husband. Her illness meant that she had to rely heavily upon family and friends who lived nearby. In spite of these factors and a very obvious arguable hardship defence, the trial court

---

52 [1974] Ch 30, p 63.

53 The importance of marriage, and the reluctance of equity to grant any remedy which might interfere with that institution, can also be seen in the fact that the marriage settlement is one of the few types of incompletely constituted trust which are enforceable by specific performance of the promises in a covenant to create a trust.

54 [1984] Ch 283.

made an order for specific performance of a long standing contract for sale of the family home to the applicants. On appeal, the court held that, although an adult who contracts to buy or sell land takes upon himself the risk of hardship to himself or his family if unexpected events occur, it is within a court's discretion to refuse specific performance of such a contract on the ground of hardship suffered by the defendant subsequent to the date of the contract. This is the case even if the hardship was not caused by the applicant and did not relate to the subject matter of the contract. It would be extreme injustice to the defendant to order specific performance of the contract, since that would have the effect of asking her to do what she had never bargained for, that is, to complete the sale after more than four years and after all the unforeseeable changes that had taken place during that period. Thus, damages would be an adequate remedy. Whilst there was little chance of specific performance splitting the family or wrecking this marriage, it was clearly within the court's mind that the woman and her children would be caused even greater suffering and hardship if the remedy were granted, and so both public policy and the rights of third parties (the children) are at play in the decision.

The second focus of this section is upon the effect of specific performance and equivalent injunctions in employment law. Courts are extremely reluctant to force a person to carry out a contract of employment, since to do so would be uncomfortably close to slavery,[55] but in a number of decisions in the field of entertainment the remedies granted have had an equivalent effect. Whilst courts will not use specific performance to compel performance of employment obligations by an employee, they will severely restrict contract workers' freedom to breach their contracts by means of positive and negative injunctions. The leading cases appear to conflict as to the desirability and effect of such injunctions, and the language of three in particular may be contrasted to demonstrate a further tentative stereotype, women who act like men.

Warner Brothers Pictures Inc v Nelson[56] represents the high point of this phenomenon. The defendant was the actress Bette Davis, who had a typically restrictive contract with Warner Brothers which forbade her to work for any other film studio or to work for any other person without the written consent of her producer. She left the US and breached the covenant by working for another studio. The court held that, although specific performance would not be available for the applicant, and the defendant could not be prevented from working to the extent that she had a choice of working for the applicant or remaining idle, an injunction could be issued to prevent the defendant from working for another employer. Branson J could find 'no discoverable reason, except that she wanted more money' behind the defendant's breach of

---

55 *De Francesco v Barnum* (1890) 45 Ch D 430.
56 [1936] 1 KB 209.

contractual term. She could be restrained from further breaching her contract by making films for anybody else as long as she was able to perform other kinds of work; so she could work in an office or as a waitress for anyone else, provided that she did not act. This was at least a partial success for the defendant, since it did not uphold the full rigour of the original blanket ban on outside work in her contract. But the judge's reasoning is not convincing:

> The defendant is stated to be a person of intelligence, capacity and means, and no evidence was adduced to show that, if enjoined from doing the specified acts otherwise than for the plaintiffs, she will not be able to employ herself both usefully and remuneratively in other spheres of activity, though not as remuneratively as in her special line. She will not be driven, although she may be tempted, to perform the contract, and the fact that she may be so tempted is no objection to the grant of an injunction.[57]

To expect a stage and film actress to be able to earn similar wages in any other form of employment, for which she might be qualified and able to undertake, seems at least naive. It is hard to understand why the court did not consider that damages would be an adequate remedy and hence find themselves to be precluded from granting the injunction. From the judgment, it appears that the defendant's 'wilfulness' and obvious capability worked against her in the eyes of the court, who could see no reason why she would breach her contract as she did. Being independent in nature and having business sense did not work in her favour. She stepped out of her expected role, and so lost the case. The decision is difficult to reconcile with a case which claimed to follow its authority, *Page One Records v Britton*,[58] where it was held that the effect of a *Warner*-style injunction would be to compel the band to continue to employ their manager, and thus would amount to enforcing the performance by the manager of his contract. Thus, the injunction was refused. It is submitted that this is a fairer and more realistic result for both parties, which recognises that, once the goodwill has disappeared from either side of an employment contract, damages would be a better remedy for all concerned than half-hearted and compulsory performance of its obligations.

In *Warren v Mendy*,[59] Nourse LJ again managed the legal trickery of simultaneously accepting that *Warner v Nelson* was an authority and finding a way to avoid its harsh result. He stated that, when considering whether granting an injunction would amount to compulsion, a court should take a realistic approach to the likely effect of an injunction on the psychological, material or physical need of the servant or performer to maintain his skill or talent; hence, presumably, the potential availability of work in a completely different field of employment would not be argued. Finding *Warner v Nelson*

---

57   [1936] 1 KB 209, p 219.

58   [1967] 3 All ER 822.

59   [1989] 3 All ER 103.

to be inconsistent with *Page One Records v Britton*, he stated on the basis of Branson J's reasoning in the former case that:

> On a first consideration, that judge's view that Miss Bette Davis might employ herself both usefully and remuneratively in other spheres of activity for a period of up to three years appears to have been extraordinarily unrealistic. It could hardly have been thought to be a real possibility that an actress of her then youth and soaring talent would be able to forgo screen and stage for such a period ... But then it is to be observed that Miss Davis did not give evidence, a feature of the case which made a great impression on the judge. In the absence of evidence from her, the judge no doubt thought that it was not for the court to assume that she could not or would not employ herself both usefully and remuneratively in other spheres of activity. From what can be gathered from the report it cannot be said with confidence that the injunction was wrongly granted.[60]

Thus, it appears that the significance of the *Warner* case should be historical, yet it finds its way into a remarkable number of legal arguments in front of judges where entertainment-related contracts are at issue. It is interesting that in no other authoritative case has the Court of Appeal upheld such a long term prohibition on outside employment (three years), nor do the other leading cases focus quite so much on characteristics of the defendant, rather than of the contract which they have breached, or the nature of the relationship between the two contracting parties. Even if *Warner* is never to be followed again, and compulsion in employment law is dead and buried as an issue, the statements and assumptions in that case are being made afresh each year in casebooks on contract law, employment law, and equity and trusts.

CONCLUSION: HOW TO SUCCEED IN EQUITABLE REMEDIES

The glib answer would be: try not to be a woman, since this automatically adds complications to a court's deliberations; avoid any situation where commercial interests may be at risk; stay away from marriage, but be vulnerable when possible and try not to step outside accepted sex roles.

This chapter has had a very broad sweep, and so concluding remarks risk a level of generalisation and cherry picking. Equitable remedies potentially affect almost every case commenced in this jurisdiction, and are an invaluable tool for providing effective and fast redress where common law would deny any remedy. Women's, and indeed all individuals', rights have been advanced by the inventive adaptation of old remedies to new situations in a manner which reacts to perceived needs far more quickly than does statutory law. But

---

60 [1967] 3 All ER 822, p 865.

there are a discomfortingly high number of situations in which the sex of the applicant or defendant appears to be of great relevance in courts' exercising of their discretion whether or not to grant a specific remedy. Equity does appear to have a 'special tenderness' for women which has resulted in some notable successes and powerful weapons against violence and abuse, yet this very tenderness is an aspect of a far broader and largely hidden tendency to view women as 'other' and in need of differential treatment. Surprise is still seen in judgments where women are independent and strong, but no remarks would be made if men carried out similar activities. Vulnerable men have no specific and declaratory protection against intrusions of their home to execute injunctions. Search orders are intrusive, whomsoever they are served against, but are difficult to obtain in precisely the cases where they could allow a court to distribute a family's assets with fairness to all parties. Where freezing orders are concerned, wives are treated with great suspicion, their assets are viewed as likely to be their husbands' in all but name, and the wives themselves are subject to exactly the same treatment as if they had been companies wholly owned by the defendant husbands. Part of this differential treatment is due to a general favouritism for business interests over the rights of individuals. The leading decisions and body of rules on granting equitable remedies are gendered, and concepts such as public policy, vulnerability, undue influence and third party rights are methods by which entrenched assumptions are hidden and reinforced. Thus, equity manages to appear to favour women unjustly, yet simultaneously tries to fit them into little boxes because of their sex and attaches labels which often work against their interests. Both for the people directly affected by this pigeonholing and for students of law, these constructions are unhelpful and stultifying. Of course, equitable remedies should be granted in a manner which protects the vulnerable, but it is difficult to see how judges and students can be wary of hidden bias and (for want of a better word) stereotyping when the accepted rules contain overt sex differentials and hidden assumptions.

CHAPTER 11

EQUITABLE PRINCIPLES OF CONFIDENTIALITY AND WHISTLEBLOWING

Catherine Hobby

So secretly, like wrongs hushed-up they went.

They were not ours:

We never heard to which front these were sent.

(The Send-Off, Wilfred Owen, 1918.)

On 10 July 2000, an employment tribunal awarded Antonio Fernandes £293,441 in compensation after he was sacked for gross misconduct for warning his company that its chief executive was claiming unauthorised expenses.[1] This award has been described as 'a wake-up call to every employer in the UK' who does not operate an effective whistleblowing policy.[2] An organisation which ignores the legitimate concerns of its workers faces the possibility of paying substantial damages and courting bad publicity under the Public Interest Disclosure Act (PIDA) 1998. The PIDA 1998 was enacted to provide protection for whistleblowers against dismissal and victimisation if they 'responsibly' raise concerns in respect of crimes, illegality, miscarriages of justice, health, safety and environmental dangers and the 'covering up' of these matters.[3]

A possible strength of the PIDA 1998 is that it provides a checklist against which an employment tribunal is required to assess an individual complaint by a whistleblower. The detailed criteria set out in the provisions reduce discretion and make it more difficult for assumptions based on gender to cloud the issue. It might be argued that women fare better when subject to strict requirements of statute than faced with the discretion of equity.[4] The establishment of a statutory test as to the credibility of a whistleblower may prevent gender bias and the negative stereotyping of female whistleblowers.

---

1   See Booth, 2000; Shaw and Demetriou, 2000; and Mason, 2000.

2   Guy Dehn, director of the charity Public Concern at Work, which supports whistleblowers, quoted in *ibid,* Booth. It should be noted that, in the same report, it was stated that the company, Netcom Consultants (UK), intended to appeal.

3   Department of Trade and Industry, *Fairness at Work,* Cm 3968, 1998, London: HMSO, para 3.3.

4   Mack, 1994.

In the past, in Britain, whistleblowing has been 'something to be condemned, not encouraged as a civic duty'.[5] However, whistleblowing and the plight of whistleblowers has received considerable attention in the last decade and whistleblowing, as an activity, has been transformed from a 'vice' to a 'virtue' worthy of protection.[6] The term whistleblower has been turned from a term of abuse to a word associated with public duty and citizenship. This change in approach can be seen in the case of *Camelot plc v Centaur Communications Ltd*,[7] decided before the enactment of PIDA 1998,[8] where the Court of Appeal ordered disclosure revealing the source of leaked documents. The court thought that there was no question of the employee acting in the public interest in that case and commented that '[t]his is not a case of disclosing iniquity, it is not a whistleblowing case'.[9]

Disasters and scandals often reveal that workers are the first to identify a potential problem within an organisation. Some workers alert their employers to difficulties and are ignored and others remain quiet through fear or disinterest.[10] Britain's industrial relations maintain a pervasive culture of secrecy[11] creating a climate where employees fear being labelled as 'disloyal' or a 'troublemaker'. The Richie Inquiry into allegations concerning consultant Rodney Ledward in June 2000 blamed senior managers for failing to investigate concerns raised by their staff and patients, and reported 'a climate of fear and retribution' which prevented colleagues from reporting their concerns about the surgical skills of a consultant. It also called for an 'open culture' that encourages whistleblowing and where employees are not afraid of 'telling tales'.[12] It is well understood that 'although the employee is well placed to sound the alarm, he or she has most to lose by raising the matter'.[13]

---

5   Ponting, 1989, p 18.

6   Vernon, 1998, p 223–24.

7   [1998] IRLR 80.

8   Judgment was given on 23 October 1997.

9   [1998] IRLR 80, *per* Schiemann LJ, p 84. See Bowers, Mitchell and Lewis, 1999, pp 103–04.

10 *Public Inquiry into the Piper Alpha Disaster*, Cm 1310, 1990, London: HMSO; *Investigation into the Clapham Junction Railway Accident*, Cm 820, 1989; *Inquiry into the supervision of the Bank of Credit and Commerce International*, Cm 198c, 1992; Court Inquiry, Department of Transport, 1987 Ct No 8074, on the Zeebrugge ferry disaster in which the *Herald of Free Enterprise* ferry sank; and the *Report of the Inquiry into the Export of Defence Equipment and Dual-Use goods to Iraq and Related Prosecutions*, 1995–96, chaired by Sir Richard Scott VC, published as HC (1995–96) 115. See Wells, 1994, Chapter 3, Wells, 1995, Chapters 2 and 3 and *ibid*, Bowers, Mitchell and Lewis, Chapter 1.

11 (1997) 563 Industrial Relations Law Bulletin, p 2.

12 The Richie Inquiry investigated allegations against Mr Ledward, a consultant gynaecologist, for inept surgery in hundreds of operations during his 16 years at William Harvey hospital in Ashworth, Kent. See (2000) *The Guardian*, 2 June.

13 Public Concern at Work's evidence to the Nolan Committee on Standards in Public Life. See *First Report of the Committee on Standards in Public Life*, 1995, para 115.

Growing awareness of the value of worker knowledge led to a campaign for the provision of practical protection for whistleblowers. The PIDA 1998 was introduced to provide employment security to those employees who disclose wrongdoing by their employers, but within limited statutory requirements. The Act seeks to facilitate an open culture in the workplace which would enable employees to feel it is 'safe and accepted' to raise concerns about malpractice.[14] It is designed to assist in the early discovery of wrongdoing within an organisation,[15] and so affords statutory recognition to the value of whistleblowing. It is widely recognised that: 'all organisations face the risk of things going wrong or of unknowingly harbouring malpractice'.[16] In this context, Borrie's definition best defines the form of whistleblowing that the proponents of the PIDA 1998 wished to encourage: 'By whistleblowing, I mean the disclosure by an employee (or professional) of confidential information which relates to some danger, fraud or other illegal or unethical conduct connected with the workplace, be it of the employer or of his fellow colleagues.'[17]

This chapter will assess the treatment of whistleblowers to determine whether gender is a factor by examining the treatment of female whistleblowers before the Act and the one case decided after it came into force. The provisions of the PIDA 1998 draw on the 'signposts from the common law'[18] reflecting the equitable principles of the law of confidence. The common law defence of 'public interest' to actions restraining disclosure will be explored, as will the extent to which its principles are represented in the Act. The PIDA 1998 will be evaluated and its impact in encouraging whistleblowing and transforming the culture of work assessed.

LAW OF CONFIDENTIALITY

All employees are under a general duty of confidence, and this duty prevents workers from making unauthorised disclosures of information.[19] The obligation may be expressly set out in the contract of employment through covenants restraining the use of confidential information during employment and after an employee has left an organisation. In the absence of a restrictive covenant in a contract, an employer may rely on the common law. The courts

---

14 Richard Shepherd MP in the Standing Committee, 11 March 1998.

15 See Public Concern at Work, *Current Law Statutes: Public Interest Disclosure Act 1998 (1999)*, 1999, London: Sweet & Maxwell, p 2. See Bowers, Mitchell and Lewis, 1999, chapter 1, for a discussion of the background to the Public Interest Disclosure Act 1998.

16 *Committee on Standards in Public Life, Second Report*, 1996, Cm 3270–1, para 41.

17 Borrie, G, quoted in (1997) 563 Industrial Relations Law Bulletin 2.

18 Public Interest at Work, *Public Concern at Work (Current Law Statutes)*, 1999, London: Sweet & Maxwell, p 3.

19 See Toulson and Phipps, 1996, Chapter 16; and Napier, 1990.

will imply into the contract a duty of confidentiality requiring an employee not to disclose confidential information to third parties, even after they have left their employment. This duty is part of the wider implied duty of good faith and fidelity owed by the employee to the employer.[20] Breach of the duty of confidence can amount to a gross breach of contract justifying summary dismissal. An employee will, therefore, be bound by an obligation of confidentiality through an express or implied term in the contract of employment. A restraint may also operate independently of a contract through the equitable principle of confidence[21] providing a person with an equitable remedy against another who seeks to abuse confidential information.[22] Indeed, the contractual duties of confidence can be seen as a reflection of the equitable principle.[23] In discussing the confidential relationship between employers and employees, Kekewich J remarked, in *Merryweather v Moore*,[24] that it is:

> ... sometimes difficult to know whether the court has proceeded on the implied contract or the confidence ... Perhaps the real solution is that the confidence postulates an implied contract: that where the court is satisfied of the existence of the confidential relation, then it at once infers or implies the contract arising from that confidential relation.[25]

Not all information received by an employee is confidential.[26] In determining whether information is confidential, certain criteria have been established.[27] Information must have the 'necessary quality of confidence'[28] and not be 'common knowledge'.[29] Information may still be confidential if it has been disclosed in the media,[30] or by another third party,[31] or has been gathered from material in the public domain.[32] Further, the communication or imparting of the information must have been done in a manner to import an

---

20 *Robb v Green* [1895] 2 QB 315; *Roger Bullivant v Ellis* [1987] ICR 464.

21 *Saltman Engineering Co Ltd v Campbell Engineering Co Ltd* [1948] 65 RPC 203. See Lord Keith in *AG v Guardian Newspapers (No 2)* [1988] 3 WLR 776, p 781.

22 See Lord Griffiths in *AG v Guardian Newspapers (No 2)* [1988] 3 WLR 776, p 793.

23 See Kekewich J in *Merryweather v Moore* [1893] 2 Ch 518, p 522.

24 [1893] 2 Ch 518.

25 *Ibid*, p 522. See Cripps, 1986, p 18.

26 See *Faccenda Chicken Ltd v Fowler* [1986] IRLR 69.

27 (1997) 563 Industrial Relations Law Bulletin, pp 4–5. See, also, Toulson and Phipps, 1996, Chapter 3.

28 Lord Greene MR in *Saltman Engineering Co Ltd v Campbell Engineering Co Ltd* [1963] 3 All ER 413, p 415.

29 Lord Buckmaster in *O Mustad & Son v S Allcock & Co Ltd and Dosen* [1963] 3 All ER 416, p 418. See *Bunn v Broadcasting Corp* [1998] 3 All ER 552.

30 *AG v Guardian Newspapers (No 2)* [1988] 3 WLR 776; *Schering Chemicals Ltd v Falkman Ltd* [1981] 2 All ER 321.

31 See *Speed Seal Products v Paddington* [1986] 1 All ER 91.

32 *Saltman Engineering Co Ltd v Campbell Engineering Co Ltd* [1963] 3 All ER 413; *Coco v AN Clark (Engineers) Ltd* [1969] RPC 41.

obligation of confidence,[33] and an unauthorised use of the information must have taken place.[34]

It is well established that the publication of confidential information can be restrained by injunction.[35] The jurisdiction is based on the duty of good faith or conscience; no person is permitted to disclose to the world information received in confidence. This exclusive equitable jurisdiction entitles a person to an injunction without establishing any proprietary right[36] and 'without the necessity of there being any contractual relationship'.[37] An injunction can restrain not only publication by the whistleblower, but by any third party to whom the information was disclosed.[38] The duty of confidence can arise in a range of relationships including husband and wife,[39] friends,[40] doctor and patient,[41] police and suspect,[42] but is of particular interest in the area of employment. In cases involving whistleblowers, employers have relied on the equitable principles of confidentiality as they sought to prevent disclosure of confidential information or the return of documents, mainly against an ex-employee, by means of an injunction.

There is a public as well as a private interest in the maintenance of confidence.[43] However, the public interest in the maintenance of confidence may be overridden whenever there is a countervailing public interest in disclosure, as there is 'no confidence to the disclosure of iniquity'.[44] A cover of confidentiality concerning his employer's business is thrown over employees by reason of their employment, but the corner of the cover can be lifted in limited circumstances to reveal iniquity.[45] Employees may be under an obligation of confidentiality not to disclose documents or information that they have received in confidence, but that is subject to an exception where disclosure can be excused or justified because it is in the public interest. In

---

33 See *Saltman Engineering Co Ltd v Campbell Engineering Co Ltd* [1963] 3 All ER 413; *Coco v AN Clark (Engineers) Ltd* [1969] RPC 41.

34 *Thomas Marshall (Exports) Ltd v Guinle* [1978] IRLR 174.

35 *Argyll v Argyll* [1965] 1 All ER 611; *AG v Guardian Newspapers* [1987] 3 All ER 316.

36 See Kekewich J in *Merryweather v Moore* [1893] 2 Ch 518, p 523.

37 *Saltman Engineering Co Ltd v Campbell Engineering Co Ltd* [1963] 3 All ER 413, p 414.

38 *Schering Chemicals Ltd v Falkman Ltd* [1981] 2 All ER 321.

39 *Argyll v Argyll* [1965] 1 All ER 611.

40 *Stephens v Avery* [1988] 2 All ER 477.

41 See *W v Egdell* [1989] 1 All ER 1089; and *X v Y* [1988] 2 All ER 648.

42 See *Hellewell v Chief Constable of Derbyshire* [1995] 1 WLR 804; *Bunn v British Broadcasting Corp* [1998] 3 All ER 552; and *Woolgar v Chief Constable of Sussex Police* [2000] 1 WLR 25.

43 *British Steel Corp v Granada Ltd* [1981] 1 All ER 417, *AG v Guardian Newspapers (No 2)* [1988] 3 WLR 776. See Browne, 2000, which reports that the confidentiality of patient records is being disregarded. See, also, *X v Y* [1988] 2 All ER 648.

44 *Gartside v Outram* [1856] 26 LJ 113, *per* Wood VC, pp 114 and 116.

45 See Salmon LJ in *Initial Services v Putterill* [1967] 3 All ER 145, p 152.

Initial Services v Putterill, Lord Denning decided that the 'iniquity' exception[46] extends to any misconduct that should be disclosed in the public interest. He argued that the exception should include 'crimes, frauds and misdeeds, both those actually committed as well as those in contemplation, provided always – and this is essential – that the disclosure is justified in the public interest'.[47]

Whether the duty of confidentiality will be upheld depends on all the circumstances of the case, and therein lies considerable flexibility. Issues such as the nature of the information, motive and the recipient are all considerations, but the essence of the defence is whether it is in the public interest for the employee to reveal the confidential material. In *Fraser v Evans,* Lord Denning stated:

> I do not look on the word 'iniquity' as expressing a principle. It is merely an instance of just cause or excuse for breaking confidence. There are some things which may be disclosed in the public interest, in which event no confidence can be prayed in aid to keep them secret.[48]

The courts will refuse to uphold an employer's right to confidence if it considers wrongdoing will be concealed,[49] but as it is an equitable remedy, the courts afford themselves considerable discretion in deciding what confidential information it is in the public interest to disclose. The Court of Appeal in *Lion Laboratories v Evans* found concerns regarding the accuracy of a breathalyser machine raised such serious issues that confidential documents should be made public and an injunction restraining publication was discharged.[50] Stephenson LJ commented that '[t]here is confidential information which the public may have a right to receive and even a duty to publish, even if the information has been unlawfully obtained in flagrant breach of confidence and irrespective of the motive of the informer'.[51] However, by way of contrast, in *British Steel Corp v Granada Ltd,*[52] a case in which British Steel sought disclosure of Granada's source of its confidential documents, the majority of the House of Lords, in language vociferously condemning the whistleblower, held mismanagement by British Steel at vast expense to the taxpayer did not reveal wrongdoing that ought to be disclosed in the public interest

It has been claimed that the court essentially conducts a balancing exercise, setting the private interest in maintaining the confidentiality of an employer (involving issues of loyalty and trust) against the public interest in disclosure

---

46 See Toulson and Phipps, 1996, Chapter 6, for a discussion of the defence of iniquity.

47 [1967] 3 All ER 145, p 148.

48 [1969] 1 All ER 8, p 11. He repeated this view in *Hubbard v Vosper* [1972] 1 All ER 1023, p 1029.

49 See Lord Griffiths in *AG v Guardian Newspapers (No 2)* [1988] 3 WLR 776, p 794.

50 [1984] 2 All ER 417.

51 *Ibid,* p 422.

52 [1981] 1 All ER 417.

of certain information.[53] However, the judicial question has also been described as the resolution of two conflicting public interests; the public interest in the preservation of an individual's or organisation's confidential information, and the interest of the public in being informed of real public concerns.[54] Sir Nicholas Browne-Wilkinson, in *AG v Guardian Newspapers*, has remarked that: 'the principles on which the law of confidence is based have never been clarified and remain, to my mind, obscure.'[55] This lack of clarity is highlighted within the employment cases, where the one firm principle is that employees are bound by an obligation not to disclose confidential information that they have acquired through their employment. Breach of this obligation justifies dismissal both at common law and under employment legislation. In the past, employment tribunals have been reluctant to utilise the public interest defence in cases of unfair dismissal[56] and the inconsistency of the defence may provide an explanation. In the few cases where the issue has arisen, tribunals have shown it was not susceptible to the defence. In *Thorley v Aircraft Research Association*,[57] the employee was dismissed for writing a letter to the editor of *The Guardian* expressing his concerns about the efficiency of the Tornado aircraft. The tribunal and EAT declined to commence an investigation into the validity of concerns expressed by Thorley. In *Byford v Film Finances*,[58] the employee passed information in a shareholders' dispute to the other side because she believed her employer was engaged in illegal conduct. The EAT expressed the view that it 'would take a great deal of persuading that there were not a number of courses which Mrs Byford could have embarked upon which did not involve the out-and-out deception of her employers'.[59]

DISLOYALTY

The courts have not always sought to shield whistleblowers from the wrath of employers who seek to punish their workers for what is seen as an act of betrayal. Indeed, in some cases, the judges have joined the employer in condemning a worker in emotive language. In the *Granada* case, the whistleblower, who disclosed confidential documents to Granada, is persistently described as a disloyal employee in contrast to the innocence of

---

53 Lord Griffiths in *AG v Guardian Newspapers (No 2)* [1988] 3 WLR 776, p 795. *Woolgar v Chief Constable of Sussex Police* [2000] 1 WLR 25.

54 See Stephenson LJ in *Lion Laboratories Ltd v Evans* [1984] 2 All ER 417, pp 422–23.

55 [1987] 3 All ER 316, p 326. See Toulson and Phipps, 1996, p 80 for a discussion of the 'true principle' of the public interest defence.

56 See Cripps, 1995, pp 523–33; and Vickers, 1995, pp 21–22.

57 14 September 1976 and 11 May 1997, EAT 669/76.

58 EAT 804/86.

59 *Ibid.*

other workers against whom suspicion is harboured.[60] In Lord Fraser's opinion:

> ...the occurrence of the leak has shown that [British Steel Corp] have a disloyal employee with access to confidential information, that their efforts to identify him have created an unpleasant atmosphere of suspicion among their employees, especially at head office, and they need to know the name of the traitor in order to clear the air.[61]

The employee is also censured as a 'miscreant',[62] in addition to accusations of theft[63] and treachery.[64] All this for an employee who Lord Salmon, in the minority, believes disclosed information which the public had a right to know. Disloyalty is a preoccupation of the courts. In the *Lion Laboratories* case, Griffiths LJ spoke of loyalty as an old fashioned virtue threatened with a shadow cast by the defence of public interest[65] and of his fear of creating a 'mole's charter'.[66]

It is well recognised that: '[I]n politics, as well as in the anxiety-pervaded corporate world, potential whistleblowers who may criticise their own organisations in public, are generally feared and punished.'[67] This may be particularly the case for public workers.[68] Condemnation and censure omit consideration of the value of whistleblowing. A whistleblower is often one brave employee who represents the collective concerns of workers. If wrongdoing is taking place within an organisation, it is unlikely that just one employee will be concerned. In the *Granada* case, Lord Salmon was of the opinion that the source was unlikely to be alone in his view that justice would be served by informing the public of the disastrous financial state of British Steel.[69] It has been suggested that British Steel believed that 'token pursuit' would be advantageous in terms of the deterrent effect on other like-minded employees.[70]

There may be a fate worse than receiving the censure of the courts. Sarah Tisdall, who was convicted under s 2 of the Official Secrets Act 1911 for disclosing government documents to *The Guardian*, was dismissed as a 'silly girl' by her own defence barrister.[71] Did she receive such poor legal advice

---

60 See Templeman LJ in the Court of Appeal in *British Steel Corp v Granada* [1981] 1 All ER 417, p 443 and Lord Fraser in the House of Lords, p 475.

61 *British Steel Corp v Granada* [1981] 1 All ER 417.

62 Lord Russell in the House of Lords, p 481.

63 See Lord Wilberforce, p 453 and Viscount Dilhorne, p 462.

64 Lord Fraser, p 474.

65 [1984] 2 All ER 417, p 432.

66 *Ibid*, p 435.

67 Flam, 1993, p 73.

68 Cripps, 1986, Chapter 3. See, also, Munro, 1990; Robinson, 1994; and Toulson and Phipps, 1996, Chapter 5.

69 [1981] 1 All ER 417, p 474.

70 Cripps, 1984, p 277.

71 See Caute, 1985, p 5.

that she pleaded guilty and presented herself as only a foolish girl? It was, in fact, pleaded that she was not a political person opposed on principle to the installation of nuclear weapons in Britain, just infuriated by the evasive tactics of the Secretary of State for Defence in announcing their arrival. Alternatively, did her defence team consider the only way for her to avoid prison was to present herself as a misguided child who did not seek to glorify her views or lead a crusade?[72] She uttered just one word in the courtroom: 'Guilty', and the articulate woman who gave a principled defence of her actions in an interview to Granada Television disappeared.[73] This is in stark contrast to the political defence mounted by Clive Ponting, who was tried under the same Act within a year of the sentencing of Sarah Tisdall. Journalists suggested the firm of Bindmans to Ponting and it fought a 'political' and 'combative' defence.[74] Norton-Taylor asks: 'Would Sarah Tisdall's fate – a six months' gaol sentence – have been the same had she gone to a more established firm of solicitors and pleaded not guilty?' As a trial would certainly have embarrassed the Government.'[75] Ponting's lawyers even persuaded the judge to allow Ponting to leave the dock after the first day as the case has 'special circumstances'.[76] He sat alongside his counsel to prevent disclosures of national security. This was an 'unusual occurrence' and a 'nice move, a psychological point in Ponting's favour'.[77] In court, Ponting's defence counsel, Bruce Laughland, emphasised an 'impeccable career and conservative values'[78] and Ponting was represented as a man of principle who put himself 'in peril and in risk'[79] by seeking to enforce the constitutional convention of ministerial accountability to Parliament. Bruce Laughland argued that Ponting suffered from a 'real crisis of conscience' and was a man of 'high seriousness and not a person who acts out of impetus or pique'.[80] Laughland distinguished Ponting from:

> ... the case of a young woman called Sarah Tisdall, who was imprisoned for giving away security sensitive material about the date of the arrival of Cruise missiles, a matter of high defence policy involving also diplomatic relations, no doubt doing it for a political motive because of her own private views about nuclear disarmament and, indeed sending the material to a newspaper. So that's a different kettle of fish altogether.[81]

---

72 Caute, 1985, p 5.
73 *Ibid.*
74 Norton-Taylor, 1985, p 12.
75 *Ibid.*
76 Ponting, 1985, p 172.
77 *Ibid,* Norton-Taylor, p 74
78 *Ibid.*
79 Closing speech of Defence Counsel, Bruce Laughland, as quoted in *ibid,* Norton-Taylor, p 100.
80 *Ibid,* p 99.
81 *Ibid,* p 94.

This line of defence succeeded with the jury in *R v Ponting*,[82] who acquitted the defendant in spite of the direction of the judge. There was no jury in *R v Tisdall*.[83] Ponting has been presented as a man of 'some distinction'[84] and 'rare conviction'[85] who provided a great 'political' trial, with Tisdall left the reputation of a foolish, if not disloyal, crown servant sentenced to six months' imprisonment.

Commentators have sought to explain the differential treatment experienced by two of the most infamous British whistleblowers. It is interesting to explore the two cases, as there are obvious parallels. Two distinctions have been drawn between the two civil servants.[86] One deals with the concept of authorisation. Ponting was a senior civil servant who had an implied discretion to disclose official documents, but Tisdall occupied a junior position and so only had a limited discretion. This argument is based on the observation of the Franks Committee in 1972 that '[s]enior civil servants exercise a considerable degree of personal judgment in deciding what disclosures of official information they may properly make and to whom'.[87] Indeed, Ponting refers to Tisdall as 'a 23 year old clerk' and himself in the third person as: 'Clive Ponting, a senior civil servant.'[88] However, Dewry comments that authorisation is a 'nebulous' concept and, in respect of Ponting, that 'the concept of self-authorisation is, by itself, an insufficient basis for justifying covert leakage to ministers' political adversaries'.[89] The other explanation for the difference in their treatment is based on the recipient of their confidential information. In passing documents designated confidential to Tam Dalyell, a Labour MP, concerning the ministerial responses to parliamentary questions about the sinking of the General Belgrano, Ponting was making a disclosure to a proper person. It was a proceeding in Parliament and, therefore, absolutely privileged.[90] Sarah Tisdall sent two documents to a component of the media, *The Guardian* newspaper and, on publication by *The*

---

82 [1985] Crim LR 318.

83 (1984) unreported, 23 March.

84 Ewing and Gearty, 1993, p 143.

85 Norton-Taylor, 1985, p 16.

86 Dewry, 1985.

87 The Frank Committee Report, *Report of Departmental Committee on Section 2 of the Official Secrets Act 1911*, Cmnd 5104, 1972.

88 Ponting, 1990, pp 63–64.

89 *Ibid*, Dewry, p 207.

90 See *ibid*, pp 209–10; and Campbell, 1985. This is based on observation of the Public Accounts Committee in 1978 involving the question of whether an official who believes a senior officer has provided misleading information to the Committee and publicises his view of the facts would be in breach of the Official Secrets Act. The Committee observed: '... if the sole publication were to the Committee or to the House, since publication in that event would amount to a proceeding in Parliament and would be absolutely privileged.' Ponting claimed he had this view in mind when he made his disclosure and sought to distinguish himself from Tisdall. See Ponting, 1985 and *ibid*, Norton-Taylor.

Guardian, disclosed to the world at large. However, Campbell quotes the Report of the House of Commons Select Committee on the Official Secrets Act in 1939, who considered the issue of a MP who receives confidential material: '... the receipt of information *per se* is not a "proceeding in Parliament" and that privilege does not apply to the receipt of information by MPs.'[91] Therefore, it seems Ponting did make an unauthorised disclosure under the Official Secrets Act 1911, arguably as 'a leaker is still a deviant'[92] and, under the most criticised s 2 of the 1911 Act, he should have been convicted and punished. The above is not intended to argue that Ponting was not a man of conscience and a brave whistleblower who risked all to disclose wrongdoing, but to present Sarah Tisdall in the same light and question their differential treatment. In October 1984, the Solicitor General spoke of the prosecution of Ponting on a BBC Radio 4 'Law in Action' programme and commented: '[I]n this particular case, it is simply a question of a very senior civil servant who has disclosed matters which, I say, that he had no right to disclose ... It rather fits with Sarah Tisdall and some others.'[93] Winfield equates Ponting and Tisdall, describing them as 'well known whistleblowers' who had 'common themes' running through their cases.[94] Both were 'valued employees' who 'acted in good faith and with justification' in raising concerns which for a 'variety of reasons ... could not be resolved internally and were eventually to be made public'.[95]

Much less well known is Ian Willmore, a whistleblower of the same period as Ponting and Tisdall. Stark similarities appear between the cases of Tisdall and Willmore.[96] Ian Willmore was also a junior civil servant who disclosed confidential information to the press. He sent an informal note to *Time Out* magazine of a meeting that took place between the Permanent Secretary to the then Department of Employment and the Master of the Rolls. The note revealed that the men discussed reform of the right to strike at a time when Sir John Donaldson was about to hear an important case concerning the sequestration of a trade union's funds following secondary picketing. Willmore gave two reasons for his action that reflect those of Tisdall. First, he was immediately concerned to publicise what he deemed an instance of constitutional 'subversion' and, secondly, he had a general concern with the government's interference with the neutrality of civil servants.[97] Tisdall was concerned that the Secretary of State for Defence's plans for the announcement of the arrival of the Cruise missiles were intended to avoid his

---

91 (1938–39) HC 101.
92 Dewry, 1985, p 210.
93 As quoted in Norton-Taylor, 1985, p 52.
94 Winfield, 1994, p 21.
95 *Ibid.*
96 See Pryer, 1985.
97 *Ibid.*

accountability to Parliament. She also had a general dislike of the impact of government policies on her as a civil servant and voter.[98] Despite these similarities, '[t]he fate which befell Ian Willmore was, however, quite different from that of Sarah Tisdall'.[99] When the article appeared, the Government commenced, as with Tisdall, an immediate internal investigation and Willmore resigned. However, he was still interviewed and offered immunity from prosecution, upon which he confessed. His resignation was accepted, as it was deemed sufficient punishment, and he left the Civil Service to begin employment with a youth organisation. Pryer has presented an explanation for the different treatment of the two junior civil servants that: '... while Sarah Tisdall's immediate "constitutional" reason for leaking seemed somewhat shaky, Ian Willmore's appeared to be of some substance.'[100] This suggests Willmore's information was of more value, but is unconvincing, for Willmore disclosed details of a meeting that occurred a year earlier. The Tisdall episode, in respect of her status, motives and actions, appears to be a mirror image of that of Willmore. Each of them leaked confidential and sensitive material that embarrassed the Government, but Tisdall received a very different sanction, with the Government even refusing consent to a summary trial.[101] Norton-Taylor argues that, although Willmore left the Civil Service, 'his manner of going weakens Heseltine's argument that Ponting had to be prosecuted because of the Tisdall precedent' and 'also provides yet another example of the inconsistent way the Official Secrets Act is applied'.[102] If the argument is weak for the prosecution of Ponting, it is weaker still for Tisdall. It has been argued that, if Ponting had been allowed to resign or been disciplined short of prosecution, it would have contrasted 'unfavourably in public with the handling of the Tisdall case, particularly given Ponting's seniority'.[103] It should also be noted that the courts played a prominent role in identifying Tisdall by ordering the return of marked government documents that led to the revelation of her identity and her subsequent prosecution.[104] The House of Lords ordered 'the immediate return of the contentious document despite the fact it did not contain information threatening to national security'.[105]

Another famous whistleblower was Cathy Massiter, a former MI5 employee who made disclosures on a Channel 4 television programme. She revealed that a leading member of the Campaign for Nuclear Disarmament

---

98 Pryer, 1985, p 74.

99 *Ibid.*

100 *Ibid.*

101 The Official Secrets Act 1991, s 2, provided for a maximum fine of £50.00 and three months' imprisonment if she had been tried at a magistrates' court.

102 Norton-Taylor, p 126.

103 *Ibid*, p 51.

104 *Guardian Newspapers Ltd v Secretary of State for Defence* [1984] 3 All ER 601.

105 Cripps, 1986, p 115.

(CND) was being bugged under a warrant from the Home Secretary. She also claimed that CND had been classed as subversive in the past and was still regarded in the 1980s as a communist dominated organisation on whom the Defence Secretary received regular briefings. The decision not to prosecute Ms Massiter under s 2 of the Official Secrets Act 1911 'gave rise to controversy',[106] as there was no legal reason to prevent it.[107] She was a former member of the security service, but owed a 'lifetime duty' of confidentiality.[108] It has been argued that she was not pursued, since she was 'open' in making her disclosures. Tisdall, Ponting and Willmore all denied leaking information when first questioned. Prosecuting counsel in *R v Ponting* questioned whether 'a man who has been acting out of high motive [would] react in that fashion'.[109] Another view is that the government did not want a repeat of the Ponting fiasco,[110] and so Massiter benefited from the acquittal of a male whistleblower.

The public interest cases all involve men, and there is an absence of material on female whistleblowers generally. Indeed, whistleblowers are 'often male, around 40 years old and married with children'.[111] There may be a number of explanations for the absence of women whistleblowers. It could be an issue of loyalty; women are more loyal and less likely to expose their organisations to adverse publicity. Another possible account is that women deal with concerns about malpractice internally and raise issues in a constructive and, therefore, unpublicised way. An alternative explanation is that women approach the whole issue of malpractice or wrongdoing within the workplace differently. A 'broader, gendered vision of organisation' reveals 'all aspects of modern organisation as infused with values, priorities and orientations that are deeply gender-biased'.[112] Such an approach recognises that 'corporations and public bureaucracies have traditionally been, and remain, dominated by males'.[113] The structure of such organisation may alienate and frustrate women. In adapting to management demands and conforming to a particular organisational pattern in order to achieve success, women may lose their 'critical consciousness'.[114] However, research has shown that 'working women, of all levels of skill and qualifications, are as, or more, demanding of their jobs and employers as are men'[115] and it is possible

---

106 Ponting, 1990, p 58.

107 *Ibid*, p 74.

108 See *AG v Guardian Newspapers* [1987] 3 All ER 316; and *AG v Guardian Newspapers (No 2)* [1988] 3 WLR 776.

109 Closing speech of Defence Counsel, Roy Amlot, as quoted in Norton-Taylor, 1985, p 84.

110 Ewing and Gearty, 1993.

111 Winfield, 1994, p 22.

112 Alvesson and Willmott, 1996, p 112. See, also, Belcher, 1997.

113 *Ibid*, Alvesson and Willmott, p 112.

114 *Ibid*.

115 Gospel and Palmer, 1993, p 95.

that women approach the issue of morality from a different perspective than that of men. Gilligan, as has been recounted widely in feminist literature, suggests that women have a 'different'[116] moral voice to that of men and approach moral questions from an 'ethic of care' rather than an 'ethic of justice'.[117] This view can be criticised for failing to provide 'a truly adequate account of morality',[118] and for presenting a 'deeply muddled voice'.[119] 'The relationship between feminism and morality has recently been one of unease and suspicion.' Some feminists see morality as 'one of the phenomena from which women should be liberated', as it can be associated with 'paternalism, restrictive regulation of women's lives, and conservatism', as well as forming an 'obstacle between tradition and freedom, between subordination and equal rights'.[120] Romain is concerned that women are being stereotyped and thinks that characteristics should not be classified as feminine or masculine 'when we have no evidence that all females or males have such characteristics'.[121] Also, there has been criticism of Gilligan's work 'for essentialism in that the voice of white women is presented as universal for all women'.[122] Of late, there has been a discussion about the possibility of a relationship between the ethics of care and justice, 'and whether they could possibly be united in a single ethical system'.[123] A worker who risks employment security by blowing the whistle on wrongdoing may possess a heightened sense of morality, 'a moral extra', that involves both a sense of caring and a sense of justice.[124] It can be argued that whistleblowers are simply 'fully morally developed' female or male workers who 'genuinely and freely sacrifice their interest for another'.[125] In raising concerns about malpractice, a worker may be influenced by an ethic of 'rebellion'.[126] Whistleblowing could be described as a form of rebellion which 'simultaneously rejects injustice and oppression and affirms human dignity'[127] and, in doing so, 'embraces the relationship' between justice and care.[128] Indeed, it could be claimed that, in raising such concerns, workers risk their economic well being in an act of 'rebellion' and 'that risk implies that these claims for which they rebel must extend beyond the individual to the

---

116 See Lim, 1996a, pp 202–04. See, also, Graham, 1994.
117 As quoted in Romain, 1992, p 27.
118 Rigternk, 1992, p 39.
119 Romain, 1992, p 34.
120 Sevenhuijsen, 1998, p 36.
121 Romain, 1992, p 35.
122 Lim, 1996a, p 203.
123 Sevenhuijsen, 1998, p 39.
124 Rigternk, 1992, p 39.
125 Romain, 1992, p 35.
126 See the account of Albert Camus' ethic of rebellion in Bartlett, 1992.
127 *Ibid*, p 84.
128 *Ibid*, p 87.

common good'.[129] No individual moral stance is absolute and 'neither sex nor gender are adequate constructions for reflecting the multiplicity of human realities'.[130] Much will depend on the situation in which an individual finds her or himself and there is a danger that a focus on what 'is most acute for female workers may obscure what is common among many employees irrespective of gender'.[131] No individual may know whether she or he will take the risk of blowing the whistle until she or he is in possession of information revealing wrongdoing.

The non-appearance of female whistleblowers in the area of confidence may, more simply, be explained by the position of women within the workplace. Until recent years, women have had limited access to information as they did not enjoy positions of responsibility. In 1986, Ponting described women as 'second class citizens in the Civil Service'.[132] The proportion of women in the labour market has grown from 41% in 1984 to 45% in 1999,[133] but almost all this increase is represented by women with young children and the 'share of women working full time has not changed since 1984, remaining constant at 56% of all female employees'.[134] Women with dependants may be reluctant to raise concerns about malpractice. Research has shown women tend 'to make pragmatic accommodations to the fact that they are less well paid, are less likely to get promotion and do in practice have to shoulder more domestic responsibilities'.[135] Also, the share of women employed in clerical, secretarial, sales and personnel occupations, traditionally associated with women, 'has remained virtually unchanged in the same period'.[136] It has been assumed that 'paid employment is less important for women' and it is a 'less central life interest for them'.[137] However, recent research reveals that: '... in terms of their orientation to work and expectations, women see paid employment as a necessary and natural component of their lives and as a complement to family life and domestic responsibilities.'[138] Women have now begun to feature more fully in the workplace, but their position in the employment hierarchy may make them reluctant to challenge the practice of senior colleagues. This could be particularly true in the health service, with women highly represented in the profession of nursing and in the ranks of

---

129 Bartlett, 1992, p 85.

130 Barnett, 1998.

131 Alvesson and Willmott, 1996, p 113.

132 Ponting, 1986, p 93.

133 See 'Continuity beats change at work' (2000) IRS Employment Trends 703, May, p 2.

134 Ibid.

135 Gospel and Palmer, 1993, p 95.

136 'Continuity beats change at work' (2000) IRS Employment Trends 703, May, p 2.

137 Gospel and Palmer, 1993, p 95.

138 Ibid.

junior doctors.[139] A nurse who planned to give evidence to the Richie Inquiry was told by colleagues: 'More fool you.'[140] The Richie Report found: '... a closed and closet atmosphere where there was and probably still is a culture of junior doctors being reluctant to criticise their seniors.'[141] The Richie Report also formed the impression that 'everyone hoped that someone else would deal with the consultant, Rodney Ledward'.[142] There may be a parallel between the nursing profession and the traditional role of women in society. Jean Orr has argued that women are often 'expected to collude in the silences and secrecy of the home and this can be translated into the hospital situation where nurses frequently know much more than they may ever disclose'.[143] She has stated that the role of nurses is to 'support the system and the doctors as the most powerful group within that system'.[144] It is possible that women are more willing to raise concerns if they act collectively. In July 2000, an employment tribunal began to hear the case of seven female care assistants who raised their concerns about the abuse of frail residents at a Bupa-run residential home for the elderly.[145] Together, they reported the abuse to the registration and inspection unit, and all were forced to resign.

Whistleblowers are often described as loners or outsiders,[146] which may be a characteristic more often associated with men. Norton-Taylor says Ponting 'was detached from, and felt uncomfortable with, the intricacies of Whitehall in-fighting and manipulations between civil servants and ministers'.[147] Whistleblowers can be 'idealists'.[148] Unlike the majority of employees who maintain 'a discreet silence', they feel compelled to speak out.[149] A whistleblower may seek to ensure an organisation conforms to its standards of morality, rather than conforming to the expectations of the organisation[150] and as a consequence 'quickly gains a reputation as a misfit or outsider'.[151] However, '[i]t is all too easy to typecast all whistleblowers as misfits'.[152] The law appears to feels more comfortable with the individual

---

139 Orr, 1995, p 55–56.

140 See Hartley-Brewer, 2000.

141 *Ibid*.

142 *Ibid*. See Stacey, 1995; Winfield, 1995; and Hunt, 1995, pp 163–64.

143 Orr, 1995, p 55. A well known exception is Graham Pink, who was a male nurse: see Hunt, 1995, pp 163–64; and Vinten, 1994b.

144 *Ibid*, Orr, p 55.

145 See 'Whistleblowers forced to resign', *The Guardian*, 14 July 2000. The full hearing will take place in March 2001.

146 See Mabey and Hooker, 1994.

147 Norton-Taylor, p 16.

148 Gobert and Punch, 2000, p 30.

149 *Ibid*.

150 *Ibid*.

151 *Ibid*.

152 Winfield, 1990, p 37.

maverick than the collective voice. Law begins with 'the individual' and, indeed, whistleblowing is 'a new name for an ancient practice, which dates from the development of the concept of individualism'.[153] The 'heritage of political liberalism' means the English legal system has 'difficulty with any concept other than that of the individual'.[154] Wells is of the view that: '[T]he dominance of liberalism which has celebrated the ultimate value of the individual person and correspondingly denounced collectivism or social welfarism has inevitably been reflected in legal accounts of responsibility.'[155] Whistleblowing may mainly be committed by a lone individual, but it is in the interests of organisations and society. The legal concern with the 'sovereignty of the individual'[156] fails to explain collective responsibility or the accountability of corporations.[157] The PIDA 1998 focuses attention on the individual by providing a worker with employment protection, subject to strict statutory requirements, but is does not guarantee the whistleblower's concerns will be heeded. There is no obligation upon an employer 'to give credence to or do anything about a whistleblower's charges'.[158] This is unfortunate as '[t]he roles of responsibility and blame allocation do not begin and end with individual moral positions'.[159]

PUBLIC INTEREST DISCLOSURE ACT 1998

The PIDA 1998 came into force on 2 July 1999[160] and amends the Employment Rights Act (ERA) 1996 to provide statutory protection to whistleblowers against dismissal and victimisation if they disclose information in respect of their employer's criminal, dangerous or damaging activities.[161] The preamble to the PIDA states that it is: '[A]n Act to protect individuals who make certain disclosures of information in the public interest; to allow such individuals to bring action in respect of victimisation; and for connected purposes.'

The protection is only afforded if a 'qualifying disclosure' is made which falls within one of the categories in the definitive[162] list provided by s 43B of

---

153 Vinten, 1994a, p 4. See, also, Vinten, 1992.

154 Wells, 1994, p 66.

155 *Ibid*.

156 *Ibid*, p 67.

157 See Wells, 1993.

158 Gobert and Punch, 2000, p 38.

159 Wells, 1993, p 67.

160 The Public Interest Disclosure Act 1998 (Commencement) Order 1999 SI 1999/1547. See the Industrial Relations Law Bulletin 621 for an analysis of the Act and Bowers, Mitchell and Lewis, 1998, Chapter 2 for its structure.

161 All references will be to the ERA 1996, as amended.

162 See Bowers, Mitchell and Lewis, 1998, p 17.

the ERA 1996, that is: 'any disclosure of information which, in the reasonable belief of the worker making the disclosure,' tends to show one or more of the following has been committed: a criminal offence; non-compliance of a legal obligation; a miscarriage of justice; a threat to the health or safety of an individual; damage to the environment; or the deliberate concealment of information concerning any of the previous categories. The requirement of 'reasonable belief' on the part of the worker does not mean the belief need be justified, but only that it was reasonable to hold it. Thus, a mistaken, but reasonable and genuine belief that a specified wrong had occurred could be a qualifying disclosure.[163] However, Gobert and Punch argue that negligence is 'the antithesis of reasonableness'.[164] It has been said that 'unsubstantiated rumours will not be considered as qualifying disclosures' as information tending to show wrongdoing is required.[165] How much information is required is not clear. Section 43B(3) of the ERA 1996 excludes a disclosure from being a qualifying disclosure 'if the person making the disclosure commits an offence by making it'. The example that most immediately comes to mind is an unauthorised disclosure under the Official Secrets Act 1989 such that a civil servant will continue to be denied protection for disclosures in the public interest.

The Act differentiates between internal disclosures to an employer and external disclosures to other persons or bodies. By virtue of s 43C(1)(a) of the ERA 1996, workers will be protected if they make a qualifying disclosure to their employer as long as they make it in 'good faith'. It has been argued that good faith simply means 'honestly', and even if information is disclosed negligently or without due care it will still be a qualifying disclosure.[166] The requirement of good faith can be criticised as 'mixed motives are common'.[167] Also, as argued earlier, an evaluation of motive may involve gender bias. The examination of motive could also 'deter' the disclosure of important information.[168] Some whistleblowers may fear that 'their motivations may be misconstrued' while others may be 'sufficiently self-aware to appreciate that their decision to blow the whistle may be prompted by a combination of factors, some of which are consistent with good faith but others of which may not'.[169] Equity did not establish the necessity of good faith. Indeed, it can be argued that the motive of the discloser is irrelevant if the allegation of wrongdoing is correct, as 'it is certainly arguable that the public interest is best served by the disclosure of all serious malpractice or wrongdoing within an

---

163 Public Interest at Work, *Public Concern at Work (Current Law Statutes)*, 1999, London: Sweet & Maxwell, p 10.
164 Gobert and Punch, 2000, p 40.
165 *Ibid*, p 11.
166 *Ibid*, p 13.
167 Vinten, 1994a, p 13.
168 Lewis, 1998, p 326.
169 Gobert and Punch, 2000, p 41.

organisation, regardless of whether the person making the disclosure is acting in good faith'.[170] The public may have a right to receive information irrespective of the motive of the whistleblower.[171] Further, even if a complaint is maliciously made and the grievance unfounded, it need not destroy the legitimacy of the concern.[172] Significant information concerning wrongdoing within organisations may be lost if an employee has to show that their intentions are strictly honourable and not driven by malice or revenge. Employees may fear the repercussions of the disclosure of confidential information and only be prepared to risk the consequences when they are pushed into revelations by the actions of their employers towards them. Lord Denning commented, in *Initial Services,* that it would be a 'great evil' if whistleblowers disclosed information for reward, and did not wish to consider the position of a whistleblower who might disclose information out of malice or spite.[173] It has been argued that the delay in introducing legislation to protect whistleblowers was the fear of inducing 'an epidemic of disloyal and aggrieved workers' who would 'rat' on their employers at every opportunity.[174] The motivation which drives a whistleblower 'may be mischievous, malevolent or even near pathological'[175] and Vinten argues that '[i]t needs to be recognised that not all whistleblowing is valid',[176] and 'ethical and unethical whistleblowing can occur leaving the employer's story "neglected"'.[177] It has been commented that one of the objectives of the PIDA 1998 is to ensure whistleblowers act 'responsibly' by drafting legislation that ensures most individuals will first raise their concerns internally or, at least, outside the workplace only with a regulator.[178] Winfield believes the law should afford protection to the worker 'acting in good faith', but notes that '[n]o matter how pure the motives, an employee who asks awkward questions or blows the whistle risks losing everything'.[179]

An employee can make a qualifying disclosure 'in the course of obtaining legal advice' under s 43D of the ERA 1996 and will be protected whether or not it is imparted in good faith. Further, a qualifying disclosure can be made 'in good faith to the Minister of the Crown' within s 43E of the ERA 1996. This applies whether the individual's employer is appointed by a minister, such as the utility regulators, or where one or more of the members of the relevant

---

170 Gobert and Punch, 2000.
171 See Stephenson LJ in *Lion Laboratories v Evans* [1984] 2 All ER 417, p 422.
172 Camp, 1999, p 47.
173 [1967] 3 All ER 145, p 149.
174 Camp, 1999, p 50.
175 Gobert and Punch, 2000, p 30.
176 Vinten, 1993, p 23. See, also, Vinten, 1994a.
177 Vinten, 1994b, p 118.
178 Camp, 1999, p 47.
179 Winfield, 1994, pp 25–26.

body is so appointed, as in NHS trusts, tribunals and other non-departmental public bodies.[180] However, the most effective and safe avenue for raising concerns externally is by making a qualifying disclosure under s 43F of the ERA 1996 in good faith to a person prescribed by an order of the Secretary of State. A worker must show that he or she reasonably believes that the relevant failure falls within any description of matters in respect of which that person is so prescribed, and that the information disclosed is 'substantially true'. An exhaustive list of prescribed persons is set out in the Public Interest Disclosure (Prescribed Person) Order 1999[181] and includes the Health and Safety Executive, the Rail Regulator, the Financial Services Authority and the Audit Commission. The order both lists the persons prescribed and specifies the matters for which they have responsibility, but does not embrace all regulators. Disclosure to a non-prescribed regulator, including to the police, would have to satisfy s 43G or s 43H of the ERA 1996, as discussed below.[182] This external disclosure imposes a further evidential burden on a worker, as the allegation must be substantially true. The legislative emphasis on the role of specified regulators in external disclosure builds from the law of confidence.[183]

It is external disclosures to non-prescribed persons that reveal the complexity of the provisions under s 43G of the ERA 1996. To illustrate the complexity and assist understanding, the detailed conditions of s 43G are fully outlined. A worker can only make a qualifying disclosure under s 43G(1) if: (a) it is made in 'good faith'; (b) they reasonably believe that the information they disclose, and any allegation contained in it, is substantially true; (c) the disclosure is not made for gain;[184] (d) any of the conditions in s 43G(2) is met; and (e) in all the circumstances of the case, it is reasonable for them to make the disclosure. The worker then has to establish one or more of the conditions that are referred to by s 43G(1)(d). These are laid down in s 43G(2): (a) at the time of disclosure, the worker reasonably believes that he or she would be 'subjected to a detriment' by the employer if he or she made a qualifying disclosure to the employer or to a prescribed person; (b) if there is no prescribed person in respect of the relevant failure, the worker reasonably believes it is likely that evidence relating to the failure could be concealed or destroyed if he or she makes a disclosure to the employer; or (c) the worker has in the past made a disclosure of 'substantially the same information' to the employer or prescribed person.

---

180 Public Concern at Work, 1999, London: Sweet & Maxwell, p 15.

181 Public Interest Disclosure (Prescribed Person) Order 1999 SI 1999/1549.

182 See discussion of *Bladon v ALM Medical Services Ltd* (1999).

183 See *Initial Services v Putterill* [1967] 3 All ER 145; *In Re A Company's Application* [1989] ICR 449; *Woolgar v Chief Constable of Sussex Police* [2000] 1 WLR 25.

184 A reward payable under any enactment will not be regarded as personal gain for the purposes of this section: ERA 1996, s 43L.

Once the worker has shown that at least one of the conditions in s 43G(2) of the ERA 1996 has been established, she or he has to establish that it was 'reasonable' to make the disclosure. Particular attention will be addressed to: (a) the identity of the person to whom the worker makes the qualifying disclosure; (b) the seriousness of the relevant failure; (c) whether the relevant failure is ongoing or is likely to occur in the future; (d) whether the disclosure is made in breach of a duty of confidentiality owed by the employer to any third party; (e) in respect of a subsequent disclosure of substantially the same information that has previously been made to an employer or prescribed person, any action which the employer or the prescribed person has taken or might reasonably be expected to have taken as a result of the previous disclosure; and (f) in respect of that previous disclosure of substantially the same information to the employer whether the worker complied with any procedure the use of which was authorised by the employer. A subsequent disclosure may be regarded as a disclosure of substantially the same information as that raised in an earlier disclosure, even though the later disclosure extends to information about action taken, or not taken, by any person as a result of the previous disclosure.

Finally, by contrast, when it involves a very serious matter, a worker can make a qualifying disclosure under s 43H of the ERA 1996 if: (a) it is done in 'good faith'; (b) it is reasonably believed that the information disclosed, and any allegation contained in it, are substantially true; (c) the disclosure is not made for personal gain; (d) the relevant failure 'is of an exceptionally serious nature'; and (e) it is 'reasonable' to make the disclosure 'in all the circumstances of the case'. In determining the reasonableness of the disclosure, particular regard shall be had to the identity of the person to whom the disclosure is made.

Both ss 43G and 43H require the employment tribunal to consider the identity of the recipient of the disclosure by the whistleblower. This preoccupation with the person who receives the unauthorised information was an issue for concern by the courts in confidentiality cases, and the tribunal may look to these cases for assistance. In *Initial Services*, Lord Denning stated that the disclosure should be to a person who had a 'proper' interest in receiving it, though he was of the view that there were misdeeds that may excuse or even demand broader publication even to the press.[185] In *Lion Laboratories*, Stephenson LJ accepted that there were cases where the public interest was best served by disclosure to the police or other responsible person,[186] but the Court of Appeal decided this was not one of them, as it was an exceptional case.[187] The House of Lords, in *AG v Guardian Newspapers (No 2)*, decided that, even if the public interest favoured publication, it did not

---

185 [1967] 3 All ER 145, p 148.
186 [1984] 2 All ER 417, p 423; and *Francome v Daily Mirror* [1984] 2 All ER 408.
187 [1984] 2 All ER 417, p 432.

necessarily follow that it should be to the whole world, though there may be some circumstances that required it. It was held that the public interest would be better assisted by a limited disclosure to the police or other responsible body that would not abuse the confidential matter in its investigation of an allegation of wrongdoing.[188] Moreover, if the allegation proved unfounded, confidentiality would be maintained. This was also the approach adopted by Scott J in *Re A Company*,[189] in which he held that an employee's duty of confidentiality did not prohibit disclosure to FIMBRA and the Inland Revenue.[190]

Protection against unfair dismissal is a primary concern for whistleblowers, since the 'ultimate deterrent'[191] to publishing a worker's concerns is the threat of dismissal, as the 'silent majority prefer the security of their jobs'.[192] Dismissal is a particular concern for a worker in such a work-ethic-based society as Britain, where work is so intrinsically caught up with the identity of an individual that unemployment is to be feared not only for loss of income, but also identity:

> [E]ven in the liberal Western regimes, no matter how low their unemployment rates and how good their unemployment and social benefits, the fundamental threat of unemployment exists. In these work-ethic societies, individuals fear both unemployment and a loss of their work identity. This fear exercises a powerful influence on the way we act.[193]

Whistleblowing 'may be desirable from an ethical point of view', but it may have 'disastrous consequences' for the employee concerned.[194] Employment protection legislation prior to the enactment of the PIDA 1998 did not provide specific protection for whistleblowers against unfair dismissal, and employees had to rely on the unfair dismissal provisions of the ERA 1996. After being employed for one year, an employee can claim unfair dismissal, in contrast with the absence of a threshold for a claim of unfair dismissal for making a protected disclosure,[195] though it should be noted that, if an employee makes a disclosure that is outside the definition of a 'qualifying disclosure', this one year bar will still apply. First, an employee has to establish that a dismissal has occurred.[196] Then, the burden shifts to the employer to show that the reason

---

188 See Lord Griffiths [1988] 3 WLR 776, p 794; and Lord Goff [1988] 3 WLR 776, p 807.

189 [1989] 1 Ch 477.

190 *Ibid.* See, also, *Woolgar v Chief Constable of Sussex Police* [2000] 1 WLR 25.

191 McHale, 1992, p 366.

192 Gobert and Punch, 2000, p 33.

193 See Flam, 1993, p 68.

194 Cover and Humphreys, 1994, p 89.

195 The threshold was lowered from two years on 1 June 1999 by the Unfair Dismissal and Statement of Reasons for Dismissal (Variation of Qualifying Period) Order 1999 SI 1999/1436.

196 ERA 1996, s 95(1).

for dismissal, or the principal reason, is potentially a fair one, contained in a list of five, that includes conduct and 'some other substantial reason'. Before the PIDA 1998, if the express reason for dismissal was an allegation of the disclosure of confidential information, it was not an onerous burden to show that the dismissal was the result of misconduct on the part of the employee.[197] In determining the reason for the dismissal, the tribunal would assess the facts of which the employer was aware, or the employer's understanding at the time of the dismissal.[198] An honest belief that an employee has breached the duty of confidentiality would usually have allowed an employer to allege misconduct, as this would 'undermine the mutual trust and confidence that must exist'.[199] Even if an employee argued that the disclosure had been in the public interest, it was still open to an employer to argue that the employee was under a mistaken belief that there had been misconduct that provided a sufficient reason to dismiss.[200] If an employer cannot prove misconduct, some other substantial reason for dismissal can be relied upon. It has been held there was no more 'potent' a reason than that of an employee who divulged confidential information.[201] If the employer presents a potentially fair reason for dismissal, the employment tribunal will decide whether the dismissal was fair. If an employer's decision is within the band of 'reasonable responses' of employers it will be fair,[202] although it should be noted that this approach has been criticised as promoting a managerial bias[203] and has recently been challenged in the Employment Appeals Tribunal and the Court of Appeal.[204]

'Rights without remedies are an illusion',[205] and the PIDA 1998 amends the ERA 1996 to offer protection to both workers and employees. By virtue of

---

197 See (1997) 564 Industrial Relations Law Bulletin, p 4.

198 *British Home Stores v Burchell* [1978] IRLR 379.

199 *Sanderson v Mirror Group Newspapers Ltd* (1986) EAT 138/86, 22 May.

200 See Vickers, 1995, p 18.

201 *Byford v Film Finances Ltd* (1987) EAT 804/86, 21 May.

202 *Iceland Frozen Foods v Jones* [1982] IRLR 439.

203 See Freer, 1998.

204 See *Haddon v Van Bergh Foods Ltd* [1999] IRLR 672, in which the EAT held that the band of reasonable responses was not helpful as the test of fairness in s 98(4) is 'clear and unambiguous and should be applied without embellishment'. This approach was endorsed by the Scottish EAT in *Wilson v Ethicon* [2000] IRLR 4. However, the EAT in *Midland Bank v Madden* [2000] IRLR 288 found it was not an option for the EAT in Haddon to challenge the test adopted by the Court of Appeal, and whilst it held the reasonable range test should be applied, noted the tribunal must have regard to the plain wording of the statute as a solution. In *Berry v West Ferry Printers* (2000) unreported, 7 July, the EAT found that the three cases 'do not alter the earlier orthodoxy'. On 31 July 2000, in joined appeals of *Post Office v Foley* (unreported) and *Midland Bank v Madden* (unreported), the Court of Appeal restated the test of 'reasonable responses' and held that tribunals should continue to apply the test. Leave to appeal to the House of Lords was refused. See Smith, 2000, p 642; and Edwards, 2000, p 393.

205 Gobert and Punch, 2000, p 46.

s 43K of the ERA 1996, an extended meaning of 'worker' is utilised to provide protection to a wide range of the workforce. A worker has the right not to be subjected to a 'detriment' if making a qualifying disclosure,[206] entitling her to complain to an employment tribunal.[207] If a tribunal concludes a worker has suffered detrimental treatment, it is required to make a declaration and has the power to award compensation[208] that is 'just and equitable in all the circumstances' with regard to the infringement and any loss the worker suffers that is attributable to the detriment.[209] An employee has the right to claim unfair dismissal if dismissed for making a qualifying disclosure.[210] No qualifying threshold in respect of period of service or restriction upon age applies. It is also unfair to select an employee for redundancy if the primary reason was the making of a protected disclosure.[211] A compensatory award for unfair dismissal or unfair selection for redundancy on the grounds of a protected disclosure is not subject to a statutory minimum,[212] in contrast to the £50,000 limit on compensatory awards for dismissal and redundancy on all other grounds.[213]

Prior to the enactment of PIDA 1998, there were no legislative guidelines to assist the courts in deciding whether a whistleblower disclosed confidential information in the public interest. It was for the courts to decide whether the confidential information disclosed wrongdoing that entitled the whistleblower to disclose it,[214] and consequently which individual received the veiled protection of the court. This appears, as suggested earlier, to be more than a mere exercise in balancing the private interest in confidentiality against the public interest in disclosure; it was an 'exercise in judicial judgment'.[215] Dispute resolution with wide discretionary power places 'those who are marginalised at a great disadvantage'.[216] A lack of procedural guidelines may lead to 'informal systems of justice' that are detrimental to women[217] and 'foster racial and ethnic bias'.[218] It has been argued that the focus of cases developing the public interest defence was on the information itself and whether it should be disclosed, and not whether protection should

---

206 ERA 1996, s 47B.

207 *Ibid*, s 48(1A).

208 *Ibid*, s 49(1).

209 *Ibid*, s 49(2).

210 *Ibid*, s 103A.

211 *Ibid*, s 105(6A).

212 Public Interest Disclosure (Compensation) Regulations 1999 SI 1999/1548, reg 3(a). *Ibid*, s 124(1A), as amended by s 37 of the Employment Relations Act (ERA)1999.

213 ERA 1999, s 124(1)(b).

214 See Lord Fraser in *British Steel Corp v Granada Ltd* [1981] 1 All ER 417, p 480.

215 Lord Wilberforce in *Science Research Council v Nasse* [1979] 3 All ER 673, p 681.

216 Lim, 1996b, p 137. See Williams, 1991, p 199.

217 *Ibid*, Lim, p 137. See Bottomley, 1993.

218 *Ibid*, Lim, p 137.

be given to the whistleblower.[219] The information must be the 'proper subject for protection'.[220] While the attention of the court was directed to the information itself, this did not preclude a judicial evaluation of the whistleblower and employer seeking to restrain disclosure. Indeed, O'Connor LJ, in the case of *Lion Laboratories*, noted that, as the relief of an equitable injunction to restrain unauthorised disclosure is discretionary: 'it can be tailored to the facts of the particular case.'[221] Lord Denning, who did much to develop the public interest exception to the duty of confidentiality, stated in *Hubbard v Vosper* that it was only in a 'proper case' that a court would intervene to prevent a person from disclosing confidential information.[222] If an employer sought an equitable remedy of an injunction to control the revelation of information, it allowed the court to assess whether they came with 'clean hands'.[223] It should be noted that 'clean hands' has lost much of its judicial meaning since the late 1970s.[224] Lord Denning returned to his assessment of a proper case in *Woodward v Hutchins*. He denied an employer an injunction restraining publication of confidential information as he employed a pop group that courted publicity.[225] This assessment as to whether an individual's case is a 'proper' one which deserves the protection of the court also involves an examination of the whistleblower. In *Schering Chemicals Ltd v Falkman Ltd*,[226] a media adviser contracted to deal with adverse publicity concerning a drug manufactured by Schering Chemicals Ltd used confidential documents acquired from his position to make a documentary about the effect of the drug. Lord Denning, in his dissenting judgment, considered the whistleblower justified in breaching his duty of confidentiality, and in Denning's view it was most unfair to accuse him of 'being a traitorous adviser'.[227] However, this contrasts with his approach in the Court of Appeal decision in *British Steel Corp v Granada*, where British Steel sought disclosure of Granada's source of leaked confidential information which revealed gross mismanagement on the part of British Steel, which was then a nationalised industry, resulting in immense losses. Lord Denning found the breach of confidence 'grave' and 'quite inexcusable'.[228] In contrast, Lord Salmon, in the minority in the House of Lords, dissented with quite a different view of the behaviour of the whistleblower. He considered the employee was

---

219 Public Concern at Work, 1999, London: Sweet & Maxwell, p 3.
220 Lord Denning in *Hubbard v Vosper* [1972] 1 All ER 1023, p 1028.
221 [1984] 2 All ER 417, p 431.
222 See Lord Denning in [1972] 1 All ER 1023.
223 See Megaw LJ in *Hubbard v Vosper* [1972] 1 All ER 1023, p 1033.
224 See *Tribe v Tribe* [1995] 4 All ER 236.
225 [1977] 2 All ER 751, p 754.
226 [1981] 2 All ER 321.
227 *Ibid*, p 329.
228 [1981] 1 All ER 417, p 436.

not guilty of wrongdoing, but revealed from a significant sense of public duty.[229] It remains to be seen whether the enactment of the PIDA 1998 will remove this kind of judicial appraisal of the whistleblower.

EVALUATION

Overall, the Act has been widely and warmly welcomed by commentators for providing protection to whistleblowers that, it has been claimed, may possibly be the best in the world.[230] Reform had long been demanded and discussed.[231] In 1985, Cripps proposed an amendment to the existing employment protection legislation to 'protect public-spirited employees',[232] and this call was repeated through the introduction of two private member's Bills until the enactment of legislation in 1998.[233] To secure the objective of reform of the workplace culture to allow the effective raising of concerns in an open environment, the PIDA 1998 has declared so called 'gagging clauses' unlawful. By virtue of s 43J of the ERA 1996, a contract or any agreement that seeks to preclude a worker from making a protected disclosure is void, as will be any agreement that restrains a worker from instituting or continuing proceedings under this Act or any proceedings for breach of contract. However, for some, this welcome comes with reservations. The PIDA 1998 has secured the extension of individual rights to whistleblowers. If there is debate on the issue as to how far it promotes good governance and an open culture at work,[234] there is concern over the complexity of the provisions:[235]

> The convoluted structure of the protection outlined, with a variety of states of belief and awareness required of the potential whistleblower, does little to promote certainty, and gives rise to the suspicion that the only workers who will be able to take advantage of the provisions are those who are usually well advised and informed.[236]

Three cases have been decided to date under the protected disclosure provisions of the amended ERA 1996: *Bladon v ALM Medical Services Ltd*

---

229 [1981] 1 All ER 417, p 436.

230 Camp, 1999, p 46.

231 See Cripps, 1984; Cripps, 1985, pp 537–38; Cripps, 1986, Chapters 13 and 14; Dehn and Rose, 1996; Lewis, 1995, pp 218–21; Vickers, 1995 pp 38–40; and Winfield, 1994, p 27.

232 Cripps, 1985, p 537.

233 Dr Tony Wright MP introduced a ten minute rule bill in 1995 and Don Touhig MP sought to introduce a private member's Bill in 1996 which gained the commitment of government legislation from Tony Blair MP, then Leader of the Opposition.

234 See Public Concern at Work, 1999, London: Sweet & Maxwell, p 3 and Lewis, 1998, p 330.

235 See Lewis, 1998; and (1998) 586 Industrial Relations Law Bulletin.

236 (1998) 586 Industrial Relations Law Bulletin, p 14.

(1999);[237] *Azmi v ORBIS Charitable Trust* (2000);[238] and *Fernandes v Netcom Consultants (UK) Ltd* (2000).[239] The case of *Azmi* involved a woman applicant and the cases of *Bladon* and *Fernandes* involve male applicants. In all three cases, the employment tribunal found that the employees had been dismissed for making a protected disclosure and thus showed the potential effectiveness of the PIDA 1998 in extending employment protection to whistleblowers regardless of gender. These cases have attracted comment highlighting the protection now available to whistleblowers, and warning others that wrongdoing will be exposed,[240] although, overall awareness of the PIDA 1998 in the working environment, particularly amongst workers, remains low. The PIDA 1998 has received limited government promotion and media attention in comparison with other employment legislation passed by the new government, including the National Minimum Wage Act 1998 and the Employment Relations Act 1999. However, this may now change with the considerable media attention generated by the substantial compensation awarded to Antonio Fernandes.

The first case to be heard by an employment tribunal under the PIDA 1998 was *Bladon v ALM Medical Services Ltd.* In this case, the applicant was employed as a charge nurse at a nursing home owned by the respondent for less than three months when he was dismissed for raising concerns in respect of mismanagement of the nursing home and the welfare of patients. Mr Bladon had initially contacted Mr Sinclair, personal assistant to the managing director of the respondent company, to express his concerns, and at Mr Sinclair's request set out his concerns in a fax. A week later, when Mr Bladon received no response, he took further action and contacted the Social Services Inspectorate, who referred the matter to the Nursing Homes Inspectorate, and an inspection officer carried out an inspection of the home within days. The respondent was sent the conclusions of the inspection, which found the concerns of the applicant to be 'substantiated in whole or in part'. However, the applicant was summoned to a disciplinary hearing and received a written warning. The managing director of the respondent company, Dr Matta, claimed the written warning was warranted as the applicant's own poor professional care was in part the cause of the home's failings, his complaint stemmed from frustration with a colleague and his concerns were untrue. Six days later, Mr Bladon was summarily dismissed on the grounds that he was 'not prepared to work with [the] company's basic interests in mind' and in the discharge of his professional duties fell below standards expected of the company's employees.

---

237 Case No 2405845/99.

238 Case No 3300624/99.

239 Case No 2200060/00.

240 See Brockes, 2000, in which Emma Brockes examines expenses fraud following the case of *Fernandes v Netcom Consultants Ltd.* See, also, (2000) 648 Industrial Relations Law Bulletin (in association with Public Concern at Work).

On 25 April 2000, the tribunal found that, while the applicant may have been 'over zealous in the steps that he took', his dismissal was automatically unfair. In sending his fax to Mr Sinclair, he was making a qualifying disclosure to a person acting in the capacity of his employer. His concerns involved the health and safety of patients and the control of drugs. This related to a possible failure to comply with a legal obligation and a potential criminal offence within the list of qualifying disclosures in s 43B. The tribunal found that the applicant was acting in good faith and that he had made a qualifying disclosure to his employer within s 43C. With regard to the disclosure to the Social Services Inspectorate, the tribunal regretted that neither the Social Services Inspectorate nor the Nursing Home Inspectorate were a prescribed person under s 43F of the ERA 1996 and considered this to be 'a significant omission from the ambit of the [Prescribed Person] Regulations'.[241] However, the tribunal found the applicant made a qualifying disclosure under s 43G of the ERA 1996. He had made a disclosure of a serious matter in good faith, acted without the purpose of personal gain and his allegations were substantially true. In addition, the applicant had already disclosed his concerns to his employer and it was reasonable, in all the circumstances, for the applicant to take his concerns to a regulatory and investigatory body. It was noted by the tribunal that Mr Bladon had acted professionally and responsibly in raising his concern and had not contacted either a Member of Parliament or the press.

The hearing was adjourned until 12 June 2000 to determine Mr Bladon's remedy. At this later stage, it was noted that the applicant had failed to secure alternative employment, although he had been short-listed twice for jobs, because he had 'blown the whistle'. The tribunal acknowledged the view of Mr Bladon that his treatment was 'unjust and unfair' and his 'unblemished employment record'. It was also accepted that the applicant was 'shocked and humiliated', and 'justified' in concluding that his disciplinary hearing was both a ploy by the respondent to avoid undertaking an investigation and to place the blame upon the applicant. The submission of the applicant's counsel that it was empowered to award not only damages for injury to feelings, but an additional sum for aggravated damages, under s 49 of the ERA 1996, was also accepted. Mr Bladon was awarded £13,075.06 as compensation for his unfair dismissal and £10,000 for injury to feelings including a substantial sum for aggravated damages.

The decision of the employment tribunal in *Azmi v ORBIS Charitable Trust* followed shortly afterwards. The applicant was employed by the respondent charity for almost five months when she was dismissed for 'poor performance'. The employment tribunal concluded the real reason for her dismissal was not her performance, but her attempts 'persistently' to raise

---

241 Public Interest Disclosure (Prescribed Person) Order 1999 SI 1999/1549.

breaches of UK trustee law by the charity with the Executive Director of ORBIS. The director did not welcome the concerns of Ms Azmi and used the excuse of poor performance to dismiss her. The tribunal concluded the dismissal was automatically unfair within s 103A of the ERA 1996 as she had made a protected disclosure to her employer. The applicant's repeated raising of her concerns in the face of a management style were accepted by the tribunal and described as 'bullying and intimidatory'.[242] ORBIS were found to be in breach of her contract and liable to pay her two months' pay in lieu of notice with the case adjourned until 17 November 2000 to determine remedy.

The third case of *Fernandes v Netcom Consultants (UK) Ltd*, which was discussed briefly in the introduction, concerned the disclosure of irregularities in respect of corporate expenses. The applicant was employed by the respondent company for over four years when he was dismissed as chief financial officer for 'shortcomings in his job'. Netcom had a policy by which senior managers had a corporate credit card and the bill was paid by the company monthly. Personal expenses could be placed on the card, but had to be repaid to the company after receipts were produced to verify business expenditure. It was Mr Fernandes' role to ensure expenditure was properly incurred on receiving the required receipts from employees. The managing director of the company, Mr Woodhouse, persistently failed between 1997 to 1999 to produce any receipts to support his expenses claims despite repeated requests from Mr Fernandes. In January 1997, Mr Fernandes faxed to Mr Palladino, his contact in the parent company, XSource Corp in America, his concerns over Mr Woodhouse's failure to submit receipts for expenditure. However, Mr Palladino telephoned him late that evening to tell him that the fax had been destroyed and to do likewise to his copy, with the warning 'You must look after your butt'. In 1999, there was a 'steep increase' in Mr Woodhouse's expenses. In November, with an impending audit, Mr Fernandes sent a detailed letter reporting on Mr Woodhouse's failings to XSource and its parent company's management board in Luxembourg. Following this disclosure, Mr Fernandes was ordered to stay at home and pressed repeatedly to resign. He was subjected to a disciplinary hearing and dismissed for approving unsupported transactions and allowing 'what he determined fraudulent activities to continue'. Mr Woodhouse was allowed to continue working until the management team of XSource Corp insisted action be taken and he resigned on request.

The tribunal decided the applicant was unfairly dismissed for making a protected disclosure in good faith to his employer. It concluded the managers had decided to 'get rid of the more junior man who disclosed the position' leaving Mr Woodhouse in place, and there had been 'a clear attempt to intimidate and pressurise Mr Fernandes to resign so that all could be hushed

---

242 Case No 2200624/99, p 14.

up'. Mr Fernandes received a record award of £293,441 in compensation for his dismissal.

In the *Azmi* case, the tribunal stated that the burden of proof fell on the applicant to show that the making of a protected disclosure was the reason or principal reason for dismissal. In the *Fernandes* case, the employment tribunal found that, if an applicant provides evidence which casts doubt on the respondent's stated reason for dismissal, the burden of proof switches to the respondent, to show the 'true reason' and the tribunal should look at the actions of the employer as a whole.

The employment tribunal demonstrated in the *Bladon* case that they not only accepted their jurisdiction to award damages for injury to feeling, but also their power to award a sum for aggravated damages and their willingness to exercise it. The tribunal were referred to, and relied on, *Cleveland Ambulance NHS Trust v Blane*[243] which held that, in awarding compensation that was 'just and equitable in all the circumstances having regard to the infringement complained of', it had the power to award damages for injury to feelings.

It is to be hoped that the protection offered to whistleblowers will be applied equally regardless of gender. However, the employment tribunal may have deployed preconceptions of gender in their approach to the *Azmi* case. The parties disputed the purpose of a lunchtime meeting on 6 August 1999 in which the applicant claimed she had raised her concerns with David Coe, the Executive Director, and he claimed he reviewed a number of matters with her and she in turn became 'extremely upset and distressed'. This attempt by an employer to dismiss the female whistleblower as an emotional and incompetent female failed but, on evidence, the tribunal found there was no witness to support David Coe's account. Following the meeting, the respondent's solicitor saw 'no signs of any distress', and the tribunal concluded that 'if the lunchtime meeting had proceeded as Mr Coe alleged,' the applicant 'would have appeared tearful and upset to Ms Middleton'. The tribunal commented: '[O]verall we prefer the evidence of the applicant and her witnesses to that in particular of David Coe.' In contrast, throughout the Bladon judgment, the tribunal emphasised the applicant's professionalism, stating, for instance, that 'he was an objective and accurate historian'. They also noted that they were particularly 'impressed by the fact that the applicant

---

243 [1997] IRLR 275. Authorities also considered included *McConnell Police Authority for Northern Ireland* [1997] IRLR 625; and *Prison Services and Others v Johnson* [1997] ICR 275.

was reluctant to describe some of the incidents that he had witnessed as 'abuse' because, in his words, 'abuse is an emotive issue'.

It would not do to make any conclusions on gender from just three cases, but it is an issue to be kept under review. In the first year of its operation, over 200 claims have been brought under the PIDA 1998.[244] In April 2000, Public Concern at Work, a charity established to assist whistleblowers, successfully sought judicial review of the decision not to allow them access to applications of complaint under the PIDA 1998 provisions.[245] Jackson J held the decision of the central office of the employment tribunal was unlawful and ruled that 'as a matter of public policy' full details of claims should be open to inspection.[246] It is hoped that information regarding the treatment of whistleblowers on grounds of gender and race will be maintained separately as part of the monitoring process.

The early operation of the PIDA 1998 is to be applauded, for it appears to guarantee protection to whistleblowers thus far. Bryan Bladon, who was the first to benefit from the PIDA 1998, considers his case may encourage others who are too frightened to disclose wrongdoing. He commented: '[T]o end up with £23,000 – it gives a message to nurses that they are not going to walk away with nothing. It also gives employers a message, that they are not going to get away with it.'[247] In addition to the three decided cases, a former secretarial assistant, dismissed for gross misconduct by the Manufacturing, Science and Finance (MSF) union, received £50,000 and legal costs in an out of court settlement in July 2000. In an unfair dismissal complaint under the PIDA 1998 provisions, Marcia Solomon alleged that Roger Lyons, the general secretary of MSF, falsified expenses and used false bank accounts to defraud the union of almost £130,000. The union argued that Ms Solomon had no evidence, but the tribunal proceedings were terminated by the chair as the union could not establish that Ms Solomon had acted maliciously.[248] Following the settlement, Ms Solomon stated: 'I maintain that I saw what I saw and acted in good faith when I brought my concerns to the attention of John Chowcat, the then assistant general secretary of MSF. I therefore regard the settlement as a vindication of my position.' The recipient of Ms Solomon's concerns, Mr Chowcat, was initially also dismissed for gross misconduct, but received £250,000 in an out of court settlement after signing a confidentiality

---

244 See Weale, 2000; and (2000) 648 Industrial Relations Law Bulletin, p 2.

245 *R v Secretary of the Central Office of the Employment Tribunals (England and Wales) ex p Public Concern at Work* [2000] IRLR 658.

246 See Dyer, 2000.

247 See Weale, 2000.

248 See Hencke, 2000a; and Hencke, 2000b.

agreement.[249] Following its settlement with Ms Solomon and Mr Chowcat, MSF had to pay £108,000 to Howell John, its north Thames regional officer, add £84,000 to Mr John's pension fund and provide him with a Ford Mondeo. In return, the union made Mr John sign a 'gagging clause' concerning the financial affairs of the union hours before he was to commence a claim for victimisation against Roger Lyons. It was agreed between the parties that Mr John should take early retirement 'on grounds of ill health'.[250] It seems companies who ignore the concerns of workers could 'pay dearly' under the whistleblowing legislation,[251] and damage their reputations. Dehn believes '[e]mployers who suppress warnings and shoot the messenger are now taking enormous risks with their reputations'.[252]

Despite these high profile cases, it is not clear that any significant change will result from workers raising their concerns. An organisation may be willing to 'pay off' what they see as a disloyal worker. Following the payment of nearly £750,000, to the whistleblowers mentioned above, Roger Lyons apologised to MSF members for 'flawed' judgment, but refused to resign.[253] A whistleblower may receive compensation, but it does not guarantee future employment. Antonio Fernandes may have been awarded over £293,000, but he is 59 years old and believes it is unlikely that he will find employment, as employers will be reluctant to employ a 'troublemaker'.[254] He suggests his compensation 'was a good award' and more than he expected,[255] but he has been unable to find alternative employment in six months and the award, which is mainly for loss of earnings, may have to cover his salary until retirement. Following the award, Mr Fernandes told reporters: '[T]here aren't many companies that are willing to employ someone who is nearly 60 and with no formal accountancy qualifications.'[256]

Gobert and Punch have concerns that the PIDA 1998 may be misused: '[W]hile there are undoubtedly sincere and well-meaning whistleblowers who deserve to be protected against reprisals, any protection offered to such individuals will also become available to employees to use as a means to fend off legitimate criticism, pending disciplinary proceedings or a threatened

249 See Hencke, 2000a.

250 Hencke, 2000c.

251 Guy Dehn, director of the charity Public Concern at Work, quoted by Shaw and Demetriou, 2000.

252 Quoted by Mason, 2000.

253 See White, 2000.

254 See Weale, 2000.

255 See Dyer, 2000b.

256 Quoted by Shaw and Demetriou, 2000.

termination of employment.'[257] However, the experience of whistleblowers does not seem to indicate that this will be the case. Antonio Fernandes found that: '[I]t is a long process. It leaves you out in the cold. You feel victimised and you lose confidence. All I did was follow my conscience. You have to do what you essentially believe is right.'[258]

THE HUMAN RIGHTS ACT 1998

The PIDA 1998 must be valued as it provides rights for the first time to whistleblowers and can be seen as part of the government's commitment to introduce 'a range of new rights at work'[259] to guarantee the 'basic fair treatment of employees'.[260] The PIDA 1998 has been presented as part of the government's commitment to extend rights to all its citizens. The government claimed that the Human Rights Act (HRA) 1998, introduced in the same parliamentary session as the PIDA 1998, would 'bring rights home', as it will 'make more directly accessible the rights which the British people already enjoy under the Convention'.[261] It has also been argued that the Act introduces 'a radical new equity of fundamental importance'.[262] The HRA 1998 came into force in October 2000 and incorporates the 'Convention rights', Arts 2–12 and 14[263] of the European Convention on Human Rights (ECHR),[264] into domestic law.[265] Legislation must be interpreted 'as far as possible' to be compatible with the Convention rights, and so the relevant provisions of the ERA 1996[266] must be read in light of Art 10 of the ECHR, which provides a right to freedom of expression. It will be unlawful for a public body to act in a way that is incompatible with the Convention rights.[267] Courts and tribunals are stated to be public bodies by the HRA 1998,[268] but some private bodies, and quasi-private bodies, will also be public bodies. Public sector employees can challenge their employers who deny them freedom of expression, and this could be a possible 'spill over' to the private

---

257 Gobert and Punch, 2000, p 32.
258 See Weale, 2000. It is possible Antonio Fernandes was also driven to blow the whistle by professional ethics: see Lovell and Robertson, 1994.
259 Department of Trade and Industry, 1998, para 2.14.
260 *Ibid*, para 1.9.
261 Home Office, 1997, para 1.19.
262 See Clements, 1999.
263 HRA 1998, s 1.
264 The European Convention of Human Rights and Fundamental Freedoms (the Convention on Human Rights) TS 71 (1953); Cmnd 8969.
265 See Bowers, Mitchell and Lewis, Chapter 13.
266 HRA 1998, s 3.
267 *Ibid*, s 6.
268 *Ibid*, s 6(3). See *Smith v Secretary of State for Trade and Industry* [2000] IRLR 6.

sector.[269] There are no cases under the European jurisprudence relating to whistleblowing, but there was a successful utilisation of Art 10 by a schoolteacher dismissed for her membership of the Communist Party in *Vogt v Germany*.[270] Preceding this case, the European Court of Human Rights had been slow to extend Art 10 to the issue of dismissal and to provide protection to public sector workers.[271] *Vogt v Germany*[272] provides for the entry of Art 10 into the realm of the workplace and the employment law of dismissal.[273] It has been argued that a possible explanation for the lack of protection for whistleblowers prior to the PIDA 1998 was the lack of respect for freedom of speech in the UK.[274] It is a matter of debate how far the PIDA extends an 'open culture' in the workplace where individuals feel free to express their concerns.[275] It is not expected that the HRA 1998 will have a significant impact on the area of labour law as a whole,[276] though it has potential to protect the free speech of whistleblowers.[277] It should be noted that Art 10 does not provide an absolute right to free speech. The article permits interference with the right of free expression if it is prescribed by law and necessary in a democratic society for one of the permitted reasons listed, which include the interests of national security and the prevention of disclosure of information received in confidence. Indeed, the criteria in the PIDA 1998 do not require a tribunal to consider whether the disclosure is a breach of a duty of confidentiality, other than for external disclosures in s 43G of the ERA 1996. In this section, the tribunal should have regard to the duty of confidentiality owed by an employer to a third party as part of its criteria. Further, any rights contained in Art 10 must be balanced against the right to respect for a person's private life and correspondence contained in Art 8.[278] This involves a right to maintain the confidentiality of confidential information,[279] as it can be argued that it is in the public interest for confidences to be respected.[280] The ECHR has been considered in cases in the

---

269 Ewing, 1998, p 284. See Morris, 1998; and Buxton, 2000.

270 *Ibid*, Ewing, p 279.

271 The European Court of Human Rights had held in both *Kosiek v Germany* [1986] 9 EHRR 328 and *Glasenapp v Germany* [1987] 9 EHRR 25 that Art 10 of the Convention did not afford protection to public sector employees in respect of dismissal.

272 [1996] 21 EHRR 205.

273 Vickers, 1997, p 597.

274 Vickers, 1995, p 37.

275 See Lewis, 1998, p 330; and Camp, 1999.

276 See *ibid*, Ewing.

277 Vickers, 1997, p 602.

278 See Toulson and Phipps, 1996, Chapter 9, on confidentiality and privacy generally. See, also, Stuckley-Clarke, 1990; and Thompson, 1990.

279 See Lord Denning in *Schering Chemicals Ltd v Falkman Ltd* [1981] 2 All ER 321, p 333.

280 Lord Keith in *AG v Guardian Newspapers (No 2)* [1988] 3 WLR 776, p 782.

law of confidence.[281] In reaching his conclusions, Lord Goff, in *AG v Guardian Newspapers*, concluded that English law in the area of freedom of speech would not have led to a different conclusion than the jurisprudence of the European Court of Human Rights.[282]

DUTY TO DISCLOSE WRONGDOING

The PIDA 1998 does not impose a duty on workers to disclose malpractice, even though the value of public interest disclosure has been recognised by legislators in drafting the Pensions Schemes Act 1993 and the Pensions Act 1995. Indeed, the 'best hope of regulating what goes on inside private and public sector enterprises is through the vigilance of individual employees'.[283] Whistleblowers can act as a 'safety net' to protect 'the workforce or the public from fraud, malpractice and preventable disasters'.[284] There is no general duty placed on a worker by the common law to report misconduct or wrongdoing,[285] but, in certain circumstances, a duty may arise out of a particular contractual relationship if an employee enjoys a senior position within the organisation.[286] An employee 'may be so placed in the hierarchy as to have a duty to report either the misconduct of his superior ... or the misconduct of his inferiors'.[287] In the *Granada* case, it was believed the whistleblower, who passed confidential documents anonymously to Granada, was part of the management at British Steel. Lord Salmon was the only Law Lord in the case who considered the public were 'morally entitled'[288] to the information and that the whistleblower believed it was his 'public duty' to make the contents of the documents public.[289] However, in *Annesley v Earl of Anglesea*, it was stated that: '... no private obligations can dispense with that universal one that lies on every member of society to discover every design which may be formed, contrary to the laws of the society, to destroy the public welfare.'[290]

281 Lord Keith in *AG v Guardian Newspapers (No 2)* [1988] 3 WLR 776, p 782; Lord Templeman in *AG v Guardian Newspapers* [1987] 3 All ER 316, p 355; and Lord Goff in *AG v Guardian Newspapers (No 2)* [1988] 3 WLR 776, p 808. See, also, Kennedy LJ in *Woolgar v Chief Constable of Sussex Police* [2000] 1 WLR 25, p 36; and Lord Woolf MR in *R v Chief Constable of North Wales ex p Thorpe* [1999] QB 396, p 428.

282 Lord Goff in *AG v Guardian Newspapers (No 2)* [1988] 3 WLR 776, p 808.

283 Winfield, 1994, p 23.

284 *Ibid.*

285 Stephenson LJ in *Sybron Corp v Rochem Ltd* [1983] IRLR 253, p 258.

286 Greene LJ in *Swain v West (Butchers) Ltd* [1936] All ER 261, p 264 and *Sybron Corp v Rochem Ltd* [1983] IRLR 253, p 258.

287 Stephenson LJ in *Sybron Corp v Rochem Ltd* [1983] IRLR 253, p 258.

288 [1981] 1 All ER 417, p 467.

289 *Ibid*, p 468.

290 (1743) 17 State Tr, 1139, pp 1223–46, quoted by Lord Denning in *Initial Services v Putterill* [1967] 3 All ER 145.

CONCLUSION

Employment protection was urgently needed to protect whistleblowers as the law relating to employees' public interest was 'unsatisfactory and difficult to ascertain'.[291] The PIDA 1998 provides workers with rights not to be dismissed or victimised and Lord Nolan congratulates those behind the Act for 'so skilfully achieving the essential but delicate balance in this measure between the public interest and the interests of employers'.[292]

The Act sought to achieve this balance by encouraging the internal raising of concerns and providing employment security to whistleblowers by encouraging 'resolution of concerns through proper workplace procedures, but it will protect those who, in the last resort, have to go public'.[293] It remains to be seen whether these objectives are fully achieved.

The treatment of Sarah Tisdall indicates that women brave enough to disclose confidential information in the public interest may receive harsher treatment than their male counterparts. The use of 'he' in the definition of whistleblowing utilised at the beginning of this chapter is a reflection of an exclusion of women from the transformed public perception of the value of whistleblowers. It is just over a year since the new legislation came into force and three whistleblowers have successfully brought complaints against their employers, but the raising of gendered stereotypes in the *Azmi* case is of concern. The PIDA 1998 gives 'a clear message'[294] that all whistleblowers should be protected if they meet the exhaustive criteria set out in its provisions. It is hoped that this will remove any bias on the part of the judicial process and ensure cases are determined without preconceived or stereotypical beliefs about the 'true' natures, roles or capacities of men and women.[295] It remains to be seen if the strict legislative requirements of the PIDA 1998 will afford equal treatment to all whistleblowers, but this is an issue that should clearly be kept under review.

It is unclear whether the legislation will transform the workplace so that whistleblowers are not viewed as disloyal or traitors, but as acting in the best interests of their organisation by highlighting malpractice. It has been stated that '[c]ultures do not change overnight, particularly firmly entrenched ones'.[296] The whistleblower, Stephen Bosin, who sought for five years to raise concerns with the authorities in respect of poor standards of paediatric heart

---

291 Cripps, 1986, conclusion.
292 *Hansard* HL, 5 June 1998, col 614, quoted in Public Concern at Work, 1999, London: Sweet & Maxwell, 1999, p 2.
293 Department of Trade and Industry, 1998, para 3.3.
294 See Mack, 1994, p 192.
295 *Ibid*, p 186.
296 Winfield, 1995, p 98.

surgery at the Bristol Royal Infirmary, was ostracised by colleagues and forced to leave the UK to work in Australia. He supports the Act, but asks whether it will alter a 'deeply entrenched culture': 'It's difficult to legislate for changes in attitudes. The medical profession is still that you don't shop your colleagues.'[297] Whistleblowing maintains its 'negative connotations for many' across industries and in organisations, despite the enactment of legal protection. It continues to be 'associated with people fighting personal battles, making anonymous leaks to newspapers. It smacks of betraying colleagues, letting the side down and people are afraid it results in victimisation and loss of employment.'[298] The limited awareness of the PIDA 1998 may further this perception. However, the recent publicity generated by the first group of cases decided under the new Act may reveal whistleblowing to be a valuable safety net[299] and promote an 'ethic of disclosure'.[300] The media attention given to Antonio Fernandes may further assist the cause of whistleblowers as '[i]t is only with clear signals like this that people will gain confidence to speak up and so break the cycle of silence, inertia and inaction behind many scandals'.[301]

---

297 *Op cit*, fn 244.
298 Guy Dehn, quoted in Weale, 2000.
299 See Winfield, 1990.
300 See O'Donnell and Johnstone, 1997, Chapter 2.
301 Guy Dehn, quoted by Shaw and Demetriou, 2000.

CHAPTER 12

OUR PROPERTY IN TRUST: THINGS TO MAKE AND DO

Anne Bottomley

The operation of implied trusts based on 'common intention' continues to receive a bad press from all sides. On the one hand, commentators who espouse certainty and clarity of principle find the whole area a rather ungodly juridical mess[1] and, on the other hand, commentators seeking redress for wronged women have a host of objections to the limitations placed on finding a trust in such a manner.[2]

This chapter will develop an approach which I have introduced before: that there is, in fact, a strong argument to be made, from a feminist perspective, in support of 'common intention' trusts.[3] This argument is based on two elements. First, I want to draw a sharp distinction between broadly seeking economic redress at the end of a relationship and specifically arguing about the parameters of the trust. In terms of redress, it is quite clear that the trust is a poor vehicle.[4] However, too often, the limitations of the implied trust, in these terms, have been counterpoised to the benefits of the so called 'remedial trust' without thinking through the consequences for a claimant who might fall within the existing trust model. Put very simply, the benefit of the present trust formulation is that it carries with it a proprietary claim, a claim that is strong enough to be thought of as a right. This distinguishes it, firmly, from an application to the court for a remedy, the form of which will be in the discretion of the court.[5] To argue that this is a central and determining feature of the trust is, I am well aware, contentious and, therefore, a major section of the chapter will deal with this issue.

The second element of my argument is that 'common intention' is as good a basis as any presently available on which to ground an implied trust obligation. There are both negative and positive elements contained within this statement, which I will begin to explore in this paper. In this context, one of the controversial aspects of my argument will be the linkage I wish to make between intention, rights and property: liberalism revisited?

---

1   See, eg, Gardner, 1993 and 1996; and O'Hagan, 1997.
2   See, eg, Wong, 1999; Lawson, 1996; and Glover and Todd, 1996.
3   Bottomley, 1998.
4   See, eg, Wong, 1999; and Dewar, 1998, p 353, in which he argues that 'ownership thinking might have become a bit of a straight-jacket' and that we should think more functionally in terms of needs.
5   See Ferguson, 1993.

DEVELOPING A STRATEGIC ENGAGEMENT WITH LAW

I have argued elsewhere[6] that a feminist engagement with law should not be limited to a critique of revelation (that is, an examination of the many ways in which law has been brought to bear in constructing particular images of, and roles for, women, and disciplining them in relation to these images and roles), but that it is a necessary function of feminist work continually to seek strategic responses to law which will enhance the position of women. Further, such work enables us to continue to seek, explore and construct images of potential, that is, potential futures, which are not riven by a gendered division more favourable to one sex than the other.[7] All of our engagements with law within these terms are necessarily contingent. It would be wrong, however, to ground this notion of contingency in an explanation which emphasises the limitations and constraints of having to engage with, and through, the legal tools immediately available to us. Nor should we limit ourselves by the argument that we have no finalised programme for the future, no blueprint of the potential we might claim to be working towards. Such an approach is fundamentally wrong: it presumes that it is both possible and desirable to design/achieve a blueprint which can then be utilised as the standard by which all incursions are to be judged and through which all strategies are to be planned. In other words, get the theory (or the political programme) right first and then, only then, begin to engage. Anything less is seen as dangerous skirmishing with no long term objective, no co-ordinated plan, no clear direction. In these terms, the best approach for an academic working with law is simply to continue to be involved in a ground clearing exercise, either the ground clearing of continuing to reveal the perfidy of law in all its many manifestations, or the ground clearing of absenting oneself from the mires of legal doctrine and taking to the heady heights of legal theory. Above the clouds the air is clear, the sun warm, and from this lofty vantage point one sends down a promise that, when the horizons become visible and the terrain mapped, then we will know what it is all about and can take the risk of returning to the mire of the lower lands, because we will have the security of the map and compass of direction.

My starting point is quite different – quite a different act of mapping.[8] It is the contention that we can only construct our maps through a process of

---

6   Bottomley, 2000.

7   This statement is necessarily written very concisely and so omits all the 'howevers', 'buts' and 'notwithstandings'; I should add, however, that I firmly believe that men, within the present regime, reap many benefits but at a great cost to their own potential.

8   'The map does not reproduce an unconscious closed in upon itself; it constructs the unconscious ... The map is open and connectable in all of its dimensions; it is detachable, reversible, susceptible to constant modification ... A map has multiple entryways, as opposed to ... tracing, which always comes back "to the same". The map has to do with performance, whereas ... tracing involves an alleged "competence" ...': Deleuze and Guattari, 1987, p 12.

continual engagement, in which we move between the hills of theory and the lowlands of law and practice as one terrain with many pathways linking the typography together. To engage with law constructively is to become increasingly aware of the need to engage, again constructively, with theory. And through these engagements, we continually re-image, re-imagine our potentials, our potential futures. We revise, we develop, we reconsider and we take, every so often, imaginative leaps. For feminists, the incentive in this approach is our commitment to seeking a better vision for a better world. It is not just that we cannot ignore the very real needs of women now, nor that we cannot stand aside from engagement with law as it continues to develop. It is that the feminist project, in both its manifestation as a scholastic concern with understanding and its political concern with change, can only be developed through such an engagement.

My purpose in this chapter is rather mundane – it is to engage with trusts law through an examination of the beneficiary principle as a context through which to pursue an argument for 'common intention' trusts. This is not to base my argument on possible benefits to individual women, but rather to begin to engage with elements of trusts law as a feminist, by which I mean using tools made available to me through feminist thinking as well as considering the normative and strategic benefits of 'common intention' trusts.

ON FOLDING AND UNFOLDING ...

One of the great problems in teaching and thinking trusts is the traditional pattern of segmenting the subject into a series of 'areas' in which one then concentrates on doctrinal detail, perhaps exploring an issue, or even a theme, in relation to that specific area but rarely standing back and looking at, or for, themes which might underpin the subject more generally. Feminist work has tended, with notable exceptions,[9] to reproduce this tendency by concentrating on those areas which most overtly address 'women's issues', most obviously the implied trust in domestic property. It could, rightly, be argued that the feminist concern with implied trust issues has, as in other areas of law, focused on an area which has been traditionally marginalised. At worst, it was an area subjected to an uncontexed rendition in simple doctrinal terms. At best, the area was one in which there was an evaluation based on policy issues which ignored the gender issues in play. I think that it would now, however, be difficult to write in this area, whether in a paper or in a student text, without taking the gender issues into account, even if feminist work is not directly referred to.

---

9   See, eg, Lim, 1996.

However, conversely, one of the great benefits of designing a course in any particular area of law is that one is able to consider not only the specific foci for lecture and seminar material, but also whether there are any underlying themes which link the material together. This may begin purely as a heuristic exercise but, in practice, what one is developing is a theoretical engagement with the area which might bring fresh insight into an engagement with the specific material: a reconsideration of our intellectual maps, a recognition not merely of the fact that all maps are contingent but, further, that the traditional acts of mapping may well obscure rich potential in the material.[10] Of course, such acts of remapping tend to be very uneven – we all, I am sure, tend to work from those areas we feel most familiar with, have a real sense of engagement with, and then tentatively move out from these points. In practice, this leaves many areas fallow, and, if we engage at all, it tends to be at the level of themes which are overtly visible within those specific areas. We may then reach a point where we turn and realise that there is a certain dissonance between themes we are 'pushing' in certain areas of work and the themes we explore in others.

It is one such scenario that has arisen for me over the last few years which forms part of the background to this chapter. In my teaching on implied trusts I argue that it is important, at this point in time, to hold to one element of the present jurisprudence of the implied trust, namely, that it is centrally a proprietary claim and that this must be firmly distinguished from the related, but clearly distinguishable, trope of equitable remedies. However, in another major section of my trusts course, I use the theme of the major changes in, indeed challenges to, the notion of the 'beneficiary principle', and I have been particularly interested in what could be characterised as the loosening up of the proprietary aspect of the beneficiary principle. It became increasingly apparent to me, as I explored and pushed these themes forward, that there seemed a disjuncture in my approach. Given the traditions of the subject area, I could simply continue with these two tropes as unrelated to each other, not needing to find an account which brings them into any kind of relation to each other. However, to avoid such an encounter would, I believe, be wrong.

---

10 This form of engagement has to be very sharply differentiated from the more orthodox act of mapping legal material, in which the author presents himself as seeking the underlying rationale for the area of law; that is, an attempt to 'uncover' the fundamental (legal) principles upon which doctrinal detail been built. This is no more than the attempt to build a coherent structure within legal discourse, holding together disparate elements by finding, either through evocations of historical origin or 'heroic acts of reification', underlying rationality. It can be thought of as a parallel to the attempt to achieve and present unitary subjectivity, and has its heritage in a seemingly scientific mode of engagement with empirical material by means of classification of objects, as well as the search for the underlying forms and principles of movement. In fact, it is probably better to recognise this as an essentially aesthetic project, the appeal of the beauty of it being in constructing a pleasing shape from the many parts, and a masculinist project in that it emphasises the power of control over what would otherwise by unruly, unboundaried, fluid elements, speaking seepage rather than containment. See, further, Bottomley, 1996.

It is necessary to context feminist work as far as we can – by this I mean that we have to resist any temptation to remain within those areas that are overtly concerned with 'women's issues'. One obvious reason for this is the need to situate our strategic incursions as carefully as possible, within a frame which can allow us to draw similarities as well as extenuate difference. But there is also a factor we all take for granted but rarely closely examine – that is, that we are teachers/scholars of trusts law as well as feminists. The question is to what extent, and in what ways, our feminism informs our approach to trusts law *per se*, as well as the extent to which our understanding of trusts law informs our project as feminists. In this sense, I am interested in pushing a feminist analysis beyond a concern with simply those areas which overtly seem 'women's issues' and thinking more broadly about a feminist approach to the subject overall.

There are a number of reasons why it is important for me, at this juncture, to emphasise approaching a subject more broadly, rather than concentrating on those areas which overtly pertain to women's issues. We need to avoid conflating work on one specific area with presumptions that this is indicative of the subject area as a whole without further, careful, inquiry. I make this point because I am concerned that too much feminist analysis to date, although not particularly in this subject area, has been prone to a kind of reasoning-out process, a globalisation of the kind which suggests here is one example, therefore this critique is true in general of this area of law, and even of law *per se*.[11] In relation to this specific area of law, we have to avoid and challenge statements made too sweepingly about equity, and specifically the use of the trust, as being a 'good' thing for women, or a 'bad' thing: it is rather a question of what use has been made of the processes of law and with what impact in any particular area at any particular time.[12] Further, it is now well established that feminist scholarship can, indeed should, go beyond a concern with how a particular subject immediately impacts upon women.[13] Feminists have, along with other critical scholars, examined basic epistemological questions concerning the construction of knowledge. In this sense, how trusts law is perceived and written is a fundamental question for feminists to address. Which then returns us to the feminist project, in which a critique of power, matched with a commitment to change, has to be played through a continual reassessment of strategies and normative values. It is not, then, simply what the law has said about women, or the impact it has had on women, but rather a feminist reassessment of the way in which we think and use law, its potential as much as its limitations, as part of the delivery of the feminist project for a better world.

---

11   See, further, Bottomley, 2000.

12   See, eg, Stretton, 1998 (especially his careful reviews of Cioni, Springer *et al* in Chapters 1 and 2) and Pottage, 1998.

13   See, eg, Richardson and Sandland, 2000.

At one level, my primary question is: within the context of emerging patterns in contemporary trusts law in this country, what is the potential for arguing, from a feminist perspective, for 'common intention' trusts? As a strategic issue, this is a shift from simply thinking about what it delivers, or does not, for women now, to a concern with how far it can be utilised to express our concerns, as feminists, with how women, as subjects, are constituted and presented through legal discourse. However, at another level, what has to be recognised is that any analysis of 'emerging patterns in contemporary trusts law' and, therefore, the extent to which there is any potential in addressing the primary question, is utterly dependent on *how* trusts law is portrayed, how stories of trusts law are told. Thus, my question about common intention trusts, and the sense of dissonance which I experienced between two sections of my course, becomes framed in this chapter through an exploration of *how* certain stories in and of trusts law have been constructed and received. I am not concerned with finding the *right* story, the truest account, but rather with examining the impact of different renditions of the law.

To give one example from my own story so far. Having experienced a strong sense of dissonance between two sections of my course, I could then take the approach of trying to silence that dissonance in order to try and achieve one grand melodic picture. I could, for instance, decide that 'common intention' trusts hold little prospect for feminists, because the central feature of them which attracts me, the proprietary right, is not only being challenged in other areas of trusts law, but could clearly be viewed as an unnecessary inhibition on useful developments in these other areas. Such an account would, however, be based on two premises. First, that trusts law is, or should be, a unitary whole in which doctrinal change in one area necessarily impacts on another. It would, clearly, be wrong not to see this very real possibility, but, equally, it would be wrong to presume it. The question is well posed by Moffat,[14] when he asks about the extent to which trusts law is fragmented or is held together by a core of basic principles. The reality, as he concludes, is that it is a field of law in which there is a continual tension between fragmentation and (re-)assessment of core or basic principles which construct and inform the thing we call a trust. But this brings me to the second premise, which is really the compulsion to want to bring order to things; to want everything to fit, neatly. For the overall structure to be harmonious, a melody with a reassuring resonance which suggests coherence and clarity. The best way to achieve this is not by simply finding themes, but by revealing underlying principles. 'Principles' suggest structure, secure foundations upon which we can build and through which we can locate the detail of doctrine. This is more than facilitative: it is a project which is about control, the need to control unruly knowledge, the unruly, untidy potential within law. The project

14 Moffat, 1993.

is necessary, it is a crucial aspect of containment as well as potential, but it is the power of the project, the way in which it can be used, and the effects it produces, which is important.[15] It is about the way in which we construct and use our understanding of law, the way in which we tell the stories of law. Thus, rather than simply trying to smooth out the dissonance, it is important to be sensitive to the dissonance, to explore it. The object of this chapter is, then, to approach my primary question, in relation to 'common intention' trusts, through an examination of the ways in which narratives of trust law are constructed; in particular, narratives of the 'beneficiary principle'.

There are two major sections to the chapter – in the first, I will consider the beneficiary principle, and in the second, I will reconsider my argument in relation to common intention implied trusts. Finally, as a consequence of these two sections, I shall conclude by returning to the idea of strategic incursions into the use of law, or rather, in this context, work with certain legal 'principles'.

I think of the two major sections of the chapter as 'surfaces'. By using the term 'surface', I am not suggesting that they are surfaces of an object which has some internality to it, some underlying *primum mobile*, of which each of these surfaces is simply a manifestation, I am using the term in quite a different sense. I am using Deleuze's figuration of surfaces brought into relation to each other through acts of folding, unfolding and refolding. In this image, there are no operative principles of external/internal: quite the contrary, the surfaces are the 'reality' we are operating with; the surfaces may have different densities and depths, and by talking of surfaces we are not, necessarily, invoking any image of continuity, all we are enabling is an image of bringing together surfaces, allowing them to touch before we unfold them again. It is a very malleable, tactile image, which helps me visualise how I want to approach this particular exercise.[16]

It will, I hope, be obvious by now, that I am purposely using a series of images which draw on the senses, oral, visual, tactile, etc, to invoke a sense of embodiment as a counter to the dominant traditions of scholarship.[17] The figuration of the fold can be understood, in this context, as one way of imaging narrative structures which challenge the dominant scholastic model of lineal narratives, but I shall also use it, in this chapter, to interrogate the models which are employed, or lie behind, current renditions of trusts law and, in particular, the beneficiary principle.

---

15 *Op cit*, fn 10, and note imagery used by Hackney, 1987, p 2, when visualising the potential excitement of studying the subject: 'The rewards, if reaped, can be immense. The student becomes the hunter, not the hunted. As the sense of participation increases, so does the pleasure; and with the pleasure comes more motivation, skill and technical mastery; with skill, more pleasure ...'

16 Deleuze, 1992. See an excellent commentary by Badiou, 1994.

17 See, eg, Bottomley, 2001, forthcoming.

FIRST SURFACE

Remembering

What is the nature of the beneficiary's interest?

At one level, the debate is so hackneyed that it is hardly worth recalling – and yet the history does open up some interesting issues. Austin, following through the project of organising the law into neat categories, attempted to use the civilian distinction, between rights *in personam* and rights *in rem*, as one system of his classification of law and declared beneficial rights to be *in rem*, that is, in the property itself, the trust fund. Maitland, very robustly, said that Austin had got it wrong, not, that is, the system of classification, but rather, where he placed the beneficiaries' rights: to Maitland, on the basis of his historical material, they were clearly *in personam*, being rights derived from the beneficiaries' rights against the trustees, and not, historically, from any specific rights in relation to the fund. However, Maitland, whilst still holding to the classification system, and insisting on the specificity of the origin of the beneficial interest, could also be very pragmatic, the right may be in analytical juridical terms personal, but: '... has been so treated that it has come to look like a true proprietary right.'[18] And:

> I believe that for the ordinary thought of an Englishman 'equitable ownership'
> is just ownership pure and simple ... so many people are bound to respect
> these rights that practically they are almost as valuable as if they were
> *dominium.*[19]

Despite the reference to 'ordinary thought of an Englishman', Maitland is not here referring to 'ordinary respect' which makes these rights 'almost as valuable', he is referring to the extensive doctrinal framework which creates such an effect, a framework which might be read as presuming such an origin. Like Austin before him, and with the full impact of Darwinian thinking behind him, he had to make each element fit within a classificatory frame. But does one try to classify through appearance or through origin? By emphasising the latter, Maitland was able to maintain an integrity for equity,

---

18 Maitland, 1936, p 115.

19 Maitland, 1911, p 349. The respect he is referring to means 'in law'. It should also be noted that this is taken from a paper addressed to civilian lawyers. As with such scholars as Dicey, Maitland tended to tailor his image of English law very much to the audience he was addressing. Thus, when addressing an English audience, he may well utilise Roman law to enhance his project of categorisation of law, whilst to a civilian audience he was keen to emphasise the uniqueness of the English. In this paper, p 322, he says: 'It is a big affair our Trust. Anyone who wishes to know England, even though he has no care for the detail of Private Law, should know a little of our trust.' And, p 325, when addressing the expectations of a civilian audience as to the efficacy of classification: 'The technical concepts with which the English lawyer will have to operate, the tools of his trade (so to speak), are of a different kind.'

equity was about actions *in personam*. The whole of equity. Then, lawyer as he was, he had to reconcile his system of classification with his knowledge of 'appearances', doctrinal reality; he did this by saying not that it was wrong, but rather, it has come to be seen this way. By attempting to recognise the pragmatic as well as the pure, he tried to have it both ways. What never occurred to him was to challenge the classification system *per se*:

> [I]t is arguable that these terms had only limited value for the civil lawyer, but in the common law they are capable of actually frustrating constructive thought by leading thinkers into mazes of intellectual aridity.[20]

Equally forcefully:

> [T]he analysis ... has treated a very complex aggregate of legal relations as though it were a simple thing, a unit. The result is no more enlightening than it would be were a chemist to treat an extraordinary complex chemical compound as if it were an element.[21]

Martin, having briefly reviewed the debate, and emphasising that equitable rights are indeed *in personam*, then, rather lamely I think, says: '[P]erhaps the better view is that the beneficiary's interest is *sui generis*.'[22]

This can, again, confirm the classificatory system (and that great father of modern equity – Maitland), whilst finding a way out of having finally to classify the interest behind the trust. Moffat, unsurprisingly, brings to the debate a much more astute historical sensitivity:

> Equity's initial view of a beneficiary's interest was that it amounted to nothing more than a right to compel the trustee to perform the trust or make good any loss arising from breach of trust – very much a right in personam. Subsequent developments extended the scope of this right to the extent that it became enforceable against everyone except the *bona fide* purchaser for value.[23]

This again confirms Maitland, in terms of origin, but without being overly restricted in terms of having to try and fit the present form within the classificatory system. It makes quite clear that we are concerned with an emerging and mutating form which, by implication, cannot be, should not be, pressed into a binary pattern of 'limited value'. Whilst I have some sympathy with Martin's view that it may be better to think of it as sui generis, the importance of Moffat is that he requires us to think more carefully about the nature of the interest rather than simply slipping into a descriptive account of what it is now.

However, what is interesting is the extent to which both contemporary judges and textbook writers are willing to speak quite categorically about the nature of the interest as 'proprietary'. Lord Browne-Wilkinson in *Westdeutsche Landesbank*:

---

20   Waters, 1967, p 223.
21   See the reference to Cook, quoted in Moffat, 1999, p 191.
22   Martin, 1997, p 19.
23   Moffat, 1999, p 191.

Once a trust is established, as from the date of its establishment the beneficiary has, in equity, a proprietary interest in the trust property, which trust interest will be enforceable in equity against any subsequent holder of the property ... other than a purchaser for value of the legal interest without notice.[24]

This classic statement of the law is not only robust, but also holds within it one of the central definitional issues. The suggestion is that it is because of the proprietary right that the beneficiaries' claims are enforced, but one can equally assert that it is because claims are enforceable against third parties that they come to be seen as proprietary. Thus, Latham argues that, although the interest a beneficiary holds is, of essence, only rights against trustees in relation to the administration of the fund, these rights can become 'attach[ed] ... to specific trust assets', particularly where there are 'problems of social and economic importance involved'.[25] Waters tries to image the nature of the interest as 'something like shot-silk',[26] which weaves together remedial threads with threads of a material interest. He argues that, at times, it is better 'to look at the substantive side of the matter'[27] rather than retain the purity of insisting on the only ownership right being in a chose in action.

Pearce and Stevens say that: '... despite some historical debate, the better view is that beneficiaries are ... entitled to proprietary rights in the trust property.'[28] This 'better view' becomes quite definitive later in their book:

[S]ince a trust creates a proprietary interest in favour of the beneficiaries, it is a cardinal principle that it must have beneficiaries who are capable of owning property and enforcing the trust.[29]

Thus, it could be argued that, at one level, despite its chequered history, the beneficiary principle, rather like the equitable maxims, has become so seemingly entrenched, naturalised, in trusts law that only the barest of citations is necessary to support the contention of its status as a 'cardinal principle'. However, even a brief glance at history suggests a much more fragile status for this 'cardinal principle'. This raises three interesting questions. First, why attempt to render strength to such a fragile 'principle'?

---

24 *Westdeutsche Landesbank Girozentrale v Islington BC* [1996] AC 699, p 705. Of course, given that the whole focus of the case was on the proprietary remedy, it is not surprising that such a rigorous account of the law was given. Lord Browne-Wilkinson's decision not to extend the parameters, and therefore the potential consequences, of the resulting trust was focused on the impact it could have on third party rights. Note (p 716) he is much less concerned about the development of a 'remedial constructive trust' 'in some future case when the point is directly in issue'. His reasoning is clear (if doctrinally confused): although this would be a 'proprietary restitutionary remed(y)', it would be 'tailored to the circumstances of the particular case' in that the restitutionary defences would be available and 'innocent third parties would not be prejudiced'.

25 Latham (later aka Korah), 1954, pp 521 and 544 respectively.

26 Waters, 1967, p 274.

27 *Ibid*, p 275.

28 Pearce and Stevens, 1998, p 116.

29 *Ibid*, p 341.

To begin to find an answer to that question leads to the second question: what effect has such an attempt had? Thirdly, presuming, for the moment, that effects have been usefully gained from such a rendition, how has this rendition of strength been constructed?

At this point, it is worth recalling Maitland's concern to classify law into rights *in personam* and rights *in rem*. However much we may doubt the validity, or usefulness, of trying to use this particular system of classification in English law, Maitland reminds us of a fundamental tension in the way in which we perceive the law of equity and trusts. Are trusts best categorised as a subset of equity or as a subset of property? This tension is beautifully revealed in Hudson's book[30] in which he, on the one hand, declares the trust to be simply a property holding device and, on the other hand, insists that equity is, necessarily, only about rights *in personam*. It is no wonder that Martin concludes that the beneficial interest is *sui generis*, because this is the only way to avoid what seems to be a fundamental conflict. The need for everything to fit, to find basic principles which define the area, hold it together and differentiate it from related areas, remains a concern for scholars, and not simply because of the heritage of Maitland. In contemporary terms, many courses have now given up on equity and placed trusts firmly within property. Given that many equity and trust courses, and most books, had given so much space to trusts and so little to other aspects of equity, this has been an understandable development. But the consequences of trying to 'fit' trusts into equity, or trusts into property, are the same. They suppress the important and useful tensions which are only revealed when, as in a Venn diagram, we accept that trusts straddle both areas, are neither finally contained nor confirmed in either, partake of both and equally have a constitutive effect in both. It is not enough to try and suppress the tensions by saying that the beneficiary principle is *sui generis*, the tensions have to be unfolded and examined. However, within the context of the overall tension between equity and property, there might lie one clue as to why the principle has been given a cardinal status. This might be an act of suppression of dissonance, rather as attack is argued as the best form of defence, a different strategy from the *sui generis* route but having, at one level at least, the same effect. How is such an effect to be achieved?

On the construction of principles

Let me suggest the image of a stool. The beneficiary principle has come down to us, like so many of its counterparts, as a series of legs which are presumed to be held together by their overall function of maintaining a seat. The seat clearly needs the legs to support it and loosening even one leg weakens the

---

30 Hudson, 1999.

overall structure – but, crucially, we make the presumption that, not only does the seat require all the legs it seems to have, but also that the legs only achieve their integrity by reference to the seat and thereby their functional value in relation to the other legs. Without either seat or other legs, they are mere sticks. By binding sticks together and adding the seat, we transform each stick into a leg. Each part is enhanced, transformed, by becoming a part of the greater sum, the stool.

The beneficiary principle has three distinctive legs, which lead to, become, a stool (or chair, or whatever). Each leg not only supports the other, but also, by being placed in relation to the other, itself becomes stronger. Hence, the rendition of the principle is usually given in three parts,[31] each part strengthened by reference to the other parts.

First leg

There must be objects.[32] This trite rule is introduced early on in a trusts course and given, usually, two rationales for its existence: (1) if there are no objects, who will enforce the trust obligations?; (2) if there are no objects, who will 'own' the trust property?

The first may well echo Maitland's contention that this is the essence of the beneficiary principle as a right *in personam*, but it does so with an interesting functional twist. Without objects (who have the right to enforce the trust), who else could argue that they have the *locus standi* to call the trustees to account? This quickly becomes a rhetorical gesture which points at the absence of other persons with such rights, or indeed interests, in enforcing the trust. Of course, the answer to that can simply be found in a pragmatic solution – either nominate a functionary who takes on this role (as had to be found with charities and, latterly, pensions trusts, and has been developed in many jurisdictions with 'protector trusts'), or develop a rather broader principle of 'interested parties' (inclusive of beneficiaries, but not limited to them) and give them the *locus standi* to appeal to a far more active and interventionist

---

31 I have followed the classical way in which the average law student on the average trusts course will be led through the law of trusts.

32 Unless, of course, the trust is charitable, or one of the accepted exceptions defined as 'purpose' trusts, of which more later! Usually cited authority is *Morice v Bishop of Durham* (1804) 9 Ves Jr 399, although, as Moffat, 1999, p 195, points out, there was not overwhelming support for the principle established in this case, and the 19th century also produced contrary authority. It is important to remember that the principle of binding precedent was not established until late in that century. See Penner, 1998, pp 210–16, for an interesting résumé of trusts established, and upheld, in the 19th century for the specific purpose of maintaining relatives and dependants. The better view is to locate the strength, in modern jurisprudence, of this rule by its reassertion in *Re Astor's Settlement Trusts* [1952] Ch 534 and to remember that this case derives from a period of high rule formalism, a period of orthodox (re)entrenchment, which can be contrasted to the more flexible, pragmatic decisions of the 1970s (enabled in part by the House of Lords' decision, in 1966, that it was no longer bound by its own precedents).

court, a potential juridical development pre-figured in such cases as *Scott v National Trust*.[33]

It is quite clear, then, that on the first count, an answer can be found. Beneficiaries might be the obvious bearers of the principle of enforcement, but they are not necessarily the only ones. This, then, leads to the second count – you still need someone to 'own' the fund. This particular point of ownership is, of course, rather problematic when placed alongside Maitland's insistence that, to think in terms of *in rem* rights is wrong. We can accept his point that, pragmatically, we think of the beneficiaries as owners, but this is rather different. This is an insistence that without 'owners' there can be no trust fund and, therefore, no trust. It has been suggested by some authors that this is best understood as trusts law having to deal with the insistence of property lawyers that there is an 'owner' to any piece of property.[34] However, at this point I am more interested in how the trusts lawyer, in student texts, deals with the issue of objects as owners and the necessary corollary that ownership (of a trust fund) without objects is an impossibility.

The presumption of the object/ownership coupling is made and reinforced by reference to another leg of the stool: the much cited, but rarely closely examined, case of *Saunders v Vautier*.[35]

Second leg

This is the right of beneficiaries who are of full age and capacity (and if more than one, all acting together) to insist on the performance of the trust by having legal title to the fund transferred to them in law.[36] In the sense that equity presumes that what should be done or can be done, has been done, the beneficiaries are already, before such a transfer, 'owners' in equity of the fund.[37] However, in a circular account, this sometimes becomes rendered as a narrative in which their right to have the property transferred at law is simply a consequence of their ownership rights in equity. Whichever point on the circle one enters, or whichever informing narrative one uses, the consequences are the same: these are the owners of the fund and without them, there will be no ownership of the fund.

The strong story line which takes as its origin *Saunders v Vautier*[38] feeds a number of important related benefits for beneficiaries, most notably rights in

---

33 [1998] 2 All ER 705.

34 Harris, 1971, p 47, says that it is 'distilled dogma' that 'ownership must be located somewhere'.

35 (1841) 4 Beav 115, affirmed Cr and Ph 240.

36 That is, if their rights in the fund are in capital rather than in income, in the latter case they may, by an extension of this principle, take control over the income.

37 Except, of course, that such rights are subject to the protection given to 'equity's darling'.

38 Although Penner asserts that the 'principle is actually of much longer standing'. See Penner, 1998, p 41.

relation to variation of a trust document and access to trust documentation deemed to be part of the property of the trust fund. As each of these juridical developments feeds from the basic principle, so that original principle becomes more deeply entrenched in, and through, a series of interwoven narratives. So, as the stool seems to be dependent for its effective functioning on all its legs, to use another metaphor, the threads become woven into what appears to be a seamless cloth. However, one does have to wonder how such a 'little' case as *Saunders v Vautier* became elevated to such canonical status. When looked at closely, both the facts of, and the judgment in, the case are much more limited than later history might suggest.

The beneficiary in *Saunders v Vautier* had a vested interest in the fund, which was held under a direction to the trustees to postpone payment (capital as well as income accumulated from dividends during the operation of the trust), but not under the condition that the beneficiary only receive the fund upon reaching the age specified, which was 25. On reaching majority (21), the beneficiary's application that the trust be brought to an end and the moneys transferred to himself, was accepted by the court and could be sustained (just) on technical arguments based on the construction of this particular trust document.[39] Why did such a 'small' case become such a big deal? Moffat suggests, and I think that he is right, that the case became a hook on which to hang one element of a much bigger narrative, the concern with the settlor's power, the 'dead hand of history', and keeping as much capital on the market as possible rather than tied up in trusts:[40]

> The decisions [which followed *Saunders v Vautier*] may ... have been influenced by a 19th century feeling that capital should be 'active', that is, freely available for entrepreneurial use beyond the limits possible for trustee investment. That the rule is the product of a doctrine of free alienability, and not a fundamental prerequisite of a law of trusts, is demonstrated by the diametrically opposite approach of the American courts.[41]

The development of the 'rule', which became a principle, from such small beginnings, can then be seen as a pragmatic exercise in response to broader socio-economic concerns. It also became a useful tool by which to counter one narrative (the power of the settlor) with another (the rights of the beneficiary). Thus Harris, over a century later, was able to write: '... fidelity to the settlor's intention ends where equitable property begins.'[42]

Later extended into the whole gamut of variation exercises, again for very pragmatic reasons, usually fiscal, this leg of the stool reinforces (if not, in fact of origin, constructs) the overall claim to a proprietary interest. Further,

---

39 See Chesterman, 1984.

40 Interestingly, the fund in *Saunders v Vautier* was held in East India stock.

41 Moffat, 1999, p 252.

42 Harris, 1975, p 2.

because of the context of its origin, it begins to sound very 'absolutist'. It needs to in order to offer a narrative of countervailing force to the rights of the settlor, to deal with his property as he wishes:

> Absolute dominion is paradoxical at the core. The freedom to do anything one likes with property implies the freedom to create restraints upon it, and thus to bind one's own hands or the hands of one's transferees. In the early modern period, perhaps the most severe form of the paradox was that of intergenerational constraints, the problem of the 'dead hand' ... the famous protracted struggle between common law and equity over which parties must be constrained to protect the freedom of others.[43]

This, then, reflects not only a pragmatic element, but an ideological one too – the construction of a narrative which both feeds from, and back into, the all too compelling trope of 'ownership' and 'property' as absolute values. As property had become focused on ownership of the 'thing', so also had the 'trust' moved from being a relationship between the parties to being focused on the ownership of the fund.[44] However, as Cotterrell points out in relation to other developments in trusts law, rather than seeing this as a lineal development in which one form replaces another, it is better to see it as, at most, a displacement. Probably more accurately, it is a layering effect, a series of accretions, in which the previous forms continue, albeit now in association with the emergent forms.[45] Thus, the notion of 'relations' between parties, whether in land law or in trusts law, remains an important informing idea. They are a continued presence available to be reasserted against a focus on the 'thing' itself, as holding the defining characteristic of property or ownership of the fund, as being the defining characteristic of the trust.

Third leg

The third leg really returns us to the first leg of the stool – in fact, it could be argued that it is wrong to figure it as a leg at all. Its function is simply to support the other legs rather than have any claim to leg status in its own right! But, as a support, and latterly a much weakened one, its functional status is aptly caught by my imaginary stool. This leg is the much fondly embraced (by students, at least!) notion of the 'certainty' rule in relation to objects. The history of the need for 'certainty of objects' is narrated as a requirement arising from both a protective element for trustees (and courts) in fulfilling their obligations within the terms of the trust and so that the

---

43 Gordon, 1996, p 102.

44 Neil Jones sees this development at a much earlier stage in the history of the trust: 'Trusts: practice and doctrine, 1536–1660', 1994, unpublished Cambridge PhD thesis. I am not disagreeing with this: I am simply suggesting that this movement is finally played out in the 19th century through the development of the notion of beneficial proprietary rights.

45 Cotterrell, 1993.

beneficiary(ies)/owner(s) can enforce their rights in relation to the fund. The story of how this simple idea became so confused is well known, and in modern law hinges on the case of *McPhail v Doulton*.[46] This case involved a pension scheme set up by employers in which: '... the trustees shall apply the net income of the fund in making at their absolute discretion grants to or for the benefit of any of the officers and employees or ex-officers or ex-employees of the company or any relatives or dependants of such persons in such amounts at such times and on such conditions (if any) as they think fit.' To refuse to uphold this instrument would have meant not only the collapse of this pension fund, but would have put into jeopardy many other such funds. A pragmatic response was called for: the terms of the trust could simply not meet the then rule that certainty of objects could only be met by being able to draw up a complete list of objects. Goff J, at first instance, took the route of declaring that this was not a trust at all, but a mere power, and therefore could be upheld.[47] The House of Lords, in an era of pragmatic law reform, took on the issue headlong. This was a trust. Although there would be clear problems in relation to how to deal with the issue of court enforcement of such provisions (should they arise), in other words, how to operate the beneficiary principle in terms of ownership of the fund, '[I] prefer not to suppose that the great masters of equity, if faced with the modern trust for employees, would have failed to adopt their creation to its practical and commercial character'.[48]

It could be done by either asserting that equity is equality and having all within the class given an equal amount, or by the courts being willing to adopt a more flexible approach, as required of the trustees. All that the court required, as did the trustees, was sufficient certainty as to who was within the class or not (as well as sufficient clarity in relation to the settlor's intention). Thus, the majority of the House of Lords felt able to extend the test for certainty of objects, and in so doing could reinforce the fiduciary obligations of the officers of the fund and the intention of the settlor, as well as signalling their own willingness to become more pro-active if called upon to enforce the trust.

The decision was clearly pragmatic, and much mileage has been made of the subsequent doctrinal 'fall-out'. It could be said that strong policy reasons and weak doctrinal reasoning was made possible by recourse to the centrality of 'settlor's intention' to trusts law and the consequent reasoning that the use of the trust form should not be over-constrained by doctrinal limitations which had been formed within quite a different context, the rationale for which was now not so much their efficacy, as their status as precedent. This was a period of willingness to 'rethink' the contemporary relevance of legal principles and, within the context of trusts law, a period of emphasising the

---

46 [1970] 2 All ER 228.
47 [1967] 1 WLR 1457.
48 *Per* Lord Wilberforce, p 242.

freedom of the settlor rather than being constrained by orthodoxy.[49] However, in this instance, the interesting paradox was that, in upholding the trust and therefore the expectations of the beneficiaries, the strong narrative of beneficial entitlement in the property of the fund had to be weakened. Under such a large discretionary trust, the full force of the proprietary element of the beneficiary principle had to be recast. It was necessary, now, to untangle, unfold, what had seemed to become one strong narrative and find the different narrative structures. Clearly, *Saunders v Vautier* had to be reworked: in such discretionary trusts, how could any one member of the class claim a right to have property vested in them? Could, however, the class act as a collective in order to enforce their rights to the property? One answer came via Inland Revenue cases, in which the court, in a protective move for the class who might benefit and whom the revenue wanted to tax, decided that, for revenue purposes, neither an individual in the class nor the class as a whole could be taxed.[50] The consequence of this protective stance was received back into trusts law as evidence that, in relation to discretionary trusts, any proprietary interest the beneficiaries might have was, at best, inchoate.[51] However, what could not be denied was that beneficiaries had a right to be properly considered by the trustees and a cause of action in turning to the courts to make sure that the fund was duly and properly administered and distributed. One could think of this as a property right, or perhaps as what remained of the greater sense of ownership of the fund itself. It is clearly easy to think of it as evidence of the proprietary aspect of the beneficiary principle being weakened or stretched. However, equally, one can present it as evidence of both the frailty of the narrative from the beginning or, more correctly, as evidence of the way in which narratives are folded, unfolded and refolded in legal discourse.

Current mutations: of unfolding rather than stretching and weakening

Unfolding requires that we recognise the functional aspect of each element of the beneficiary principle, the context in which it arose and was operationalised, and then ask whether any of these functional aspects is still useful to us (whoever, at this point, the 'us' is!). To be able really to engage with this, we need to kick away the image of the stool, the structure which either stands or falls, and take the much more fluid image of cloth folding and

---

49   See, eg, *Pettitt v Pettitt* [1970] AC 777; and *Gissing v Gissing* [1971] AC 886.

50   *Gartside v IRC* [1968] 1 All ER 121.

51   *Sainsbury v IRC* [1970] Ch 712, but it is emphasised in many texts that *Saunders v Vautier* (1841) 4 Beav 115 still applies in relation to discretionary trusts as long, of course, as all the beneficiaries act together. In relation to large discretionary trusts, it would be interesting to see this actually happening!

unfolding as the apposite figuration. As in land law, the stool supported by the legs of the doctrine of conversion, the trust for sale and over-reaching seemed to have become one inextricably linked (functionally and analytically) object. Case law and then statute (Trusts of Land and Appointment of Trustees Act 1996) unhinged, unfolded, and all that remained was the pragmatic decision to keep over-reaching despite the demise of the other two elements.

This suggests that structural images which seem to construct principles by reference to specific elements of the principles are inherently fraught. The paradox is that, by suggesting that each element is part of a wider whole, the sum total being larger than the sum of the parts, then any weakening of one element threatens the whole structure. Hence, we are led into a rendition of a narrative of first stretching and then weakening the thing that we have come to think of as 'the beneficiary principle'. This narrative is suggested, at one level of reading, in Moffat's approach to the subject.[52] However, such an approach necessarily presumes that, at some point in time, the 'beneficiary principle' was strong and that the stool was a stable object upon which we could sit with no fear of falling. In fact, Moffat himself throws doubt upon this construction of history. Within his text, he not only makes clear the 'uneven' histories of *Saunders v Vautier* (see above, p 269) and *Morice v Bishop of Durham*,[53] but he also reminds us of the 'Maitland debate'. Moffat himself adopts the term *sui generis* to signal the complexities of the proprietary aspect of the principle.[54] Thus, maintaining a reading of the principle, in terms of stretching and weakening, cannot be sustained by an historical account – why, then, continue to partake of a narrative which suggests that this is a useful way to picture legal change?

It could be argued that it is simply a heuristic device to enable students not only to locate 'basic principles', but also to begin to understand the ways in which such principles may impede or enhance certain developments. However, it is then too easy to allow students to presume a basic core of trusts law, from which deviations from are either to be learned as 'exceptions' (and, as we all know, exceptions can be simply manipulated to confirm the basic rule), or 'developments', which it might be best to think of as emerging from the trust form, seemingly using the trust form, but not 'really' trusts at all. This problem was well expressed by Moffat himself in a review article, when he asked whether there was a 'trusts law' or rather a law of 'trusts'.[55]

Is there a basic core which holds the form together? The answer to this, that is, a description of what the basic constituents of the form might be, surely does not depend upon a presumption that the private express trust,

---

52 Moffat, 1999, pp 195ff.
53 (1804) 9 Ves Jr 399. *Op cit*, fn 32.
54 Moffat, 1999, p 192.
55 Moffat, 1993.

developed and used within the family economy over a number of centuries, is necessarily the 'true form'. Simply because so much of the heritage of our jurisprudence addresses this form of trust, and the many issues which arose from this form of trust, it does not mean that we have to presume that this form is the model from which we must necessarily work. Historically, it has been received by us as the dominant model – but does modern jurisprudence require that we continually rework it as the 'true form'?

It is surely better to understand the beneficiary principle as a pliable, malleable field of practices which are to be worked on and with, as one aspect of how we might think and use the 'trust'. In this sense, it is important to return both to the aspect of the need for objects as well as the proprietary aspect. It is really a question of matching narrative strengths with a functional, contextual approach. In relation to the requirement of objects, this must now clearly be in contention. The functional requirements of public interest non-charitable trusts calls for a rereading of *Re Denley*,[56] a more proactive and imaginative approach to issues of enforcement, whether through a statutory base or through developments in case law.[57] The question of any necessary proprietary aspect to the fund (that is, if the beneficiaries are not the owners, can it be possible to have property without ownership vested in it?) has to be directly faced and reasoned, as it has been with the ownership issue in unincorporated associations. None of these 'principles' needs to hold back the proactive development of trusts into areas where a form of co-operation between group members and the need to impose fiduciary obligations on officers makes the trust form an obvious (although not the only) potential vehicle.

However, invoking the image of the 'true trust' against certain developments in the trust form has become an important contemporary issue. Matthews has invoked the 'true trust' model in just such a way. Pointing out that, if the proprietary interest had not developed as a core definition of trust, then we would simply be dealing with a branch of obligations, he says:

> We must see trusts – and the purpose trust in particular – in this light. It is a product serving a commercial need. To some extent, like all law and legal institutions, it is a conjuring trick. It is a way of making another legal institution – ownership – disappear, or half disappear. First it is refracted into legal ownership and beneficial enjoyment, and then beneficial enjoyment seems to disappear into thin air.[58]

The loss of beneficial enjoyment, by which he means ownership, means that this cannot be a true trust. In a series of articles[59] in which he takes issue with

---

56 *Denley's Trust Deed, Re, Holman v H Martyn and Co Ltd* [1969] 1 Ch 326. See Kohler, 1999; and Matthews, 1996.

57 In relation to statutory changes (especially 'protector' trusts), see Moffat, 1999, p 204; and Matthews, 1996.

58 Matthews, 1996, p 31.

59 Matthews, 1997, 1998.

Duckworth, supporting the Cayman Islands' development of STAR trusts (Special Trusts (Alternative Regime)), he invokes the usual tripartite model of the beneficiary principle combining issues of enforcement, enjoyment and *Saunders v Vautier* to argue that this is the basic characteristic of the trust form. Duckworth responds very pragmatically: '[W]e recognise that there are various manifestations of the English trust idea, and we do not describe any of them as anomalous. We are interested in the practical application of the trust idea.'[60]

To what extent it will be decided that the beneficiary principle, especially in its proprietary aspect, does remain fundamental to the trust form we shall have to see. Whether this will be an issue which can be answered in a global way, we shall also have to see. The interests of offshore tax havens may throw up one response, but equally, as we try and reason trusts in relation to civilian law, it may throw up quite a different response.[61] Browne-Wilkinson LJ was quite vehement in his definition of the trust form.[62] We have to recognise that his strong stand was taken in the context of an appeal to the court to extend what they understood to be a resulting trust, in a context in which the argument was specifically designed to benefit one commercial party and which would hold crucial consequences in commercial relations. Invoking a strong statement of trusts law allowed Browne-Wilkinson LJ to draw a line, find a boundary. (Ironically, the sub-plot of Birk's argument, that resulting trusts were actually a species of restitution, would have returned us to the argument invoked by Matthews, that this could have been a branch of obligations if it were not for the proprietary interest.)

Where does this leave us? I think we are left with two crucial points:

(1) That, in trying to pin down the content of the beneficiary principle, we are continually engaged in a series of crucial slippages – between the doctrinal detail of each element, between the way in which each element is used to invoke a general principle which is never 'quite there', and between the policy rationales for each element and the contexts within which those rationales have had a particular resonance.

(2) Therefore, it is better to see the beneficiary principle as a narrative, a story with a number of plots and subplots, but essentially a story through which we can invoke and think through the (power) relations between the characters in the story and the themes which continually play through the relationships of trust. Thus, within trusts law, the beneficiary principle is a narrative which provides a counterbalance to the narrative of 'settlor's intention'. In relation to other legal forms, it is a narrative which allows us

---

60 Duckworth, 1998, p 24.
61 See, eg, Moffat, 1999, p 192.
62 *Op cit*, fn 24.

to ask questions about the possibilities and limitations of the trust form as opposed to other legal institutions. In terms of narrative, it is crucial that the principle is malleable enough to be invoked with strength (through reference to doctrinal detail or history, for instance) when needed as well as marginalised or dismissed (through reference to pragmatic concerns or lack of certainty in history, for instance) when not needed. In this sense, it is an important and continuing reference point, a narrative, which allows for a series of concerns to be spoken (and tests to be applied) when faced with new developments in specific contexts.

The importance is to see its functional aspect, which is very different from saying it 'is' a fundamental principle or 'has been' a fundamental principle: it has been invoked as a fundamental principle when it has been useful. The difficulty we have is that, as with many legal principles, it can be drawn too solidly, become an unnecessary constraint, and then be revealed as not as strong as it looked and therefore rendered as fragile. If we see it, rather, as a functional story, we can ask when and how it still operates usefully.

For instance, although I have characterised, above, Matthews' argument as a rather old fashioned holding to 'true trust' principles, it could well be argued that there is a very ethical motive or concern informing his approach. In one of his papers, I sense a distaste on his part with the use of trusts to further the facilitation of commercial gain and the avoidance of taxation to the extent to which they are being developed off-shore, which 'could truly be said to belong to no one beneficially and which could be slotted into commercial transactions without difficulty'.[63] This approach is taken further in Willoughby, who, when describing 'user friendly trust legislation' refers to it as part of a 'quarter of a century of creative abuse of the trust form'.[64] This continues the theme of using the beneficiary principle as a way of talking about power, in this context not so much power between the parties, but rather the power of the use of law, another aspect to the power of the settlor.

However, Moffat questions how far 'statutory evasions of the Beneficiary Principles do succeed in subverting the purity of the conceptual notion that, under any division of ownership, it must be possible to locate both legal and beneficial ownership'.[65] Thus, we return to not only 'the Principle' in capitals, but also, I think, to a sense (nostalgic?) of preference for 'conceptual purity'. We must recognise that there are a number of factors in play which operate on a reading of the notion of 'principles'. One of these is the role of the text book

---

63 Matthews, 1996, p 28.
64 Willoughby, 1999, p 26. I am grateful to Hilary Lim for drawing this to my attention. See, also, Rendell, 1999.
65 Moffat, 1999, p 204.

writer. It is very difficult for text book writers to break from the canon which dominates the 'text of law'. Their role is to bring together doctrinal detail into a map of chapters which leads the student reader through the area.

One of the most attractive ways to present oneself as a really good map reader/creator is to be able to provide coherence, combining the virtues of a scholar with the promised virtues of law, to be able to locate and use underlying principles as fundamental trig-points on the map. This can cause certain 'principles' to be overwritten, to become too seemingly fixed. Rather than markers to help us find our way around, they become the very terrain. Further, by locating ourselves in relation to these principles, we then want everything to 'fit' as neatly as possible. Those aspects of doctrine or legal development which do not neatly fit, have to be marginalised and neutralised. The more the author tries to take control of the texts of law by producing a text of law, the more the author has to try and suppress dissonance. Thus, in Moffat, the unruly and difficult aspect of trusts in relation to domestic property is held in a separate chapter and written by one of the co-authors of the book. There is a strong argument for this, as there is now with treating pensions in a separate chapter, but there is also a message that something different is going on here and, indeed, the argument leads into the virtues of the remedial trust form.

In Hudson, the material on implied trusts is rather more integrated. However, Hudson's overall theme of trusts being a part of equity and equity being about rights *in personam* sets up the argument, for him, that implied trusts in relation to domestic property should be dealt with as a species of equitable remedies. In the case of both books, using quite different strategies, not only is the conclusion in relation to domestic property the same, but something else is achieved as well: the holding together of core material through basic principles. I recognise that this is a function and a *modus vivendi* of text books which is difficult to avoid. Indeed, one could argue that it is an important function, in that it introduces another narrative to law: the need to try and keep open the possibility of underlying principles, of some coherence to doctrine, just as judges do, must do, in their decisions. This is emerging as a fashionable exercise in texts on equity, in which the subject is being recast as an exercise in a new geography of underlying principles, principles which unify the subject area and which suggest a coherence behind (and sometimes despite) the detail of doctrine: an almost 'back to basics' approach.[66] Whether using historical material and/or comparative material, this emerging trend does meet a certain spirit of the times: the increasingly dominant trope of a constitutionalist approach to legal reasoning in our higher courts. Hudson, rightly, identifies this movement as one in which the courts are more concerned with finding and using 'general principles' in their judgments, but

---

66 See the excellent essay review of Halliwell by Dunn, 1999.

he, like others 'tuned into' this trend, does not investigate what is actually meant by 'principles'.[67] There is a suggestion that they are the structure, often the structure which requires some act of revelation, upon which doctrine is built. But I would suggest that this requires much more careful consideration about the many ways in which the notion of 'principles' are, and can be, used. Is it to be simply another rendition of the idea of doctrine, albeit at a higher level of abstraction, as a set of established, cohesive 'rules'; or rather a more fluid account of narratives and ideas which give expression to the informing concerns of the subject area, a set of ideas through which we can explore the potentials of law? It is surely the role of text book writers to explore these issues. Moffat has made a major contribution to the teaching of trusts by giving context and (readable) history to the subject: now we should go one step further and think about the ideas, the narratives expressed through principle, which are associated with the development of (equity and) trusts law. To think more sharply about underlying patterns is not difficult: the material and the tools are readily available. Yet to do so is to break the pattern of the promise of scholarship in law, that if we dig deeply enough, we will find coherence in doctrine and the fear of scholarship in law; that if we look too closely, we will find none, or rather not enough.

My conclusion is that the beneficiary principle is an important narrative which does not, necessarily, finally define a trust, but helps us think about trusts and about the relations of trust. In certain areas of development it can simply work as a warning to make sure, for instance, that there are proper procedures for enforcement and a reminder that the notion of ownership of the fund is still moot. In other areas, it may well remain as fundamentally important, in a discursive sense, and functional in the effects it produces in particular contexts. It allows us to think about power. What we have to realise, from the above account, is that, as a fixed principle, it is not to be presumed upon. In fact, the paradoxical danger is that, if we render a narrative of general trends in trusts law as one simply of 'weakening' the beneficiary principle, and then add to that a return to the assertion that, as in equity all rights are in personam anyway, then the implied trust, par excellence, is the candidate that is most vulnerable, at this point in time, to being recast as a remedy rather than a right.

---

67 Hudson, 1999. I should add that I do not agree with his particular characterisation of the differences between cases decided in the 1970s and cases decided in the 1990s, but he opens up a very interesting area for analysis and debate.

SECOND SURFACE

The present juridical confusions surrounding the implied trust, paradoxically, in great part arise from the robust attempts made by the judiciary in the past two decades to clarify both the scope of the implied trust and the basic principles upon which the details of rules are grounded. How are we to try and reconcile Lord Bridge's template for what he calls 'constructive trusts'[68] with Lord Browne-Wilkinson's outline[69] of the basic principles of what he calls 'resulting trusts'?[70] Are we to categorise 'common intention' trusts as constructive trusts or, given one reading of the formulation made by both judges, a species of resulting trusts in which 'intention' followed by contribution, or contribution as evidence of 'intention', rather than 'contribution' without an intention to make a gift, is the key index of the presence of a trust? This is not the place to pursue the many formulations which can be gleaned from the present juridical muddle, but it is important to note two things:

(1) At some point, there is going to have to be a decision made, in the courts, as to whether it is possible to formulate and hold together a set of principles, and doctrinal detail, which cover all the contexts in which implied trusts operate.

(2) As part of that account, there is going to have to be another struggle with the extent to which any aspect of the implied trust formulation veers towards a 'remedy'-based formula, rather than a 'rights'-based one. It is probably better to think of this as a continuum – in which those aspects designated as 'resulting' and 'institutionally constructive' will be at the 'rights'-based end, carrying a proprietary aspect, and those designated at the 'constructive trust' end will by seen as remedial, in which any proprietary aspect may be awarded, along with other possible remedies, at the discretion of the court.

The significance of how the area is mapped, therefore, both in terms of nomenclature and basic principles, will be very important. The mapping will determine when and where the narrative of property/right will be sustained and when, conversely, the trust formulation will simply become one option within the overall gamut of equitable remedies.

Meanwhile, it is significant that most textbook writers now locate 'common intention' trusts within a chapter on the family home. Thereby, they avoid the issue of how to integrate the *Rosset* formulation with Lord Browne-Wilkinson's account of the resulting trust, tied, as it is, so closely in his

---

68 In *Lloyds Bank v Rosset* [1991] 1 All ER 107, p 132.
69 In *Westdeutsche Landesbank* [1996] AC 699, p 708.
70 See the very interesting discussion in Hudson, 1999, in Part V.

judgment with an orthodox rendition of rights *in rem*.[71] Focusing on the family home as context does allow the particular issues which arise in this sphere to be examined. It also unhinges 'common intention' trusts from a more mainstream analysis. In so doing it opens up a narrative which leads very neatly from an account of their limitations to the contemporary fashion for looking at the more flexible remedial forms available in other Commonwealth jurisdictions. In such a way, one can only applaud what has been achieved elsewhere and lament the poor state of affairs in this country. For those too cautionary to support one of the Commonwealth approaches, two modes of exit appear attractive. One is to move as close as is possible to a family law model, and the other is simply to call for statutory reform (which may well be the same exit).

What might seem an honourable attempt (and indeed set out to be such) to deal with the specific issues relating to the family home, which would otherwise be lost in a more doctrinally based analysis, seems to me to end up, too often, in a marginalisation which can be very detrimental. The focus shifts from a more standard trusts analysis to one which features the wronged women and addresses the question of how best to attain a remedy for her at the end of a relationship. She becomes a dependant to be protected. What is taken from her is a narrative of rights based on a property claim. Further, it expels the difficulties, confusions and muddles of trying to tie a trust model into a difficult social context and offers the possibility of ridding the body of trusts law of this unruly confusion, this place of difficulty. Pushed to the margins, with the possibility of being pushed over the edge, the family home trust (code for trusts dealing with women's issues) becomes the site by which expulsion will, it is hoped, confirm the purity and doctrinal clarity of 'real' trusts law.[72] Once again, that which is associated with the female, becomes the place on to which the masculinist project of order and containment is projected.[73]

I am not dismissing either the very real doctrinal limitations of the 'common intention' trust,[74] or the very real possibilities of finding other ways of offering economic redress to women at the end of a relationship. What I am saying is that we will lose many advantages offered in the model of the 'common intention' trust if we do not think carefully about the implications of moving too rapidly towards a remedial model.

---

71 See, eg, Moffat, 1999.

72 Dewar, 1998, pp 330–33, identifies this trend, but the sentiment is one I would not associate with him, but rather with authors such as Gardner, 1993; and Hudson, 1999 (despite his final pages!).

73 See, eg, Grosz, 1994, p 203; and Bottomley, 2001.

74 Especially as expressed in *Rosset*, but see later developments as outlined in Bottomley, 1998, pp 207–14; and Bottomley, 1994.

First, by keeping the trust formulation within its rights/property aspect, we partake of a strong narrative in which we come to the court demanding a right rather than requesting a remedy. If we construct narratives around the request for a remedy, we run into two dangers. The first is doctrinal, on what basis are we going to ground our request? The general formula used in such circumstances is either the current family law focus on need, but mitigated by reference to past contributions and detriment, or a mixture of expectations arising from the nature of the marriage-like relationship and contributions made to the economy of the relationship. Both these reference points feed from, and into, an approach which tends to award women in relationships that look most marriage-like and in which the women have played the role of a good and supportive wife figure. The second danger, then, is that we feed into a discourse which, whilst recognising dependency, can only continue to reproduce a model of dependency. The further we move into these realms, the more open we are to a discretionary model in which judges can too easily slip into the prejudices of what is to be expected of a good woman. This is exemplified in Lord Denning's judgment in *Eves v Eves*,[75] which should be remembered as a warning to us all. Denning's approach in *Eves* is as fraught as Lord Bridge's judgment in *Rosset*, when he refused to recognise the contributions made by the wife as anything more than any wife would do.[76]

All these approaches emphasise the social role expected of women. Going in the other direction, the only other obvious alternative, which would maintain a strong proprietary right narrative, is one based on economic exchange. Under the current *Rosset* formulation (in the absence of express agreement), a direct financial contribution to the purchase of the property is the only contribution recognised. Given the reality of many women's financial dependency in domestic relationships, especially when children are involved, this counts for little for many women. Further, one classic counter to this, in which the exchange/contribution model is stretched to include domestic services (and one could even push this to sexual services) simply brings us back to a model based on roles and the expectation that women should perform such roles.

So, my argument is that we have to resist this pressure to be excluded and marginalised, to be cast yet again as 'wives' and mothers in need of the protection of the law, and turn to look more closely at the benefits of the 'common intention' model. In juridical terms, we have already seen, in the cases following *Rosset*, that a sympathetic reading of the ideas of 'common intention' does not have to be so constrained by the spirit of the *Rosset* approach.[77] More importantly, for my purposes at this point, 'common intention' can be used to emphasise an approach which is based on the need

---

75 (1975) 3 All ER 768.

76 See Bottomley, 1993.

77 Bottomley, 1998.

to recognise us as individuals within the context of a familial relationship. It looks not to roles, but rather to our attempts to find our own way of entering into relationships: 'most of us live our lives within a continuum of a relationship which is based on a precarious balance between the need for individuality as well as a need for communality. Thus, we recognise a split subjectivity, ourselves as individuals (however fragile this account may be) and ourselves as related to others.'[78]

Thus, however fragile the account of 'common intention' in practice, it invokes, for me, a strong sense of both the possibility, and the need, to give an account of my self for myself as well as the possibility, and the need, to give an account of myself in relation to significant others. It speaks the need to try and communicate, whilst recognising that, in practice, that is, in the case law, many factors militate against communication. 'Common intention' covers a continuum from the rare parties who have really sat down and talked and planned their legal relations, through to those who have been tricked and misled. It allows for the aspiration of dialogue as well as the reality of power.

It treats us, in the full liberal sense, as citizens. The linkage of the narratives of rights/property/citizenship become available to us. At root, we are drawing on that combination, of such historical and political strength, to construct a demand for recognition. In an important sense, by invoking the rights/property combination, we are invoking a discourse of citizenship. Such an invocation can only be contingent and strategic, most importantly because, essentially, it is an appeal backwards rather than forwards. It is not pushing at new forms, but rather looking back to old ones and demanding inclusion.[79] Why is this important? Because, at the present time, the only immediate alternative is a remedy-based one in which we appeal to the court, in their conscience, to grant us relief.

'WHY WHISTLE THE TUNE WHEN YOU SHOULD BE SINGING?'

I can well imagine that many readers will have read my previous paragraph in horror and disbelief. Not only have I defended the 'common intention' trust by an expansive reading of its possibilities, but also I have done so by invoking the triumvirate of the liberal bogies of rights/property/citizenship.

---

78 Bottomley, 1998, p 225.

79 See Kingdom, 1999, for a useful overview of current debates on citizenship. My point here is simply that, as with the claim to subjectivity (see below), there is no point in vacating an area or idea simply because we have established a thorough critique of its failure to deliver what it seemed to promise, especially when we have reached the point of having some purchase, however fragile, onto it. Whilst the discourse of property/right/citizenship still holds a political sway, then use it, but use it clearsightedly, knowing its weaknesses as well as recognising the power of its allure.

Everything that good feminists (let alone radical critics of law) have tested and found wanting at every level. They do not deliver, they cover continued inequalities and, anyway, they feed from and into discourses of power and individualism which we have struggled against.[80] This paper lacks any good theoretical project, let alone any true radical edge ... it is as if I can hear the cacophony of dismissive rejection. What I can actually hear is one of my, at present, favourite music tracks from the latest Moloko album.[81]

Against a very seductive and persuasive beat, a women's voice begins to wonder whether the man she fancies will want to sleep with her, what he would think and say if she were to tell him and, equally, how he will approach her. She recognises him as a seductive male character who will presume to make all the moves. We then hear him approaching her and, indeed, presuming to seduce her by his words as well as his invitations; come and dance, come and lay down by me. He calls her 'sweet child'.[82] He is so certain that he is in control. She sings what she thinks, he sings what he says to her. They do not sing together, but, as so often in opera, the music rather than the libretto plays the possibilities of the scene, the possible coming together, counterpoised by the lack of a coming together in what is actually sung.[83] We hear him as she hears him. He sings to her, completely failing to see where she is coming from, and yet so invitingly offering her the chance to 'become' through him: 'Why whistle the tune when you should be singing?'

I am reminded so much of Rosi Braidotti's insistence that, at the very same time as knowing, recognising and insisting that the presumption of the unitary subject[84] could no longer be sustained[85] and yet that this form of subjectivity was/is fundamental to philosophy, that, whilst struggling to find pathways to significant transformations in the act of thinking about thinking, we have, for now, to hold to those elements in the construction of subjectivity, and therefore philosophy, which are, at present, enabling to us.[86] In the Deleuzian sense, we have continually to ask, does this help me think my way

---

80 Critical race theory has, of course, recognised the potential strategic value of such an approach but there is still, I believe, a marked reluctance amongst feminists writing within the critical legal 'tradition' to examine the radical potential of this position.

81 'Someone, somewhere', track from *Things To Make and Do*, 2000, London: Echo.

82 There is a possibility, which I recognise, that it may not be simply a gender (ir)relation at play here but also that he might be much older than her and even a 'forbidden' object of desire.

83 See, Clement, 1997.

84 The rational man in intellectual control of his decisions, who could frame choice, intention and responsibility, the key axioms upon which modern law and scholarship are based.

85 As, in Braidotti's view, such a conception requires the most violent acts of repression and denial and the projection onto the feminine of the elements of disorder and muddle which cannot be so contained, and the consequent valorisation of the feminine as the place of danger and desire.

86 Braidotti, 1991. See discussion in Bottomley, 2000.

towards new ways, does this hold a potential? Is this productive? What effect might this have? For Braidotti, it is also very clearly a sense of having reached a point at which we can begin to partake in some of the dominant discursive practices, a point at which we have achieved some sense, however fragile, of a subjectivity, to be told that it no longer exists (sorry, you're too late), or to refuse to see the potential in its strategic, contingent uses (this isn't pure enough for me, its not 'real' and I'm still seeking 'reality'), is to vacate the little purchase we have, as well as to deny any potential value in the tools available to us. For both Braidotti and Deleuze, this is both political and scholastic suicide. We all want to sing, and with our own voice; however, it is through whistling that we may begin to imagine the full potential of that voice. What must be avoided is a search for song which actually results in a very long silence.

So, what tune(s) am I whistling? What song(s) might it begin to invoke? Sometimes the position to take, or rather the approach to take up, is not very grand. To argue in defence of a particular position in law can seem very restrictive: no great imaginative leaps here! But, the position of defending 'common intention' trusts from a feminist perspective is one which not only alerts us to the potential dangers of the all too seemingly attractive alternatives, but also requires that we focus on those aspects of the present narrative structures within law which give us some entry point around which we can begin to think about potential songs. We have increasingly recognised, as feminists, how difficult it is to try and find strategies in law which will be of benefit to all women, given the many and diverse circumstances that women find themselves in. Thus, we have begun, cautiously and unevenly, to approach our work in terms of a broader project: to try and find patterns in the jurisprudence of law which allow us to talk not just of how badly certain, indeed many, women have suffered as a consequence of both present legal forms and practices (including the operation of judicial discretion), or how certain forms and practices might enhance our individual struggles as women, but rather a sense of what we might mean by a feminist politics in relation to law. What kind of legal forms might be conducive to grounding a feminist engagement? What forms and practices might be more malleable, in terms of our commitment as feminists, in trying to find ways of beginning to speak of how we want to relate to each other?

Rendering an account of the genealogy of the 'beneficiary principle' has become important to me for two reasons. First, it is simply, yet again, evidence of the plasticity of law: to trace its development is to understand the very functional contexts in which it arose and operated. It is also to understand that too often, having rendered the history in absolutist terms, that is, in having clothed (shrouded) the history in doctrinal adornment, and thus in removing the figure from the landscape in which it arose and took form, it can become a constraint upon further functional development. But this is the very stuff of law: the constant tension between legal clarity (doctrine or principle) and delivering forms which have socio-economic viability given changes in circumstance. The tensions between principle and pragmatism are continually played through, mediated by the prevailing political sensitivities within legal discursive practices in any one period. Sometimes, rule formalism holds sway; sometimes, a much more pragmatic approach. We now seem to have entered an era in which there is not only a concern to ground doctrine more overtly in principle, but also to be much more concerned with a constitutionalist approach to decision making in the higher courts. We have to be sensitive to these developments and much more grounded in emerging forms and practices, rather than simply critiquing what has already been.

So, secondly, in emphasising fluidity, we become more aware of the ways in which principles and doctrines are enfolded, unfolded and refolded, to (re)produce narratives of legal forms. These narratives, the ways in which a story can be rendered, can be utilised to produce strong or weak renditions. My prediction is that the strong narrative of the 'beneficiary principle' will become recast to allow new forms of trust to develop – ones which are not constrained by a need for objects or by a need to vest ownership of a fund (however tenuously) in the beneficiaries. However, unless and until restitution law does take a real grip on both our jurisprudence and our imagination, holding to certain aspects of the beneficiary principle for certain types of trust will remain important. As I have argued above, it remains an important narrative which reminds, when necessary, of the power relations between the parties to a trust. It functions to produce a counterbalance to the narrative of 'settlor's intention' and helps feed the development of the narrative of the fiduciary obligations of the trustee. Within that context we are faced, as feminists, with two questions: (1) is there still some purchase for us in holding to a trusts formula for dealing with domestic property during and at the end of a relationship? (which is not to deny other forms of claim); and (2) if so, what should be the major characteristics of such a trust?

The trusts formula, in this context, for me, remains attractive whilst it holds not merely the characteristic of fiduciary obligations, but also the characteristic of a right rather than a remedy. That is, it is grounded in a proprietary claim. Recall Water's image of the interest as 'something like shot-silk' and Latham's argument that rights tend to become attached to assets when there are 'problems of social and economic importance' involved.[87] The emphasis, then, is that this is an area in which it is important to keep open the narrative of beneficial interests, to keep open the claim to property as right. Further, to base such a claim, it is better to utilise the narrative of 'intention'

---

87 *Op cit*, fns 25 and 26.

rather than a narrative based on exchange. Intention focuses on individual circumstances, within the context of social circumstances, rather than invoking social roles and/or a philosophy of rights based on principles of exchange (of money or labour, rather than the exchange of promises). Intention is fragile, not merely because of social circumstances, but also because of our recognition of the fraught notion of subjectivity. However, by focusing on 'intention', as with focusing on the notion of responsibility in criminal law, or the notion of equality, we can begin to tease out this fragility as well as begin to consider the potential aspirational values which might be contained in such a notion. We should not think of 'intention' as a simple idea which stands or falls on whether it can be proved in practice, judged by some empirical notion of its sustainability in descriptive terms, but rather as a complex idea which needs to be worked with and through. It has been called a fiction – to which my response is, is it a good fiction to work with?

So, finally, two points to emphasise. Engagement with law is not simply about issues of critique or reform, it is about becoming more sensitive to the processes of legal change and through that beginning to talk about legal forms and practices which may be conducive to feminist thinking. It is not about being absolute – any more than it is about trying to argue that one form will be 'good for women' or not. It is a process of engagement which tries to have something to say now, about law now, as well as beginning to think about future potentials. To emphasise the fluidity of law is not, of course, to suggest that it is totally open, rather it is to counter an approach to law which only speaks of constraints. This is a narrative of potential and engagement, it is not a promise of deep structural change. This narrative moves between instances of constraint and instances of potential. In this context, sensing and using developments in legal discourse, which includes the way in which stories of law are told, is part of a process of accessing the potential of engagement. It is all a process, not an end. Secondly, to whistle is always to consider the possibility of singing. To sing requires that we find voice(s), but learning to whistle well is also difficult. To give up on the resources we have, is, potentially, to neither whistle nor sing. They may not have been 'our' tunes, but what can we do with them?[88]

---

88 With many thanks to the editors of the volume for all their help and useful comments, also to Nathan Moore for all the discussions we had on these issues during the time we taught trusts together. Finally, during a difficult period, my thanks to Sheila and Devan Noonan, Ali Twyford and Bea Bottomley and, as always, to Belinda and Derek Meteyard.

BIBLIOGRAPHY

Ahmed, L, *Women and Gender in Islam*, 1992, New Haven: Yale UP.

Alban-Metcalfe, B and West, M, 'Women managers', in Firth-Cozens, J and West, M (eds), *Women at Work*, 1991, Milton Keynes: Open UP.

Alcorso, C, '"And I'd like to thank my wife ...": gender dynamics and the ethnic "family business"' (1993) 17 Australian Feminist Studies 93.

Aldag, R and Brief, A, *Managing Organisational Behaviour*, 1981, St Paul: West.

Alexander, G, 'The transformation of trusts as a legal category 1800–1914' (1987) 5(2) Law and History Review 303.

Ali, SA, *The Law Relating to Gifts, Trusts and Testamentary Dispositions Among the Mahommedans (According to the Hanafi, Maliki, Shafei and Shiah Schools)*, 1885, Calcutta: Thacker, Spink.

Allen, PH and Reynolds, RG, *Australian Executorship Law and Accounts*, 1942, Sydney: LBC.

Alvesson, M and Willmott, H, *Making Sense of Management: A Critical Introduction*, 1996, London: Sage.

Anderson, S, 'Land law texts and the explanation of 1925' (1984) 37 CLP 63.

Arjava, A, *Women and Law in Late Antiquity*, 1996, Oxford: OUP.

Atherton, R, 'Family and property: a history of testamentary freedom in New South Wales with particular reference to widows and children', 1993, unpublished PhD thesis, University of New South Wales.

Atiyah, PS, *Rise and Fall of Freedom of Contract*, 1979, Oxford: Clarendon.

Atiyah, PS, *Essays on Contract*, 1986, Oxford: Clarendon.

Austin, RP, 'Constructive trusts', in Finn, PD (ed), *Essays in Equity*, 1985, London: Sweet & Maxwell.

Australian Digest 1825–1933, 1940, Sydney: LBC.

Australian Law Reform Commission, *Equality Before the Law: Justice for Women*, 1994, Land Reform Commission, Sydney.

Australian Law Reform Commission, *Equality Before the Law: Women's Equality Report*, 1994, No 69, Part II, Sydney, Commonwealth of Australia.

Avini, A, 'The origins of the modern English trust revisited' (1996) 70 Tulane L Rev 1139.

Badiou, A, 'Gilles Deleuze: the fold: Leibniz and the Baroque', in Boundas, C and Olkowski, D (eds), *Gilles Deleuze and the Theater of Philosophy*, 1994, New York: Routledge.

Baer, G, 'Women and *waqf*: an analysis of the Istanbul tahrir of 1546' (1983) 17 Asian and African Studies 9.

Baer, G, *Studies in the Social History of Modern Egypt*, 1969, Chicago: Chicago UP.

Bailey, JD, *A Hundred Years of Pastoral Banking: A History of the Australian Mercantile Land and Finance Company*, 1966, Oxford: Clarendon.

Baird, J and Bradley, P, 'Styles of management and communication' (1979) 46 Communication Monographs 101.

Baker, JH, *An Introduction to English Legal History*, 3rd edn, 1990, London: Butterworths.

Ballaster, R, Beetham, M, Frazer, E, and Hebron, S, *Women's Worlds: Ideology, Femininity and the Woman's Magazine*, 1991, Basingstoke and London: Macmillan.

Bankton (Lord), *An Institute for the Law of Scotland in Civil Rights; with Observations upon the Agreement or Diversity Between them and the Laws of England*, 1751, Edinburgh.

Barnett, H, *Introduction to Feminist Jurisprudence*, 1998, London: Cavendish Publishing.

Baron, P, 'The free exercise of her will: women and emotionally transmitted debt' (1996) 13 Law in Context 23.

Bartlett, E, 'Beyond either/or: justice and care in the ethics of Albert Camus', in (Browning) Cole, E and Coultrap-McQuin, S (eds), *Explorations in Feminist Ethics: Theory and Practice*, 1992, Indianapolis: Indiana UP.

Bartlett, KT and Kennedy, R (eds), *Feminist Legal Theory: Readings in Law and Gender*, 1991, Boulder: Westview.

Bass, B and Avolio, B, *Shatter the Glass Ceiling*, 1993, Binghamton, NY: State University of NY.

Beard, M, *Women as Force in History*, 1946, New York: Macmillan.

Beatson, J and Friedman, D, *Good Faith and Fault in Contract Law*, 1995, Oxford: OUP.

Becker, G, 'Human capital, effort and the sexual division of labor' (1985) 3 Journal of Labor Economics 33.

Beddoe, D, *Back to Home and Duty: Women Between the Wars 1918–1939*, 1989, London: Pandora.

Belcher, A, 'Gendered company: views of corporate governance at the Institute of Directors' (1997) 5 FLS 57.

Belcher, A, 'A feminist perspective on contract theories from law and economics' (2000) 8 FLS 29.

Bell, GJ, *Principles of the Law of Scotland*, 4th edn, 1839, Edinburgh: T Clark.

Bigwood, R, 'Undue influence: "impaired consent" or "wicked exploitation"' (1996) 16 OJLS 503.

Birks, P, 'Mareva injunctions and third parties' (1999) 62 MLR 539.

Birks, P and Chin NY, 'On the nature of undue influence', in Beatson, J and Friedman, D (eds), *Good Faith and Fault in Contract Law*, 1997, Oxford: Clarendon.

Blackmore, K, 'War, health and warfare', 1994, unpublished doctorate: Macquarie University.

Bodichon, BLS, *Brief Summary, in Plain Language, of the Most Important Laws Concerning Women*, 1854, in Lacey, CA (ed), *Barbara Leigh Smith Bodichon and the Langham Place Group*, 1987, London: Routledge & Kegan Paul.

Bonsall, D, *Securitisation*, 1990, Edinburgh: Butterworths.

Booth, J, 'Man who shopped boss wins £290,000' (2000) *The Times*, 11 July.

Borkowski, A, *Deathbed Gifts*, 1999, London: Blackstone.

Bottomley, A, 'Self and subjectivities: language of claim in property law' (1993) 20 JLS 56.

Bottomley, A, 'Production of a text: *Hammond v Mitchell*' (1994) 2 FLS 83.

Bottomley, A, 'Figures in a landscape: feminist perspectives on law, land and landscape', in Bottomley, A (ed), *Feminist Perspectives on the Foundational Subjects of Law*, 1996, London: Cavendish Publishing.

Bottomley, A, 'Women and trust(s): portraying the family in the gallery of law', in Bright, S and Dewar, J (eds), *Land Law: Themes and Perspectives*, 1998, Oxford: OUP.

Bottomley, A, 'Theory is a process, not an end', in Richardson, J and Sandland, S (eds), *Feminist Perspectives on Law and Theory*, 2000, London: Cavendish Publishing.

Bottomley, A, 'The many appearances of the body in feminist scholarship', in Bainham, A, Richards, M, and Schlater, SD (eds), *Body Lore and Laws*, 2001, Oxford: Hart.

Bowers, J, Mitchell, J and Lewis, J, *Whistleblowing: The New Law*, 1999, London: Sweet & Maxwell.

Braidotti, R, *Patterns of Dissonance*, 1991, Cambridge: Polity.

Brentnall, T, *My Memories*, 1938, Melbourne: Robertson.

Bridges, A, 'History of farm recording 1785–1072', MEC dissertation, University of New England, Armidale.

British Institute of Management Report, *Management Development into the Millennium*, 1994, London: British Institute of Management.

Broad, R and Fleming, S (eds), *Nella Last's War: A Mother's Diary 1939–45*, 1981, London: Falling Wall.

Brockes, E, 'Who dares swindles' (2000) *The Guardian*, 21 June.

Brown, B, 'Contracting out/contracting in: some feminist considerations', in Bottomley, A (ed), *Feminist Perspectives on the Foundational Subjects of Law*, 1996, London: Cavendish Publishing.

Browne, A, 'Lives ruined as NHS leaks patients' notes' (2000) *The Guardian*, 25 June.

Brownsword, R, 'The limits of freedom of contract and the limits of contract theory' (1995) 22 JLS 259.

Brownsword, R, Hird, NJ and Howells, G (eds), *Good Faith in Contract: Concept and Context*, 1999, Aldershot: Ashgate/Dartmouth.

Budd, L and Whimster, S (eds), *Global Finance and Urban Living: A Study of Metropolitan Change*, 1992, London: Routledge.

Bulbeck, C, *Re-Orienting Western Feminisms*, 1998, Cambridge: CUP.

Butt, P, *Land Law*, 1996, Sydney: LBC.

Buxton, R, 'The Human Rights Act and private law' (2000) 116 LQR 48.

Caine, B, *Destined to be Wives, the Sisters of Beatrice Webb*, 1988, Oxford: OUP.

Callinicos, A, *Against Post Modernism: A Marxist Critique*, 1989, Oxford: Polity.

Camilleri, M, 'Lessons in law from literature: a look at the movement and a peer at her jury' (1990) 39 Catholic University L Rev.

Camp, C, 'Openness and accountability in the workplace' (1999) 149 NLJ 46.

Campbell, A, 'Ponting and privilege' (1985) PL 212.

Cannadine, D, *Aspects of Aristocracy*, 1994, New Haven: Yale UP.

Carnegie, GD, 'Pastoral accounting in pre-federation Victoria: a case study of the Jamieson family' (1993) 23 Accounting and Business Research 204.

Carnegie, GD, 'The structure and use of accounting information in pre-federation pastoral management in western districts of Victoria 1836–1900', 1994, Flinders: doctorate thesis.

Carnegie, GD, 'Pastoral accounting in pre-federation Victoria: a contextual analysis of surviving business records' (1995) 8 Accounting Auditing and Accounting Journal 3.

Cattan, H, 'The law of *waqf*', in Khadduir, M and Liebsney, HJ (eds), *Law in the Middle East*, 1955, Richmond: William Byrd.

Caute, D, 'A political trial misfires' (1985) New Socialist 1.

Cavarero, A, *In Spite of Plato: A Feminist Rewriting of Ancient Philosophy*, Anderline- D'Onofrio, S and O'Healy, A (trans), 1995, Cambridge: Polity.

Charity Commission, *Responsibilities of Charity Trustees*, Leaflet CC3, 1999, London: Stationery Office.

Charles, N, 'Food and family ideology', in Jackson, S and Moores, S (eds), *The Politics of Domestic Consumption: Critical Readings*, 1995, Hemel Hempstead: Prentice Hall/Harvester Wheatsheaf.

Chedzoy, A, *A Scandalous Woman, The Story of Caroline Norton*, 1992, London: Allison & Busby.

Chell, E and Baines, S, 'Does gender affect business performance?' (1998) 10 Entrepreneurship and Regional Development 117.

Chesterman, MR, 'Family settlements on trust: landowners and the rising bourgeoisie', in Rubin, G and Sugarman, D (eds), *Law Economy and Society 1750–1914: Essays in the History of English Law*, 1984, Abingdon: Professional.

Chua, WF and Poullaos, C, '"The dynamics of closure" amidst the construction of market, profession, empire and nationhood: an historical analysis of an Australian accounting association 1886–1903' (1998) 23 Accounting Organizations and Society 155.

Cioni, M, *Women and Law in Elizabethan England with Particular Reference to the Court of Chancery*, 1985, New York: Garland.

Clement, C, *Opera and the Undoing of Women*, Wing, B (trans), 1997, London: Tauris.

Clements, L, 'The Human Rights Act – a new equity or a new opiate: reinventing justice or repackaging state control?' (1999) 26 JLS 72.

Collins, J, Gibson, K, Alcorso, C, Castles, S and Tait, D, *A Shop Full of Dreams: Ethnic Small Business in Australia*, 1995, Sydney: Pluto.

Committee on the Financial Aspects of Corporate Governance, *Report and Code of Best Practice*, 1992, London: Gee.

Committee on the Modernization of the Trustee Act, *Report on Trustee Investment Powers*, 1999, Vancouver: British Columbia Law Institute.

Conaghan, J, 'Enhancing civil remedies' (1999) 7 FLS 203.

Conaghan, J, 'Equity rushes in where tort law fears to tread: the Court of Appeal decision in *Burris v Azadani*' (1996) 4 FLS 221.

Connell, RW and Irving, TH, *Class Structure in Australian History: Documents and Arguments*, 2nd edn, 1992, Melbourne: Longman.

Corrigan, P and Sayer, D, *The Great Arch: English State Formation as Cultural Revolution*, 1985, Oxford: Blackwell.

Cotterrell, R, 'Power, property and the law of trusts: a partial agenda for critical legal scholarship', in Fitzgerald, P (ed), *Critical Legal Studies*, 1987, London: Blackwell.

Cotterrell, R, 'Trusting in law; legal and moral concepts of trust' (1993) 46 CLP 75.

Cover, M and Humphreys, G, 'Whistleblowing in English law', in Vinten, G (ed), *Whistleblowing – Subversion or Corporate Citizenship?*, 1994, London: Paul Chapman.

Cretney, SM, 'The little woman and the big bad bank' (1992) 109 LQR 534.

Cripps, Y, 'The public interest defence to the action for breach of confidence and the Law Commission's proposals on disclosure in the public interest' (1984) 4 OJLS 361.

Cripps, Y, 'Protection from adverse treatment by employers: a review of the position of employees who disclose information in the belief that disclosure is in the public interest' (1985) 101 LQR 506.

Cripps, Y, *The Legal Implications of Disclosure in the Public Interest*, 1986, Oxford: ESC.

Dalpont, G and Chalmers, D, *Equity and Trusts in Australia and New Zealand*, 1996, Sydney: LBC.

Dalton, C, 'Deconstructing contract doctrine', in Bartlett, KT and Kennedy, R (eds), *Feminist Legal Theory: Readings in Law and Gender*, 1991, London: Westview.

Davidoff, L, 'Regarding some "old husbands' tales": public and private in feminist history', in Landes, JB (ed), *Feminism in the Public and Private*, 1998, Oxford: OUP.

Davidson, G, *The Rise and Fall of Marvellous Melbourne*, 1978, Carlton, Victoria: Melbourne UP.

Davidson, M and Cooper, C, *Stress and the Woman Manager*, 1983, Oxford: Martin Robertson.

Davies, M, 'Feminist appropriations: law, property and personality' (1994) 3 Social and Legal Studies 365.

De Groot, JK and Nickel, B, *Family Provision in Australia*, 1993, Sydney: Butterworths.

Deacon, D, 'Political arithmetic: the nineteenth century Australian census and the contrition of dependent women' (1985) Signs 27.

Deakins, D, Hussain, G and Ram, M, 'Ethnic entrepreneurs and commercial banks' (1994) 29 Regional Studies 95.

Dean, M and Hindess, B, 'Introduction: government, liberalism, society', in Dean, M and Hindess, B (eds), *Governing Australia: Studies in Contemporary Rationalities of Government*, Sydney: CUP.

Dehn, G and Rose, N, 'The case for the Public Interest Disclosure Bill' [1996] PL 235.

Delaney, H, *Equity and the Law of Trusts in Ireland*, 1996, Dublin: Round Hall, Sweet & Maxwell.

Deleuze, G, and Guattari, F, *Capitalism and Schizophrenia: A Thousand Plateaus*, 1987, Minneapolis: Minnesota UP.

Deleuze, G, *The Fold: Leibniz and the Baroque*, 1992, Minneapolis: Minnesota UP.

Denning (Lord), 'The equality of women' (the Eleanor Rathbone Memorial Lecture), 1960, Liverpool: Liverpool UP.

Denning (Lord), *The Family Story*, 1981, London: Butterworths.

Denning, Sir Alfred, *The Changing Law*, 1953, London: Sweet & Maxwell.

Denoon, D, *Settler Capitalism: The Dynamics of Dependent Development*, 1983, Oxford: Clarendon.

Department of Trade and Industry, *Fairness at Work*, Cm 3968, 1998.

Dewar, J, 'Land, law and the family home', in Bright, S and Dewar, J (eds), *Land Law: Themes and Perspectives*, 1998, Oxford: OUP.

Dewry, G, 'The *Ponting* case – leaking in the public interest' [1985] PL 203.

Dicey, AV, *Lectures on the Relation Between Law and Public Opinion in England During the Nineteenth Century*, 2nd edn, 1962, London: Macmillan.

Dickson, SF, 'Good faith in contract, spousal guarantees and *Smith v Bank of Scotland*' 1998 SLT 39.

Doggett, ME, *Marriage, Wife-Beating and the Law in Victorian England*, 1993, Columbia: South Carolina UP.

Draper, MJ, 'Undue influence: a review' (1999) 63 Conv 176.

Drinkwater, M, 'Visible actors and visible researchers: critical hermeneutics in an actor perspective' (1992) 32 Sociologia Ruralis 367.

DuBois, E, Dunlap, MC, Gilligan, C, MacKinnon, C and Menkel-Meadow, CJ, 'Feminist discourse, moral values, and the law – a conversation' (1985) 34 Buffalo L Rev 74, reprinted in Olsen, FE (ed), *Feminist Legal Theory 1: Foundations and Outlooks*, 1995, Aldershot: Dartmouth.

Duckworth, A, 'Star wars: the colony fights back' (1998) 12 Trusts Law International 16.

Dunlop, R, '*Smith v Bank of Scotland*, spouses, caution and the banks' (1997) 42 JLSS 446.

Dunn, A, 'Adjusting the scales? Independent advice and partial mortgage enforcement' (1995) Conv 325.

Dunn, A, 'Equity is dead: long live equity!' (1999) 62 MLR 140.

Duxbury, N, 'Robert Hale and the economy of legal force' (1990) 53 MLR 421.

Dyer, C, 'Judge lifts lid on tribunals' (2000) *The Guardian*, 20 April.

Dyer, C, '£293,000 for whistleblower' (2000b) *The Guardian*, 11 July.

Edwards, M, 'Unfair dismissal update' (2000) SJ 393.

Eekelaar, J, 'A woman's place – a conflict between law and social values' (1987) Conv 93.

El Guindi, F, *Veil*, 1999, Oxford and New York: Berg.

Engender, Gender Audit, 1997, 1998–99, 2000, www.engender.org.uk.

Erickson, AL, *Women and Property in Early Modern England*, 1995, Padstow: Routledge.

Ewing, K and Gearty, C, *Freedom Under Thatcher: Civil Liberties in Modern Britain*, 1993, Oxford: Clarendon.

Ewing, K, 'The Human Rights Act and public law' (1998) 27 ILJ 275.

Fehlberg, B, 'The husband, the bank, the wife and her signature' (1994) 58 MLR 467.

Fehlberg, B, 'Stand by your man?: legal protection for wives who charge the family home to secure their husbands' business debts' (1995) 2 Cardozo Women's LJ 3.

Fehlberg, B, 'The husband, the bank, the wife and her signature – the sequel' (1996) 59 MLR 675.

Fehlberg, B, *Sexually Transmitted Debt: Surety Experience and English Law*, 1997, Oxford: Clarendon.

Ferber, M and Nelson, J, *Beyond Economic Man: Feminist Theory and Economics*, 1993, Chicago: Chicago UP.

Ferguson, P, 'Constructive trusts: a note of caution' (1993) 10 LQR 114.

Finch, J *et al*, *Wills, Inheritance and Family*, 1996, Oxford: Clarendon.

Finch, V, 'Company directors: who cares about skill and care?' (1992) 55 MLR 179.

Finn, FJ and Ziegler, PA, 'Prudence and fiduciary obligations in the investment of trust funds' (1987) 61 ALJ 329.

Fisher, HAL (ed), *Collected Papers of Frederic William Maitland*, 1911, Cambridge: CUP.

Fitzherbert, L, Addison, D and Rashman, F, *A Guide to the Major Trusts Vol 1, 1999/2000*, 1999, London: Directory of Social Change.

Flam, H, 'Fear, loyalty and greedy organizations', in Fineman, S (ed), *Emotion in Organizations*, 1993, London: Sage.

Fleming, MA, 'Secret trusts' (1947) 1 Conv 28.

Flynn, L and Lawson, A, 'Gender, sexuality and the doctrine of detrimental reliance' (1995) 3 FLS 105.

Ford, HAJ and Lee, WA, *Principles of the Law of Trusts*, 1990, Sydney: LBC.

Forrest, R and Murie, A, 'Accumulating evidence, housing and family wealth in Britain', in Forrest, R and Murie, A (eds), *Housing and Family Wealth: Comparative International Perspectives*, 1995, London, Routledge.

Forte, A, 'Good faith and utmost good faith: insurance and cautionary obligations in Scots law', in Forte, A (ed), *Good Faith in Contract and Property Law*, 1999, Oxford: Hart.

Foucault, M, '*Omnes et singulatim*: towards a criticism of political reason', in McMurrin, S (ed), *The Tanner Lectures in Human Value*, 1983, Vol 11, Utah: Utah UP.

Foucault, M, *Discipline and Punish: The Birth of the Prison*, 1977, London: Allen Lane.

Foucault, M, 'Governmentality', in Burchell, G *et al*, *The Foucault Effect: Studies in Governmentality*, 1991, London: Harvester.

Fowler, J, 'A note on capital and income in the law of trusts', in Edey, HC and Yamay, BS (eds), *Debts, Credits, Finance and Profits*, 1974, London: Sweet & Maxwell.

Fraser, A, *The Weaker Vessel – Women's Lot in Seventeenth-Century England*, 1989, London: Methuen.

Fraser, N and Gordon, L, 'Decoding "dependency": inscriptions of power in a keyword of the US welfare state', in Lyndon Shanley, M and Narayan, U (eds), *Reconstructing Political Theory*, 1997, Cambridge: Polity.

Fraser, N, and Nicholson, LJ, 'Social criticism without philosophy: an encounter between feminism and postmodernism', in Nicholson, LJ (ed), *Feminism/Postmodernism*, 1990, London: Routledge.

Frazer, E and Lacey, N, *The Politics of the Community; A Feminist Critique of the Liberal-Communitarian Debate*, 1993, London: Harvester Wheatsheaf.

Freer, A, 'The range of reasonable responses test – from guideline to statute' (1998) 27 ILJ 335.

Fricke, GL and Strauss, OK, *The Law of Trusts in Victoria*, 1964, Sydney: Butterworths.

Frug, MJ, *Postmodern Legal Feminism*, 1992, New York: Routledge.

Gandhi, L, *Postcolonial Theory*, 1998, Edinburgh: Edinburgh UP.

Gardner, S, *An Introduction to the Law of Trusts*, 1990, Oxford: OUP.

Gardner, S, 'Rethinking family property' (1993) 109 LQR 263.

Gardner, S, 'Fin de siècle' (1996) 112 LQR 378.

Gaudiosi, M, 'The influence of the Islamic law of *waqf* on the development of the trust in England' (1988) 136 U Pa L Rev 1231.

Gerber, H, 'Position of women in Ottoman Bursa, 1600–1700' (1980) 12 International Journal of Middle Eastern Studies 231.

Giliker, P, '*Barclays Bank v O'Brien* revisited: what a difference five years can make' (1999) 62 MLR 609.

Gilligan, C, *In a Different Voice: Psychological Theory and Women's Development*, 1993, Cambridge, Mass: Harvard UP.

Gilligan, C, Ward, JV and Taylor, J McL (eds), *Mapping the Moral Domain*, 1988, Cambridge, Mass: Harvard UP.

Gloag, W, *Law of Rights In Security*, 1897, Edinburgh: Green.

Gloag, W, *The Law of Contract – A Treatise on the Principles of Contract in the Law of Scotland*, 2nd edn, 1929, Edinburgh: Green.

Glover, N and Todd, P, 'The myth of common intention' (1996) 16 LS 325.

Gobert, J and Punch, M, 'Whistleblowers, the public interest and the Public Interest Disclosure Act 1998' (2000) 63 MLR 25.

Goodchild, P, *Deleuze and Guattari: An Introduction to the Politics of Desire*, 1996, London: Sage.

Goodhart, W, 'Trust law for the twenty-first century', in Oakley, AJ (ed), *Trends in Contemporary Trust Law*, 1996, Oxford: OUP.

Goodrich, P, 'Gender and contracts', in Bottomley, A (ed), *Feminist Perspectives on the Foundational Subjects of Law*, 1996, London: Cavendish Publishing.

Goodwin, CDW, *The Image of Australia: British Perception of the Australian Economy from the Eighteenth to the Twentieth Century*, 1974, Durham: Dale University.

Gordon, R, 'Paradoxical property', in Brewer, J and Staves, S, *Early Modern Conceptions of Property*, 1996, London: Routledge.

Gospel, H and Palmer, G, *British Industrial Relations*, 1993, London: Routledge.

Gover, WHA, *Concise Treatise on the Law of Capital and Income as Between Life Tenant and Remainderman*, 1933, London: Sweet & Maxwell.

Gow, J, *The Mercantile and Industrial Law of Scotland*, 1964, Edinburgh: Green.

Graham, P, 'The Registrar in the John Lewis Partnership plc: corporate conscience', in Vinten, G (ed), *Whistleblowing – Subversion or Corporate Citizenship?*, 1994, London: Paul Chapman.

Grant, J, 'Women as managers: what they can offer to organisations' (1988) 16 Organizational Dynamics 56.

Gray, J and Fennell, E, 'Theoretical perspectives on regulatory enforcement' (1996) 3 Journal of Financial Crime 334.

Gray, K, 'Property in common law systems', in van Maanen, GE, van der Walt, AJ and Alexander, GS (eds), *Property Law on the Threshold of the Twenty-First Century*, 1996, Antwerp: Maklu.

Green, K, 'The Englishwoman's castle' (1988) 51 MLR 187.

Green, K, 'Being here: what a woman can say about land law', in Bottomley, A (ed), *Feminist Perspectives on the Foundational Subjects*, 1996, London: Cavendish Publishing.

Greenberg, J, Minow, M and Schneider, 'Contradiction and revision: progressive feminist legal scholars respond to Mary Joe Frug' (1992) 15 Harvard Women's LJ 37.

Gregg, P and Machin, S, 'Is the glass ceiling cracking? Gender compensation differentials and access to promotion among UK executives' (1993) National Institute of Economic and Social Research Discussion Paper 50.

Gretton, G, 'Sexually transmitted debt' 1997 SLT 195.

Gretton, G, 'Good news for bankers – bad news for lawyers?' 1999 SLT 53.

Griggs, L and Lowry, J, 'Finding the optimum balance for the duty of care owed by the non-executive director', in Macmillan Patfield, F (ed), *Perspectives on Company Law 2*, 1997, London: Kluwer.

Grimwood, C and Popplestone, R, *Women, Management and Care*, 1993, Basingstoke: Macmillan.

Grosz, E, *Volatile Bodies*, 1994, Bloomington: Indiana UP.

Grosz, E, *Sexual Subversions: Three French Feminists*, 1989, Sydney: Allen & Unwin.

Gunning, IR, 'Arrogant perception, world travelling and multicultural feminism: the case of female genital surgeries' (1991–92) 23 Columbia Human Rights L Rev 189.

Habakkuk, J, *Marriage, Debt and the Estates System, English Landownership 1650–1950*, 1994, Oxford: Clarendon.

Hackney, J, *Understanding Equity and Trusts*, 1987, London: Fontana.

Hadfield, G, 'The dilemma of choice: a feminist perspective on the limits of freedom of contract' (1995) 33 Os HLJ 337.

Hakim, C, 'Five feminist myths about women's employment' (1995) 46 Journal of Sociology 429.

Halliwell, M, 'Equity as injustice: the cohabitant's case' (1991) 20 Anglo-Am L Rev 550.

Halliwell, M, *Equity and Good Conscience in a Contemporary Context*, 1997, London: Old Bailey.

Harris, JW, 'Trust, power and duty' (1971) 87 LQR 31.

Harris, JW, *Variation of Trusts*, 1975, London: Sweet & Maxwell.

Hartley-Brewer, J, 'Arrogant, intimidating and lacking compassion' (2000) *The Guardian*, 2 June.

Hartsman, A, *Victorian Divorce*, 1985, London: Croom Helm.

Hayton and Marshall, *Commentaries and Cases on the Law of Trusts*, 10th edn, 1996, London: Sweet & Maxwell.

Hayton, DJ, *The Law of Trusts*, 1998, London: Sweet & Maxwell.

Heinzelman, SS and Wiseman, ZB (eds), *Representing Women: Law, Literature, and Feminism*, 1994, Durham: Duke UP.

Hencke, D, 'Union chief in £130,000 fraud, claims whistleblower' (2000a) *The Guardian*, 4 July.

Hencke, D, 'Union pays £140,000 over expenses claim' (2000b) *The Guardian*, 8 July.

Hencke, D, 'Third tribunal payout gags MSF allegations' (2000c) *The Guardian*, 18 July.

Herbert, A and Kempson, E, *Credit Use and Ethnic Minorities*, 1996, London: Policy Studies Institute.

Herman, S, '*Utilitas Ecclesiae*: the canonical conception of the trust' (1996) 70 Tulane L Rev 2239.

Heward, E, *A Victorian Law Reformer, A Life of Lord Selborne*, 1998, Chichester: Barry Rose.

Hirsch, KL, 'Inflation and the law of trusts' (1983) 18 Real Property, Probate and Trust Journal 601.

Hirschman, LR, 'The book of "A"' (1992) 70 Texas L Rev 985, reprinted in Olsen, FE (ed), *Feminist Legal Thought II: Positioning Feminist Theory Within the Law*, 1995, Aldershot: Dartmouth.

Hirschmann, NJ, 'Difference as an occasion for rights: a feminist rethinking of rights, liberalism, and difference', in Hekman, S (ed), *Feminism, Identity and Difference*, 1999, London and Portland, Or: Frank Cass.

Hirschon, R, *Women and Property – Women as Property*, 1984, London: St Martin's.

HM Treasury, *Investment Powers of Trustees* Consultation Document, 1996, London: HM Treasury.

Holcombe, L, *Wives and Property*, 1983, Toronto: Toronto UP.

Holdsworth, WS, *A History of English Law*, 1922, London: Methuen.

Holdsworth, WS, 'Secret trusts' (1937) LQR 501.

Holdsworth, WS, *A History of English Law*, 3rd edn, 1945, London: Sweet & Maxwell.

Home Office, *Rights Brought Home: The Human Rights Bill*, Cm 3782, 1997, London: HMSO.

Hopwood, AG and Miller, P (eds), *Accounting as a Social and Institutional Practice*, 1994, Cambridge: CUP.

Houlbrooke, RA, *The English Family 1450–1700*, 1984, London: Longman.

Howell, N, '"Sexually transmitted debt": a feminist analysis of laws regulating guarantors and co-borrowers' (1994) Australian Feminist Law Journal 93.

Hudson, A, *Principles of Equity and Trusts*, 1999, London: Cavendish Publishing.

Hungerford, C, 'The accounts of sheep stations managed by trustees' (1922) *Public Accountant*, March 275 and April 289.

Hunt, A and Wickham, G, *Foucault and Law: Towards a Sociology of Law as Governance*, 1994, London, Pluto.

Hunt, G, 'Conclusion: a new accountability', in Hunt, G (ed), *Whistleblowing in the Health Service*, 1995, London: Arnold.

Industrial Relations Law Bulletin 563, 'Whistleblowing at work 1: contract, confidentiality and the public interest' (1997) IRS 2.

Industrial Relations Law Bulletin 564, 'Whistleblowing at work 2: the statutory context' (1997) IRS 2.

Industrial Relations Law Bulletin 586, 'Public Interest Disclosure Bill' (1998) IRS 12.

Industrial Relations Law Bulletin 621, 'Public Interest Disclosure Act 1998' (1999) IRS 2.

Industrial Relations Law Bulletin 648, 'Whistleblowing: the early view from the tribunals' (2000) IRS 2.

Jackson, S, and Moores, S (eds), *The Politics of Domestic Consumption: Critical Readings*, 1995, Hemel Hempstead: Prentice Hall/Harvester Wheatsheaf.

Jennings, RC, 'Women in early 17th century Ottoman judicial records – the Sharia Court of Anatolian Kayseri' (1975) 18 Journal of the Economic and Social History of the Orient 53.

Johnson, AH, *The Disappearance of the Small Landowner* (Ford Lectures 1909), 1909, London: Merlin.

Kames, *Principles of Equity*, 5th edn, 1825, Edinburgh: Bell & Bradfute.

Kaye, M, 'Equity's treatment of sexually transmitted debt' (1997) 5 FLS 35.

Kendall, G, 'Governing at a distance: Anglo-Australian relations 1840–70' (1997) 32 Australian Journal of Political Science 223.

Kennedy, H, *Eve Was Framed: Women and British Justice*, 1992, London: Chatto & Windus.

Kennedy, I, *How the Family Court Deals with Trusts*, 1996, Sydney: College of Law, papers 96/3.

Kenny, CS, *The History of the Law of England as to the Effects of Marriage on Property and on the Wife's Legal Capacity*, 1879, London: Reeves and Turner.

Kerber, LK, Greeno, CG, Maccoby, EE, Luria, Z, Stack, CB and Gilligan, G, 'On *In A Different Voice*: an interdisciplinary forum' (1986) 11 Signs: Journal of Women in Culture and Society 304.

Kingdom, E, 'Citizenship and democracy: feminist politics of citizenship and radical democratic politics', in Millns, S and Whitty, N (eds), *Feminist Perspectives on Public Law*, 1999, London: Cavendish Publishing.

Kingdom, E, 'Cohabitation contracts and the democratization of personal relations' (2000) 8 FLS 5.

Kohler, P, 'Common property and private trusts', in Holde, J and McGillivray, D (eds), *Locality and Identity: Environmental Issues in Law and Society*, 1999, London: Dartmouth.

Lacey, N, *Unspeakable Subjects, Feminist Essays in Legal and Social Theory*, 1988, Oxford: Hart.

Lando, O and Beale, H, *The Principles of European Contract Law Part 1: Performance, Non-Performance and Remedies*, 1995, London: Martinus Nijhoff.

Landow, GP, 'William Holman Hunt's "Oriental mania" and his Uffizi self-portrait III' (1982) 64 Art Bulletin 646.

Langbein, JH, 'The twentieth-century revolution in family wealth transmission' (1988) 86 Michigan L Rev 722.

Latham, V, 'The rights of the beneficiary to specific items in the trust fund' (1954) 32 Can BR 520.

Latour, B, 'The power of association in law', in Law, J (ed), *Power, Action and Belief: A New Sociology of Knowledge*, 1986, London: Kegan Paul.

Latour, B, *Science in Action: How to Follow Scientists and Engineers Through Society*, 1987, Cambridge: CUP.

Laurence, A, *Women in England 1500–1760: A Social History*, 1994, London: Phoenix.

Law Commission, Consultation Paper No 146, *Trustees Powers and Duties*, 1997, London: Stationery Office.

Law Commission, *Trustees' Powers and Duties*, Law Com No 260, 1999, London: Stationery Office.

Law Reform Committee, 23rd Report, *The Powers and Duties of Trustees*, Cmnd 8733, 1982, London: Stationery Office.

Law, J, 'On the methods of long-distance control: vessels navigation and the Portuguese route to India', in Law, J (ed), *Power, Action and Belief: A New Sociology of Knowledge*, 1986, London: Routledge & Kegan Paul.

Lawson, A, 'The things we do for love: detrimental reliance in the family home' (1996) 16 LS 218.

Lee, TA, 'The early debate on financial and physical capital', in Parker, IRH (ed), *Accounting History: Some British Contributions*, 1994, Oxford: Clarendon.

Leneman, L, *Alienated Affections – The Scottish Experience of Divorce and Separation, 1684 –1830*, 1998, Edinburgh: Edinburgh UP.

Levin, L, 'Toward a feminist, post-Keynesian theory of investment', in Kuiper, E and Sap, J (eds), *Out of the Margin: Feminist Perspectives on Economics*, 1995, London: Routledge.

Lewis, D, 'Whistleblowing and job security' (1995) 58 MLR 208.

Lewis, D, 'The Public Interest Disclosure Act 1998' (1998) 27 ILJ 325.

Leyshon, A and Thrift, N, *Money, Space: Geographies of Monetary Transformation*, 1997, London: Routledge.

Lim, H, 'Messages from a rarely visited island: duress and lack of consent in marriage' (1996a) 4 FLS 195.

Lim, H, 'Mapping equity's place: here be dragons', in Bottomley, A (ed), *Feminist Perspectives on the Foundational Subjects of Law*, 1996b, London: Cavendish Publishing.

Lister, R, *Citizenship: Feminist Perspectives*, 1997, London: Macmillan.

Loden, M, *Feminine Leadership: How to Succeed in Business Without Being One of the Boys*, 1985, London: Times.

Lovell, A and Robertson, C, 'Charles Robertson: in the eye of the storm', in Vinten, G (ed), *Whistleblowing – Subversion or Corporate Citizenship?*, 1994, London: Paul Chapman.

Lumis, T and Marsh, J (eds), *The Woman's Domain*, 1990, London: Viking.

Lush, M, 'Changes in the law affecting the rights, status, and liabilities of married women', in *A Century of Law Reform*, Council of Legal Education, 1901, London: Macmillan.

McGlynn, C and Graham, C, *Soliciting Equality – Equality and Opportunity in the Solicitors' Profession*, 1995, London: Young Women Lawyers.

McGlynn, C, *The Woman Lawyer – Making the Difference*, 1998, London: Butterworths.

McGregor, L, 'The House of Lords "applies" *O'Brien* north of the border' (1998) 2 Edin LR 90.

McHale, J, 'Whistleblowing in the NHS' (1992) JSWFL 363.

McIntyre, S, *Winners and Losers: The Pursuit of Social Justice in Australian History*, 1985, Sydney: Allen & Unwin.

McKendrick, E, 'The undue influence of English law', in MacQueen, HL (ed), *Scots Law into the 21st Century: Essays in Honour of WA Wilson*, 1996, Edinburgh: Green/Sweet & Maxwell.

McNay, L, *Foucault: A Critical Introduction*, 1994, Oxford: Polity.

McWhorter, L, 'Foucault and the paradox of bodily inscriptions' (1989) 86 Journal of Philosophy 601.

Mabey, C and Hooker, C, 'What does it mean to be a committed employee?', in Vinten, G (ed), *Whistleblowing – Subversion or Corporate Citizenship?*, 1994, London: Paul Chapman.

Mack, K, '*B v R*: negative stereotyping and women's credibility' (1994) 2 FLS 183.

Mackenzie, R, 'Beauty and the beastly bank – what should equity's fairy wand do?', in Bottomley, A (ed), *Feminist Perspectives on the Foundational Subjects of Law*, 1996, London: Cavendish Publishing.

MacKinnon, CA, *Toward a Feminist Theory of the State*, 1989, Cambridge, Mass and London, England: Harvard UP.

Macneil, IR, 'Adjustments of long-term economic relations under classical, neoclassical, and relational contract law' (1978) 72 Northwestern University L Rev 854.

Macneil, IR, *The New Social Contract*, 1980, New Haven: Yale UP.

MacQueen HL (ed), *Scots Law into the 21st Century: Essays in Honour of WA Wilson*, 1996, Edinburgh: Green/Sweet & Maxwell.

MacQueen, H, 'Good faith in the Scots law of contract: an undisclosed principle', in Forte, ADM (ed), *Good Faith in Contract and Property Law*, 1999, Oxford: Hart.

Madigan, R and Munro, M, 'Ideal homes: gender and domestic architecture', in Puttnam, T and Newton, C (eds), *Household Choices*, 1990, London: Future Publications.

Maitland, FW, *Collected Papers*, Vol III, 1911, Cambridge: CUP.

Maitland, FW, *Equity and the Forms of Action and Common Law*, 1932, Cambridge: CUP.

Maitland, FW, *Equity and Course of Lectures*, 2nd edn, 1936, Cambridge: Bungate.

Makdisi, G, 'The guilds of law in medieval legal history: an inquiry into the origins of the Inns of Court' (1985) 34 Clev St LR 3.

Manchester, AH, *A Modern Legal History of England and Wales 1750–1950*, 1980, London: Butterworths.

Manitoba Law Reform Commission, *Trustee Investments: The Modern Portfolio Theory*, 1999, Winnipeg: Manitoba Law Reform Commission.

Marshall, J, *Women Managers: Travellers in a Male World*, 1984, Chichester: Wiley.

Marsot, al-Sayyid, AL, 'Entrepreneurial women', in Yamani, M (ed), *Feminism in Islam, Legal and Literary Perspectives*, 1996, Reading: Ithaca.

Martin, G, *Bunyip Aristocracy: The New South Wales Constitution Debate of 1883 and Hereditary Institutions in the British Colonies*, 1986, Sydney: Croom & Helm.

Martin, J, *Hanbury and Martin Modern Equity*, 15th edn, 1997, London: Sweet & Maxwell.

Mason, A, 'The place of equity and equitable remedies in the contemporary common law world' (1994) 110 LQR 238.

Mason, J, 'Whistleblower wins £293,000' (2000) *Financial Times*, 11 July.

Matthews, P, 'The new trust: obligations without rights?', in Oakley, AJ (ed), *Trends in Contemporary Trust Law*, 1996, Oxford: Clarendon.

Matthews, P, 'Shooting star: the new specialist trusts regime from the Cayman Islands' (1997) 11 Trusts Law International 67.

Matthews, P, 'STAR: big bang or red dwarf?' (1998) 12 Trusts Law International 98.

Maudsley, RH, *Trusts and Trustees, Cases and Materials*, 5th edn, 1996, London: Butterworths.

Meagher, RP and Gummow, WMC, *Jacob's Law of Trusts*, 1993, Melbourne: Butterworths.

Menkel-Meadow, C, 'Portia in a different voice: speculations on a woman's lawyering process' (1985) 1 Berkeley Women's LJ 39.

Mepham, JJ, 'The Scottish enlightenment and the development of accounting' (1998) 15 Accounting Historian Journal 151.

Meriwether, ML and Tucker, JE (eds), *Women and Gender in the Modern Middle East*, 1999, Boulder and Oxford: Westview.

Mill, JS, 'The subjection of women', in Schneir M (ed), *The Vintage Book of Historical Feminism*, 1996, London: Vintage.

Miller, P and Rose, N, 'Governing economic life' (1990) 19 Economy and Society 3.

Miller, P, 'Accounting as social and institutional practice: an introduction', in Hopwood, AG and Miller, P (eds), *Accounting as Social and Institutional Practice*, 1994, Cambridge: CUP.

Millet, P, 'Equity's place in the law of commerce' (1998) 114 LQR 214.

Millett, P, 'Equity – the road ahead' (1995) 9 Trust Law International 35.

Mingay, G, *English Landed Society in the Eighteenth Century*, 1963, London: Routledge.

Minow, M, *Making All the Difference: Inclusion, Exclusion, and American Law*, 1990, Ithaca: Cornell UP.

Moffat, G, 'Trusts: a song without ending?' (1993) 56 MLR 471.

Moffatt, G, Bean, G and Dewar, J, *Trust Law: Test and Materials*, 1994, London: Butterworths.

Moffat, G, *Trust Law: Text and Materials*, 3rd edn, 1999, London: Butterworths.

Morris, D, 'Volunteering, a nice little job for a woman', in Morris, A and O'Donnell, T (eds), *Feminist Perspectives on Employment Law*, 1999, London: Cavendish Publishing.

Morris, G, 'The Human Rights Act and the public/private divide in employment' (1998) 27 ILJ 293.

Munro, C, 'Confidence in government', in Clarke, L (ed), *Confidentiality and the Law*, 1990, London: Lloyds of London.

Murphy, T, 'Bursting binary bubbles: law, literature and the sexed body', in Morison, J and Bell, C (eds), *Tall Stories? Reading Law and Literature*, 1996, Aldershot: Dartmouth.

Murphy, T, 'Review of Spring, E, Law, Land and Family' (1996) 59 MLR 625.

Musson, CT, 'Book-keeping for farmers and orchardists' (1893) 4 Agricultural Gazette of NSW 162.

Naffine, N, *Law and the Sexes: Explorations in Feminist Jurisprudence*, 1990, London: Allen & Unwin.

Napier, B, 'Confidentiality and labour law', in Clarke, L (ed), *Confidentiality and the Law*, 1990, London: Lloyds of London.

Neave, M, 'Living together – legal effects of the sexual division of labour in four common law countries' (1991a) 17 Monash Univ L Rev 14.

Neave, M, 'The unconscionability principle – property disputes between de facto partners' (1991b) 5 Australian Journal of Family Law 185.

Nelson, E, 'Tennyson and the Ladies of Shalott', 1979, The Victorian Web, http://landow.stg.brown.edu/victorian (15/7/2000).

Nelson, J, 'Economic theory and feminist theory', in Kuiper, E and Sap, J (eds), *Out of the Margin: Feminist Perspectives on Economics*, 1995, London: Routledge.

Nicholson, LJ (ed), *Feminism/Postmodernism*, 1990, London: Routledge.

Noddings, N, *Caring: A Feminine Approach to Ethics and Moral Education*, 1984, Berkeley, Los Angeles: California UP.

Normanton, H, *Everyday Law for Women*, 1932, London: Ivor Nicholson and Watson.

Norton-Taylor, R, *The* Ponting *Affair*, 1985, London: Cecil Woolf.

Nussbaum, MC, *Poetic Justice: The Literary Imagination and Public Life*, 1995, Boston: Beacon.

O'Donnell, A and Johnstone, R, *Developing a Cross-Cultural Curriculum*, 1997, Sydney and London: Cavendish Publishing.

O'Sullivan, J, 'Lawyers, conflicts of interest and Chinese walls' (2000) 16 Professional Negligence 88.

Oakley, AJ, *Constructive Trusts*, 3rd edn, 1997, London: Sweet & Maxwell.

Oehr, RT, 'How to become a skilled accountant' (1899) *Bankers' Magazine of Australasia* 291, 29 December.

Offer, A, *Property and Politics, 1870–1914 (Landownership, Law, Ideology and Urban Development in England)*, 1981, Cambridge: CUP.

O'Hagan, P, 'Quantifying interests under resulting trusts' (1997) 60 MLR 420.

Okoth-Ogendo, H, 'The imposition of law in Kenya', in Burman, S and Harrell-Bond, BH, *The Imposition of Law*, 1979, New York: Academic.

Oldham, M, '"Neither a borrower nor a lender be" – the life of *O'Brien*' (1995) 7 CFLQ 104.

Olsen, FE, 'The family and the market: a study of ideology and legal reform' (1983) 96 Harv LR 1560.

Opie, R (compiler), *The 1930s Scrapbook*, 1997, London: New Cavendish.

Opie, R (compiler), *The 1950s Scrapbook*, 1998, London: New Cavendish.

Orr, J, 'Nursing accountability', in Hunt, G (ed), *Whistleblowing in the Health Service*, 1995, London: Arnold.

Paccioco, D, 'The remedial constructive trust: a principles basis for priorities over creditors' (1989) 68 Can BR 315.

Pahl, J, 'Household spending, personal spending and the control of money in marriage' (1990) 24(1) Journal of British Sociological Association 119.

Pahl, J, *Money and Marriage*, 1989, Basingstoke: Macmillan.

Pahl, J 'Women and money', in *For Richer or Poorer: Feminist Perspectives on Women and the Distribution of Wealth*, 1995, Feminist Legal Research Unit, University of Liverpool Working Paper No 2.

Pahl, J and Vogler, C, 'Money, power and inequality within marriage' (1994) 42(2) Sociological Review 263.

Palmer, G, *Trustee Investment: The Relative Merits of the 'Legal List' and 'Prudent Man' Approaches to Trustee Investment*, 1986, Wellington, NZ: Department of Justice.

Panter-Downes, M, *One Fine Day*, 1985, London: Virago.

Pateman, C, *The Sexual Contract*, 1988, Cambridge: Polity.

Pawley, M, *Home Ownership*, 1978, London: Architectural Press.

Pearce, R and Stevens, J, *The Law of Trusts and Equitable Obligations*, 2nd edn, 1998, London: Butterworths.

Penner, JE, *The Law of Trusts*, 1998, London: Butterworths.

Perrins, B, 'Can you keep half a secret?' (1972) 88 LQR 225.

Pierce, LP, *The Imperial Harem*, 1993, New York and Oxford: OUP.

Plant, S, 'The future looms: weaving women and cybernetics', in *Theory, Culture and Society, Cyber Space, Cyber Bodies, Cyber Punks*, 1995, London: Sage.

Pohjonen, S, 'Partnership in love and business' (2000) 8 FLS 47.

Pollock, F, *The Land Laws*, 1896, Littleton, Colo: Rothman.

Ponting, C, *The Right To Know*, 1985, London: Sphere.

Ponting, C, *Whitehall: Tragedy and Farce*, 1986, London: Hamish Hamilton.

Ponting, C, *Whitehall: Changing the Old Guard*, 1989, London: Unwin.

Ponting, C, *Secrecy in Britain*, 1990, London: Blackwell.

Posner, RA, 'Conservative feminism' (1989) University of Chicago Legal Forum 191, reprinted in Weisberg, DK (ed), *Feminist Legal Theory: Foundations*, 1993, Philadelphia: Temple UP.

Posner, RA, *Law and Literature*, 1998, Cambridge, Mass: Harvard UP.

Pottage, A, 'Proprietary strategies: the legal fabric of aristocratic settlements' (1998) 61 MLR 162.

Potter, H, *An Introduction to the History of Equity and its Courts*, 1931, London: Sweet & Maxwell.

Pryer, R, 'Sarah Tisdall, Ian Willmore, and the civil servant's "right to leak"' (1985) 56 Political Quarterly Journal 72.

Ramsay, I, 'Consumer credit law, distributive justice and the welfare state' (1995) OJLS 177.

Redgewell, C, *Intergenerational Trusts and Environmental Protection*, 1999, Manchester: Manchester UP.

Reid, M, *A Plea for Women*, 1988, Edinburgh: Polygon.

Reiter, Y, 'Family *waqf* entitlements in British Palestine 1917–1948' (1995) Islamic Law and Society 174.

Rendell, C, *Intergenerational Trusts and Environmental Protection*, 1999, Manchester: Manchester UP.

Rhode, DL, 'Feminist legal theories' (1990) 42 Stanford L Rev 617, reprinted in Bartlett, KT and Kennedy, R (eds), *Feminist Legal Theory: Readings in Law and Gender*, 1991, Boulder: Westview.

Richardson, J and Sandland, R, 'Introduction to feminist perspectives on law and theory', in Sandland, R and Richardson, J (eds), *Feminist Perspectives on Law and Theory*, 2000, London: Cavendish Publishing.

Richardson, M, 'Protecting women who provide security for a husband's, partner's or child's debts: the value and limits of an economic perspective' (1996) 16 LS 368.

Rigternk, R, 'Warning: the surgeon moralist has determined that claims of rights can be detrimental to everyone's interests', in (Browning) Cole, E and Coultrap-McQuin, S (eds), *Explorations in Feminist Ethics: Theory and Practice*, 1992, Indianapolis: Indiana UP.

Riley, C, 'The company director's duty of care and skill: the case for an onerous but subjective standard' (1999) 62 MLR 697.

Ringle, R, 'What is a secretary?', in McDowell, L and Pringle, R (eds), *Defining Women: Social Institutions and Gender Divisions*, 1992, Blackwell: Polity and The Open University.

Rizzi, J, 'Trustee investment powers: imprudent application of the prudent man rule' [1975] Notre Dame Lawyer 519.

Robinson, R, 'Official secrecy: civil servants, secrecy and the defence of the realm', in Vinten, G (ed), *Whistleblowing – Subversion or Corporate Citizenship?*, 1994, London: Paul Chapman.

Roded, R (ed), *Women in Islam and the Middle East*, 1999, London and New York: Tauris.

Romain, D, 'Care and confusion', in (Browning) Cole, E and Coultrap-McQuin, S (eds), *Explorations in Feminist Ethics: Theory and Practice*, 1992, Bloomington and Indianapolis: Indiana UP.

Rose, N and Miller, P, 'Political power beyond the State, problematics of government' (1992) 43 British Journal of Sociology 173.

Rosener, J, 'Ways women lead' (1990) Harvard Business Review 199.

Rowland, C and Tamsitt, G, *Hutley's Australian Will Precedents*, 1994, Sydney: Butterworths.

Ruben, GR and Sugarman, D (eds), *Law, Economy and Society*, 1984, Abingdon: Professional.

Ryde, NB, Rainsford, WD and Arnott, JF, *Australian Executor's Law and Accounts*, 1928, Sydney: LBC.

Scane, R, 'Relationships "tantamount to spousal", unjust enrichment and constructive trusts' (1991) 70 Can BR 260.

Seltzer, LH, *The Nature of Tax Treatment of Capital Gains and Losses*, 1951, New York: NBER.

Sevenhuijsen, S, *Citizenship and the Ethics of Care: Feminist Considerations on Justice, Morality and Politics*, Savage, L (trans), 1998, London: Routledge.

Shatzmiller, M, 'Women and property rights in Al-Andalus and the Maghrib: social patterns and legal discourse' (1995) 2 Islamic Law and Society 220.

Shaw, T and Demetriou, D, '£293,000 awarded to whistleblower who was dismissed' (2000) *The Daily Telegraph*, 11 July.

Sheridan, LA, 'English and Irish secret trusts' (1951) 67 LQR 314.

Shurmer-Smith, P and Hannam, K, *Worlds of Desire, Realms of Power: A Cultural Geography*, 1994, London: Edward Arnold.

Sifris, A, 'Part IX of the Property Law Act 1958 (Vic): what constitutes a just and equitable order?' (1998) 12 Australian Journal of Family Law 179.

Simpson, AWB, *A History of the Land Law*, 1986, Oxford: OUP.

Smart, C and Brophy, J, 'Locating law', in Brophy, J and Smart, C (eds), *Women in Law*, 1985, London: Routledge.

Smart, C, *Feminism and the Power of Law*, 1989, London: Routledge.

Smith, I, 'Employment law brief' (2000) 150 NLJ 642.

Smith, TB, *A Short Commentary on the Law of Scotland*, 1962, Edinburgh: Green.

Snell, *Principles of Equity*, 29th edn, 1990, London: Sweet & Maxwell.

Sombert, W, *Der Moderne Kapitalismus*, 6th edn, 1924, Vol 2, 1 Munich.

Spivak, GC, 'Can the subaltern speak? Speculations on widow sacrifice?' (1985) Wedge 120.

Spivak, GC, *Outside in the Teaching Machine*, 1993, New York: Routledge.

Spring, D, *European Landed Elites in the Nineteenth Century*, 1977, Baltimore: Johns Hopkins UP.

Spring, E, 'The heiress-at-law: English real property law from a new point of view' (1990) 8 Law and History Review 273.

Spring, E, *Studies in Legal History, Law, Land and Family: Aristocratic Inheritance in England, 1300–1800*, 1993, Chapel Hill and London: Carolina UP.

Srivastava, KK, 'Wakf: historical perspective', in Singh, SK (ed), *Wakf Administration*, 1998, Rohtak: Spellbound.

St Joan, J and McElhiney, AB (eds), *Beyond Portia: Women, Law and Literature in the United States*, 1997, Boston: Northeastern UP.

Stacey, M, 'Medical accountability', in Hunt, G (ed), *Whistleblowing in the Health Service*, 1995, London: Arnold.

Stanley, C, *Urban Excess and the Law – Capital, Culture and Desire*, 1996, London: Cavendish Publishing.

Staves, S, *Married Women's Separate Property in England, 1660–1833*, 1990, Cambridge, Mass: Harvard UP.

Stogdill, R, 'Personal factors associated with leadership: a survey of the literature' (1948) 25 Journal of Psychology 35.

Stone, E, 'Infants, lunatics and married women: equitable protection in *Garcia v National Australia Bank*' (1999) 62 MLR 604.

Stone, L, *The Family, Sex and Marriage in England 1500–1800*, 1977, London: Weidenfeld & Nicolson.

Stone, L, *The Road to Divorce, England 1530–1987*, 1990, Oxford: OUP.

Stone, L, *Uncertain Unions and Broken Lives*, 1995, Oxford: OUP.

Strachey, R, *'The Cause': A Short History of the Women's Movement in Great Britain*, 1928, London: Bell.

Stratchen, W, 'Economic and legal differentiation of capital and income' (1910) 26 LQR 40.

Strawson, J, *Encountering Islamic Law*, 1996, University of East London Research Publications No 1.

Stretton, T, *Women Waging Law in Elizabethan England*, 1998, Cambridge: CUP.

Stuckley-Clarke, J, 'Freedom of speech and publication in the public interest', in Clarke, L (ed), *Confidentiality and the Law*, 1990, London: Lloyds of London.

Sugarman, D, 'Simple images and complex realities: English law years and their relationship to business and politics 1750–1950' (1993) 3 Law and History Review 259.

Sugarman, D and Rubin, GR, 'Towards a new history of law and material society in England', in Rubin, G and Sugarman, P (eds), *Law, Economy and Society 1750–1914: Essays in the History of English Law*, 1984, London: Professional.

Thompson, FML, *English Landed Society in the Nineteenth Century*, 1963, London: Routledge & Kegan Paul.

Thompson, M, 'Breach of confidence and privacy', in Clarke, L (ed), *Confidentiality and the Law*, 1990, London: Lloyds of London.

Thompson, S, 'Suburbs of opportunity: the power of home for migrant women', in Watson, S and Gibson, K (eds), *Metropolis Now: Planning and the Urban in Contemporary Australia*, 1994, Sydney: Pluto.

Thomson, A, 'The law of contract', in Grigg-Spall, I and Ireland, P (eds), *The Critical Lawyers' Handbook*, 1991, London: Pluto.

Thomson, J, 'Error revised' 1992 SLT 215.

Thomson, J, 'Misplaced concern' (1997) SLG 124.

Thrift, N, *Spatial Formations*, 1996, London: Sage.

Tierney, B, 'Villey, Ockham and the origin of individual rights', in White, J and Alexander, FS, *The Weightier Matters of the Law: Essays in Law and Religion*, 1988, Georgia: Scholars.

Tjio, H, '*O'Brien* and unconscionability' (1997) 113 LQR 10.

Todd, P, *Cases and Materials on Equity and Trusts*, 3rd edn, 2000, London: Blackstone.

Toulson, R and Phipps, C, *Confidentiality*, 1996, London: Sweet & Maxwell.

Trebilock, MJ, *The Limits of Freedom of Contract*, 1993, Cambridge, Mass: Harvard UP.

Trinh T Minh-Ha, *Woman, Native, Other*, 1989, Indianapolis: Indiana UP.

Tucker, JE, *In the House of Law*, 1998, Berkeley: California UP.

Tucker, JE, *Women in Nineteenth Century Egypt*, 1985, Cambridge: CUP.

Van Nostrand, C, *Gender Responsible Leadership*, 1993, Newbury Park, Calif: Sage.

Vernon, S, 'Legal aspects of whistleblowing in the social services', in Hunt, G (ed), *Whistleblowing in the Social Services*, 1998, London: Arnold.

Vickers, L, 'Whistleblowing in the public sector and the ECHR' (1997) PL 594.

Vickers, L, *Protecting Whistleblowers at Work*, 1995, London: Institute of Employment Rights.

Vigars, FE, *Station Book-keeping: A Treatise on Double Book-keeping for Pastoralists and Farmers*, 1914, Sydney: Brooks.

Ville, S, 'Networks and venture capitals in the Australian pastoral sector before World War Two' (1996) 38 Business History 48.

Vinten, G (ed), *Whistleblowing – Subversion or Corporate Citizenship?*, 1994, London: Paul Chapman.

Vinten, G, 'Whistleblowing – fact and fiction. An introductory discussion', in Vinten, G (ed), *Whistleblowing – Subversion or Corporate Citizenship?*, 1994a, London: Paul Chapman.

Vinten, G, 'Enough is enough: an employer's view – the Pink affair', in Vinten, G (ed), *Whistleblowing – Subversion or Corporate Citizenship?*, 1994b, London: Paul Chapman.

Vinten, G, *Whistleblowing Auditors: A Contradiction in Terms?*, 1992, London: Technical and Research Department of the Chartered Association of Certified Accountants.

Vinten, G, *Whistleblowing, Race Relations and the Manager*, 1993, London: City University Business School.

Voyce, MB, 'Pension entitlements of farmers: mean(s) test or mean test' (1993a) 18 Alternative LJ 75.

Voyce, MB, 'The impact of testator's family maintenance legislation as law and ideology on the family farm' (1993b) 7 Australian Journal of Family Law 191.

Voyce, M, *A Life Estate or a Family Discretionary Trust?*, 1996, Sydney: College of Law.

Wajcman, J, *Managing Like a Man: Women and Men in Corporate Management*, 1998, Cambridge: Polity.

Walker, DM, 'Equity in Scots law' (1954) 66 JR 103.

Walker, D, *The Scottish Legal System*, 7th edn, 1997, Edinburgh: Green/Sweet & Maxwell.

Waters, D, *Law of Trusts in Canada*, 2nd edn, 1984, Toronto: Carswell.

Waters, DMW, 'The nature of the trust beneficiary's interest' (1967) 45 Can BR 219.

Weale, S, 'Is it safe to speak out' (2000) *The Guardian*, 3 July.

Weiss, EB, *In Fairness to Future Generations: International Law, Common Patrimony, and Intergenerational Equity*, 1988, Transnational.

Wells, C, *Corporations and Criminal Responsibility*, 1993, Oxford: Clarendon.

Wells, C, *Negotiating Tragedy: Law and Disasters*, 1995, London: Sweet & Maxwell.

Welstead, M, 'Domestic contributions and constructive trusts: the Canadian perspective' (1987) Denning Law Journal 151.

West, R, 'Submission choice and ethics: a rejoinder to Judge Posner' (1986) 99 Harv LR 1449.

West, R, *Narrative, Authority, and Law*, 1993, Ann Arbor: Michigan UP.

Wexley, K and Hunt, P, 'Male and female leaders: comparison of performance and behaviour patters' (1974) 35 Psychological Reports 867.

White, J and Summers, R, *Uniform Commercial Code*, 4th edn, 1995, St Paul, Minn: West.

White, M, 'Union leader apologises for flawed judgment but refuses to quit' (2000) *The Guardian*, 7 August.

Wightman, J, 'Intimate relationships, relational contract theory, and the reach of contract' (2000) 8 FLS 93.

Wightman, J, *Contract: A Critical Commentary*, 1996, London: Pluto.

Williams, JC, 'Deconstructing gender' (1989) 87 Michigan L Rev 797, reprinted in Bartlett, KT and Kennedy, R (eds), *Feminist Legal Theory: Readings in Law and Gender*, 1991, Boulder: Westview.

Williams, P, *The Alchemy of Race and Rights: Diary of a Law Professor*, 1991, Harvard UP.

Willoughby, P, *Misplaced Trust*, 1999, London: Gostick Hall.

Wilson, F, *Organisational Behaviour and Gender*, 1995, London: McGraw-Hill.

Winfield, M, 'Whistleblowers as corporate safety net', in Vinten, G (ed), *Whistleblowing – Subversion or Corporate Citizenship?*, 1994, London: Paul Chapman.

Winfield, M, *Minding Your Own Business*, 1990, London: Social Audit.

Winfield, M, 'Self-regulation through employee vigilance', in Hunt, G (ed), *Whistleblowing in the Social Services*, 1998, London: Arnold.

Witz, A, 'Women and work', in Robinson, V and Richardson, D (eds), *Introducing Women's Studies: Feminist Theory and Practice*, 2nd edn, 1997, Basingstoke: Macmillan.

Women and Credit Task Force, *How to Get Out of Sexually Transmitted Debt*, 1990, Melbourne: Consumer Credit Legal Service.

Wong, S, 'Constructive trusts over the family home: lessons to be learned from other commonwealth jurisdictions?' (1998) 18 LS 369.

Wong, S, 'When trust(s) is not enough: an argument for the use of unjust enrichment for home-sharers' (1999) 7(1) FLS 47.

Woolman, S, 'Error revisited' 1986 SLT (News) 317.

Worden, KC, 'Overshooting the target: a feminist deconstruction of legal education' (1985) American University LR 34, reprinted in Olsen, FE (ed), *Feminist Legal Thought II: Positioning Feminist Theory Within the Law*, 1995, Aldershot: Dartmouth.

Wright, J, *The Generations of Men*, 1988, Sydney: Harper.

Yamani, M, 'The power behind the veil' (1996) (4) Index on Censorship 80.

Yegenoglu, M, *Colonial Fantasies*, 1998, Cambridge, CUP.

Young, IM, *Justice and the Politics of Difference*, 1990, Princeton, NJ: Princeton UP.

Young, R, *White Mythologies*, 1990, London: Routledge.

INDEX

Balfour - [1919] 2 KB 571

Gissing [1971] AC 886

Pettitt - [1970] AC 777

Rosset [1991] 1 AC 107